Reprints of Economic Classics

BIBLIOGRAPHY

OF

WORKS ON ACCOUNTING
BY AMERICAN AUTHORS

BIBLIOGRAPHY

OF

WORKS ON ACCOUNTING BY AMERICAN AUTHORS

BY

HARRY C. BENTLEY

AND

RUTH S. LEONARD

TWO VOLUMES IN ONE

VOLUME I

1796-1900

[1934]

REPRINTS OF ECONOMIC CLASSICS

AUGUSTUS M. KELLEY · PUBLISHERS

NEW YORK 1970

FIRST EDITION 1934
(BOSTON: HARRY C. BENTLEY, *921 Boylston Street*, 1934)

REPRINTED 1970 BY
AUGUSTUS M. KELLEY · PUBLISHERS
NEW YORK NEW YORK 10001

I S B N 0 678 00648 2
L C N 72 115313

PRINTED IN THE UNITED STATES OF AMERICA
by SENTRY PRESS, NEW YORK, N. Y. 10019

PREFACE

THE need for a bibliography of works on accounting by American authors became apparent to the writer many years ago when a search for such a publication disclosed that nothing approximating a complete bibliography existed. It was then that he decided to undertake the task of compiling one, little realizing how much time it would require and the difficulties it would entail.

After devoting considerable time to the project he found it necessary to have skilled assistance, and in October, 1930, Miss Ruth S. Leonard, S.B., a graduate of the School of Library Science of Simmons College, was engaged for this purpose. It has required nearly four years to complete the work. This reveals to some extent the time element involved in such a compilation.

Miss Leonard spent sixteen months in Washington, D. C., examining the records in the Library of Congress and the Copyright Office and several months in New York, the major part of which time was given to examining the records placed at her disposal through the courtesy of the American Institute of Accountants. In the course of her research she examined bibliographical data and works on accounting in public libraries, private libraries, subscription and society libraries, and business and technical libraries in many of the large cities throughout the country; and also the libraries connected with such universities as Harvard, Yale, Columbia, New York, Princeton, Johns Hopkins, Pennsylvania, Illinois, Northwestern, Chicago, and Catholic University of America. In addition, she examined the Union Catalog and every other source of pertinent bibliographical information available.

It was ultimately decided to publish the bibliography in two volumes. The present volume (Volume I) is a complete bibliography of works on accounting by American authors which were copyrighted prior to January 1, 1901. It may be called a *19th century bibliography* because, with the exception of two works by Mitchell and Cobb, it is restricted to works published during the one hundred years ended December 31, 1900. The distinction of being the pioneer American author on accounting falls to William Mitchell, and his work heads the list of titles. His "New and complete system of book-keeping by an improved method of double entry" was published in Philadelphia in 1796, and William Cobb's "The country trader's assistant" was published in Brookfield, Massachusetts, in 1799. These two books are the only works on accounting by American authors published prior to the 19th century.

Works on accounting is a term used to comprehend bound volumes, pamphlets, etc., devoted exclusively or primarily to an exposition of or a treatise on some one phase of accounting, such as elementary bookkeeping theory and practice, advanced bookkeeping principles and practice, subjects in advanced accounting, and accounting for some one business, profession, or service.

No articles on accounting appearing in periodicals, bulletins, year books, and proceedings of societies are included unless they were issued as separate works on accounting.

Many books on various subjects published during the 19th century contained a superficial treatise on single or double entry bookkeeping, the portion allotted to this subject ranging from eight to fifty pages. These books are not included because they are not separately bound works on accounting. The following will serve to illustrate the various classes of books omitted: arithmetics, home study courses in business education, encyclopedias of business and commercial knowledge, manuals for merchants, shipmasters, lawyers, etc., and works on business correspondence, business methods, business and legal forms, etc.

Of this group, arithmetics deserve special mention. Approximately twenty-five arithmetics written by American authors and published in the United States prior to 1851 contained treatises on elementary bookkeeping, usually by single entry. Though some of these works have been referred to in check-lists of early texts on bookkeeping, they have been excluded from this bibliography because they are not essentially "works on accounting."

It is of some interest, however, to know that the first arithmetic by an American author to contain a treatise on double entry bookkeeping was written by Chauncey Lee and published in Lansingburgh, New York, in 1797. Lee's "American Accomptant" contained 297 pages of which forty-two were devoted to "a compendium of the Italian mode of book-keeping agreeable to *Gordon's system of accomptantship" and two pages only to a method of single entry called "The farmer's book-keeping." This work is said to be the first to use the dollar mark ($).

A well-known arithmetic text which contained a short treatise on

* Gordon, William. The universal accountant, Edinburgh, 1863.

bookkeeping both by single and double entry was written by Benjamin Greenleaf in 1835. Among the authors who included a section on single entry bookkeeping in their arithmetics the following may be mentioned: Francis Nichols, 1797; William Kinne, 1807; James Robinson, 1825; Zadock Thompson, 1826; Michael Walsh, 1826; Roswell C. Smith, 1827; Oliver Welch, 1827; William Slocomb, 1828; Lyman Cobb, 1832; Daniel Parker, 1833; and George Willson, 1836. In addition, there were several authors whose bookkeeping treatises were bound with arithmetics which they did not write. For example, Samuel Green's treatise on single entry bookkeeping, "The practical accountant; or, Farmer's and mechanic's best method of book-keeping," was bound with "Daboll's schoolmaster's assistant" in 1823 and was included as a part of this work each time that it was reprinted.

Other works not considered as "works on accounting" but commonly classified and cataloged under bookkeeping were omitted from this bibliography. Approximately 150 such works were eliminated. They include check systems, ready reckoners, equation of payments, and other mathematical aids for bookkeepers; keys and handbooks for teachers of bookkeeping; charts and diagrams; classification of accounts and office manuals for private use; uncopyright works on accounting procedure issued by railroad companies for their exclusive use; publications of the Interstate Commerce Commission and several state railroad commissions; government bulletins for the use of departments in municipal, state, and federal administration; and account books and bookkeeping forms for farmers, mechanics, merchants, lawyers, dentists, doctors, housekeepers, etc., consisting chiefly or wholly of ruled forms, although, in some cases, containing brief instructions for using the forms. No record is made of auxiliary books, such as ledgers, journals, etc., designed to accompany textbooks on bookkeeping.

A person who, while residing in the United States, wrote a work on accounting particularly adapted to American practice, and had it copyrighted and published in the United States, is regarded as an *American author*, regardless of whether or not he was a citizen of the United States and notwithstanding that he may have later returned to his native country. Considerable time was spent and an intensive search was made in order to establish that each author listed was "American."

All works by American authors which were found to be verbatim copies of works by foreign authors or other American authors, as the case may be, were eliminated, but many works plagiarized in part from foreign or American works were not eliminated. Such plagiarisms of contemporary works, particularly during the latter half of the 19th century, did not take the form of verbatim copying but were sufficiently disguised so that the material appropriated does not obviously appear to be copied from another author's work. One example of a so-called American work eliminated will suffice: "The mercantile manual; or, Accountant's guide; exhibiting a clear and comprehensive view of the science of book-keeping . . . principally extracted from the encyclopedia." New Haven, Printed by O. Steele, 1810. 21p. 21½cm. This work was published anonymously, but was deposited for copyright by Henry Sherman (District of Connecticut) April 13, 1810. It is a verbatim copy of an article on book-keeping in "The new and complete American encyclopedia; or, Universal dictionary of arts and sciences . . ." N. Y. 1805–11, which, in turn, was copied from the "Encyclopaedia Perthensis; or, Universal dictionary of knowledge . . . " published in Perth, Scotland [18–?].

Another class of books eliminated is editions of works by foreign authors (Irish, Scottish, and English) printed in the United States. This group includes not only foreign works reprinted and "copyrighted" in the United States by American publishers and booksellers, but also foreign works revised and adapted to American practice by American authors; that is, "American editions" of foreign works. The authors whose works were reprinted or adapted to American practice and published in the United States are: Thomas Dilworth, Charles Hutton, William Jackson, Edward Thomas Jones, Patrick Kelly, and Richard Turner.

An especial effort was made to establish the correct dates of birth and death for each American author listed. In addition to a search of secondary sources of biographical information such as biographical dictionaries, college necrologies, printed genealogies, local histories, and city directories, much research was undertaken by means of correspondence, scrutiny of original records, and personal visits. The following primary sources of biographical information were used: court records (wills and letters of administration), real estate records, printed and manuscript church and cemetery records, vital statistics, newspapers, authors' own works, and miscellaneous manuscripts.

It is recognized that this bibliography has little or no practical value as a source of reference to works on accounting for present-day use. It should, however, be of interest to university, college, public, and private libraries, collectors, and students of accounting who are interested in the historical and bibliographical background of American literature on accounting.

The publication of this volume will be followed by the second volume containing a complete bibliography of works on accounting by American authors published from January 1, 1901, to January 1, 1935. This volume will have a practical value for reference purposes. It will contain a classification of works on accounting under the following headings:

1. Accounting Principles and Practice for schools of secondary grade
2. Accounting Principles and Practice for schools of college grade and for reference purposes
3. Financial Statements, their preparation and interpretation
4. Cost Accounting:
    (a) General principles and practice
    (b) Principles and practice for a specific business, profession, or service
5. Constructive Accounting:
    (a) General principles and practice
    (b) Principles and practice for a specific business, profession, or service
6. Auditing:
    (a) General principles and practice
    (b) Principles and practice for a specific business, profession, or service
7. C. P. A. Examination Questions and Answers
8. Miscellaneous

In addition, the works on accounting will be listed chronologically and indexed alphabetically by the author.

Some of the problems and difficulties encountered in this effort to present a complete bibliography of works on accounting by American authors copyrighted prior to 1901 are set forth in the Introductory Chapter which the writer hopes will have significance and value for those interested in bibliographical research, particularly that relative to the 19th century. The table of contents indicates the scope of the work and the introduction to each part is a detailed explanation of that part.

The writer is grateful to many librarians and other individuals who cooperated in the compilation of this bibliography. The courtesies and the expert advice of the staff of the Library of Congress and the Copyright Office are particularly appreciated.

HARRY C. BENTLEY

October, 1934.

TABLE OF CONTENTS

INTRODUCTORY CHAPTER

Copyright Laws and Administration — Their Significance to Bibliographers

THE customary bibliographical sources were found inadequate for the compilation of a complete bibliography of 19th century works on accounting by American authors. The discovery that there were titles and editions known to have been copyrighted which could not be located and about which there was no complete bibliographical information led to an inquiry into the records of copyright, and finally to the study of the copyright laws and administration.

A review of the legislation and administration pertaining to copyrights will give some idea of the problems and difficulties encountered in an attempt to have a record of every work on accounting by an American author copyrighted prior to 1901. It should dispel the popular notion that the Library of Congress contains a copy of every work copyrighted.

Only the acts and the sections of each act which have particular significance to the bibliographer are reviewed; that is, the law relating to the deposit of the printed title and the law relating to the deposit of the published work.

The original federal copyright act of May 31, 1790, "an act for the encouragement of learning by securing the copies of maps, charts, and books to the authors and proprietors of such copies during the times therein mentioned," prescribed that an author or proprietor in order to obtain copyright protection must deposit a printed title in the clerk's office of the local United States district court in which he resided; and that an author or proprietor must deposit one copy of the published work in the office of the Secretary of State of the United States within six months of the date of publication.

The act of February 3, 1831, *the first revision,* "to amend the several acts respecting copyrights," prescribed that one copy of the published work must be deposited in the clerk's office of the local United States district court within three months of the date of publication; and that it should be the duty of the clerk of each district court to transmit to the Secretary of State at least once a year the works deposited in his office, together with a certified list of titles recorded. The provisions of this act remained in force until 1870 except that the Secretary of the Interior became the custodian of the copyright deposits and records under the act of 1859.

The act of August 10, 1846, "to establish the Smithsonian Institution for the increase and diffusion of knowledge among men," required the deposit of one copy of the published work in the Smithsonian Institution and one copy in the Library of Congress within three months of the date of publication. An author or copyright proprietor was, therefore, required by law to deposit three copies of his published work, one in his local United States district court, another in the Smithsonian Institution, and a third in the Library of Congress. This act, however, was generally disregarded and a court decision held that the deposit of copies in the two libraries was not a prerequisite to copyright.

The act of February 5, 1859, "for keeping and distributing all public documents," expressly repealing the provision of 1846 for deposit of copies at the Smithsonian Institution and the Library of Congress, provided that all books heretofore deposited in the Department of State, together with all records of the Department of State, should be removed to and be under the control of the Department of the Interior; and that hereafter all publications of every nature should under the present laws and regulations be left with and kept by the Secretary of the Interior. The duties thus transferred to the Department of the Interior were administered by the Patent Office under the direction of the Commissioner of Patents. Under the act of 1831, still in force, the deposits and certified lists of titles were transmitted yearly by the clerks of the district courts to the Commissioner of Patents.

The act of March 3, 1865, supplemental to an act entitled "an act to amend the several acts respecting copyrights," approved February 3, 1831, provided that one copy of the published work be deposited in the Library of Congress within one month of the date of publication. Thus, prior to 1870 the Library of Congress during two periods, 1846 to 1859 and 1865 to 1870, was entitled by law to receive one copy of each copyright work. The Library of Congress received also the copyright deposits of the Smithsonian Institution transferred under an act of Congress, April 5, 1866.

The act of July 8, 1870, *the second revision,* "an act to revise, consolidate, and amend the statutes relating to patents and copyrights," prescribed that the deposit of the printed title be made in the office of the Librarian of Congress and that the author must deposit two copies of the published work within ten days of the date of publication. It further provided that all books and records which were removed from the Department of State to the Department of the Interior be removed to and be under the control of the Library of Congress and that the clerk of each United States district court transmit to the Librarian of Congress all the books not heretofore sent to the Department of State and to the Department of the Interior and all the records of copyright in his possession.

The act of March 3, 1891, the so-called international copyright act extending the copyright privilege to citizens of other nations (provided that the work be manufactured in the United States) required that two copies of the published work be delivered at the office of the Librarian of Congress not later than the day of publication.

The act of February 19, 1897, "making appropriations for the legislative, executive, and judicial expenses of the government," in force July 1, 1897, provided for the appointment of a Register of Copyrights to perform all the duties relating to copyrights under the supervision of the Librarian of Congress. Thus the Copyright Office, located in the Library of Congress as it is today, was created.

The act of March 4, 1909, in force July 1, 1909, which with amendments is in effect today (1934) provides an entirely new basis for securing copyright registration. The author or proprietor must (1) publish the work with the prescribed copyright notice and (2) send promptly after publication two copies of the best edition of the work with an application for registration.

SUMMARY OF THE COPYRIGHT LAWS

1790 Printed title to be deposited in United States district court. In force until 1870.

One copy to be deposited with Secretary of State within six months of date of publication. In force until 1831.

1831 One copy to be deposited in United States district court within three months of date of publication; copies thus deposited to be transmitted at least yearly to Secretary of State together with certified list of printed titles deposited. In force until 1870 (except that Secretary of Interior became copyright custodian in 1859).

1846 One copy to be deposited in Smithsonian Institution within three months of date of publication. In force until 1859.

One copy to be deposited in Library of Congress within three months of date of publication. In force until 1859.

1859 All deposits and records to be transferred from Department of State to Department of Interior. (From 1859 to 1870 Commissioner of Patents, appointed by Secretary of Interior, received and cared for deposits and records transmitted by the clerks of district courts.) In force until 1870.

1865 One copy to be deposited in Library of Congress within one month of date of publication. In force until 1870.

1870 Printed title to be deposited in office of Librarian of Congress (Copyright Custodian). In force until 1909.

Two copies to be deposited in Library of Congress within ten days of date of publication. In force until 1909 (except that by the act of 1891 the two copies were required to be deposited not later than day of publication).

1909 Publication of work with the prescribed copyright notice.

Deposit of two copies of published work in Copyright Office together with an application for registration.

The administration of the copyright law has particular significance for the bibliographer of works published in the 19th century. Prior to 1870 the titles submitted for copyright were recorded chronologically by the clerks of the various United States district courts in record books provided for the purpose. Each record showed the date of registration, name of author, and title. The majority of volumes were indexed by author or by author and title. An incomplete file of the record books of the district courts, consisting of 312 volumes, is located in the archives of the Copyright Office. Those record books which are missing may be assumed not to have been received from the clerks of the district courts when requested according to law in 1870. Many had doubtless been lost or mislaid and some had been destroyed during the Civil War.

The Copyright Office has, in addition, an incomplete file of the certified lists of titles and duplicate copyright title-entry records which were transmitted by the clerks of the district courts to the Department of State from 1831 to 1859 and to the Patent Office from 1859 to 1870. These records are fragmentary but in many cases supplement the district court record books inasmuch as title lists are on file for districts whose original records are lost. In many instances the records indicate the works which were transmitted to the Department of State and later to the Patent Office, but these records were not kept uniformly in the various districts.

The record books of copyright accessions to the Department of State, Patent Office, and Library of Congress before 1870 are also in the Copyright Office archives. This file, like the file of original copyright title entries and certified title lists, is incomplete. Moreover, it is not possible to determine that all books deposited according to law were credited and added to the various depository libraries by their custodians.

It is unfortunate that the various provisions for the deposit of copies of the published work prior to 1870 were difficult to enforce and, in fact, practically unenforceable. The lapse of time allowed between the date of publication and the deposit of the work indicates that, in practice, deposit was not made a condition precedent to copyright protection. Sometimes the work whose title was deposited for copyright was not published, but more often authors neglected to send a copy or copies of their published works to the proper designated place or places through carelessness, ignorance, or disregard of the law. Thus it happened that the number of copies deposited in the various district courts, the Department of State, Smithsonian Institution, Library of Congress, and Patent Office was considerably less than the number of copyright title entries recorded in the district courts.

Moreover the deposited books were not properly cared for by the custodians. When the law required the removal of all copyright deposits to the Library of Congress in 1870, the library received only a small proportion (some 23,000 volumes) of the number deposited prior to 1870.

Mr. A. R. Spofford, former Librarian of the Library of Congress, expressing satisfaction that the act of 1870 centralized registration of copyright at the Library of Congress and provided for the deposit of two copies of each published work in the national library, said: "The advantage of securing to our national library a complete collection of all American copyright publications can hardly be overestimated. If such a law as that enacted in 1870 had been enforced since the beginning of the government, we should now have in the Library of Congress a complete representation of the product of the American mind in every department of science and literature."

The act of 1870 was, indeed, a step in the right direction in making the Library of Congress the depository for the registration for copyright of the printed title instead of the many district courts. Between July 8, 1870, and December 31, 1899, the titles submitted for copyright were recorded chronologically in record books. The complete file of the annual series of record books in the copyright office consists of 615 volumes. For the year 1900 the titles submitted for copyright were recorded in four separate classes. Class A (books and dramatic compositions) was recorded in sixty-five volumes. Each entry showed the date of registration, name of author, copyright owner, title, and in most cases the place of residence of the copyright owner. Since 1870 the copyright entries have been indexed on cards under the names of the claimants of copyright. From 1870 to 1895 they were also indexed by author and title, but since 1895 they have been indexed by author in the case of books and by title in the case of anonymous books, periodicals, and dramatic compositions. The act of 1891 provided for the publication of a catalog of title entries.

During the period from 1870 to 1899 the record of the deposit of the published work was noted on the title entry in the record books when the title and book were sent at one time and many deposits received at later dates were credited on their respective entries. It is possible, however, that some books were received but not credited as deposited in the record books.

From 1870 to 1897 when the law required the deposit of two copies of the published work with the Librarian of Congress, the Copyright Custodian, and from 1897 to 1900 when the deposit of two copies in the Copyright Office was required, the total receipts of copyright publications always fell far short of the total of titles deposited for copyright. There were several reasons for this: (1) the laxity and carelessness of the authors and publishers; (2) the intention of publication abandoned or deferred; (3) the deposit of several titles for one projected work, the final entry of which was used as the title in the published work. Though penalties were imposed and provision was made for a demand in writing by the Librarian of Congress within twelve months of date of publication, there is no record that the Librarian of Congress ever instituted a prosecution for violation of the law in this respect.

For many years prior to 1897 when the Library of Congress moved to its new building, the library located in the Capitol was appallingly overcrowded. A great mass of copyright deposits uncredited and uncataloged was allowed to accumulate. In 1897 a storage room was provided for the Copyright Office to keep the accumulations which had never become a part of the Library of Congress collection. From time to time material of value has been turned over to the Library of Congress. In 1932 the remainder of the storage collection was formally transferred to the Library of Congress reading room to be weeded out and added to the permanent collections of the Library of Congress. There still remain approximately eighty thousand articles unclassified and uncataloged.

SUMMARY

Reasons why the Library of Congress does not have a copy of every title deposited for copyright during the 19th century

1. Some titles deposited for copyright but not published.

2. Many works copyrighted but not deposited.

3. Deposits not properly cared for and preserved in United States district courts, Department of State, and Patent Office prior to 1870 (Library of Congress received only 23,070 volumes).

4. Overcrowded conditions at Capitol unfavorable for safe preservation of copyright deposits from 1870 to 1897.

5. Inevitable loss of books from Library of Congress collection before 1900 through fire, water, carelessness, theft, and deterioration.

6. Accumulation of copyright deposits from 1870–1900, unclassified and uncataloged, still in process of being weeded out and added to Library of Congress permanent collection.

It is obvious that the limitations imposed by the copyright law and its administration have caused many copyright deposits to be doomed to oblivion, unless it is possible to locate them in libraries other than the Library of Congress.

It is obvious, too, that the aim to present a final, definitive bibliographical record of every work on accounting by an American author, copyrighted prior to 1901, could not be accomplished until a complete search of all existing copyright records and copyright deposits in the reserve storage collection of the Library of Congress had been made. This task was accomplished.

Since the indexes to the copyright record books are incomplete and inadequate, it was necessary for the period from 1790 to 1900, inclusive, to make a page-by-page search of over one thousand copyright record books of the district courts, the Department of State, the Patent Office, and the Library of Congress. The search of the copyright deposits in reserve storage necessitated the examination of over eighty thousand articles, including books and unbound material.

The copyright record books revealed actual dates of copyright and other valuable bibliographical information concerning editions of works known to exist. These additional data were added to Part One, the main bibliography.

The few works which were located among the copyright deposits still in reserve storage were added to the main bibliography since they come under the category of works on accounting "known to exist in one or more libraries."

In addition, many titles were recorded in the copyright record books which were not found to exist in any library and about which there is no complete bibliographical information available. All these titles are listed in Part Four. Since the completeness and accuracy of the copyright records cannot be determined it is impossible to know in many cases whether these titles were ever published. Furthermore, there are published works credited with having been deposited which doubtless have been lost or destroyed. Other titles not credited with having been deposited may have been published but not deposited according to law.

In spite of their limitations the records of copyright are an important source of bibliographical information. That they were of value to the compilers of this work is evidenced by the supplementary bibliography, Part Four.

REFERENCES

Ashley, Frederick William.
Three eras in the Library of Congress. [New Haven, Yale university press, 1929]

Bishop, William Warner.
Library of Congress. Chicago, American library association publishing board, 1911.
Later editions issued by the Library of Congress for its own use.

Bowker, Richard Rogers.
Copyright, its law and its literature; being a summary of the principles and law of copyright; with special reference to books; with a bibliography of literary property by Thorvald Solberg. New York, Office of the Publishers' weekly, 1886.

—Copyright, its history and its law; being a summary of the principles and practice of copyright with special reference to the American code of 1909 and the British act of 1911. Boston, Houghton Mifflin, 1912.

Curtis, George Ticknor.
A treatise on the law of copyright in books, dramatic and musical compositions, letters and other manuscripts, engravings and sculpture; as enacted and administered in England and America; with some notices of the history of literary property. Boston, C. C. Little and J. Brown, 1847.

DE WOLF, Richard Crosby.
An outline of copyright law . . . introduction by Thorvald Solberg. Boston, J. W. Luce [c1925]

DRONE, Eaton Sylvester.
American copyright . . . Boston, Little, Brown, 1877.

—A treatise on the law of property in intellectual productions in Great Britain and the United States . . . Boston, Little, Brown, 1879.

ELLSWORTH, William Wolcott.
A copy-right manual; designed for men of business, authors, scholars, and members of the legal profession. Boston, O. Ellsworth, 1862.

GRISWOLD, William McCrillis.
A synopsis of copyright decisions. Bangor, Me. Q. P. index; New York, J. W. Christopher, 1883.

JOHNSTON, William Dawson.
History of the Library of Congress; volume 1, 1800–1864. Washington, Government printing office, 1904.

PUTNAM, George Haven, editor.
The question of copyright: a summary of the copyright laws at present in force in the chief countries of the world . . . New York, G. P. Putnam's sons, 1891.

SMITHSONIAN INSTITUTION.
Annual report . . . Washington, Government printing office [1847]–1870.
The fifth and sixth reports, 1850 and 1851, include information concerning the Smithsonian collection of copyright deposits, the copyright law, etc.

SPOFFORD, Ainsworth Rand.
Copyright in its relation to libraries and literature. (In the Library journal, v.1, no.1, p.85–89, 1877)

—The copyright system of the United States — its origin and growth [an address delivered at the celebration of the beginning of the second century of the American patent system at Washington, D. C., April 8, 9, 10, 1891] Washington, Press of Gedney-Roberts, 1892.

U. S. Copyright office.

Annual report . . . Washington, Government printing office, 1928 — date.

Annual reports, 1897–1927, were bound with the annual report of the Librarian of Congress. From 1910 to 1920 each report was also reprinted as a separate publication.

—Copyright enactments, 1783–1900; comprising the copyright resolution of the Colonial Congress, 1783; the copyright laws of the original states, 1783–1786; the constitutional provision concerning copyright legislation; and the public and private copyright laws enacted by Congress from 1790 to 1900 . . . comp. by Thorvald Solberg, register of copyrights. Washington, Government printing office, 1900. (Its Bulletin no.3)

—Copyright in Congress, 1789–1904: a bibliography and chronological record of all proceedings in Congress in relation to copyright from April 15, 1789, to April 28, 1904, First Congress, 1st session, to Fifty-eighth Congress, 2d session; prepared by Thorvald Solberg, register of copyrights . . . Washington, Government printing office, 1905. (Its Bulletin no.8)

—Report on copyright legislation; by the register of copyrights . . . Washington, Government printing office, 1904.

Reprinted from the Report of the Librarian of Congress for the fiscal year ending June 30, 1903.

U. S. Library of Congress.

Annual report . . . Washington, Government printing office, 1866 — date.

Title varies.

Includes annual report of the copyright office, 1897–1927.

Weil, Arthur William.

American copyright law; with especial reference to the present United States copyright act . . . Chicago, Callaghan and company, 1917.

Wyeth, Samuel Douglas.

History of the Library of Congress; compiled from official documents. Washington, Gibson brothers, printers, 1868.

PART ONE

PART ONE

A chronological bibliography of copyright works on accounting by American authors which were published for general distribution prior to 1901. At least one edition of each work is known to exist. Additional reprints and editions are recorded insofar as they have been verified.

INTRODUCTION

THE historical and bibliographical record of the accounting literature of the 19th century is presented through the use of the chronological method. Each work is listed under the date of publication and the reprints and editions of each work are listed chronologically under the date of their respective first editions.

At least one edition of each work listed in Part One was copyrighted, was published for general distribution, and is known to exist in one or more libraries.

The works are called " copyright works " because all those located which were for general distribution were copyrighted. It was decided not to burden this bibliography with works which were restricted for private use. Indeed, it would be impossible to make a complete list of uncopyright works prepared for private use only. (See, however, Part Three for *copyright* works each of which was prepared for use in some one school or correspondence course.)

It is impossible to have a complete record of all the reprints and editions of each work. The copyright law did not require the registration of reprints and editions unless new material were added, and editions with added or revised material sometimes failed to be copyrighted. Moreover many small issues of reprints and editions have long since disappeared. A determined effort, however, was made to discover and verify as many reprints and editions of each work as possible in order to have an accurate historical record of each work. Twentieth century editions of 19th century works are included to make the bibliographical record for each work complete.

It was customary, especially during the first half of the 19th century, for publishers to reprint a work many times, calling each "reprint" an "edition." In the majority of cases these editions did not represent revisions of the original edition or of a subsequent edition. No attempt was made to distinguish between reprints and editions and it may be assumed, unless otherwise indicated, that when the paging is the same as that of a previous edition no new material was added. Each reprint is called "another edition" unless it is numbered.

This bibliography is presented with the convenience of the user in mind, avoiding both the fullness and detail of the so-called scholarly bibliography and the extreme brevity and resulting confusion of the mere check-list.

The title is given in the fullness necessary to identify and explain the content and purpose of the work. Three dots, . . . , indicate an omission on the title-page.

The following cities are so well known that they are given without appended state designation. (In some cases abbreviations only are given.)

Albany (Alb.)
Atlanta

Baltimore (Balt.)
Boston (Bost.)
Brooklyn
Buffalo

Chattanooga
Chicago (Chic.)
Cincinnati (Cin.)
Cleveland

Dallas
Denver
Des Moines
Detroit

Fort Wayne

Grand Rapids

Hartford

Indianapolis

Los Angeles

Memphis

Milwaukee (Milw.)
Minneapolis

Nashville
New Haven
New Orleans (N.O.)
New York (N.Y.)

Omaha

Philadelphia (Phil.)
Pittsburgh
Providence

Richmond

St. Louis (St. L.)
St. Paul
Salt Lake City
San Antonio
San Francisco (San Fran.)
Savannah
Scranton
Seattle

Toledo
Trenton

Washington, D.C. (Wash.)

Prior to 1876 the names of publishers, publishing firms, printing houses, etc., are given in full whenever known, except that initials of forenames are used.

In general since 1876 only the surnames of well-known firms are given (e.g. Harper). Both surnames are given if they are hyphenated in the firm name (e.g. Bobbs-Merrill).

In the case of personal firms, the words "publishing company" and "and company" are omitted.

If the publisher is the author, the surname only is repeated.

If unchanged, the place of publication and the name of the publisher are not repeated for each reprint or edition; but if one or both change, both are repeated.

Brackets, [], are used when (1) the date is not on the title-page; (2) the pages are not numbered; and (3) the insertion does not appear on the title-page.

The letter "c" before a date signifies "copyrighted."

Common abbreviations are used throughout.

STATISTICS

NUMBER OF TITLES LISTED IN PART I

By Decades

1791–1850

1791–1800	2
1801–1810	2
1811–1820	9
1821–1830	8
1831–1840	23
1841–1850	24

Total = 68

1851–1900

1851–1860	26
1861–1870	20
1871–1880	59
1881–1890	106
1891–1900	113

Total = 324

Total number of titles listed in Part I 392

The total number of authors, including joint authors, listed in Part I is 366.

Part One

Main Bibliography

1796

MITCHELL, William, 1763–1854.
A new and complete system of book-keeping by an improved method of double entry; adapted to retail, domestic and foreign trade . . . the whole comprised in three sets of books . . . to which is added a table of the duties payable on goods, wares, and merchandise, imported into the United States of America; the whole in dollars and cents. Phil. Printed by Bioren & Madan, 1796. 454p. 21½cm.

1799

COBB, William, jr., 1770–1853.
The country trader's assistant; or, Young clerk's directory in the art of book-keeping on a new and approved plan; to which is added a record of trade, a record of notes and bills; also a few forms of notes, orders, receipts, bills, &c. Brookfield [Mass.] Printed for the author [by E. Merriam & co.] 1799. 48p. 12½ x 10½cm.

1804

TURNER, Thomas.
An epitome of book-keeping by double entry; delineated on a scale suited to the faculties and comprehension of senior school boys and youth; designed for the mercantile line; comprising systematic and unerring rules for the forming of monthly statements of books, as well as those for opening, conducting, adjusting and closing them . . . to which are added rules for keeping retail books by double entry . . . Portland [Me.] Printed by Jenks & Shirley for T. Clark (Proprietor) 1804. 148p. 17cm.

1808

E., O. (probably Francis Nichols, 1758?–1839)
Book-keeping by the method of single entry for the use of young persons. Phil. Printed for F. Nichols by T. & G. Palmer, 1808. [38]p. 24cm.

Francis Nichols, bookseller of Boston and Philadelphia, compiled and published various mathematical works. In 1797 he

E., O. (continued)

published in Boston an arithmetic containing twenty-four pages devoted to single entry bookkeeping.

The work listed above, "printed for F. Nichols" with the preface signed by O. E., contains the same form and names in the day book and ledger that are found in the part of the arithmetic devoted to single entry bookkeeping. Several pages of explanation were added and the day book and ledger were expanded.

1813

DAVIES, Benjamin.

A new and concise system of book-keeping according to the Italian method of double entry; adapted to the commerce of the United States.

The title of this work was deposited for copyright (District of Pennsylvania) October 30, 1813, by Benjamin Johnson, proprietor of the copyright.

2d ed. Phil. B. Johnson, 1819. [64]p. 22cm.
At head of title on cover: Davies' book-keeping.

1815

SHEYS, Bryant, 1750–1835.

The American book-keeper; part the first; comprising a system of book-keeping by single and double entry; adapted to the merchant, farmer, and mechanic, with the principal auxiliary books annexed . . . designed for the use of schools and private persons in the United States. N. Y. Printed by N. Van Riper, 1815. 160p. 22cm.

Another ed. N. Y. Printed by Collins & co. 1818. 333p. 22½cm.
Complete edition.

Another ed. N. Y. D. D. Smith, 1822. 160p. 22cm.
Part the first, reprinted.

1817

GALE, Edmund, 1788–1824.

An epitome of book-keeping by single entry; particularly calculated for mechanics and retail dealers; to which are added forms of the most important writings used in business. Nantucket [Mass.] Printed by A. G. Tannatt, 1817. 40p. 17½cm.

The first twenty-seven pages are devoted to single entry bookkeeping; the remaining pages, to forms.

GERISHER, Charles, 1773–1832.
Modern book-keeping by double entry; adapted to commission business as it is conducted in the United States of America; designed for mercantile young men. N. Y. Printed by E. Conrad, 1817. [158]p. 24cm.

MAGINNESS, James, 1780–1829.
The family clerk or students' assistant; containing a neat, concise, and plain method of book-keeping by single entry; and a variety of useful forms . . . and directions to a young scholar . . . Harrisburg [Pa.] Printed by W. Greer, for the author, 1817. 194p. 22cm.
About one third of the book is devoted to bookkeeping.

1818

ROSCOE, David C.
A new and compendious system of book-keeping by double entry; adapted to the commerce of the United States; and calculated, as well to exonerate the accountant from the tedious, complex and laborious operations of the Italian system now in use, as to enable the merchant easily to ascertain the true state of his affairs. Hagers-Town [Md.] Printed by W. D. Bell, 1818. [49]p. 20cm.

STANIFORD, Daniel, 1766–1820.
Practical arithmetic . . . to which is added a new and concise system of book-keeping both by single and double entry; the former calculated for the use of traders in retail business, farmers, and mechanics; and the latter for wholesale, domestic, and foreign trade as conducted in the United States. Bost. Printed by J. H. A. Frost for West, Richardson & Lord, 1818. 324p. 18½cm.
The title of this work was first deposited for copyright (District of Massachusetts) November 24, 1817. It was again deposited for copyright in the same district, November 16, 1818.
Contents.—[pt. 1] Practical arithmetic . . . p.[9]–196.—[pt. 2] A short and plain system of book-keeping by single entry . . . p.[197]–233.—[pt. 3] A new and concise system of book-keeping by double entry . . . p.[235]–324.
2d ed. Bost. Printed by J. H. A. Frost for West, Richardson & Lord, 1820. 324p. 18½cm.
This work is a reprint of the first edition.

1820

ALGER, Israel, 1787–1825.
The young merchant's manual, or practical book-keeper; containing the fundamental principles of mercantile science . . . by double entry. Bost. Printed for the author, 1820. [48]p. 32½cm.

ALGER (continued)

—Key to book-keeping; or, A practical illustration of the fundamental principles of mercantile science; being the second part to The young merchant's manual . . . the whole comprising a new and easy method of self-instruction . . . Bost. Printed for the author, by True & Greene, 1823. 104p. 25½ x 21cm.

BENNET, James Arlington, 1788–1863.

The American system of practical book-keeping; adapted to the commerce of the United States . . . exemplified in one set of books kept by double entry; designed for the use of schools; to which are added forms of the most approved modern auxiliary books [and] a copperplate engraving . . . exhibiting the final balance of the leger. N.Y. Printed by A. Paul, 1820. xx+[72]p. 24cm.

Paging in various copies of the first edition varies.

Title in later editions varies.

Preliminary matter varies.

The editions published before 1841 give the author's name as James Bennett. In 1841 James Bennett changed his name to James Arlington Bennet.

The author deposited for copyright (Southern District of New York) March 4, 1815, the following title: "The new and complete American system of practical book-keeping; exemplified in three sets of books . . . with the highly approved method of keeping a journal and of forming a journal balance . . . " Benjamin Franklin Foster in his "Origin and progress of book-keeping," London, Souter, 1852, lists Bennett's work, published in 1814. It is possible that the work, copyrighted in 1815, had 1814 on the title-page. It may have been a manuscript copy which Bennett used in his lectures on bookkeeping between 1815 and 1820.

It is probable that the 1820 edition is the first edition which was published for general distribution. An advertisement, dated 1846, in the 1848 edition states: "This work has been six and twenty years before the public . . . "

James Bennett deposited for copyright (Southern District of New York) February 25, 1817: "A balance chart; exhibiting a complete and final balance of the accounts in a merchant's leger kept by double and single entry."

This chart appears as a copperplate engraving in the 1820 edition.

With one issue of the first edition is bound: Jackson's book-keeping; adapted to the coin and commerce of the United States . . . by James Bennett. N.Y. Printed by A. Paul, 1821. [82]p. 24cm.

6th ed.	1824.
7th ed.	N. Y. Collins & Hannay, 1824. xxiv + [64]p. 24cm.
8th ed.	1826. xxiv + [64]p. 24½cm.
9th ed.	1826. xxiv + [64]p. 23½cm.
10th ed.	1828. 96p. 24cm. List of subscribers: p.[91]–96.
11th ed.	1828. 96p. 24½cm. List of subscribers: p.[91]–96.
12th ed.	1829. 96p. 24½cm. List of subscribers: p.[91]–96.
14th ed.	1831. 104p. 24½cm.
15th ed.	1833. 104p. 26cm.
16th ed.	N. Y. B. & S. Collins, 1835. 104p. 26cm.
17th ed.	1836. 104p. 26cm.
18th ed.	N. Y. Collins, Keese & co. 1837. 104p. 25cm.
19th ed.	1839. 104p. 26cm.
21st ed.	N. Y. Collins, bro. & co. 1842. 104p. 26cm.
22d ed.	N. Y. Harper & bros. 1843. 128p. 27cm.
24th ed.	1846.
28th ed.	N. Y. M. H. Newman, 1848. 160p. 25½cm.
30th ed.	1852. 160p. 25cm.
31st ed.	N. Y. Ivison & Phinney, 1855. 160p. 25½cm.
41st ed.	[N. Y. c1862] 126p. 25½cm. The title of this work was deposited for copyright (Southern District of New York) March 31, 1862, by James Arlington Bennet.

1821

GODDARD, Thomas Henry, 1787–1832.

The merchant; or, Practical accountant; being a series of mercantile accounts . . . in single and partnership business . . . to which are added tables of moneys, weights, and measures, of the commercial world. N. Y. C. Starr, 1821.

201 + [1]p. 28 x 23cm.

The title of this work was deposited for copyright (Southern District of New York) January 13, 1819. It was again deposited for copyright (Southern District of New York) August 23, 1821, by Charles Starr, proprietor of the copyright. It is known that Goddard taught bookkeeping between 1818 and 1821. It may be that the work copyrighted in 1819 was not issued for general distribution but used only in his classes; that the work issued in 1821 was the first published edition. The journal entries in the 1821 edition are dated 1818.

The following titles, possibly preliminary parts of "The mer-

GODDARD (continued)

chant; or, Practical accountant . . . " were deposited for copyright in 1818:

"The partnership; or, A system of book-keeping commenced in partnership, carried on and concluded, and the concern closed . . . "

"The trial balance . . . shewing a complete system of book-keeping; commenced, carried on and closed and new books opened . . . "

2d ed. N. Y. 1828. 144+9+p.145–201+[1]p. 28 x 23cm.
A section: "An improved merchant's journal" has been interpolated; with special title-page and separate paging.

3d ed. N. Y. H. C. Sleight, 1831. 144+9+p.145–201+[1]p. 28 x 23½cm.
A section: "An improved merchant's journal" has been interpolated; with special title-page and separate paging.

4th ed. N. Y. Moore & Payne; Collins & Hannay, 1834. 144+9+p.145–201+[1]p. 28 x 23½cm.
A section: "An improved merchant's journal" has been interpolated; with special title-page and separate paging.

5th ed. Trenton, B. Davenport; Phil. George & Byington; Balt. Cushing & sons, 1837. 188p. 28 x 23cm.

1822

WILLETTS, Jacob, 1785–1860.

Book-keeping by single entry. Poughkeepsie [N. Y.] Printed & pub. by P. Potter, 1822. 21p. 18cm.

The title of this work was not deposited for copyright (Southern District of New York) by P. Potter until February 27, 1824. The copy of the first edition owned by the Boston public library contains the printed copyright notice pasted on the back of the title-page.

Another ed. 1830. [43]p. 18cm.
This work is called a new edition revised and corrected.

1823

CHAPMAN, William.

Practical book-keeping by double entry; comprised in twelve books . . . forming a complete system of the transactions of a trader of eminence; conformable to the prevailing usages of regular counting-houses in the United States, with the most efficacious method of teaching that useful science. Phil. Printed for the author by J. Young, 1823. [125]p. 20½cm.

HITCHCOCK, Ira Irvine, 1793–1868.

A new method of teaching the art of book-keeping by the use of: 1. Necessary definitions and universal rules; 2. Interrogatory exercises or oral journalizing; 3. Practical exercises . . . and directions for using them; 4. Instructions for the adjustment and closure of the leger . . . accompanied by a key . . . the whole comprised in fifteen lessons and the rules and instructions exemplified in two sets of books kept by double entry . . . Phil. Pub. by E. Littell, Clark & Raser, printers, 1823.

The title of this work was deposited for copyright (Eastern District of Pennsylvania) April 28, 1823. It is the first edition. The printed title-page deposited in the district court in 1823 and now located in the rare book department of the Library of Congress contains the imprint added above.

Various editions of the Journal, Leger, and the Key are wanting. Only those which were located are listed.

2d ed.	Phil. Pub. by the author, 1826. 42p. 27cm. Though the title-page of the second edition has the date 1826 the title was deposited for copyright (Eastern District of Pennsylvania) August 27, 1825. The subsequent editions bear the copyright date 1825. The journal entries in the second edition are dated 1822.
5th ed.	Phil. Pub. by the author, 1829. 42p. 27cm.
7th ed.	Balt. Pub. by the author, 1832. 42p. 27½cm.
Another ed.	Bost. Nichols & Hall [1836?] 42p. 25½cm. On cover: Revised edition, Journal of Hitchcock's new method of teaching book-keeping.
Other eds.	Bost. B. B. Mussey & co. 1844; 1852; 1853. 42p. 27cm. On cover of each edition: Revised edition, Journal of Hitchcock's new method of teaching book-keeping. Stereotype editions.
Another ed.	Bost. Sanborn, Carter & Bazin, 1855. 42p. 25½cm. On cover: Revised edition, Journal of Hitchcock's new method of teaching book-keeping.
Another ed.	Hartford, Belknap & Hamersley [n. d.] 42p. 27cm. On cover: Revised edition, Journal of Hitchcock's new method of teaching book-keeping.

HITCHCOCK (continued)

Another ed. Phil. Pub. by the author [n. d.] Stereotyped by L. Johnson.

Another ed. Bost. Chase, Nichols & Hill [n. d.] 42p. 27cm. On cover: Revised edition. Journal of Hitchcock's new method of teaching book-keeping.

—Leger of Hitchcock's new method of teaching book-keeping. Phil. Pub. by the author, 1828. 40p. 27cm.

Another ed. 1829. 40p. 27cm.

Other eds. Balt. Pub. by the author, 1831; 1832; 1835. 40p. 27cm.

Other eds. Bost. B. B. Mussey & co. 1844; 1853. 40p. 27cm.

Other eds. Bost. Sanborn, Carter & Bazin, 1855; 1858. 40p. 27cm.

Another ed. Hartford, Belknap & Hamersley [n. d.] 40p. 27cm.

Another ed. Bost. Chase, Nichols & Hill [n. d.] 40p. 27cm.

—Key of Hitchcock's new method of teaching book-keeping. Phil. Pub. by the author, 1826. 56p. 21½cm.

Another ed. 1829. 56p. 22cm.

Other eds. Balt. Pub. by the author, 1831; 1832. 56p. 22cm.

Another ed. Bost. B. B. Mussey & co. 1851. 56p. 23cm.

Another ed. Bost. Sanborn, Carter & Bazin, 1856. 56p. 23cm.

Another ed. Hartford, Belknap & Hamersley [n. d.] 56p. 23cm.

Another ed. Bost. Chase, Nichols & Hill [n. d.] 56p. 23cm.

Hitchcock's plan as outlined in his preface to "A new method . . . " is as follows: "After the proper preliminary description of the books to be used, and a statement of the rules of the art, interrogatory exercises in journalizing to be answered . . . are introduced (but the answers withheld) they are succeeded by two series of original entries of day-books (but the journal expression of them is not given). Blank paper neatly ruled and prepared is given him for a Leger (but he must form it himself from his own Journal). The answers to the interrogatories, the journal expression of every original entry and the result of the posting to the Leger . . . are all contained in the Key to which there is a perfect system of reference by numbers from the questions and original entries."

1826

GIBSON, John.

A new and improved system of practical book-keeping; applicable to all kinds of business; exemplified in one set of books of individual and partnership concerns; arranged on the principles of double entry by a new method, which obtains the same results by two entries as the present practice by four . . . designed for the use of schools and counting houses. Phil. Pub. by the author, 1826. 12+[120]p. 23½cm.

1827

PRESTON, Lyman, 1795–(?)

Preston's manual on book-keeping; or, Arbitrary rules made plain; in two parts; adapted to the use of academies and common schools . . . the first part being designed for the use of mechanics of all classes; the second, arranged more particularly for the instruction of young men who contemplate the pursuit of mercantile business; shewing the method of keeping accounts by double entry . . . Utica, N.Y. Printed by Dauby & Maynard, 1827. 94+[2]p. 22cm.

2d ed. N.Y. Printed by Elliott & Palmer, 1829. 102+[2]p. 22cm.

—Preston's treatise on book-keeping; or, Arbitrary rules made plain; in two parts . . . N.Y. Sleight & Robinson, printers [c1831] 174+[2]p. 23cm.

The third edition of the "Manual . . ."

With this work is bound the author's "Equation of payments."

Another ed. Hartford, D.F. Robinson & co. 1833. 184+13p. 24cm.
This work includes the author's "Cubical estimates."

Another ed. N.Y. R. & G. S. Wood, printers [1833?] 184+[12]p. 25cm.
Testimonials dated 1833.

Another ed. Hartford, Robinson & Pratt, 1834. 184+13p. 23½cm.
Stereotyped by A. Chandler.
This work includes the author's "Cubical estimates."
A short semi-humorous biographical sketch of the author is also bound with the 1834 edition.

PRESTON (continued)

Other eds. N. Y. Robinson, Pratt & co. 1835; 1836; 1837. 184+13p. 25cm.
The author's "Cubical estimates" is bound with each edition.
A short semi-humorous biographical sketch of the author is also bound with the 1835 edition.

Other eds. 1838; 1841; 1842. 168+32+13p. 25cm.
The author's "Book-keeper's diploma" and his "Cubical estimates" are bound with each edition.

Other eds. N. Y. Collins, bro. & co. 1844; 1846; 1848; 1849; 1850. 224+40p. 25½cm.
The author's "Book-keeper's diploma" is bound with each edition.
The 1846 edition is called the 21st edition.

Other eds. N. Y. R. B. Collins, 1852; 1853; 1856; 1857. 280p. 24½cm.
The 1857 edition is called the 44th edition.

Other eds. N. Y. Collins & bro. 1860; 1867. 280p. 24½cm.
The 1860 edition is called the 46th edition.

—Preston's treatise on book-keeping by single entry; adapted to the use of retailers, farmers, mechanics, and common schools; being taken from Preston's larger work on book-keeping which contains both double and single entry. N. Y. Collins, bro. & co. 1844. [80]p. 25½cm.

—Preston's district school book-keeping; affording an interesting and profitable exercise for youth; being especially designed for classes in our common schools.
The title of this work was deposited for copyright (Southern District of New York) February 9, 1846.
This work is probably based upon "Preston's treatise . . ."

1828

KNOWLTON, Joseph.
A new system of book-keeping by single entry; particularly calculated for mechanics and retail dealers. Bost. Printed & pub. by J. H. Eastburn, 1828. 37p. 12 x 11cm.
This work is obviously based upon Gale's work published in 1817. The preliminary matter and forms for the day book and ledger are in most details the same but the names and articles are different. The descriptive material in "Gale" is omitted.

1830

MARSH, Christopher Columbus, 1806–1884.
The science of double-entry book-keeping; simplified by the in-

troduction of an infallible rule for dr. and cr. . . Phil. J. Towar & D. M. Hogan, 1830. 54+136p. 22½cm.

2d ed. Balt. G. M'Dowell & son, 1831. 211p. 23cm.
Other eds. Phil. Hogan & Thompson, 1834; 1836; 1839; 1841; 1843; 1846; 1847; 1848. 199p. 23cm.
Another ed. [1847?] 199p. 23cm.
Revised by the author in 1847.
Another ed. Phil. Parrish, Dunning & Mears [1847?] 199p. 23½cm.
Another ed. Phil. Hogan & Thompson, 1851. 218p. 23½cm.
The title of this edition was deposited for copyright (Southern District of New York) November 5, 1850.
Other eds. N.Y. J.C. Riker, 1853; 1854; 1855; 1856; 1857. 218p. 21½cm.
Other eds. N.Y. D. Appleton & co. 1858; 1859; 1860; 1862; 1864; 1866; 1868. 232p. 24cm.
Other eds. 1870; 1871; 1875; 1878; 1884; 1886. 235p. 23½cm.

—La ciencia de la teneduría de libros, simplificada por la aplicacion de una regla infalible para acertar el deudor y el acreedor . . . traducido de la 20 ed. inglesa, por A. G. Beck . . . N.Y. J. C. Riker, 1849. 195p. 23cm.

(Adolphus G. Beck, translator)
Another ed. 1851. 192p. 23cm.
Another ed. N.Y. D. Appleton & co. 1852. 195p. 23cm.
Other eds. 1855; 1857; 1863. 196p. 23½cm.
Another ed. 1880. 211p. 24cm.
At head of title: Nueva ed.—augm. con suplemento [etc.]

1831

BECK, Frederick, 1779–1831.

The young accountant's guide; or, An easy introduction to the knowledge of mercantile book-keeping . . . with rules and marginal notes; adapted to the use of academies and counting-rooms . . . Bost. Stimpson & Clapp, 1831. 116p. 27½ x 23cm.

The author deposited for copyright (District of Massachusetts) October 21, 1820, the following title: "The accountant's first part; containing the requisite rules in book-keeping . . . " The preface to "The young accountant's guide . . . " states that the rules contained therein "were first published about ten years since in a pamphlet form, mostly for the convenience of young gentlemen . . . since which they have been sought for, and approved of, both by teachers and clerks . . . " This work was not located.

MORISON, B.

Book-keeping improved; or, A short and regular system of keeping the accounts of retailers of merchandise; with an appendix; containing the most approved precedents for receipts, bonds, and promissory notes, and a vocabulary, explaining most of the abstruse words and terms that occur in merchandise. Milton, Pa. Pub. by the author; Frick, Bennett & Correy, printers, 1831. [127]p. 23cm.

ROBINSON, James, 1781–1877.

A compend of book-keeping by single entry; designed for the use of schools . . . Bost. Hilliard, Gray, Little & Wilkins, 1831. 28p. 23cm.

2d ed.	Bost. Hilliard, Gray & co. 1833. [28]p. 22½cm.
Another ed.	Bost. Ide & Dutton, 1837. [28]p. 24cm. Stereotype edition with improvements.
Another ed.	Bost. C. Stimpson, 1837. [28]p. 22cm. Stereotype edition with improvements.
Other eds.	Bost. Hilliard, Gray & co. 1837; 1838; 1839. [28]p. 22cm. Stereotype editions with improvements.

1832

MARSH, Christopher Columbus, 1806–1884.

The art of single-entry book-keeping; improved by the introduction of proof or trial-balance, &c. Balt. G. M'Dowell & son, 1832. 118p. 18½cm.

[2d ed.?]	N.Y. J.C. Riker, 1836.	130p. 23cm.
3d ed.	1839.	126p. 22½cm.
3d ed.	1843.	128p. 23cm.
4th ed.	1844.	128p. 23cm.
4th ed.	1847.	128p. 23cm.
6th ed.	1849.	128p. 23cm.
6th ed.	1850.	128p. 23cm.
6th ed.	1852.	128p. 23cm.
6th ed.	1854.	128p. 23cm.

ROCHE, Martin.

Compendious rules for book keeping; exhibiting the peculiar properties of every account throughout that science and teaching the most simple and elegant methods of closing books; to which are annexed the most convenient forms of bill books; precisely adapted to the most extensive business of counting house. Phil. Printed by Garden & Thompson, 1832. 9+[3]p. 18cm.

WALSH, Michael, 1763–1840.

Book-keeping, suited to the business of traders, farmers, and mechanics; mostly by single entry . . . to which is added a key to certain parts of the Mercantile arithmetic. Bost. Carter, Hendee & co. 1832. 78p. 23cm.

The author copyrighted a work on bookkeeping in 1804 and again in 1826. The first was not located. The second is bound with several editions of the author's "Mercantile arithmetic." The content, however, is not the same as the author's "Book-keeping . . ." published in 1832. Several editions of Walsh's "Mercantile arithmetic" published prior to 1826 include "A new introduction to book-keeping after the Italian method of debtor and creditor . . . on the plan of R. Turner . . ." The content is different from Walsh's works mentioned above.

1833

BUCKLIN, Isaac B.

Bucklin's counting house journal; or, Book-keeping by double entry, simplified . . . Troy, N.Y. Printed by N. Tuttle for I.B. Bucklin & W. Jones, proprietors, 1833. 150p. 28 x 36½cm.

The title of this work was deposited for copyright (Northern District of New York) November 16, 1832.

The printed title-page deposited in the district court in 1832 and now located in the rare book department of the Library of Congress contains the imprint: Troy, N.Y. The Troy press, 1832.

MARSH, Christopher Columbus, 1806–1884.

A lecture on the study of book-keeping; with a lithographic balance sheet.

The title of this work was deposited for copyright (District of Maryland) October 26, 1833. No copy of either the first or the second edition was located.

—A lecture on the study of book-keeping with the balance sheet; being an easy introduction to double entry book-keeping; 3d ed. N.Y. C. Shepard; Providence, Shepard, Tingley & co. 1837. 38+7p. 20½cm.

With this work is bound the author's "Prospectus; the study of book-keeping . . ." in which he outlines his course of instruction given in his school room, 74 Cedar Street, New York.

1834

EDWARDS, William.

The book-keeper's atlas; or, A perfect system of book-keeping by double entry; founded on principles of real business . . . de-

EDWARDS (continued)
signed for the use of counting-houses and schools . . . N.Y. Harper & bros. 1834. 205+[1]p. 28 x 23cm.

HARRIS, Levi, and PHETTYPLACE, Eddy W.
Directions for book keeping in which the principles of that science are familiarly explained and adapted to the comprehension of young pupils . . . and designed for the use of merchants, mechanics, farmers and gentlemen of every profession; to which is added the most approved forms of blank books, the manner of making entries, debit and credit . . . Norwich, N.Y. Pellet & Cooke, printers, 1834. 252p. 18½cm.

The title of this work was deposited for copyright (Northern District of New York) June 10, 1833.

2d ed. Utica [N.Y.] Press of W. Williams, 1836. 264p. 19cm.
The second edition does not mention Phettyplace as joint author.

1835

MARSHALL, John Jones, 1800–1866.
The public school account book; designed to afford exercises in book-keeping by single entry; furnished with materials and blank pages for two series of accounts . . . Framingham [Mass.] Boynton & Marshall, 1835. 28p. 21 x 17cm.

Forty blank ledger leaves interspersed.

2d ed. 1839. 18+[40]p. 20½ x 17½cm.
Twenty blank ledger leaves added to the text.

3d ed. 1846. 18+[40]p. 20½ x 17½cm.
Twenty blank ledger leaves added to the text.

—Ledger of the public school account book; with plates and exercises for writing accounts. Framingham [Mass.] Boynton & Marshall, 1839. [23]p. 21 x 17cm.

Forty blank ledger leaves interspersed.

—Diary and key . . . 1839. 10+[32]+17p. 21 x 17cm.

Sixteen blank ledger leaves interspersed.

ROCHE, Martin.
The American combined system of book-keeping; or, Science of commerce by double entry; in two complete sets of books . . . and an appendix; containing legal and appropriate explanations, and accurate calculations of insurances,—bottomry and respondentia,—anonymous copartnerships . . . Phil. Printed by T. B. Town, 1835. 136p. 23½cm.

Another ed. 1836. 136p. 23½cm.

WINSLOW, Ezra Spooner, 1806–(?)
A system of book-keeping by double entry; adapted to the business transactions of merchants and mechanics, particularly in the retail trade . . . Albany, Hoffman & White, 1835. 32p. 22cm.
2d ed. Woodstock, Vt. J.B. & S.L. Chase & co's power press off. 1836. 47+[1]p. 21½cm.

1836

COFFIN, James Henry, 1806–1873.
Progressive exercises in book keeping by single and double entry; designed to furnish the scholars in common schools an interesting and useful mode of applying their knowledge of penmanship and arithmetic; also to afford the farmers and mechanics an easy mode of acquiring a knowledge of this important branch. Greenfield, Mass. A. Phelps; Bost. Crocker & Brewster, 1836. 84p. 22½cm.
2d ed. 1841. 89p. 21½cm.

FOSTER, Benjamin Franklin.
A concise treatise on commercial book-keeping; elucidating the principles and practice of double entry and the modern methods of arranging merchants' accounts. Bost. Perkins & Marvin; Phil. H. Perkins, 1836. 171p. 23½cm.
2d ed. 1837. 200+12p. 24cm.
With this edition is bound the author's "Prospectus of the commercial academy."
3d ed. 1839. 184+[8]p. 23½cm.
The last eight pages include advertising matter.
5th ed. Bost. T.R. Marvin, 1845. 184p. 22½cm.
5th ed. 1846. 184p. 23cm.
6th ed. Bost. Phillips & Sampson; C. Tappan, 1848. 184p. 22½cm.
7th ed. Bost. T.R. Marvin, 1851. 184p. 23cm.
8th ed. 1853. 184p. 23cm.

1838

COLT, John Caldwell, 1810–1842.
The Italian science of double entry book-keeping; simplified, arranged and methodized . . . containing a key, explaining the manner of journalizing, and the nature of the business transaction of . . . the day-book entries; together with practical forms for keeping books . . . Cin. N.G. Burgess & co. [etc.] 1838. 209p. 25½cm.
The author deposited for copyright (Southern District of New

COLT (continued)

York) November 17, 1837, the title of a chart: "Double entry rules for book-keeping."

The subsequent editions omit the word "Italian" from the title-page.

Public addresses: p.175–209.

2d ed.	1838. 209p. 25½cm. Public addresses: p.175–209.
3d ed.	1838. 209p. 25½cm. Public addresses: p.175–209.
4th ed.	Phil. T. Cowperthwait & co. 1839. 105p. 24½cm. Part 1, school edition, published separately. Part 2, teachers' and clerks' edition, p.107–209, has not been found.
7th ed.	N.Y. B.W. Foster & co.; D. Appleton & co. 1841. 188p. 25½cm. Public addresses are omitted in this and subsequent editions.
11th ed.	N.Y. Nafis & Cornish, 1845. 188p. 25½cm.
12th ed.	1846. 188p. 23½cm.
13th ed.	1849. 188p. 23½cm.
13th ed.	[n. d.] 253p. 23½cm. Public addresses: p.189–253.
45th ed.	N.Y. Lamport, Blakeman & Law, 1853. 188p. 24½cm.
45th ed.	N.Y. Lamport, Sheldon & Blakeman, 1855. 188p. 24½cm.

HARRIS, Nicholas, 1810–1879.

A complete system of practical book keeping in four sets of books . . . applicable to all kinds of business, both individual and partnership concerns . . . also a series of concise rules for performing various computations in business; designed for the counting house and schools. Hartford, Brown & Parsons, 1838.
222+[2]p. 23½cm.

Other eds.	1839; 1840; 1841; 1842; 1843; 1845. 230p. 22cm. The 1841 edition is called the third edition. Each edition contains six sets of books.
Other eds.	1846; 1848. 238p. 22cm. Each edition contains eight sets of books.
Another ed.	1852. 238p. 23½cm. Contains eleven sets of books.
Other eds.	N.Y. Clark, Austin & Smith, 1854; 1855; 1856; 1857. 238p. 23½cm. Each edition contains eleven sets of books.

Another ed.	N.Y. Clark, Austin, Maynard & co. 1860. 250p. 22½cm. Contains thirteen sets of books.
Other eds.	N.Y. Clark & Maynard, 1868; 1872. 250p. 22½cm. Each edition contains thirteen sets of books.

1839

SHEA, John H., 1800?–1855.
Book-keeping by single and double entry; simplified and arranged according to the present practice of well regulated counting-houses in the United States . . . Balt. The author, 1839. 160p. 24cm.

2d ed.	1841.	184p. 24cm. Subscribers' names and testimonials are given, p.173–184, in this edition and subsequent editions.
3d ed.	1845.	184p. 23½cm.
4th ed.	1847.	184p. 23½cm.
4th ed.	1848.	184p. 23½cm.
4th ed.	1849.	184p. 23½cm.
Another ed.	1851.	184p. 23½cm.

STONE, Eli.
The steam boat clerk: a complete systematic and concise manual of accounts; for the use of steam boats. Cin. E. Lucas & co. 1839. 24p. 26½cm.

1840

ALEXANDER, Henry, 1806–(?)
An exposition of book-keeping by single or double entry . . . Balt. Printed by R. Neilson, 1840. 24p. 17½cm.

CLARKE, Francis Gedney, 1792–1843.
A synthetic and inductive system of book-keeping by double entry; designed particularly for schools and academies and as a reference for the young accountant . . . also directions and illustrations for the ship master in arranging ship accounts . . . Portland [Me.] S.H. Colesworthy; Bost. B.B. Mussey, 1840. 82p. 19cm.
At head of title: Clarke's book-keeping.
On cover: Directions for Clarke's book-keeping.
—A synthetic and inductive system of book-keeping by double entry . . . to which is appended two complete sets of waste book entries . . . with a full set of ship masters' accounts; with ex-

CLARKE (continued)
planations . . . Portland [Me.] S. H. Colesworthy; Bost. B. B. Mussey, 1841. 150p. 24cm.
This work is part 2 of "Clarke's book-keeping."
In 1830 the author published "The seaman's manual" which contains a section devoted to shipmaster's accounts. This work includes more bookkeeping for shipmasters than does his general bookkeeping text listed above.

FOSTER, Benjamin Franklin.
The theory and practice of book-keeping, illustrated and simplified. Bost. Perkins & Marvin; Phil. H. Perkins, 1840.
112p. 23 x 18½cm.
At head of title: Foster's school book-keeping.
"The present volume bears the same relation to the author's . . . 'A concise treatise on commercial book-keeping,' published in 1835, as a manual of arithmetic to the key . . . designed expressly for learners, to be used in schools and academies. Each work is complete in itself; but the one will serve as a key to the other." — Pref.
This work was also published in London by J. Souter in 1840.
Another ed. Bost. T. R. Marvin, 1845.
112p. 21½ x 18cm.

SHEPARD, John.
The science of double-entry book-keeping, simplified; designed for the use of schools and seminaries and private instruction . . . to which is added important rules, tables and supplementary matter to aid the accountant in every emergency. Lansingburgh [N. Y.] Printed by W. B. Harkness, 1840. 216p. 22½cm.

1841

HARRIS, Nicholas, 1810–1879.
First lessons in book-keeping; exhibiting simple and approved methods of recording farmers' and mechanics' accounts by single entry, accompanied by valuable suggestions in doing business; introductory lessons in double entry; followed by a series of mathematical tables and rules for performing computations in business; designed for common schools. Hartford, Brown & Parsons, 1841. 104p. 22½cm.
Another ed. 1842. 104p. 22½cm.

JONES, Thomas, 1804–1889.
The principles and practice of book-keeping; embracing an entirely new and improved method of imparting the science; with

exemplifications of the most concise and approved forms of arranging merchants' accounts. N. Y. Wiley & Putnam, 1841. 160p. 23½cm.

1842

DANDO, Joseph.

A complete and infallible system of practical book-keeping by double entry; expressly arranged for conducting the business of importers, manufacturers, and dealers generally . . . with sectional instructions and treatises for the regulation of trade on systematic and scientific principles; also, tables of foreign exchanges, mercantile arithmetic, accounts current, &c. . . Phil. Pub. by the author, 1842. 80+79+[20]p. 28 x 22cm.

The author deposited for copyright (Eastern District of Pennsylvania) May 11, 1835, the following title: "Dando's newly discovered system of book-keeping by double books and double entry; comprised by a journal of merchandise, a journal of settlements and a ledger; adapted to the commerce of the United States; embracing a form of books suitable to jobbing, auction, commission and shipping houses generally; also annexed a form of balancing sheets . . ."

A circular was published in 1836 describing this work, quoting a recommendation by the Franklin institute of Dando's system and soliciting subscribers for the published work "soon to appear." It is doubtful that this manuscript copy of Dando's system was ever published. No copy was located.

It is probable that Dando's work published in 1842 under a different title is a revised and enlarged edition of the manuscript copy of Dando's system prepared and copyrighted in 1835.

1843

FOSTER, Benjamin Wood, 1810–1881.

A practical system of book-keeping by double and single entry, both in single and copartnership business; exemplified in three sets of books; with the most approved forms of exchanges, calculations . . . Bost. Saxton, Peirce & co.; N.Y. Saxton & Miles, 1843. 150p. 22½cm.

Another ed.	Bost. J. French; Saxton, Peirce & co.; N. Y. Saxton & Miles, 1843. 150p. 22½cm.
2d ed.	Bost. J. French; N. Y. Saxton & Miles, 1843. 150p. 23cm.
3d ed.	Bost. J. French; Saxton, Peirce & co.; N. Y. Saxton & Miles, 1843. 150p. 23cm.
4th ed.	Bost. J. French, 1844. 150p. 23cm.

FOSTER (continued)

5th ed.	Bost. Saxton & Huntington; N.Y. Saxton & Miles, 1845. 150p. 23½cm.
6th ed.	Bost. J. French, 1847. 150p. 23cm.
7th ed.	1848. 150p. 23½cm.
8th ed.	1850. 150p. 23cm.
11th ed.	1853. 150p. 24cm.
12th ed.	1854. 150p. 24cm.
13th ed.	1855.
15th ed.	1858. 184p. 24cm.
16th ed.	Bost. O.L. Briggs [c1860] 184p. 24½cm.
17th ed.	[1860] 184p. 24½cm.
17th ed.	[n.d.] 202p. 24½cm. A revised edition containing additional matter on custom house business.

—A practical system of book-keeping by single entry; exemplified in two sets of books . . . Bost. J. French; Saxton, Peirce & co. 1843. [32]p. 22½cm.

2d ed.	Bost. J. French, 1843. [31]p. 22cm.
4th ed.	1845. [31]p. 22cm.

1845

CRITTENDEN, A. F., and CRITTENDEN, Samuel Worcester, 1823?–1884.

An inductive and practical system of double entry book-keeping on an entirely new plan . . . Phil. E.C. & J. Biddle, 1845. 208p. 25½cm.

Counting house edition.

Contains twelve sets of books.

3d ed. 1848. 208p. 25½cm.

—An inductive and practical system of double entry book-keeping on an entirely new plan . . . Phil. E.C. & J. Biddle, 1845. 131p. 23½cm.

School edition, abridged from the counting house edition.

CRITTENDEN, Samuel Worcester, 1823?–1884.

An inductive and practical treatise on book-keeping by single and double entry . . . Phil. E.C. & J. Biddle, 1849. 248p. 25½cm.

Counting house edition.

Contains nine sets of books and a set of steamboat books.

Other eds.	1850; 1851; 1852. 248p. 25½cm.
Other eds.	1853; 1854; 1856. 288p. 25½cm. Each edition contains four sets of books by single entry and six sets by double entry, and a set of steamboat books.

—An inductive and practical treatise on book-keeping by single and double entry . . . Phil. E. C. & J. Biddle, 1849. 152p. 25½cm.

School edition, abridged from the counting house edition.

Other eds. 1851; 1853. 152p. 25½cm. School editions.

—An inductive and practical treatise on book-keeping by single and double entry . . . Phil. E. C. & J. Biddle, 1853. 174p. 25½cm.

High school edition.

Contains four sets of books by single entry and seven sets by double entry.

Another ed. 1856. 175p. 25½cm. High school edition.

—An elementary treatise on book-keeping by single and double entry; designed for common schools. Phil. E. C. & J. Biddle, 1853. 192p. 19½cm.

The title of this work was deposited for copyright (Eastern District of Pennsylvania) 1852.

Contains four sets of books by single entry and six sets by double entry.

Other eds. 1854; 1856; 1859; 1860; 1862; 1871. 192p. 19½cm.

—Single entry book-keeping; explained in four sets of books. Phil. E. C. & J. Biddle, 1854. 96p. 18cm.

The single entry part of "An inductive and practical treatise on book-keeping by single and double entry . . ." 1853.

Other eds. Phil. W. S. Fortescue & co. 1877; 1878. 104p. 28cm. Each edition contains five sets of books.

—and Crittenden, Salmon Hodges, 1829–1864.

An inductive and practical treatise on book-keeping by single and double entry . . . Phil. E. C. & J. Biddle, 1857. 314p. 25½cm.

Counting house edition.

Contains four sets of books by single entry, and six sets by double entry, and a set of steamboat books.

Other eds. 1859; 1860; 1865; 1866; 1867; 1869. 314p. 25½cm.

Another ed. 1870. 376p. 25½cm. Counting house edition. A set on banking by John Groesbeck has been added.

Another ed. Phil. W. S. Fortescue & co. 1875. 376p. 25½cm. Counting house edition.

CRITTENDEN (continued)

A set on banking by John Groesbeck has been added.

Other eds. 1878; 1881; 1883; 1885. 432p. 26cm.
Counting house and commercial college editions.
Each edition contains five sets of books by single entry and six sets by double entry.

—An inductive and practical treatise on book-keeping by single and double entry . . . Phil. E. C. & J. Biddle, 1857.
175p. 25½cm.
High school edition.
Other eds. 1861; 1864; 1866; 1867. 175p. 25½cm.
Another ed. Phil. W. S. Fortescue, 1870. 175p. 25½cm.
Another ed. 1878. 288p. 26cm.
High school and college edition.
Contains five sets of books by single entry and six sets by double entry.

FLEMING, John.

The national system of book-keeping; containing the art and science thereof . . . applicable to all kinds of business . . . exemplified in two sets of books kept by double entry . . .

The title of this work was deposited for copyright (Western District of Pennsylvania) February 6, 1845. This work is in later editions referred to as the first edition.

Another ed. Pittsburgh, M'Donald & Elliott, 1846.
117p. 26cm.
The title varies slightly from the 1845 edition.
This edition contains an appendix with separate title-page: The steam-boat book-keeper's assistant . . . Pittsburgh, M'Donald & Elliott, 1846.

3d ed. Cin. B. Davenport; Pittsburgh, M'Donald & Beesom, 1848. 141p. 25cm.

—Fleming's book-keeping by double entry; in five sets . . . with an appendix; containing a complete system of steamboat book-keeping, as now practiced on western rivers; together with many useful rules and calculations in equation of payments, partnerships &c.; designed for the use of schools and colleges, and a very useful companion in the counting-house. Pittsburgh, W. S. Haven; Phil. Cowperthwait, Desilver & Butler, 1854.
209p. 25½cm.

"This work is an expansion of the author's 'National system of book-keeping . . . ' published in 1845 and now in its fifth edition." — Pref.

The author introduced four short sets and omitted the set for

retailers. It contains the same introductory and preliminary matter as the 1846 edition.
It is practically a new work.
Appendix has separate title-page: The steamboat book-keeper's assistant . . . 5th ed. Pittsburgh, W. S. Haven; Phil. Cowperthwait, Desilver & Butler, 1854.

MOODY, Paul, 1804–1866.
A practical plan of book-keeping by double entry; adapted to a large or small business, with or without cash or other auxiliary books to daily journal and ledger . . . Phil. J. B. Lippincott & co. 1845. [49]p. 25½ x 20cm.
The title of this work was deposited for copyright (Eastern District of Pennsylvania) November 30, 1844.
A copy was deposited in the Clerk's office of the Eastern District of Pennsylvania, August 12, 1845. The title-page of the work is dated 1845.

NORTHEND, Charles, 1814–1895.
The common school book-keeping; being a simple and practical system by single entry; designed for the use of public schools and adapted to the wants of mechanics, farmers, and retail merchants . . . Bost. W. J. Reynolds, 1845.
2v. 20½ x 17cm. (v. 2: 26 x 21cm.)
Vol. 1, Day book, 8p.+24 blank ledger leaves.
Vol. 2, Ledger, 9+6p.+17 blank ledger leaves.
Other eds. 1849; 1850. 2v.
Another ed. Bost. Brown, Taggard & Chase, 1856.

1846

BENNET, James Arlington, 1788–1863.
A system of book-keeping by single entry; as applied in practice to the business of jobbing merchants, city retail merchants, and country merchants . . . being a self-instructor, and for the use of schools. N. Y. J. A. Bennet & co. 1846. 127p. 25½cm.

COMER, George Nixon, 1816–1877.
A simple method of keeping books by double-entry, without the formula or trouble of the journal; adapted to the most extensive wholesale, or the smallest retail business; to which is added a number of the most rapid and accurate methods of making commercial calculations. Bost. W. D. Ticknor & co. 1846.
104p. 23½cm.
2d ed. 1847. 104p. 24½cm.
3d ed. 1847. 104p. 24½cm.
4th ed. 1848. 104p. 24½cm.

COMER (continued)

5th ed.	Bost. Tappan, Whittemore & Mason, 1849. 104p. 23½cm.
6th ed.	1850. 104p. 23½cm.
11th ed.	Bost. Tappan & Whittemore, 1855. 104p. 23cm.
Other eds.	Bost. Whittemore, Niles & Hall, 1856; 1857. 103+[5]p. 23cm. Advertising matter: p.[104]–[109]
Another ed.	Bost. J. M. Whittemore & co. 1859. 103+[5]p. 23½cm.

DUFF, Peter, 1802–1869.

The western steamboat accountant: a new and complete system of book keeping; arranged and practically adapted for the use of steamers navigating the great western rivers and lakes; exemplified in one set of books kept by double entry . . . designed for the use of schools, book keepers, steamboat masters and owners. Pittsburgh, Pub. by the author, 1846. 63p. 26cm.

Another ed. N. Y. Pub. by the author, 1847. 63p. 28cm. This edition was published under the title: "The steamboat accountant . . . "

WINCHESTER, George W., 1808?–(?)

Winchester's book-keeping; or, The teacher's guide; containing the principles of single entry; embracing a clear, elementary and concise system of keeping accounts . . . accompanied by a journal and ledger.

The title of this work was deposited for copyright (Southern District of New York) February 10, 1846.

—Journal to Winchester's new method of teaching book-keeping by single entry; it being an accompaniment to The teachers' guide. Hartford, J. H. Mather & co. c1846. 30p. 27 x 22cm.

—Ledger to Winchester's new method of teaching book-keeping by single entry . . . Hartford, J. H. Mather & co. c1846. 35p. 27 x 22cm.

The Journal and the Ledger were deposited for copyright (Southern District of New York) November 20, 1846.

—Winchester's book-keeping; or, The teacher's guide; containing the principles of double entry; embracing a clear, elementary and concise system of keeping accounts . . . accompanied by a journal and ledger.

The title of this work was deposited for copyright (Southern District of New York) February 10, 1846.

Another ed. Hartford, J. H. Mather & co. c1848. 92p. 28 x 23cm.

—Journal to Winchester's new method of teaching book-keeping by double entry . . .
The title of this work was deposited for copyright (Southern District of New York) December 30, 1846.
Another ed. Hartford, J. H. Mather & co. c1848. 48p. 27 x 22cm.
Another ed. Hartford, H. H. Hawley & co.; Utica [N. Y.] Hawley, Fuller & co. c1848. 48p. 27 x 22cm.

—Ledger to Winchester's new method of teaching book-keeping by double entry . . .
The title of this work was deposited for copyright (Southern District of New York) December 30, 1846.
Another ed. Hartford, J. H. Mather & co. c1848. 47p. 27 x 22cm.

1847

BATCHELDER, Jacob, 1806–1876.
The national accountant: an improved system of book-keeping by single and double entry . . . comprising nine sets of books . . . Bost. J. P. Jewett & co.; Cin. E. D. Truman, 1847.
56p. 27½ x 22cm.
The title of this work was deposited for copyright (District of Massachusetts) December 21, 1846.
Another ed. Bost. Brown & Taggard, 1861. 56p. 27½ x 22cm.

BECKER, George J., 1816–1903.
A treatise on the theory and practice of book-keeping by double entry . . . Phil. Stereotyped by G. Charles, 1847.
180p. 23½cm.
Other eds. Phil. E. H. Butler & co. 1851; 1854; 1864; 1865; 1868. 184p. 23cm.

—A complete and practical system of double entry book-keeping; containing three sets of books . . . designed as a key to Becker's treatise on the theory and practice of book-keeping and as a guide for teachers and accountants; to which is added a complete set of practical business forms . . . Phil. S. Williams, 1848.
204p. 27cm.
Other eds. Phil. E. H. Butler & co. 1851; 1860. 204p. 27cm.

M'LAUGHLIN, Daniel.
A treatise on book-keeping by double entry, theoretical and practical. N. Y. Printed for the author by Davis & Trumbull, 1847.
128p. 23½cm.

Ross, William Parsons Meeker, 1815–(?)

A practical system of double entry book-keeping; adapted to the business of importing, shipping, and commissioned merchants . . . exemplified in four sets of books . . . designed for the use of schools and accountants. Phil. G. B. Zieber & co. 1847. 111p. 26½cm.

The title of this work was deposited for copyright (Eastern District of Pennsylvania) August 7, 1847.

—The theory and practice of book-keeping by double entry; arranged for conducting the business of importers, manufacturers, and wholesale and retail dealers generally.

The title of this work was deposited for copyright (Eastern District of Pennsylvania) March 20, 1847.

No copy of this work was located. It is not known whether the content of this work differs from "A practical system . . . " listed above, or whether it is a preliminary issue deposited for copyright under a different title.

1848

Duff, Peter, 1802–1869.

Duff's North American accountant; embracing single and double entry book-keeping; practically adapted to the inland and maritime commerce of the United States . . . N. Y. Pub. by the author, 1848. 192p. 26½cm.

Complete in two parts.

Other eds.	N. Y. Harper & bros. 1850; 1852; 1854; 1855. 192p. 26cm. Each edition is complete in two parts.
Another ed.	1854. 120p. 26cm. Part 2 is omitted.
10th ed.	1856. 222p. 25½cm. Complete in three parts.
Other eds.	1858; 1859; 1861; 1863; 1865. 222p. 25½cm. Each edition is complete in three parts.

—Duff's book-keeping by single and double entry; practically illustrating merchants', manufacturers', private bankers', railroad and national bank accounts; 20th ed. enl. & rev. N. Y. Harper & bros. 1868. 398p. 25½cm.

Cover-title: Mercantile, bank, and railroad bookkeeping.

The title of this work was deposited for copyright (Western District of Pennsylvania) 1867.

Based upon Duff's North American accountant and called 20th edition enlarged and revised.

The fourth part, p.227–383, is devoted entirely to railroad and bank bookkeeping.

It is practically a new work.

Other eds.	1869; 1870; 1871; 1873; 1876; 1882; 1896. 400p. 25½cm.

FULTON, Levi S., 1825–1895, and EASTMAN, George Washington, 1815–1862.

A practical system of book-keeping by single entry; containing three different forms of books; designed respectively for the farmer, mechanic, and merchant . . . N. Y. A. S. Barnes & co.; Cin. H. W. Derby & co. 1848. 232p. 18½cm.

2d ed.	1848. 232p. 18½cm.
3d ed.	1849. 232p. 18½cm.
3d ed.	1850. 230p. 18½cm.
4th ed.	1850. 232p. 18½cm.
5th ed.	1851. 296p. 19cm. The first edition of the work to include both single and double entry; called the fifth edition, revised.
6th ed.	1852. 296p. 19cm.
7th ed.	1853. 296p. 19cm.
Other eds.	1854; 1855; 1856; 1857. 296p. 19cm. Each reprint is called the seventh edition.
7th ed.	N. Y. A. S. Barnes & Burr, 1859. 296p. 19cm.
7th ed.	N. Y. S. A. Rollo & co. 1859. 296p. 19cm.
Another ed.	Troy, N. Y. Moore & Nims; N. Y. A. S. Barnes & Burr [c1863] 268p. 19cm. The date of the second preface is 1863.
Another ed.	1868.
Other eds.	Troy, N. Y. H. B. Nims & co. 1876; 1881; 1883. 253+[1]p. 19cm.
Another ed.	Troy, N. Y. Nims & Knight, 1888. 252+[2]p. 19cm. In 1875, a revised edition of this work was published in Toronto by A. Miller & co.

WILSON, Clement A.

A treatise on book keeping in a concise and practical form; for the tradesman, mechanic, lawyer, physician, dentist, clergyman, teacher, farmer &c.; and adapted for beginners in schools . . . Phil. Lindsay & Blackiston, 1848. 103p. 23½cm.

1849

FRENCH, John Homer, 1824–1888.

Book-keeping; containing a lucid explanation of the common method of book-keeping by single entry . . . methods of keeping

FRENCH (continued)
books by figures; short methods of keeping accounts in a limited business; exercises for the pupil; and various forms necessary for the transaction of business . . . designed for schools and academies. Keene, N. H. J. W. Prentiss & co. [c1849]
141p. 23cm. (Adams's arithmetical ser. no. 5)

At head of title: Adams's book-keeping.

J. Homer French, claiming to be author and proprietor of the copyright, deposited the title of this work (District of New Hampshire) March 21, 1849.

An advertisement dated August, 1848, signed by Daniel Adams and inserted in this work states: "The Primary arithmetic, the Treatise on mensuration and the Bookkeeping have been mainly prepared under my supervision by Mr. J. Homer French, of New York . . . "

This work, however, is chiefly known as "Adams's book-keeping" and authorship has been attributed to Daniel Adams (1773–1864).

J. Homer French and C. B. Galentine deposited for copyright (Northern District of New York) March 27, 1847, the following title: "Book-keeping analytically explained and practically applied to every department of business; the whole system of accounts made plain and familiar by numerous explanations and examples . . . designed for the use of schools, academies, and private learners."

This work is undoubtedly a forerunner of the work which French prepared for Daniel Adams.

Another ed. Keene, N. H. J. H. Spalter & co. [c1849]
141p. 21½cm. (Adams's arithmetical ser. no. 4)

JONES, Thomas, 1804–1889.
Book-keeping and accountantship, elementary and practical; in two parts; with a key for teachers . . . the whole being adapted to schools, self-instruction, or counting-house reference. N. Y. J. Wiley, 1849. 205p. 26½cm.

Each part was also published separately.

Another ed. 1850. 207p. 25½cm.

Another ed. 1853. 245p. 25cm.
Exercises, accounts of a banking house, and further material on equation of payments were added.

Other eds. 1855; 1857; 1860; 1864. 245+[1]p. 25cm.

1850

MACGREGOR, Patrick.
A practical treatise on book-keeping by single and double entry . . . containing: i. General book-keeping; for the use of farmers,

mechanics . . . ii. Retailers' book-keeping; iii. Merchants' book-keeping; with an appendix of definitions, directions, and practical forms; for the use of seminaries and self-instructors. N.Y. M.H. Newman & co.; Chic. S.C. Griggs & co. 1850. 274p. 19cm

Another ed. N.Y. Newman & Ivison; Chic. S.C. Griggs & co. 1852. 120p. 18½cm.
Contents as in entry above: p.1–115, parts 1 and 2; part 3, abridged and adapted for the use of common schools.

MUIR, John.
Muir's American accountant, mercantile manual, and instructor; comprising a concise method of book-keeping . . . Alexandria, Va. Printed at the Alexandria gazette off. 1850. 72p. 15cm.

1851

FAIRBANKS, Lorenzo Sayles, 1825–1897.
A complete system of practical book-keeping by double entry . . . arranged with special reference to public and private instruction . . . Bost. Pub. for the author, 1851. 189+[1]p. 22½cm.

MAYHEW, Ira, 1814–1894.
A practical system of book-keeping by single and double entry . . . N.Y. Cady & Burgess, 1851. 144p. 19cm.

Other eds.	N.Y. D. Burgess & co. 1852; 1853; 1855; 1856. 144p. 19cm.
[20th ed.]	Bost. Bazin & Ellsworth [1856] 144p. 18½cm.
Another ed.	Bost. Sanborn, Carter, Bazin & co. 1857. 144p. 20cm.
[60th ed.]	Bost. Nichols & Hill, 1860. 228p. 18½cm. Part 2 and part 3 are entirely new.
Other eds.	Bost. Chase, Nichols & Hill, 1861; 1862; [n.d.] 224p. 19cm.
Other eds.	Bost. Chase & Nichols, 1863; 1864. 228p. 19cm.
Other eds.	Bost. S.F. Nichols, 1865; 1866; 1867; 1868. 228p. 19cm.
Other eds.	Bost. Nichols & Hall, 1870; 1872; 1873; 1874; 1875. 228p. 19cm.
[140th ed.]	Phil. E.H. Butler & co.; Bost. C.H. Whiting [1880] 228p. 19½cm.
Another ed.	[c1888] 228p. 19½cm.

1852

Foster, Benjamin Franklin.
Double entry elucidated. Bost. T. R. Marvin, 1852.
152p. 21½ x 17½cm.
The author published a work with the same title in London in 1843. The content of the English work differs from that of the American work.

Keller, Henry.
An improved plan for day book, cash book, and journal. Columbus [Ohio] Printed by Scott & Bascom, 1852. 6p. 24cm.
The title of this work was deposited for copyright (District of Ohio) December 15, 1851.

Lowell, Daniel W., 1816–1897.
A treatise upon the theory and practice of book-keeping by double entry . . . and a copious glossary of commercial words and customs; the whole designed to afford to the merchant, the clerk, and the student at the academy an explanation of how business is done . . . Auburn [N. Y.] D. W. Lowell, 1852.
144p. 25cm.
The title of this work was first deposited for copyright (Northern District of New York) March 5, 1851, and again, March 22, 1852.
A series of diagrams illustrating "Lowell's book-keeping" were copyrighted and published separately.

Palmer, Joseph Howard, 1824–1892.
A treatise on practical book-keeping and business transactions; embracing the science of accounts and their extensive applications; designed as a class book for academies and schools.
N. Y. Pratt, Woodford & co. 1852. 167p. 19cm.
The title of this work was deposited for copyright, November 22, 1851. It is probable that the work was not published until 1852.
3d ed. 1852. 167p. 19cm.
4th ed. 1853. 167p. 19cm.
5th ed. 1853. 167p. 19cm.
13th ed. 1857. 167p. 19cm.
16th ed. N. Y. Pratt, Oakley & co. 1859. 167p. 19cm.
18th ed. N. Y. Sheldon & co. 1866. 167p. 18½cm.
18th ed. 1867. 167p. 18½cm.
20th ed. 1867. 172p. 19cm.
50th ed. 1884. 172p. 19cm.

—Palmer's elementary course: first lessons in book-keeping; introductory to A treatise on practical book-keeping and business transactions . . . N. Y. D. Appleton & co. 1852. 28p. 19cm.

—Common school book-keeping. N.Y. Farmer, Brace & co. [n.d.]

1853

MARSH, Christopher Columbus, 1806–1884.
A course of practice in single-entry book-keeping; improved by a proof or balance, and applied to partnership business; designed for the use of merchants, clerks, and schools . . . N.Y. J.C. Riker, 1853. 142+[2]p. 23cm.
Another ed. 1855. 142+[2]p. 23cm.
Other eds. N.Y. D. Appleton & co. 1859; 1861; 1864; 1868; 1876. 142p. 23½cm.

—Curso práctico de teneduría de libros por partida sencilla, con la mejora de un balance-prueba . . . traducido de la 4. ed. Americana; rev. y corr. por Gaspar Betancourt. N.Y. D. Appleton & co. 1857. 144p. 23½cm.
(Betancourt Cisneros, Gaspar, 1803–1866, editor)
Another ed. 1889. 144p. 24cm.

SMITH, John Coley, 1823–1883.
Practical book-keeping; or, Double entry adapted to the business of retail merchants and manufacturers. Cin. H.W. Derby & co. 1853. 55p. 24cm.

1854

EATON, William H.
Book-keeping by double entry; simplified and adapted to the business of both merchants and manufacturers . . . to which is added a single entry form . . . Worcester [Mass.] Printed by C. Hamilton, 1854. 106p. 22½ x 20cm.

NIXON, James.
The rudiments of book-keeping; designed for schools and self-instruction; with an address to students on the essentials to success in mercantile pursuits. N.Y. F.J. Huntington & Mason bros. 1854. 167p. 18½cm.
Thomas Jones attributes this work to Benjamin Franklin Foster. (Jones, Thomas. Book-keeping and accountantship . . . N.Y. J. Wiley, 1855. p.[246] Also, subsequent editions)
This work includes a list of works on bookkeeping (referred to as "Nixon's list") p.[155]–167. It is preceded by this note: "The most extensive and complete collection of works on book-keeping extant is in the possession of B.F. Foster of New York from whose recent pamphlet the following list of publications in the English language has been extracted."

SUTHERLAND, Hector.

Sutherland's national practical columnar system of mercantile book-keeping by double entry; combining theory and practice on an entirely new plan; comprising seven original columnar monthly methods of recording; completely adapted to individual and partnership business . . .

The title of this work was deposited for copyright (Western District of Pennsylvania) June, 1854.

—Sutherland's national practical columnar system of mercantile book-keeping by double entry . . . comprising fifteen original columnar monthly methods of recording; completely adapted to individual and partnership business . . . with an appendix containing practical examples and exercises in opening and balancing individual and partnership books . . . Pittsburgh, Printed by Singerly & Myers, 1857. 238p. 24cm.

The title of this work which is the same as the title listed above (except that there are fifteen instead of seven columnar methods and an appendix) was deposited for copyright (Western District of Pennsylvania) December, 1857. The preface to the 1857 edition, signed Pittsburgh, 1857, states that the author took out his first copyright for the columnar . . . system, May 4, 1835.

A record of the following titles by Sutherland deposited for copyright (Western District of Pennsylvania) was found: "Book-keeping; or, The ne plus ultra of the Italian method of double entry . . . simplified and condensed . . . so as to exhibit on the face of the day book separately and collectively the state of each branch of the merchant's business . . ." May 4, 1835.

"The American system of practical book-keeping; designed for mechanics in particular and merchants in general . . ." December, 1836.

"Book-keeping; or, The science of accounts illustrated and defined by a new, concise system of mercantile book-keeping by double entry applicable to all kinds of business . . ." May 2, 1839.

All these titles undoubtedly set forth the author's columnar system of bookkeeping.

1856

HERRIMAN, Ambrose.

Herriman's condensed system for self-instruction in rapid writing and book-keeping . . . adapted to the use of the farmer, mechanic, merchant and professional man . . . Lewiston [Me.] W. H. Waldron, printer, 1856. 18+[26]p. 18 x 21½cm.

MARSH, Christopher Columbus, 1806–1884.
The theory and practice of bank book-keeping and joint stock accounts; exemplified and elucidated in a complete set of bank account books; arranged in accordance with the principles of double entry; embracing the routine of business from the organization of a company to the declaration of a dividend; with all the forms and details and an original diagram. N.Y. D. Appleton & co. 1856. 292p. 31cm.

Other eds. 1859; 1863. 292p. 31cm.
4th ed. 1864. 292p. 31cm.
5th ed. 1866. 292p. 31cm.
7th ed. 1875. 300p. 31cm.
The seventh edition contains a supplement: Examples of entries in opening books of joint stock companies under different organizations.
Another ed. 1884. 292p. 31cm.

1858

COCHRAN, William D.
Agricultural book-keeping; being a concise and scientific system of keeping farm accounts; divested of all technical terms, and accompanied with blank books ruled and adapted to the system. Detroit, Daily advertiser steam presses, 1858.
67+[1]p. 24½cm.
The title of this work was deposited for copyright (District of Michigan) November 28, 1857.

HANAFORD, Lyman Brooks, 1818–1896, and PAYSON, Jesse Wentworth, 1815–1889.
Book-keeping by single and double entry; for schools and academies; adapted to Payson, Dunton & Scribner's combined system of penmanship. Bost. Crosby, Nichols & co. [c1858]
106p. 18 x 22½cm.
The day book and ledger leaves, copyrighted, 1858, were published separately.

Another ed. 1859. 144p. 18 x 22½cm.
Another ed. Bost. Crosby, Nichols, Lee & co. 1861. 140+[4]p. 18 x 22½cm.
Other eds. Bost. Crosby & Nichols, 1862; 1863; 1864. 140+[4]p. 19 x 22½cm.
Other eds. 1864; 1866. 256p. 19 x 22cm.
Academic editions with new sets added; p.207–256 contain his Mercantile arithmetic.
Other eds. Bost. Crosby & Ainsworth, 1867; 1868. 140+[4]p. 19 x 22cm.
Another ed. N.Y. Chic. Woolworth, Ainsworth & co. [186–?] [c1872] 140+[4]p. 18½ x 22½cm.

HANAFORD (continued)
—Book-keeping by single entry; for common schools; adapted to Payson, Dunton & Scribner's combined system of penmanship. Bost. Crosby, Nichols & co. [c1858] 63+[1]p. 19x22cm.
On cover: Common school edition.
Another ed. Bost. Crosby & Ainsworth [c1858] 53+[10]p. 19x22cm.
Another ed. N.Y. Woolworth, Ainsworth & co. [c1858] 53+[10]p. 17½x21cm.
Another ed. 1871. 53+[10]p. 17½x21cm.
This work bears the copyright date, 1858.

HAYDEN, Samuel Denton, 1801–1865.
The common school writing and account book; designed for youth . . . being a complete system of book-keeping; adapted to the business of every man . . . 4th ed. Bost. R.S. Davis & co.; Springfield [Mass.] C.R. Chafee & co. [c1858]
24p. 25½x20½cm.
The copyright record for the first, second, and third editions could not be located in the copyright record books of the District Court of Massachusetts nor of any other district court.

HILL, John J.
A concise method of keeping the accounts and stock transfers of railroads and other corporate agencies in the city of New York. N.Y. N. Lane & co. 1858. 92p. 23½cm.

1859

CHURCH, A. B.
Single entry book-keeping in an entirely new form; improved by the introduction of the proof or balance . . . school ed. Cin. Longley bros. 1859. 112p. 23½cm.

GOLDSMITH, Oliver B., 1815–1888, and Renville, Willis J.
Goldsmith's system of double entry book-keeping . . . also a vocabulary of mercantile terms and various commercial calculations. N.Y. Sheldon, Blakeman & co. 1859. 133p. 24½cm.

HOIT, Daniel.
Book-keeping by single and double entry. Bost. Pub. by the author, 1859. 156p. 23½cm.
The title of this work was deposited for copyright (District of Massachusetts) March 16, 1858.

JONES, Thomas, 1804–1889.
Paradoxes of debit and credit demolished; double entry results obtained from single entry; equation of payments in a nutshell;

principles versus rules, with an effervescence from the contact of common sense; "commercial colleges" and patronage; prepared for "those who think." N.Y. J. Wiley, 1859. 74p. 24cm.

POTTER, Stephen A., 1823?–1897, and HAMMOND, William Pool, 1827–1901.

Potter and Hammond's system of book-keeping by single and double entry for common and high schools; in three numbers . . .

The title of this work was deposited for copyright (Eastern District of Pennsylvania) August 2, 1859. Number 2 in the series of three numbers copyrighted was deposited August 24, 1859.

Another ed. Phil. Schermerhorn, Bancroft & co. [c1862] 3 nos. 18½ x 22½cm.
On cover of no. 2: Common school edition . . .
On cover of no. 3: High school edition . . .

Another ed. Phil. Cowperthwait & co. c1866. 3 nos. in 2v. 18½ x 22½cm.

Another ed. N.Y. Chic. Potter, Ainsworth & co. [n.d.] 76p. 18½ x 24cm.
Common school edition.

SELDEN, Charles.

Selden's condensed ledger; or, Book-keeping simplified: the condensed ledger combines the journal, ledger and balance-sheet, so as to present numerous accounts at a glance; and is peculiarly adapted to governmental or corporate company transactions.

The title of this work was deposited for copyright (Southern District of Ohio) in 1859, 1860, and 1861.

The 1861 edition was published in Cincinnati by Moore, Wilstach, Keys & co.

The author also deposited for copyright (Southern District of Ohio) in 1860 and 1861 his "Condensed memorandum book;" "Forms of record for vouchers and money orders;" and "Forms of mercantile ledger," each of which was designed to accompany the work listed above.

This work consists of an introductory essay explaining Selden's system of bookkeeping and certain forms or blanks, consisting of ruled lines and headings, illustrating the system. Selden claimed that William C. M. Baker (See 1874; 1876; 1881) infringed the copyrights of his books by publishing a similar system with a different arrangement of columns and headings. The famous United States Supreme Court decision (Baker vs. Selden, U.S. reports, v. 101, p. 99, 1880) held that there is a clear distinction between the book as such (describing the art, and thus entitled to copyright) and the art itself which it is intended to illustrate. "The object of the one is explana-

SELDEN (continued)
tion; the object of the other is use. The former may be secured by copyright. The latter can only be secured . . . by letters-patent." The conclusion of the decision was that blank account books were not the subject of copyright. This court decision is still cited in refusing for copyright blank account books and other form books illustrating a bookkeeping system.

SMITH, William W., 1827?–1874, and MARTIN, Edward.
Book-keeping by single and double entry; simplified and adapted to the use of common schools. N.Y. A.S. Barnes & Burr, 1859. 98+[2]p. 22½ x 19cm.
At head of title: Practical book-keeping for youth.
Another ed. 1860. 98+[2]p. 22½ x 19cm.
Other eds. N.Y. A.S. Barnes & co. 1873; 1874; 1887. 108p. 23 x 19cm.

1860

BRYANT, Henry Beadman, 1824–1892, STRATTON, Henry Dwight, 1824–1867, and PACKARD, Silas Sadler, 1826–1898.
Bryant & Stratton's national book-keeping: an analytical and progressive treatise on the science of accounts and its collateral branches; prepared as a book of reference for the counting-house, and also as a text-book in high schools and academies. N.Y. Ivison, Phinney & co.; Chic. S.C. Griggs & co. 1860. 216p. 26cm.
This work is also known as "High-school book-keeping."
Other eds. [186–?] 1863. 216p. 26cm.
Other eds. N.Y. Ivison, Phinney, Blakeman & co. 1867; 1868; 1870. 216p. 26½cm.

—The new Bryant & Stratton high-school book-keeping; adapted to use in business colleges and the higher grades of public and private schools. N.Y. Ivison, Blakeman, Taylor & co. 1881. 166p. 26cm.
S.S. Packard and H.B. Bryant appear on the title-page as joint authors.
"This book is a revision of Bryant & Stratton's high-school book-keeping, as first published in 1860 . . . "—Pref.
This work is also known as "Bryant & Stratton's national book-keeping."
Another ed. N.Y. Amer. bk. co. [c1909] 166p. 26cm.
This edition was copyrighted by H.W. Bryant.

COTHEAL, William, 1822–1870.
New method of keeping accounts. N.Y. J. W. Amerman, printer, 1860. 15p. 22½cm.

1861

BRYANT, Henry Beadman, 1824–1892, STRATTON, Henry Dwight, 1824–1867, and PACKARD, Silas Sadler, 1826–1898.
Common school book-keeping; embracing single and double entry. N. Y. Ivison, Phinney & co. 1861. 192p. 20½cm.
Other eds. N. Y. Ivison, Phinney, Blakeman & co.; Chic. S. C. Griggs & co. 1864; 1866; 1867; 1868. 192p. 21½cm.
Other eds. N. Y. Ivison, Blakeman, Taylor & co. 1871; 1876. 192p. 21½cm.
—The new Bryant & Stratton common school book-keeping; embracing single and double entry; adapted to individual and class instruction in schools and academies. N. Y. Ivison, Blakeman, Taylor & co. [c1878] 208p. 21cm.
S. S. Packard and H. B. Bryant appear on the title-page as joint authors.
"This little book almost in its entirety, was prepared and published more than seventeen years ago." — Pref.
Other eds. 1880; 1881. 208p. 21½cm.
Another ed. N. Y. Ivison, Blakeman & co. [n. d.] 208p. 21½cm.
Items in appendix dated 1879.
Another ed. N. Y. Cin. [etc.] Amer. bk. co. [189–?] 208p. 21cm.

COMER, George Nixon, 1816–1877.
Book-keeping rationalized; adapted to all kinds of business,—personal and partnership, commission and corporate; together with entirely new and rapid methods of computing interest, exchange, average accounts, etc.; a copious appendix . . . Bost. Comer & co. 1861. 168p. 20cm.
2d ed. 1862. 168p. 20cm.
3d ed. Bost. F. A. Brown & co. 1863. 168p. 19½cm.
Other eds. 1864; 1865. 168p. 19½cm.
Other eds. Bost. Comer's commercial college, 1866; 1867; 1869; 1871; 1873; 1875; 1878; 1880; 1884; 1885. 168p. 19½cm.
The 1885 edition is called the 53d edition.

DAY, Henry Noble, 1808–1890.
The art of book-keeping, methodically unfolded in its principles and illustrated by copious exercises; for use in schools and for private study. Cin. Moore, Wilstach, Keys & co. 1861. 161p. 20cm.
At head of title: The systematic accountant.
Another ed. 1868. 161p. 20cm.

SHORES, J. F., jr.
Exercises in book-keeping by double entry. Portsmouth [N. H.] J. F. Shore, jr. 1861. 35p. 19cm.
"This work has been prepared at the request of Dr. Robert D. Treadwell, chairman of the high school committee of this city . . . J. F. Shores, jr. Portsmouth, Sept. 1861." — Introd.
3d ed. Portsmouth [N. H.] W. G. Myers, 1878. 46p. 19cm.

1862

SARGENT, Aaron, 1822–1913.
The theory and practice of book-keeping combined. Bost. Swan, Brewer & Tileston, 1862. 44p. 23 x 18cm.
The title of this work was deposited for copyright (District of Massachusetts) December 30, 1861.
Another ed. 1863. 44p. 22½ x 17½cm.
Another ed. Bost. Brewer & Tileston [c1861] 44p. 22½ x 17½cm.

1863

BRYANT, Henry Beadman, 1824–1892, STRATTON, Henry Dwight, 1824–1867, and PACKARD, Silas Sadler, 1826–1898.
Bryant & Stratton's counting-house book-keeping; containing a complete exposition of the science of accounts in its application to the various departments of business . . . N. Y. Ivison, Phinney & co. 1863. 375p. 26½cm.
Other eds. N. Y. Ivison, Phinney, Blakeman & co. 1866; 1867; 1868; 1869. 375p. 26½cm.
—Advanced sheets of The new Bryant & Stratton universal book-keeping. [N. Y.] c1878. 75p. 25½cm.
"Advance sheets of the new counting-house edition." — Pref.
S. S. Packard appears on the title-page as author.
—The new Bryant & Stratton counting-house book-keeping; embracing the theory and practice of accounts . . . N. Y. Chic. Ivison, Blakeman, Taylor & co. 1878. 304p. 26cm.
S. S. Packard & H. B. Bryant appear on the title-page as joint authors.
"The book is intended to supplant 'Bryant & Stratton's counting-house book-keeping,' first published in 1863. It can hardly be said to be a revision . . . as there are few things in common." — Pref.
Other eds. N. Y. Ivison, Blakeman, Taylor & co. 1879; 1880; 1881; 1883; 1885. 304p. 26cm.
Other eds. N. Y. Cin. [etc.] Amer. bk. co. [c1878] [189–?] 304p. 26cm.

1865

SMITH, John Coley, 1823–1883, and JENKINS, Friend W., 1825?–1888.

The national accountant: a treatise on the theory and practice of book-keeping by double and single entry; complete in three parts . . . specially adapted to the use of schools, academies, colleges, and private learners; also as a work of reference for the counting-room. Pittsburgh, Printed by A. H. English & co. 1865. 320p. 26cm.

Other eds. Phil. Lippincott, 1891; 1893; 1905. 320p. 26cm.
Smith appears on the title-page of each edition as the sole author.
The 1893 and 1905 editions were copyrighted by Elizabeth A. Smith and Charles J. Smith.

1866

FAIRBANKS, Lorenzo Sayles, 1825–1897.

The science and practice of book-keeping by double and single entry . . . Phil. Sower, Barnes & Potts; Chic. Speakman & Proctor, 1866. 448p. 26cm.

The title of this work was first deposited for copyright (Eastern District of Pennsylvania) December 27, 1865, and was again deposited for copyright in the same district, November 6, 1866. Though the title-page states that this work is "a part of the course of instruction in the science of accounts" of Quaker City Business College of Philadelphia the preface indicates that the work was prepared for general use.

Other eds. 1869; 1881. 448p. 26cm.

ROHRER, Louis.

Definitions and explanations of the science of book-keeping; compiled from the best authorities and arranged by Louis Rohrer . . . for the use of teachers, accountants, and students; 3d enl. ed. Phil. J. B. Lippincott & co.; St. L. J. M. Crawford, 1866. 154p. 26cm.

The copyright record for the first and second editions could not be found.
The third edition was deposited for copyright (Eastern District of Missouri) December 3, 1865.
The same title was again deposited for copyright in the same district, April 21, 1866.

Another ed. 1867. 324p. 26cm.
Counting house edition.

ROHRER (continued)

This edition was deposited for copyright, November 20, 1866.

10th ed.	St. L. W. J. Gilbert, 1872. 324p. 26cm. Counting house edition.
10th ed.	1873. 270p. 26cm. School edition.
Another ed.	1875. [51]p. 27cm. Primary school edition.
Another ed.	1877. 324p. 26cm. Counting house edition.
11th ed.	St. L. Gilbert bk. co. 1883. 324p. 26cm.
11th ed.	1886. Counting house edition.
Other eds.	Lebanon, Ohio, c1888. The various editions of Rohrer's work were revised and enlarged by Josiah Holbrook and deposited for copyright in 1888 by Alfred Holbrook who claimed proprietorship of the copyright. The title varies.

WRIGHT, William.

The national system of book-keeping; containing the elements, practice, and science . . . for the use of schools; carefully prepared and adapted for the mercantile and commercial business of the United States . . . in which the true principles are set forth . . . in seven sets of books kept by double entry . . . Phil. J. B. Lippincott & co. 1866. 167p. 18 x 23cm.

Another ed. N. Y. W. Wright, 1875. 167p. 18 x 23cm.

1867

DAY, Henry Noble, 1808–1890.

Day's book-keeping without a master; comprising the rudiments of double and single entry, and plain instructions in condensed and general book accounts. N. Y. Dick & Fitzgerald, 1867. 56p. 22cm.

MAYHEW, Ira, 1814–1894.

Mayhew's university book-keeping: a treatise on business and accounts; designed as a text-book for commercial colleges and seminaries of learning; for use in the counting-room and for private study . . . Bost. Nichols & Hall, 1867. 318p. 22½cm.

Other eds.	1870; 1871; 1872; 1879. 318p. 22½cm.
Another ed.	Bost. C. H. Whiting [1880?] 318p. 22½cm.
Another ed.	N. Y. Bost. [etc.] Silver, Burdett, 1899. 318p. 22½cm.

—and WALWORTH, Charles A.
Manual of business practice for teachers and students; adapted to Mayhew's university book-keeping; used with Walworth's business practice drawer; and containing complete directions for their joint use. Detroit, Mayhew, 1870. 60p. 19½cm.
—New manual of business practice for teachers and students . . . Detroit, The author [c1880] 69+[1]p. 21½cm.
MAYHEW, Ira, 1814–1894.
Five double-entry sets of Mayhew's university book-keeping to which are adapted currency and papers for actual business practice . . . Bost. C.H. Whiting [c1883] p.195–278, 22cm.

1868

DYHRENFURTH, Julius, 1814–1890.
American autodidactic; or, Self-teaching system of book-keeping. Chic. G. & C.W. Sherwood, 1868. 71p. 22½cm.

ELLSWORTH, Henry William, 1837–1924.
Ellsworth's single and double entry book-keeping and business manual; for schools, academies, business colleges or private instruction. N.Y. Ellsworth; D. Appleton & co. 1868.
132p. 18x22½cm.
In two parts; each part also published separately.
2d ed. 1869. 133p. 18x22½cm.
3d ed. 1870. 132p. 18x22½cm.
Another ed. 1873. 132p. 18x22½cm.

PACKARD, Silas Sadler, 1826–1898.
Manual of theoretical training in the science of accounts; prepared for use in, and respectfully dedicated to, the several institutions comprised in the International business college association.
[N.Y.] The author, 1868. 47p. 22cm.
Another ed. 1876.
Another ed. N.Y. Packard pub. co. 1882. 47p. 22½cm.

1869

BRYANT, John Collins, 1821–1901.
Bryant's book-keeping: a treatise on the science of accounts in two parts, elementary and practical; containing a thorough explanation of the principles and practice of double entry book-keeping; adapted to the use of universities, business colleges, academies, public schools and self-instruction. Buffalo, Pub. by the author, 1869. 60p. 19cm.

BRYANT (continued)

2d ed. 1872. 120p. 23cm.

3d ed. 1874. 160p. 23cm.

5th ed. 1876. 160p. 22½cm.
On cover: Bryant's commercial book-keeping.

Another ed. 1876. 309p. 23cm.
On cover: Bryant's counting house book-keeping.
The complete work: counting house edition.
Contents as in the fifth edition: p.1–160; with the addition of manufacturing and modern banking sets: p.161–309.

Another ed. 1877. 309p. 23cm.
This edition is like the 1876 edition.

—Bryant's new elementary book-keeping; designed for common schools, elementary departments of academies, commercial and business colleges, and for self-instruction. Buffalo, Pub. by the author [1876] 96p. 21cm.

Added title-page: Bryant's book-keeping: a treatise on the science of accounts . . . 5th ed. rev. & enl.
Contents as in the fifth edition: p.1–96.

—Bryant's new book-keeping, elementary and practical; containing a thorough explanation of the principles and practice of double and single entry . . . 6th ed. 1880. 312p. 23½cm.

The complete work: counting house edition.
Part 1, p.1–160, was also published separately with the cover title: Bryant's new commercial book-keeping.

7th ed. [1881] 312p. 23½cm.
Counting house edition.
Part 1, p.1–160, was also published separately with the cover title: Bryant's new commercial book-keeping.

8th ed. [1882] 312p. 23½cm.
Counting house edition.
Part 1, p.1–160, was also published separately with the cover title: Bryant's new commercial book-keeping.

10th ed. 1883. 312p. 23½cm.
On cover: Bryant's new counting house book-keeping.
Part 1, p.1–160, was also published separately with the cover title: Bryant's new commercial book-keeping.

—The new standard counting-house book-keeping, theoretical and practical; containing a thorough exposition of the principles and practice of double and single entry, and a full illustration of modern business forms . . . Buffalo, J. C. Bryant, 1885. 312p. 23½cm.

—The new standard commercial book-keeping, theoretical and practical; containing a thorough elucidation of the principles of double and single entry, and illustrating the modern practical forms used in business . . . Buffalo, J. C. Bryant, 1885. 160p. 23cm.

Part 1 of "The new standard counting-house book-keeping . . ." published separately under the above title.

Other eds. 1887; 1890; 1892. 160p. 23cm.

—The new standard elementary book-keeping, theoretical and practical; containing a thorough explanation and illustration of the principles and practice of double and single entry . . . Buffalo, J. C. Bryant, 1885. 104p. 22½cm.

2d ed. 1886. 104p. 22½cm.

—The new standard practical and progressive book-keeping, double and single entry; for use in business and other colleges, and for self-instruction. Buffalo, The author, 1893. 223p. 29½cm.

Counting house edition.

"The present revision is by far the most radical one that has been made." — Pref.

Based upon "The new standard counting-house book-keeping . . ." published in 1885.

Other eds. 1896; 1901; 1911; 1916. 223p. 30cm.
Counting house editions.

Other eds. 1893; 1894. 112p. 30cm.
Commercial editions.

Another ed. 1896. 148p. 30cm.
Commercial edition.

Another ed. 1916. 155p. 30cm.
Commercial edition.

FODELL, William P., 1833–1906.

A system for keeping the histories and accounts of gas-light companies; with forms, etc. usual for such companies. Phil. Printed by W. K. Bellows; N. Y. M. L. Callender & co. 1869. 43p. 23cm.

METTENHEIMER, H. J.

Auditor's guide; being a complete exposition of book keeper's frauds . . . also containing a new and safe method of managing the cash department of retail stores, and a purchase account for commission houses. Phil. The author [c1869] 16p. 14cm.

—Safety book-keeping; being a complete exposition of book-keepers' frauds . . . Cin. R. Clarke & co. 1875. 64p. 17cm.

Another ed. 1877.

1870

NELSON, Richard, 1822–1900.

Nelson's book-keeping: a text book for schools and colleges, and a book of reference for merchants, book-keepers, clerks, and secretaries . . . part 1. Louisville, Ky. J. P. Morton & co. 1870. 119+[1]p. 23½cm.

Another ed. Cin. The author, 1882. 120p. 23½cm. Part 1.

—Nelson's new book-keeping: a text-book for schools and colleges, and a book of reference for accountants. Cin. R. Nelson, 1885. 351p. 27cm.

The complete work.

4th ed. Cin. Cincinnati & Springfield pub. co. 1890. 351p. 27cm. The complete work.

—Nelson's book-keeping for schools and colleges. Cin. Cincinnati & Springfield pub. co. 1886. 178p. 26cm.

Abridgment of the author's complete work.

WALKER, Harvey Day, 1817–1912.

Book-keeping for the million; book-keeping by single entry: a text-book for public schools and academies. Phil. Claxton, Remsen & Haffelfinger, 1870. 114p. 26½cm.

The title of this work was deposited for copyright (Eastern District of Pennsylvania) October 20, 1869.

1871

CALKINS, Storrs Seabury.

Calkins's business instructor; containing rules, definitions and explanations for keeping every kind of account books and doing business generally; also, the most wonderful and practical business lightning calculations ever discovered; also, the rules of commercial law epitomized for convenient reference. Oberlin [Ohio] R. Butler, printer, 1871. 156+[2]p. 22cm.

—Supplement to Calkins's business instructor . . . [Oberlin, Ohio, c1872] 122p. 22cm.

—Calkins's business instructor . . . rev. ed. Cleveland, Home companion pub. co. 1881. 329+[7]p. 22½cm.

HASWELL, Charles Haynes, 1809–1907.

Book-keeping by double entry; explained and practically illustrated in a complete record of mercantile and financial transactions . . . designed for schools, counting-houses, and private instruction; in two parts. N. Y. D. Appleton & co. 1871. 203p. 27cm.

Part 2 also published separately.

JOHNSON, Martin R., and KENNEDY, P. W.
The accountant's guide: a practical work on double entry bookkeeping . . . designed for the use of business men and schools. [N. Y. J. O. Dobelbower, printer, c1871] 212p. 26cm.
This work is probably the basis for the work by M. R. Powers and M. R. Johnson, published in 1875. Powers bought the copyright of Johnson's book in 1875.

PHILLIPS, Joseph Monroe, and LOSIER, E. K.
Actual business instruction; designed for the use of colleges to conduct a course of instruction in bookkeeping, or the science of accounts and business affairs; based entirely on the operations of finance and trade, wholly discarding the use of text books. Balt. Actual business college, 1871. 17 l. 24cm.
Other eds. 1872; 1873; 1874.
The title of this work was deposited for copyright, 1872, 1873, 1874 by Joseph M. Phillips as sole author.
The title, deposited for copyright, 1874, is called the fifth edition.

PHILLIPS, Joseph Monroe, WILLIAMS, Thomas M., and SCOTT, Robert C.
Actual business accountant . . . 6th ed. Pittsburgh, Actual business college, 1882. [319]p. 27½cm.
College edition.
Also issued under the title: "Williams, Phillips & co.'s actual business accountant."
(Counter forms adapted to Williams, Scott and Phillips' actual business accountant; part first; first settlement—sole proprietor. Pittsburgh, Actual business college, 1882. [37]p. 37½cm.)
7th ed. 1885. [586]p. 27½cm.
Library edition.
Another ed. 1891.

PHILLIPS, Joseph Monroe, and WILLIAMS, Thomas M.
Actual business accountant . . . Pittsburgh, c1892. [312]p. 28cm.

PHILLIPS, Joseph Monroe, and CONNER, Matthew J.
Revised actual business accountant . . . 9th ed. [Pittsburgh] 1896. [481]p. 28cm.

PHILLIPS, Joseph Monroe, WILLIAMS, Thomas M., and SCOTT, Robert C.
Actual business accountant . . . Pittsburgh, Pittsburgh & Allegheny actual business colleges, 1897. [181]p. 26½cm.
Also issued under the title: "Williams, Phillips & co.'s actual business accountant."

1872

JORDAN, Joseph B., 1836?–1900.

Jordonian short method of double entry book-keeping; for the use of schools, colleges and private learners. Toledo, Spear, Johnson & co. printers, 1872. 52p. 22cm.

—Jordan's practical book-keeping; for the use of schools, colleges and private learners; 10th ed. Toledo [c1888] 142p. 22½cm.

"Jordan's practical book-keeping was first published in 1872. In 1875 the work was enlarged, and in 1878 it underwent another revision. The present edition has been carefully revised . . . "—Pref.

PACKARD, Silas Sadler, 1826–1898.

A complete course of business training; embracing instruction and materials for practice in book-keeping, arithmetic, commercial law and correspondence; and adapted to use in business colleges. N.Y. The author, 1872. 87p. 23½cm.

Another ed. N.Y. Packard pub. co. 1873. 248p. 23½cm. Includes the Key.

Other eds. 1875; 1876; 1877; 1882; 1884. 93p. 23½cm.

—Advanced sheets of Packard's new manual of book-keeping. N.Y. S.S. Packard, 1883. 118p. 23½cm.

—Packard's new manual of book-keeping and correspondence. N.Y. S.S. Packard, 1884. 158p. 23cm.

A new edition of "A complete course of business training . . ." "To some extent, supersedes the old book."

Other eds. 1885; 1888; 1890; 1894. 158p. 23cm.

SHROCK, Jonathan.

Shrock's theoretical guide to double entry book-keeping; with definitions, principles and rules: a manual for the use of teachers and students. Mt. Pleasant [Ia.] Mt. Pleasant journal print, 1872. 13+[1]p. 14cm.

WAITT, David M., 1831–1875.

A self-instructor on the science and practice of book-keeping by double and single entry. Augusta, Me. 1872. 130p. 23cm.

Another ed. Augusta, Me. Waitt & Reynolds, 1872. 134p. 23cm. The author states in his preface (1872 edition) that in 1865 he published a small treatise on bookkeeping entitled "Student's guide" for use in the Augusta commercial college. The copyright record of this work could not be found.

1873

DREW, William A., 1829–1901.

Practical book-keeping; containing thorough instruction in journalizing, posting, and closing . . . Chic. G. Sherwood & co. [c1873] 138p. 23½cm.

At head of title: For common schools, business colleges, and the counting house.

Another ed. 1876.

FOLSOM, Ezekiel Gilman, 1821–1897.

Folsom's logical bookkeeping; the logic of accounts: a new exposition of the theory and practice of double-entry bookkeeping, based in value as being of two primary classes commercial and ideal . . . for students and business men. N.Y. A.S. Barnes & co. 1873. 442p. 21cm.

The title of this work was deposited for copyright, September, 1871, by A.S. Barnes & co., proprietor of the copyright. Two copies of the work were not deposited until 1873.

—The revised logic of accounts: a new, practical and scientific exposition of universal book-keeping, based on principles of political economy. Albany, Weed, Parsons & co. printers, 1881. 29p. 23½cm.

On cover: Advance sheets of Folsom's logic of accounts, revised.

GARBER, Samuel.

The science of double-entry book-keeping; abridged and stripped of its absurdities . . . Greenville post off. Pa. S. Garber & co. [c1873] 23p. 26½ x 34cm.

At head of title: A novelty for the investigation and criticism of accountants and the instruction of inquirers . . .

NICHOLS, Benjamin E., 1826–1889.

Practical book-keeping by single and double entry; for the common school, the high school and the commercial college. Ann Arbor, Mich. Courier steam print. house, 1873. 104p. 24cm.

Another ed. Ann Arbor [Mich.] Register steam print. house, 1876. 136p. 22cm.
Brief chapters on commercial law, prepared under the supervision of T.M. Cooley, have been added.

Another ed. 1879. 152p. 22cm.

Another ed. [c1879] 80p. 22cm.
Abridgment of the 1876 edition.

Another ed. [c1884] 224p. 22½cm.

Another ed. 1888.

1874

BAKER, William C. M.

Baker's self-instructive book-keeping; short method; how to keep accounts of merchants, wholesale and retail, manufacturers, physicians, attorneys, justices, clerks of courts, insurance agents, hotels, boarding houses, traders, business men, clerks, mechanics, printers, salaried or commissioned men, and farmers. Columbus, Ohio, W. C. M. Baker, publisher, 1874. 24+[11]p. 20½cm.

The title of this work was deposited for copyright, 1873.

Various books used in Baker's new self-instructive and short system of book-keeping, the memorandum book, synoptic ledger, sales book, etc., were published separately.

BROTHERS OF THE CHRISTIAN SCHOOLS.

Questions on bookkeeping; with exercises in journalizing. West Chester, N. Y. Printed at the Boys' Catholic protectory, 1874. 31p. 19cm.

—Questions on book-keeping; with practical exercises in single and double entry, and business forms. N. Y. De LaSalle institute, 1884. 72p. 21cm.

A revised and enlarged edition of the work published in 1874. The 1884 edition was copyrighted by John P. Murphy (Brother Isaac John).

Another ed. N. Y. LaSalle bur. of supplies [c1884] 102p. 18cm.

RICE, Thomas A.

The accountant's manual; embracing instruction and materials for practice in book-keeping, business forms, and correspondence; and adapted for use in schools and colleges. St. L. The author, 1874. 80p. 22½cm.

—Rice's practical book-keeping . . . St. L. The author, 1879. 120+[2]p. 22cm.

The second edition of "The accountant's manual . . . "

—Practical single and double entry book-keeping . . . designed as a book of reference for business men, building associations and corporations; as a text book for schools, academies and colleges, and for self-instruction. St. L. The author [c1889] 319p. 22cm.

The fourth edition of "The accountant's manual . . . "

1875

ANONYMOUS (possibly Thomas Faulkner*)

Book-keeping made easy, by single and double entry; containing

* The Library of Congress attributes authorship to Thomas Faulkner.

full instructions whereby the whole art of book-keeping may be acquired without the aid of a master. N.Y. Hurst & co. [c1875] 54p. 17½cm.

Though the book bears the copyright date, 1874, the title was actually copyrighted, 1875.

The proprietor of the copyright was Hurst & co.

No author is named on the title-page.

—The American business man and book-keeper's practical guide: a manual for the store, office, and counting-room. N.Y. Hurst & co. [c1878] 100p. 19cm.

The contents of this work include fifty-two pages of definitions plus "Book-keeping made easy . . . " listed above, copyrighted in 1875. This title was copyrighted in 1878. The proprietor of the copyright was Hurst & co. No author is indicated in the copyright record or on the title-page.

Clark, W. S.

Clark's short and easy method of double-entry book-keeping; containing brief and simple rules, thoroughly explaining the system . . . and information for the accountant. Cin. W. S. Clark, 1875. 45p. 18cm.

Fink, Albert, 1827–1897.

Cost of railroad transportation, railroad accounts, and governmental regulation of railroad tariffs . . . extract from the annual report of the Louisville and Nashville railroad co. for the year ending June 30, 1874. Louisville [Ky.] Printed by J. P. Morton & co. 1875. [48]p. 23½cm.

Popularly known as "The Fink report" and "The famous twenty-third annual report of the Louisville and Nashville."

2d ed. N.Y. Railroad gazette [187–?]
p.[51]–95+p.[19]–48, 23½cm.
This work was reprinted several times.

Groesbeck, John, 1834–1884.

Practical book-keeping, single and double entry; in accordance with the best forms and methods in actual use among business men. Phil. S.H. Crittenden & co. 1875. 225p. 25cm.

High school edition.

Other eds. Phil. Eldredge & bro. 1876; 1884.
255p. 25½cm.
College editions.

Other eds. 1878; 1879. 197p. 19cm.
School editions.

Lamb, W. F.

The double entry game of accounts. Springfield, Mass. C. W. Bryan & co. printers, 1875. 22p. 14½cm.

MESERVEY, Atwood Bond, 1831–1901.

Meservey's book-keeping without a master. New Hampton, N.H. C.D. Thyng [c1875] 135p. 21cm.

—Meservey's book-keeping, single and double entry. Bost. Thompson, Brown & co. [c1877] 156p. 21cm.

Contents as in entry above: p.1–129.

Another ed. 1878. 156p. 21cm.

Another ed. [c1882] 216p. 20½cm.

Other eds. [c1882] [c1893] [c1895] 222p. 21cm.

—Meservey's book-keeping, single entry; for grammar schools. Bost. Thompson, Brown & co. [c1882] 96p. 20½cm.

Part 1 of the author's "Book-keeping, single and double entry . . ." copyrighted in 1877.

Another ed. [c1882] 110p. 20½cm.

Another ed. Bost. Thompson, Brown & co. [c1895] 116p. 20½cm.

Another ed. [c1895] 64p. 20cm. Abridged edition.

—Meservey's book-keeping, double entry. Bost. Thompson, Brown & co. [c1882] p.95–222, 20½cm.

Part 2 of the author's "Book-keeping, single and double entry . . ." copyrighted in 1877.

Another ed. 1889.

MUSGROVE, Thomas C.

Musgrove's manuscript book-keeping; for business colleges, academies, and all schools where book-keeping is taught. Phil. Miller's Bible & pub. house, 1875. [51]p. 25½cm.

PILSEN, John G.

Reform system of double entry book-keeping; designed for business men, book-keepers and teachers; containing a new classification of accounts . . . N.Y. G. Lauter, printer, 1875. 24p. 26cm.

The author also deposited for copyright, 1875: "Pilsen's text-book on counting-house book-keeping; containing a new classification of accounts . . . in two parts; containing also a new plan of keeping a current stock book . . ."

—Complete reform of book-keeping; producing, by the shortest possible process, even at a moment's notice, infallibly correct balance sheets; supplying business men with an accurate permanent control of their stock; and establishing a standard system of practical book-keeping . . . designed for business men, book-keepers and teachers. N.Y. S.W. Green, printer, 1877. 109p. 27cm.

The first twenty-four pages of the work listed above are included in this work.

POWERS, Millard R., 1849– , and JOHNSON, Martin R.
The complete accountant; for the use of schools and private study. Chic. W. B. Keen, Cooke & co. 1875. 177 + 22p. 25cm.
M. R. Powers and O. M. Powers are named as proprietors of the copyright for the 1875, 1876, and 1877 editions.
Other eds. 1876; 1877. 320+22+[2]p. 27cm.
—The accountant; for public schools and academies. N. Y. Chic. A. S. Barnes & co. 1877. 155p. 22cm.
The title of this work was deposited for copyright, January 2, 1878.
It is an abridgment of "The complete accountant." M. R. Powers appears on the title-page as sole author.
Another ed. 1878. 155p. 22cm.

POWERS, Orville Marcellus, 1852– , and HOWE, Granville L.
The complete accountant; designed for the use of schools and private study . . . Chic. Jansen, McClurg & co. 1879. 329+22p. 26½cm.
This work is called the fourth edition. O. M. Powers appears on the title-page for the first time as author. M. R. Powers retired from business and his brother, O. M. Powers, continued for many years to revise and publish "The complete accountant." Reprints, not recorded in the bibliography, were published in the first decade of the 20th century by Powers & Lyons (later J. A. Lyons & co.)

Another ed.	Chic. Howe & Powers, 1882. 164p. 26½cm. Abridged edition.
12th ed.	Chic. O. M. Powers, 1885. 329+ 22p. 26½cm.
Another ed.	1886. 329p. 28cm.
Another ed.	1887. 301p. 26½cm.
Other eds.	1887; 1891; 1892. 171p. 26½cm. Abridged editions.
Another ed.	1893. 301p. 28cm.
Other eds.	1894; 1896; 1897; 1898; 1899. 296p. 28cm. No author is named on the title-page of these editions.
Another ed.	1898. 179p. 28cm. Abridged edition.

RAILEY, James A., 1822–1892.
Philipp & Railey's key to book-keeping; explained and illustrated in a brief, easy, clear and correct manner . . . N. O. Rea's steam bk. & job print. off. 1875. 49 + [1]p. 23cm.

WAGGENER, Daniel B.
Book-keeping simplified; the double entry system briefly, clearly,

WAGGENER (continued)
and concisely explained; with valuable rules and tables for counting-room use. Phil. D. B. Waggener & co. 1875.
62p. 16½cm.
The title of this work was deposited for copyright, 1874.
2d ed. 1875. 80p. 17cm.
3d ed. 1875. 77p. 16½cm.
4th ed. Phil. C. R. Deacon, 1885. 77p. 16½cm.
4th ed. 1887. 77p. 16½cm.
Another ed. Phil. W. M. Christy's sons & co. 1889. 77p. 16½cm.

WELSH, George B.
A key to book-keeping; double and single entry explained; valuable hints to students, teachers, and business men. Savannah, G. N. Nichol's steam-power presses, 1875. 50p. 21½cm.

1876

BAKER, William C. M.
Baker's labor-saving system of accounts; with complete instructions; combining all the safeguards contained in methods of accounts heretofore in use, and requiring but one-third the labor; also containing all the information necessary for a complete knowledge of book-keeping. Columbus, Ohio, The author, 1876.
190p. 26cm.
The title of this work was deposited for copyright, 1874. It is doubtful that the work was published before 1876. Two copies were deposited, 1876.
Another ed. 1878. 190p. 26cm.

ELLSWORTH, Henry William, 1837–1924.
The steps of book-keeping for teachers and learners; single and double entry. [N. Y.] Taintor bros.; Merrill & co. 1876.
65p. 17 x 14cm.
Another ed. N. Y. Boorum & Pease [c1890] 82p. 19 x 16cm.

McCLAIN, William, 1817–1877.
Business forms and book-keeping by single entry; in two parts; designed for use in both public and private schools; parts 1st and 2d. Iowa City, Ia. The author, 1876. 118p. 22½cm.
Part 1, p.[1]–75, was also published separately in 1876 and 1877.
2d ed. 1883. 93p. 22½cm.
Part 1, revised.

MATTHERN, C. Otto E.
The seven-account system of book keeping; introducing an original system of recording mercantile transactions under seven accounts . . . also, a treatise on the first principles . . . Chic. M. Stern, Goldsmith, typographers, 1876.
2v. 24½cm. (v.2: 16 x 25½cm.)
Vol. 2 consists of forms.
Another ed. 1882. 2v. 24½cm. (v.2: 16 x 25½cm.)
—Catalogue comprising a condensed and self-instructive treatise for the seven-account system of book-keeping . . . [Chic. Seven-account system co. c1883] 120p. 26 x 35½cm.
On cover: Condensed treatise and catalogue of the seven-account system book-keeping.
The author also deposited for copyright in 1882 and 1883 various ledgers and journals to be used with "The seven-account system."

SOMMER, Max M., 1826–1890.
A practical guide to double entry bookkeeping in tabular form, and commercial calculations; adapted to the comprehension of every body. Newark, N.J. M.R. Dennis, 1876. 34p. 23cm.

1877

BRYANT, John Collins, 1821–1901.
Bryant's common school book-keeping; embracing single and double entry; illustrated with practical business forms . . . containing practical exercises for use in primary schools, academies, commercial departments and business colleges. Buffalo, Pub. by the author, 1877. 128p. 22½cm.
Also published under the title: "Manual of book-keeping for instruction in single and double entry." Buffalo, Pub. by the author, 1877. 128p. 22½cm.
Another ed. Buffalo, Pub. by the author [c1878] 128p. 22½cm.

DUFF, Charles Peter, 1837–1907, DUFF, William Henry, 1838–1927, and DUFF, Robert Peel, 1845–1924.
Duff's common school book-keeping; book-keeping by single and double entry: a text-book for schools and a manual of practical instruction for business men. N.Y. Harper, 1877.
192p. 17 x 13½cm.
Other eds. 1878; 1880; 1881; 1882. 192p. 17 x 13½cm.
Another ed. N.Y. Amer. bk. co. [c1904] 192p. 17½cm.

FELTER, Stoddard A., 1830–(?)
The elements of book-keeping for common schools. Topeka, Kan. G.W. Martin, 1877. 213p. 19 x 15cm.

FELTER (continued)

"The first text-book for public schools written and published in Kansas." — Dedication.

KIRKMAN, Marshall Monroe, 1842–1921.

Railway disbursements and the accounts into which they are naturally divided. N. Y. Railroad gazette, 1877.
264p. 18½cm.

"A revised and enlarged edition of a small volume published in January last [1876] for private distribution." — p.[iii]

—Railway revenue and its collection; containing rules and regulations necessary to ensure faithful accounting; and explaining, generally, the object and extent of railway accounts and the necessity of their being organized upon scientific principles. N. Y. Railroad gazette, 1877. 499p. 18½cm.

2d ed. 1879. 595p. 18½cm.

SAVAGE, George.

The labor saving method of book keeping; single and double entry and writing exercises. N. Y. Amer. news co. c1877.
[16]p. 27 x 22cm.

This work was copyrighted by the "Savage Brothers" and George Savage is named as author on the title-page to the journal.

WALKER, J. H.

Walker's analytical book-keeping. Worcester, Mass. A. B. Adams, job printer, c1877. [16]p. 27 x 22cm.

Another ed. 1880.
F. W. Blacker, claiming proprietorship, deposited the title for copyright, 1880.

WRIGHT, Henry C., 1843–1909.

Manual of rules and definitions; for use in double-entry bookkeeping . . . Brooklyn, Daily times print, 1877.
20p. 22½cm.

The preface states that this work was published for "commercial students and teachers of book-keeping."

5th ed. Brooklyn, A. C. Huene & bro. 1884.
73p. 23cm.

1878

MILLS, E. S.

Public accounts; with practical suggestions for keeping them, and for making examinations, settlements, annual financial statements, and official reports. St. Paul, Pioneer press co. 1878.
27p. 23cm.

PALMER, Joseph Howard, 1824–1892.
Elements of book-keeping; embracing single and double entry; with a great variety of examples for practice. N.Y. Sheldon, 1878. 180p. 19cm.
Other eds. 1879; 1881; 1882; 1883; 1884. 180p. 18½cm.
Another ed. N.Y. Butler, Sheldon [n.d.] 180p. 19cm.

VAN SICKLE, John Waddell, 1835–1895.
A practical system of book-keeping by single and double entry; as applied to the various departments of business; embracing an improved and progressive plan of instruction . . . designed as a text book for universities, business colleges, academies, public schools, and for private instruction. Springfield, Ohio, The author, 1878. 212+[4]p. 26cm.

WOOLLEY, Edward J., and WOOLLEY, Smith R, 1840?–1886.
Woolleys' improved system of book-keeping: a treatise on bank books, mercantile books and domestic books . . . Indianapolis, Indianapolis journal co., printers, 1878. 29+[3]p. 23cm.
Another ed. Detroit, S.R. Woolley, 1885. 52p. 23½cm. Published under the title: "Woolleys' expert book-keeping . . ."

1879

BISBEE, Albert J., 1824?–1890.
Manual of debits and credits in double entry account keeping; prepared to promote class or self instruction in the science and routine of business. [Minneapolis] The author, 1879. 33+[1]p. 22½cm.
3d ed. 1880. 78p. 22½cm.

BROOKE, William.
Brooke's trial balance proof and method of preventing and finding errors in double entry book-keeping: a synopsis of book-keeping generally; including mercantile books and fundamental book-keeping . . . N.Y. 1879. 31p. 22cm.

GOODYEAR, Samuel Horatio.
Book-keeping and business practice; containing an explanation of the principles of single and double entry; together with forms and instructions for business practice in retailing, buying, shipping, milling, manufacturing, wholesaling, commission, brokerage, and banking. Dansville, N.Y. The author, 1879. 128p. 24cm.
The title of this work was deposited for copyright, 1880.

HOPKINS, Selden R.
Manual of exhibit book-keeping; introducing a simplified method of keeping and auditing accounts. N. Y. Hopkins co. 1879. 193p. 18½cm.
2d ed. 1881. 193p. 18½cm.

MCCLENAHAN, J. C., and WOODRUFF, Joab H., 1856–
The national system of double entry book-keeping; being a complete course of theoretical and practical business training . . . designed for the use of public and private schools, business colleges, and self-instruction. [Columbus, Ohio] Columbus steam print. works, 1879. 148p. 22½cm.

MUSSELMAN, De Lafayette, 1842–1910.
Musselman's practical book-keeping: a thorough and comprehensive treatise of the science of accounts; designed for the use of business colleges, schools, private learners, accountants, and business men generally. Quincy [Ill.] D. Wilcox & sons, 1879. 203p. 25½cm.
Another ed. Quincy [Ill.] Press of the Modern argo, 1881. 206p. 25½cm.
Another ed. [Quincy, Ill. Cadogan & Hatcher, printers] 1891. 218p. 25½cm.
Another ed. 1893. 225p. 26cm.

SCHOFIELD, S. C.
Schofield's universal combination system of book-keeping [for merchants] Freeport, Ill. [Journal steam print. co. c1879] [32]p. 23cm.

1880

ARMSTRONG, Augustus, 1855–
Book-keeping at a glance: a correct treatise on double entry book-keeping; simplified so as its principles are readily understood and a thorough knowledge quickly acquired . . . useful to the accountant . . . N. Y. E. Liebertz, 1880. 20p. 24cm.
—Double entry book-keeping self-taught; being a complete system of double entry as used in the largest commercial houses; so simplified that this useful art can be readily mastered . . . N. Y. E. G. Rideout, 1881.
The title of this work was deposited for copyright, 1881. It may be a revised and enlarged edition of the work published in 1880.

GREGORY, Walter P.
Gregory's practical book-keeping: a complete and thorough explanation of double and single entry book-keeping . . . fully illus-

trated by actual business transactions; designed for use in business colleges, public and private schools . . . Easton, Pa. Knapp & Finch, printers, 1880. 120p. 22½cm.
Another ed. Easton, Pa. West & Everett, printers, 1882. 134p. 22cm.
Another ed. Easton, Pa. M. J. Riegal, 1884.

KIRKMAN, Marshall Monroe, 1842–1921.
Railway expenditures; their extent, object and economy . . . Chic. Railway age pub. co. [1880] 2v. 18½cm.

LYTE, Eliphalet Oram, 1842–1913.
Practical book-keeping: a text-book for the use of schools; containing a full treatment of the subject of business papers; a complete course in single entry book-keeping; and a short course in double entry. Lancaster, Pa. Normal pub. co. 1880. 224p. 17½cm.
Other eds. Phil. C. Sower, 1891; 1906. 224p. 17½cm.
Another ed. Phil. Sower, Potts [n. d.] 224p. 17½cm.

MARRIOTT, James Hamilton Wilson, 1853–1912.
Book-keeping in a few hours: a correct treatise on single and double entry book-keeping; simplified so that the principles are easily understood and a thorough knowledge easily and quickly acquired . . . by Wm. Haddon [pseud.] Balt. Marriott, 1880. 35p. 22½cm.

MESERVEY, Atwood Bond, 1831–1901.
Meservey's manual of higher book-keeping, double entry. Bristol, N. H. R. W. Musgrove, 1880. 68p. 22cm.
Another ed. Bost. Thompson, Brown, 1895. 64p. 20½cm.

RICE, Thomas A.
Rice's prevention, detection and correction of errors in trial balances; embracing improved styles of trial balance, four complete sets of books, single and double entry . . . adapted to the use of book-keepers, accountants, commercial lawyers, merchants . . . St. L. Pub. by the author, 1880. 111p. 22½cm.

SCHOLFIELD, Albert G., 1808–1901.
Essay on debit and credit; embodying an elementary and practical treatise on book-keeping. Providence, Press of J. A. & R. A. Reid, 1880. 236p. 23½cm.
Counting house edition in two parts.
Another ed. 1880. 96p. 24cm.
Part 1, school edition.

SCHOLFIELD (continued)

Another ed.	1880. 100p. 24cm.
	Part 1, school edition, with "Synopsis of the . . . essay of debit and credit" added.
Another ed.	1889. 239p. 24cm.
	Counting house edition in two parts.
Another ed.	1895. 242p. 24cm.
	Counting house edition in two parts.

1881

BAKER, William C. M.
Book-keeping pocket chart; with instructions for teaching by Baker's short system; how to keep a mercantile, manufacturing, or business set of books. Columbus, Ohio, Baker short-method pub. co. 1881. 19p. 14½cm.

BARNARD, Henry.
Science of accounts; the principles of double entry book-keeping illustrated in their application to the solution of cash investments; adapted to the use of teachers of public schools. San Fran. Barnard & bros. 1881. 24p. 24½cm.

EATON, Abijah H., 1840–1917, and BURNETT, Elijah, 1840–1893.
Eaton & Burnett's theoretical and practical book-keeping; embracing the theory and practice of accounts; and arranged for use in business colleges, the higher grades of public and private schools, for self-instruction, and as a reliable reference book for the counting house [part 1, theory] Balt. Eaton & Burnett, 1881. 166p. 23½cm.

Another ed.	1882. 258p. 24cm.
	Two parts bound in one volume.
Another ed.	1889. 305p. 24cm.
5th ed.	Balt. Eaton, 1904. 257+[1]p. 24½cm.
	A. H. Eaton appears on the title-page as author. The fifth edition is a thorough revision of the work first published in 1881.
6th ed.	Balt. Eaton, 1910. 263+[1]p. 24½cm.
	A. H. Eaton again appears on the title-page as author. The wording of the title differs from that of the first edition.

FAERBER, Emanuel, 1844–1887.
A self correcting system of double entry book-keeping; dispensing entirely with the tedious work of a trial balance; avoiding the possibility of errors . . . for book-keepers and mercantile men generally. N.Y. Steam press industrial school, 1881. 55p. 25½cm.

GOODWIN, Joseph Henry, 1854–1912.
Goodwin's improved book-keeping and business manual; being a new system of showing what accounts are debited and what credited for the different transactions in business . . .
N.Y. [Goodwin] 1881. 137p. 24cm.
2d ed. 1881. 137p. 25½cm.
3d ed. 1882. 137p. 24cm.
4th ed. 1882. 137p. 24cm.
6th ed. 1884. 137p. 24cm.
7th ed. 1885. 137p. 24cm.
8th ed. 1887. 280p. 24cm.
9th ed. 1888. 279p. 25cm.
10th ed. 1889. 293p. 26cm.
11th ed. 1890. 293p. 24cm.
13th ed. 1892. 293p. 24cm.
14th ed. 1892. 293p. 26cm.
16th ed. 1893. 293p. 26cm.
17th ed. 1895. 293p. 24cm.
18th ed. 1896–97. 293p. 24cm.
19th ed. 1899–1900. 293p. 24cm.
20th ed. 1899–1900. 293p. 24cm.
22d ed. 1903–04. 297p. 26cm.
23d ed. 1904–05. 301p. 26cm.
24th ed. 1905–06. 301p. 26cm.
25th ed. 1907. 301p. 26cm.
26th ed. 1908. 301p. 26cm.
27th ed. 1909–10. 301p. 26cm.
28th ed. 1913. 301p. 26cm.

HARRIS, Jacob Benjamin, 1830–1912.
Book-keeping for the masses; elementary and practical. Wilton, Ia. [J. M. Rider, printer, c1881] 100p. 26½cm.
Another ed. [c1884] 100p. 26½cm.
[3d ed.] Muscatine, Ia. [Davenport, Ia. Egbert, Fidlar & Chambers, printers] 1889. 121p. 26½cm.

KIRKMAN, Marshall Monroe, 1842–1921.
Hand book of railway expenditures; explaining in the form of specific rules how the labor, material, fuel, and other items of expenditure should be kept . . . Chic. Railway age pub. co. [1881] 111+[62]p. 19cm.

SOULÉ, George, 1834–1926.
Soulé's scientific and practical system of book-keeping in two parts . . . N.O. The author, 1881. 279p. 23cm.
A preliminary edition containing the first 168 pages was published early in the year 1881.
Another ed. 1883.

SOULÉ (continued)

—Soulé's new science and practice of accounts; containing a full exposition . . . of double and single entry book-keeping . . . N.O. The author, 1887. 415p. 26cm.

This work is called a revised and enlarged edition of the first edition, published in 1881.

3d ed.	1891.	564p. 27cm.
4th ed.	1895.	716p. 27½cm.
5th ed.	1897.	716p. 28cm.
6th ed.	1901.	726p. 27½cm.
7th ed.	[1903]	749p. 27cm.
8th ed.	1906.	782p. 24cm.
9th ed.	1911.	784p. 24cm.
10th ed.	1919.	773p. 24cm.
11th ed.	1923.	567p. 23cm.
12th ed.	1932.	567p. 23cm.

—The novel manner in which Mr. D.A. Keister attests to the superior merits of Soulé's new science and practice of accounts. [N.O. 1900?] 9+[1]p. 30 x 24cm.

Examples to prove that Keister plagiarized Soulé's book. See 1894, Keister, David Armel.

TANNER, Henry T., 1842–1918.

Tanner's business guide; giving practical definitions, explanations and rules for opening, conducting and closing all kinds of account books; with instructions for doing business generally . . . Cleveland [c1881] 134p. 24cm.

On cover: Part first.

Another ed. [c1881] 103p. 24cm.
On cover: Part first.

WRIGHT, Prince Albert, 1850?–1925.

Book-keeping simplified; or, Journalizing made easy: a multum in parvo edition of double entry . . . N.Y. 1881. 15p. 22½cm.

Afterwards incorporated in "Wright's business methods; or, The Wright key to double-entry bookkeeping" (1891) and in "Wright's bookkeeping simplified" (1896).

—Book-keeping simplified; or, Journalizing made easy: a key to double entry. N.Y. 1885. 169p. 24cm.

Afterwards incorporated in "Wright's business methods; or, The Wright key to double-entry bookkeeping" (1891) and in "Wright's bookkeeping simplified" (1896).

—Wright's business methods: a three weeks course of practice in modern double entry book-keeping . . . N.Y. Wright [c1888] 122p. 23cm.

"This course of practice . . . is the additional part of the revised and improved edition of our Bookkeeping simplified." — Pref.

—30 pages of new features of Wright's book-keeping simplified. N.Y. [1890] [32]p. 23cm.

—Wright's business methods; or, The Wright key to double-entry bookkeeping . . . N.Y. 1891. 293+[2]p. 24cm.

The second part (p.[149]–293) has special title-page: Wright's business methods: a three weeks course of practice in modern double entry book-keeping . . . N.Y. Wright [n.d.]

Afterwards published under title: "Wright's bookkeeping simplified: a complete encyclopedia of business methods."

—Wright's bookkeeping simplified: a complete encyclopedia of business methods . . . the Wright key to double entry . . .
N.Y. Wright, 1896. 313+[1]p. 24cm.

"Business methods: a three weeks course of practice:" p.[151]–313.

Another ed. N.Y. Wright, 1901. 368p. 24cm.
Wall Street edition.

1882

Dow, Dwight S., 1855?–1885.

Keeping books: a new and original treatment of the logic of accounts for students and business men. N.Y. D.A. Curtis, 1882. 103p. 23cm.

—Twin entry book-keeping: a new and original treatment of the logic of accounts.

The title of this work was deposited for copyright, 1884. It may be a revised and enlarged edition of the work published in 1882.

Geer, George P., 1814–1896.

Geer's analysis of the science of accounts; its theory, principles and practice, as adapted to modern book-keeping . . . Holyoke, Mass. C. W. Bryan, 1882. 294p. 24½cm.

2d ed. 1883. 294p. 24½cm.

Goodman, Frank, 1853–1910.

Goodman's book-keeping simplified: a work thoroughly explaining the theory of single and double entry . . . adapted to the use of any university, college, academy, public or private school, and the preparatory department of any business or commercial college. Nashville, Wheeler & Osborn, 1882. 112p. 23cm.

Another ed. 1884. 112p. 23cm.

Goodyear, Samuel Horatio.

Actual business for the school room; containing model forms of book-keeping and business composition . . . Cedar Rapids, Ia. E. J. Hubbell, 1882. 97p. 16cm.

HALL, Edwin A.
Hall's book-keeping and business manual; embracing single and double entry; designed for the use of schools, for the private student, and business men. Logansport, Ind. [Press of W. N. Hall] 1882. 186p. 26½cm.
3d ed. Logansport, Ind. [Press of Longwell & Cummings] 1894. 228p. 26½cm.

HYDE, Cornelius Willet Gillam, 1838–
A course in accounts; designed to teach the principles of single-entry and double-entry bookkeeping; as applied to professional, mercantile and farm accounts . . . [St. Cloud, Minn. Journal-press, 1882] 55p. 21½cm.
Another ed. 1883. 57p. 21½cm.

KIRKMAN, Marshall Monroe, 1842–1921.
The track accounts of railroads and how they should be kept . . . Chic. C. N. Trivess, printer, 1882. 45p. 23cm.
[2d ed.] 1889. 50+[2]p. 19½cm.

LAUDEN, Martin K., 1838–1922.
Lauden's book-keeping; embracing the theory and practice of accounts. [Oakland, Calif.] The author [Pacific press, printers] 1882. 104p. 22cm.

SEYMOUR, George E., 1833–1898.
A new method in double entry book-keeping . . . designed as a hand-book for schools and teachers' institutes. St. L. Amer. school bk. co. 1882. 128p. 21cm.

VOGEL, David.
Laws of book-keeping. [Poughkeepsie, N. Y. c1882] 15p. 22½x13cm.

WILLIAMS, Louis Lafayette, 1841–1919, and ROGERS, Fernando E., 1842–1920.
Theoretical and practical book-keeping; for use in business colleges, and in common schools, high schools, and academies, and for self-instruction. Rochester, N. Y. [E. R. Andrews, printer] 1882. 160p. 30½cm.

The authors deposited for copyright, 1880 and 1881: "Rochester business university book-keeping; adapted especially for self-instruction and for use in common schools, high schools, academies, and business colleges." This work was the basis for "Theoretical and practical book-keeping . . . " listed above.

"Business practice for business colleges" was copyrighted in 1883 by Williams & Rogers.

Other eds. 1883; 1884; 1887; 1888; 1889; 1890.
Various editions issued; varying in paging and content.

—First lessons in book-keeping by single and double entry . . . Rochester, N.Y. Williams & Rogers, 1889. 80p. 27½cm.
Other eds. 1890; 1892; 1894. 80p. 27½cm.
An enlarged edition of this work, consisting of one hundred pages, published by the American book company, is still in print (1934).

—The new theoretical and practical book-keeping by double and single entry . . . [Rochester, N.Y. E. R. Andrews, printer] 1890. 250+xxxvii+[1]p. 30cm.
Short title: "New complete book-keeping."
Formerly published under title: "Theoretical and practical book-keeping."
Other eds. 1892; 1893; 1894; 1896; 1898.
250+xxxvii+[1]p. 28½cm.
Another ed. N.Y. Amer. bk. co. [c1907]
250+xxxviiip. 28½cm.
Title: "New complete bookkeeping."
An enlarged edition of this work, consisting of 131 pages, published by the American book company, is still in print (1934).

—New introductive book-keeping. [Rochester, N.Y. E.R. Andrews, printer] 1890. 119+xiip. 28½cm.
The first part of "The new theoretical and practical book-keeping . . . " or "New complete book-keeping," c1890.
Another ed. N.Y. Amer. bk. co. [c1907]
119+xiip. 28½cm.
This work, published by the American book company, is still in print (1934).

—Book-keeping and business practice . . . Rochester, N.Y. Williams & Rogers, 1895. 234p. 28½cm.
2d ed. 1896. 234p. 28½cm.
3d ed. 1898. 234p. 28½cm.

—Advanced book-keeping and banking . . . Rochester, N.Y. Williams & Rogers, 1897. 110p. 28½cm.
The subject matter of this work is taken from "The new theoretical and practical book-keeping . . . " c1890.

—Supplementary exercises in book-keeping. N.Y. Amer. bk. co. [c1908] 22p. 25cm.
This work was first copyrighted in 1890.
The titles above listed are all in the Williams and Rogers series. For other titles in the same series see 1896; 1897, Wells; 1897, Schwartz; 1899, Neal; and 1900, Neal and Cragin.

1883

BAILEY, H. C.

Book-keeping simplified: a valuable book for those who wish to learn book-keeping at home . . . [Saratoga, N. Y. c1883] 24p. 22cm.

CHAMBERS, Henry Edward, 1860–

Twenty lessons in book-keeping: a book for beginners . . . Little Rock, Ark. Kellogg pub. co. 1883. 191p. 18cm.

Another ed. N. O. F. F. Hansell & bro. [c1883] 191p. 18cm.

GOAD, J. M.

Business at a glance: a practical treatise on business and double-entry book-keeping . . . Lynchburg, Va. J. B. Bell, 1883. 111p. 14½cm.

GOODYEAR, Samuel Horatio.

Manual of business for home and school; containing a compendium of business penmanship, a dictionary of mercantile terms, book-keeping by single entry, forms and rules for business letters, commercial forms, laws of commercial paper, and elements of book-keeping by double entry . . . Cedar Rapids, Ia. E. J. Hubbell, 1883. 176+[4]p. 24cm.

Another ed. 1884. 256p. 24cm.

Contents as in entry above with additional sets on double entry bookkeeping in special lines of business.

—Book-keeping by single entry . . . 1884. 120p. 22½cm.

Part 1: The first 120 pages of Goodyear's "Manual of business . . . " 1883.

—Book-keeping by double entry; containing the standard forms of double entry . . . 1885. p.[117]–212, 22½cm.

Pages 118–180 are taken from his "Manual of business;" the contents following page 180 have been prepared expressly for this volume.

—Book-keeping by single and double entry; school ed.; containing standard forms of single and double entry . . . Cedar Rapids, Ia. Goodyear & Palmer, 1887. 167p. 24cm.

The title of this work was deposited for copyright, 1888.

The author also deposited for copyright in 1898 "Directory and business routine for inter-communication business practice" which may have been designed to accompany this work.

Other eds. Cedar Rapids, Ia. Goodyear pub. co. 1891; 1892; 1896; 1900. 167p. 24cm.

School editions.

—Book-keeping by single and double entry; college ed.; containing standard forms of single and double entry . . . Cedar Rapids, Ia. Goodyear & Palmer, 1887.
The title of this work was deposited for copyright, 1888.
Another ed. 1892.
College edition.

HENDERSON, John Alexander.
Henderson's real self-teaching book-keeping; embracing the theory and actual practice . . . [Harrodsburg, Ky.] The author, 1883. 16p. 20cm.

HUTCHINSON, Calvin G., 1836–1924, and PARKER, Walter Scott, 1846–1931.
The principles and practice of book-keeping; single and double entry. Bost. W. Ware, 1883. 240p. 23x19½cm.
Other eds. 1884; 1886. 240p. 22½x19cm.
—Elementary principles and single entry. Bost. W. Ware, 1883. 88p. 22½x19cm.
Part 1 of his "Principles and practice of book-keeping; single and double entry."
Another ed. 1884. 88p. 22½x19cm.

KAUFFMAN, Luther S., 1846–
Kauffman's manual for book-keepers; with special forms and instructions for keeping books of mining and other stock companies; also for keeping books of private firms in general business. Greeley, Col. Kauffman, c1883. 240p. 15½cm.

WARD, James Murphy.
Hand-book on bookkeeping and commercial law; with a treatise on the history of money; how to distinguish the spurious from the genuine bank note. Carthage, Mo. Banner steam print. house, 1883. 93p. 18cm.

WEST, Orlando C., 1848–1930.
Short road to results in book-keeping . . . Syracuse, N.Y. [Moser & Lyon, printers, 1883] 32p. 23cm.

WOODRUFF, Joab H., 1856–
The student's assistant: a text book on the science of book-keeping; for use in schools and colleges, and for self-instruction. Columbus, Ohio, Capital city commercial college, 1883. 72p. 22cm.

WOOLLEY, Smith R., 1840?–1886.
Woolley's practical book-keeping: a text book for public schools, colleges and private students. Detroit, T. Nourse, 1883. 223p. 23½cm.
Another ed. Detroit, Woolley, 1885. 223+68p. 23½cm.
Contains a supplement: Bank book-keeping.

1884

CARNES, Andrew J., 1836–1889.
Carnes' manual on opening and closing the books of joint stock companies: a work designed for experienced book-keepers . . . Cin. Carnes, 1884. 42p. 23cm.
2d ed. 1888. 42p. 23cm.
3d ed. Balt. [J. Murphy & co. printers] 1891. 42p. 22½cm.

GACKS, Frederick A.
The complete instructor in book-keeping and business forms. Phil. The author [Press of G. H. Buchanan] 1884. 81+[1]p. 22½cm.

GIBBS, L. E.
People's text book for double entry book-keeping; adapted to all kinds of business. Chic. 1884. 44p. 27cm.
The title of this work was deposited for copyright, 1881 and 1884.

HULL, William Newell, 1839–
Book-keeping. [Cedar Falls, Ia. 1884] 20p. 23½cm.
Printed on ten cards; unbound.
—Self-instructing book-keeping . . . adapted to schools and colleges . . . rev. ed. [Cedar Falls, Ia.] 1884. 34p. 24cm.

MAYHEW, Ira, 1814–1894.
The eclectic complete book-keeping. Cin. Van Antwerp, Bragg [c1884] 156p. 19cm.

SCHOLFIELD, Albert G., 1808–1901.
Elementary and practical treatise on book-keeping; prepared to serve as a self-educator. Providence, Scholfield, 1884. 110p. 25½x20cm.
Counting house edition.
Another ed. 1884. 106+[2]p. 24½x19½cm. Counting house edition.
Another ed. 1884. [78]p. 26x20½cm. School edition.
Another ed. 1895. 110p. 25½x20cm. Counting house edition.

1885

ALLEN, George, 1833–1912.
Allen's forty lessons in practical double entry book-keeping; arranged as a text book for use in graded and high schools and as a

book of reference for business men. Newbern, N. C. N. S. Richardson, 1885. 96p. 23cm.

2d ed. Raleigh, N. C. Edwards, Broughton, 1886. 96p. 23cm.

3d ed. 1886. 136p. 23cm.
Includes a model set of books which was published separately in 1887.

4th ed. 1888. 136p. 23cm.

5th ed. 1891. 136p. 23cm.

BRYANT, Henry Beadman, 1824–1892.
The new manual of book-keeping, theoretical and practical; for the use of business colleges, normal and high schools, and for learners generally. Chic. H. B. Bryant & son, 1885. 44p. 22cm.
Another ed. 1885. 54p. 22cm.

DEANE, Willard, 1841?–1897.
How to open, post and close a ledger. Phil. A. T. Zeising, 1885. 14p. 14cm.

ELLIS, James J.
Ellis' cash book and new and rapid system of double entry bookkeeping; including an infallible trial balance error detector. Pittsburgh, Ellis & Clark, 1885. 32p. 22½cm.

HARKINS, Francis A.
Bookkeeping by single and double entry: a business manual specially adapted to the wants of the Catholic clergy. Balt. Foley bros. 1885. 191p. 20cm.
The title of this work was deposited for copyright, 1882.

KEMPTON, P. S.
Seven weeks in actual business: a series of practical business transactions; systematically arranged for the guidance of students engaged in business in the practical departments of business colleges. Streator, Ill. Daily monitor print, 1885. 40p. 23cm.

MANNING, Richard H.
Book-keeping simplified; for common schools and private students. N. Y. Appleton, 1885. 100p. 22cm.
Published also under the title: "Bookkeeping by single and double entry . . . " 1885.
Another ed. 1886. 112p. 22½cm.

METCALFE, Henry, 1847–1927.
The cost of manufactures and the administration of workshops, public and private. N. Y. Wiley, 1885. 322p. 24cm.

2d ed. 1890. 322p. 24cm.

3d ed. 1894.

Another ed. 1907. 366p.

PADDACK, James R.
Tabular book-keeping: a system of keeping accounts by tabulation . . . intended especially for practical accountants and business men. Cin. R. Clarke, 1885. 72p. 32cm.
The author also deposited for copyright in 1884 and 1885 the titles of various forms and examples of accounts contained in "Tabular book-keeping . . . "

PALMER, James Henry, 1836–1886.
A lesson in book-keeping: a statement of first principles. [Jacksonville, Ill. c1885] 12p. 15cm.
Authorship has been erroneously attributed to Joseph Howard Palmer.

SCHOLFIELD, Albert G., 1808–1901.
Criticism on the hitherto popular method of recording interest in double-entry book-keeping; its fallacies exposed; a new system matured and submitted . . . Providence, Scholfield, 1885. 6p. 24cm.

SMITH, Ephraim Waldo, 1820–1895, and SMITH, Wilbur Rush, 1853–1923.
The text-book on book-keeping and general business education, which received the highest honor at the World's exposition, 1885 . . . Cin. R. Clarke, 1885. 269p. 26cm.
Though the author's first name is spelled "Ephriam" on the title-page of the book, an authentic biographical sketch of the author contained in "Ancestry, life and reminiscences of General Wilbur R. Smith . . . " edited by the Philemporium society of the commercial college of Kentucky university spells his name "Ephraim."
22d ed. 1907. 302p. 26cm.

SMITH, William H.
A manual of bank book-keeping; designed for the use of schools and private study . . . N. Y. Smith, 1885. 93+[2]p. 23cm.
The title of this work was deposited for copyright, 1884.

STEINER, J. C.
The blackboard system and abbreviated book-keeping: a system for teaching book-keeping to large classes by ruled forms on blackboards or on slated and ruled walls . . . [Cleveland, Hatch print. co. c1885] 118p. 26½cm.
No author is named on the title-page. J. C. Steiner, claiming to be author and proprietor of the copyright, deposited the title of this work for copyright, 1885.

The authorship has been erroneously attributed to John Lendy who bought the proprietorship of the copyright in 1889.
See also note under Southard, 1892.
Another ed. 1889.

1886

CLARK, Harold Chauncey, 1856– , and SPAULDING, Samuel S.
Clark's progressive book-keeping; elucidating the principles of double entry in a common sense manner; specially arranged for use in business colleges, public schools, academies, and for self instruction. Erie, Pa. Clark & Johnson, 1886. 2v. 23cm.
A revised edition of this work, presumably the second edition, was deposited for copyright, 1890.
3d ed. Erie, Pa. Clark's business college, 1893. 2v. 23cm. Title varies.

DUTTON, Charles, 1838–1928.
Dutton's analytical bookkeeping chart: a complete exhibit in tabular form of the science of accounts. N.Y. Office co. 1886. 47p.+fold. chart, 11 x 21½cm.
The chart was also published separately.
Another ed. N.Y. Office co. 1886. 47p.+fold. chart, 11 x 21½cm.

GILPIN, Charles.
The theory of double-entry book-keeping. Phil. Porter & Coates, 1886. 12p. 24cm.

GOODYEAR, Samuel Horatio.
Goodyear's business practice; set one, change 1–12; for business colleges and academies. Cedar Rapids, Ia. Hubbell pub. co. 1886. 12v. 22½cm.
Twelve sets of transactions, each numbered consecutively, were deposited for copyright, 1887.

JENNINGS, Robert William, 1838–1922.
Book-keeping in a nut-shell; and quick business methods . . . Nashville, Marshall & Bruce, printers, 1886. 51+[1]p. 28cm.

KINSLEY, W. J.
Students' guide; for the use of actual business departments of business colleges and commercial departments, and business students. Indianapolis, Normal pub. house, J. E. Sherrill, proprietor, 1886. 29p. 23cm.
Later editions have title: "Business practice guide; for the use of business practice departments of business colleges . . ."

KINSLEY (continued)
Another ed. Shenandoah, Ia. Kinsley & Stephens, 1890. 60p. 19½cm.
2d ed. 1891. 54p. 19½cm.

KIRKMAN, Marshall Monroe, 1842–1921.
Division of railway expenses and earnings, and the limitation of accounts in connection therewith. Chic. C. N. Trivess, printer [1886] 75p. 23½cm.

LILLIBRIDGE, David R., 1839–1896, and ROOSE, Franklin F., 1855–
Modern book-keeping, theoretical and practical . . . adapted to the use of business colleges, public and private schools . . . and self-instruction. Lincoln, Neb. Lillibridge & Roose [State journal co., printers, c1886] 139p. 26cm.
2d ed. [c1888] 160p. 26cm.

MOORE, Benjamin F.
Moore's practical book-keeping and business manual; designed as a text-book for schools, business colleges and self-instruction . . . Atlanta, W. H. Scott, printer, 1886. 162p. 22½cm.

PLUMB, Charles M., 1831–1899.
The business-standard system of double-entry book-keeping; using only one book of accounts. Phil. Cowperthwait, c1886. 80p. 19cm.
—and FELLOWS, Aaron N.
The business-standard system of double-entry book-keeping and business manual. Phil. Cowperthwait [c1890] 128p. 19cm.
Contents as in entry above as far as page 72.
Part 2, p.85–128, is a business manual.

SOURBEER, William B.
The acme book-keeping charts: a simple system of keeping books . . . St. L. Sourbeer [c1886] 21p. 18x22cm.

WITTER, Charles Asa, 1839–1913.
Witter's book-keeping and business forms; for public schools and home use . . . Norwich, Conn. Witter, 1886. 102p. 18½cm.
6th ed. 1910. 112p. 18½cm.

1887

BROWNE, Thomas Robert, 1834–1912.
Browne's manual of practical exercises; specially designed for students of business colleges; consisting of forms and practice in book-keeping by double and single entry . . . [Brooklyn] Browne, 1887. 187p. 23cm.

CHILD, Frederick W.
Elements of cost and methods of accounting in steam engine works. N.Y. Office co. 1887. 20p. 18½cm.
A paper read before the Institute of accounts.

CURTISS, Charles Carroll.
The Curtiss manual of book-keeping; for common schools. St. Paul, D.D. Merrill [c1887] 128p. 23cm.
Another ed. N.Y. Amer. bk. co. [n.d.] 128p. 22½cm.

DENMAN, Jacob S.
A practical system of accounts; or, Book-keeping for the people . . . designed for schools and private learners . . . N.Y. Baker & Taylor, 1887. 48p. 20cm.

GOODYEAR, Samuel Horatio.
A new method of business training for public schools, academies, and business colleges. Cedar Rapids, Ia. Goodyear & Palmer, 1887. 18v. 23½cm.
Eighteen sets of transactions, each numbered consecutively.
Set no. 1 was deposited for copyright, 1887; the remaining sets, 1888.

GUTHRIE, Charles W.
Practical instruction at home in the science of accounts; comprising instructions in actual business transactions by means of representative property . . . complete in thirty parts. St. L. Lloyd, 1887. [4]p. 30cm.
Part 1 only was located.

HORNER, John B., 1856–
Eight essential business papers; or, Bookkeeping for beginners . . . [2d ed.] Salem, Or. F.C. Baker, state printer, 1887. [12]p. 17½cm.
The second edition was the only one copyrighted.
A chart, "Bookkeeping for beginners," was also deposited for copyright, 1887.

SCRIBNER, William M., 1824–1902.
Scribner's common school book-keeping exercises; single entry, part one. N.Y. Potter, Knight, Ainsworth, c1887. 32+16p. 27½cm.
Part 2 and part 3, each containing double entry bookkeeping and each published separately, were copyrighted, 1887.

SLATER, Franklin A., 1843–
The people's book-keeping; or, Double entry in a nut shell . . . Judsonia, Ark. Slater pub. co. [c1887] 64p. 17½x24cm.

SPEER, J. P.
The expert accountant (business man's vade mecum) and book-keeping in four lessons; 2d ed. Birmingham, Ala. Caldwell print. works, 1887. 231p. 26cm.
The second edition, copyrighted, 1886, was the only one copyrighted.

WAGGONNER, Austin B., 1841–1914.
Waggonner's practical book-keeping . . . the principles of double entry explained as the result of twenty years' practical experience. [Hamilton, Ill. c1887] 38p. 20cm.

1888

BARDEEN, Charles William, 1847–1924.
Question book of book-keeping; containing all the questions and problems in this subject given at the first fifteen New York examinations for state certificates; with full answers, solutions, and entries. Syracuse, N. Y. Bardeen, 1888. p.[47]–73, 17cm. (Dime ser. no. 22)
Another ed. 1910. p.[47]–73, 17½cm.

CASTLES, William H.
Grocers' gains and how to adjust them: a short and complete system of double-entry book-keeping; applicable to the wants of wholesale and retail dealers, or merchants in the grocery or other trade . . . Newark, N. J. Grover bros. printers, 1888. 66p. 23cm.

CHILDS, C. W.
Essentials of book-keeping for public schools; single and double entry. San Fran. Bancroft co. 1888. 158p. 21½cm.
Another ed. 1893. 158p. 21½cm.
—New essentials of book-keeping . . . San Fran. Whitaker & Ray, 1896. 158p. 21cm.

DILL, Anson J., 1850–1904.
Book-keeping, single and double entry, and commercial law; designed for the use of schools. Indiana, Pa. State normal school, 1888. 210+[8]p. 20½cm.

DUQUE, Joseph Lewis.
Stock system: a practical method for taking a balance sheet at any time, without inventory. San Fran. Bancroft co. 1888. 37p. 18½cm.
English text followed by German and Spanish versions with separate title-pages.

GRINGHUIS, Geert, 1850–1915.
Double-entry book-keeping condensed; five or more books into one. Grand Rapids, Eaton, Lyon & Allen print. co. 1888.
119+[3]p. 21½cm.

MAYHEW, Ira, 1814–1894.
Standard book-keeping; for business colleges, commercial departments, the counting-room, and self-instruction. Chic. J. C. Buckbee, 1888. 300p. 22½cm.
—Reference book of business knowledge, and self-educator in standard book-keeping . . . Chic. J. C. Buckbee, 1889.
300+213p. 22½cm.
The text of this work is the same as that of " Standard book-keeping," with the Key added.
—Standard book-keeping; for business colleges, commercial departments, the counting-room and self-instruction. N. Y. Silver, Burdett, 1892. 308p. 23½cm.
A revised edition of the work published in 1888.

WATTERS, James M.
James M. Watters' manual for teaching book-keeping by single and double entry as applied to all branches of mercantile business; bringing into requisition . . . all the books of record and of accounts as they are used in actual business. Cin. [c1888]
90p. 29½cm.

1889

BROTHERS OF THE CHRISTIAN SCHOOLS.
The student's manual of book-keeping: a comprehensive treatise on single and double entry . . . [new series] N. Y. F. S. C. Procure, 1889. 300p. 23cm.
This work was copyrighted by John P. Murphy (Brother Isaac John) and printed at the New York Catholic protectory, West Chester, N. Y.
3d ed. N. Y. Christian brothers' depository, 1892. 300p. 23cm.
4th ed. 1895. 300p. 23cm.

CAMPBELL, Edward P.
System of freight accounts; reporting, auditing, and settlements between railroads, of revenue on through way-bills; with samples of blanks, etc. [N. Y. M. B. Brown, 1889] 51p. 23½cm.

DRAUGHON, John Franklin, 1863–1921.
Draughon's system of book-keeping.
The title of this work was deposited for copyright, 1889.

DRAUGHON (continued)
—Draughon's new system of book-keeping.
The title of this work was deposited for copyright, 1891.
—Draughon's new system of book-keeping; double entry made easy; simple and short advanced book-keeping and legal adviser. [Nashville, c1894] 62p. 31x23½cm.
"Third edition." — Pref.

FRITCH, Edouard Henri, 1857–1930.
The unique manual of bookkeeping. Wichita, Kan. Eagle print. house, 1889. 76p. 22½cm.

GRIFFITTS, D. A.
Book-keeping; or, The science of accounts in a nut-shell. Dallas, Chase print. co. [c1889] 7 numb. l. 9½ x 23cm.

HART, Walter.
Hart's precise system for building and loan associations. N.Y. Press of H. J. Ronalds [c1889] 28p. 16cm.

MOORE, Elder Denny, 1854–
Principles of the science of accounts. East Liverpool, Ohio, Moore, 1889. 36p. 23½cm.

1890

BAYLESS, Cornelius, 1839–1927.
Book-keeping: outline of practical business training in the science of accounts; 3d ed. rev. Dubuque, Ia. Pub. by the author, 1890. 144p. 23cm.
The third edition was the only one copyrighted.
Another ed. 1890. 194p. 24½cm.
This work is also called the third edition but, in addition, it includes: "Practical banking; adapted to state and national banks . . ." p.[145]–189.

GOODYEAR, Samuel Horatio.
The theory of accounts; containing a complete exhibit of the principles of bookkeeping; for use in business colleges and other commercial schools. [Cedar Rapids, Ia. Goodyear, 1890] 228p. 26cm.
—The new theory of accounts; containing a complete exhibit of the principles of bookkeeping; high-school ed. . . [Chic. Goodyear pub. co.] 1893. 136p. 27½cm.
Other eds. 1893; 1894. 225p. 27½cm.
Complete editions.
Contents as in the high school edition, with additional sets.

—The essentials of bookkeeping. Chic. Goodyear pub. co. 1895. 136p. 28cm.

Contents as in the high school edition but published under the above title.

Another ed. 1896. 136p. 28cm.

—The theory of accounts; containing the essentials of bookkeeping and forms of higher accounting . . . Chic. Goodyear pub. co. 1899. 206p. 27½cm.

Contents as in "The essentials of bookkeeping," p.1–136. The second part is devoted to higher accounting.

Other eds. Cedar Rapids, Ia. Goodyear-Marshall pub. co. 1901; 1907. 206p. 27½cm.

GOTTSCHALL, John Brough, 1863–

300 questions and answers on book-keeping . . . Ada, Ohio, J.L. Nefe, c1890. 52p. 15cm.

This work was deposited for copyright, January 26, 1891.

—500 questions and answers; or, The book-keepers' friend . . . 2d ed. rev. and enl. Ada, Ohio, S.B. Wagner, 1894. 75+[1]p. 15½cm.

GRIM, Washington S., 1830–1902.

The modern "expert" book-keeper; embracing the "expert" journal . . . the "expert" method of maintaining the ledger balance without trial balance; the "expert" short methods for the counting room. Springfield, Ohio, Winters print & litho co. [1890] 87+[1]p. 23cm.

GROVER, Elizabeth F., 1849–

Short course in book-keeping; prepared especially for use in normal schools, common schools and teachers' institutes. [Chic. Donohue & Henneberry, printers, c1890] 37p. 26cm.

The title of this work was first deposited for copyright, 1889.

HUDSON, Lycurgus Leonidas, compiler, 1857–1911.

G. W. Michael's text book on theoretical and practical book-keeping. Delaware, Ohio, G. W. Michael [1890] 143p. 22 x 23½cm.

On cover: Michael's theoretical and practical book-keeping.

The title of this work was deposited for copyright, 1890, by George Washington Michael, author and publisher of several works on penmanship.

Hudson evidently compiled this work under Michael's supervision.

KIRKMAN, Marshall Monroe, 1842–1921.

Hand book of freight accounts . . . Chic. C. N. Trivess, printer, 1890. 157+[52]p. 18½cm.

KIRKMAN (continued)
—Hand book of passenger traffic and accounts . . . Chic. C. N. Trivess, printer, 1890. 170+[30]p. 18cm.

MACNAIR, Charles Stewart, 1844–1906.
Self-instruction in practical book-keeping . . . self-instruction in practical business qualifications . . . self-instruction in telegraph operating . . . Detroit, Macnair, 1890. 244p. 28 x 22½cm.
The section on bookkeeping, p.[12]–138, has a separate title-page: Macnair's book-keeping: book-keeping simplified . . . double entry book-keeping for the ordinary daily business. This title was deposited for copyright, 1889.

NELSON, Richard, 1822–1900.
Accounts and business for the use of book-keepers, schools and colleges. Cin. Cincinnati & Springfield pub. co. [c1890] 186p. 27cm.

OSBORN, Frank E., and MILLER, William C.
Manual of instruction in actual business practice for schools. La Porte, Ind. Osborn, Miller, 1890. 36p. 21cm.

PIPES, Joseph.
Book-keeping simplified; a short method of book-keeping by double entry . . . adapted to the wants of the student, the accountant, and the business man in general . . . Shreveport, La. Times job print [c1890] 23p. 25½ x 20cm.

RICHMOND, Charles S., 1855–
Practical book-keeping . . . [Savannah] Press of Robinson steam print. co. 1890. 149p. 24cm.

RILEY, Cornelius.
The "abstract" system of book-keeping; combining all the advantages of double entry. N.Y. [c1890] 31p. 19½ x 25½cm.
The title of this work was first deposited for copyright, 1889.

ROBERTSON, Alexander.
The elements of double-entry bookkeeping . . . [South Orange, N.J. Press of the South Orange bulletin, c1890] 50p. 23cm.
—Advance sheets . . . 1890. 38p. 23cm.

SLATER, Franklin A., 1843–
Business practice and how to keep accounts by the iron-clad system . . . Fenton, Mich. Pub. by the author [c1890] 26p. 20½cm.

1891

BRUNNER, David B., 1835–1903.
A practical treatise on single entry bookkeeping; adapted to the wants of farmers, mechanics and merchants. Reading, Pa. Eagle bk. print, 1891. 52p. 23½cm.

CATON, Martin Jennings, 1863–
The counting house book-keeping, theoretical and practical; containing a thorough elucidation of the principles and a complete exemplification of the modern practice of double and single entry; adapted to the use of business colleges, high schools, academies, commercial departments and for self-instruction. Cleveland, Caton business college co. 1891. 336p. 29½cm.

COX, Alanson.
A new, simple and easy method of keeping books by double and treble entry . . . Shreveport, La. Caucasian print, 1891. 19p. 21cm.

DUDLEY, A. W.
The new rapid theory and practice of double-entry book-keeping; adapted to the use of business colleges, high-schools, academies . . . Buffalo, 1891.
A. W. Dudley, claiming authorship, deposited this title for copyright, 1891.
Another ed. [Buffalo] Buffalo pub. co. 1892. 161p. 28cm. This work, which is the same as the 1891 edition, was deposited for copyright, 1892, by Charles O. Perrin. No author is named on the title-page. Authorship has been attributed to Charles O. Perrin who became proprietor of the copyright.

FRENCH, Charles, 1826–1920.
Practical bookkeeping and accounts simplified. Bost. Beale pub. co. c1891. 143+[1]p. 20 x 15½cm.

GAY, George E., 1848–1927.
Business book-keeping: a manual of modern methods in recording business transactions; common school ed., single entry. Bost. Ginn, 1891. 93p. 26cm.
Another ed. 1892. 226p. 26cm.
High school edition, single and double entry.
Other eds. 1897; 1900. 226p. 26cm.
High school editions, single and double entry.
Another ed. 1893. p.91–231, 26cm.
Part 2, double entry bookkeeping, published separately.

GOTTSCHALL, John Brough, 1863–
Gottschall's new theoretical book-keeping embracing single and double entry; for schools and business colleges and for self instruction. Ada, Ohio, The author, 1891. 127p. 29cm.
The title of this work was deposited for copyright, November 15, 1890.
Two copies of this work were deposited, May 14, 1891.
Another ed. 1892. 134p. 29cm.

GRAHAM, G. H.
A manual of actual business for common and high schools. York, Neb. Graham school pub. co. [c1891] 50p. 16½cm.

HARRIS, E. D., 1840–1921.
Business practice applied to elements of book-keeping without a teacher . . . prepared for use in state and county teachers' institutes. Lincoln, Neb. [State journal co. printers] c1891. 36p. 23cm.
This work is part 3 of a work entitled "Business practice" published in four separate parts.

MACY, George J.
Condensed system of accounts and general entry book . . . Indianapolis, Macy, c1891. 36p. 21½ x 17½cm.

STEADMAN, Andrew H.
Actual business practice book-keeping: a complete guide to a thorough practical knowledge of the science of accounts; adapted to the use of schools and business colleges. Toledo, Van Wormer & Tiedtke, printers, 1891. 124p. 19½cm.

1892

ATKESON, Thomas Clark, 1852–
Bookkeeping for farmers: a treatise on farm accounts; to which is added the Stockbridge system accounts; ed. by Herbert Myrick. N.Y. Judd, 1892. 40p. 19cm.
Other eds. 1905; 1920. 40p. 19cm.

BRUNNER, David B., 1835–1903.
A practical treatise on double entry bookkeeping; adapted to the wants of commercial and high schools as well as to self instruction. Reading, Pa. Eagle bk. print, 1892. 90p. 23½cm.

BRYANT, Thomas J.
Science of accounts and detection of counterfeit gold and silver coin and bank bills. St. Joseph, Mo. Posegate print. co. c1892. 36p. 15½cm.

CRAIGE, A. S.
Organization and management of private corporations; with notes on corporation bookkeeping. Chic. Bankers' stationery supply co. 1892. 128p. 20cm.
Practically one half of this work is devoted to accounting.

DAVIS, J. M., and WILSON, H. E.
A guide for students in business practice departments of business colleges. Oakland, Calif. [Pacific press pub. co.] 1892. 46p. 20cm.

ELLIOTT, George W., 1843–1913.
The counting house book-keeping; embracing the theory and practice of accounts . . . for use in business colleges, business offices, banks, normal and high schools, and for self-instruction. Burlington, Ia. Elliott, 1892. 224+38+[1]p. 28½cm.

ELLIS, Charles L., 1856–1897.
The guide to the Ellis system of actual business practice and practical bookkeeping; including single entry, double entry, joint stock companies, and corporations . . . designed for the use of students, teachers, accountants and expert bookkeepers. San Fran. Ellis pub. co. [c1892] 214p. 37cm.
This Guide is to be used in connection with the instructions contained in the Cabinet which accompanies each edition of this work. The actual business practice as arranged in the Cabinet, together with the forms and customs, practical suggestions and references contained in the Guide, gives an outline of the Ellis system of commercial training as developed by Charles L. Ellis.
3d ed. Battle Creek, Mich. Ellis pub. co. [c1892] 223p. 37cm.
Vol. 1, abridged.

—Hints and suggestions to teachers of the Ellis system of actual business practice and practical bookkeeping, by Charles E. Howard. [San Fran. Ellis pub. co. 1893] 75p. 23½cm.

—The new business practice; prepared expressly for the use of business colleges. San Fran. Ellis pub. co. [c1893]

—Outline of instructions for intercommunication practice. Battle Creek, Mich. Ellis pub. co. [c1894]

—The guide to the new business practice or tablet system of bookkeeping; special abridged ed. for the shorter course. c1895.

—The new business practice; or, Tablet system of teaching business and the science of accounts by actual business methods . . . [c1895]

—The guide: a manual of instructions and business forms to accompany the tablet system of bookkeeping and business training . . . Battle Creek, Mich. Ellis pub. co. [c1896] 2v. 36cm.
Contents.—Elementary course.—Intermediate course.

ELLIS (continued)

—The guide: a manual of instructions and business forms to accompany the tablet method of bookkeeping and business training. [c1897] 3v. 36cm.

Contents.—Elementary course.—Intermediate course.—Complete course.

ELLIS publishing company, Battle Creek, Mich.

The guide: a manual of instructions and business forms to accompany the tablet method of bookkeeping and business training . . . [c1906] 3v. 35½ x 22cm.

Contents.—Elementary course.—Intermediate course.—Complete course.

—Guide to the Ellis system of actual business training and practical accounting: a full course of instruction in business practice and elementary and advanced accounting for the use of commercial schools; rev. ed. [c1906] 224p. 28½cm.

—Student's guide to accompany the Ellis tablet method of teaching bookkeeping and business practice . . . 1908. 3v. 29cm.

Contents.—Elementary course.—Intermediate course.—Complete course.

Other eds. 1909; 1910; 1911. 3v. 35½ x 22cm.

—Student's guide to accompany the Ellis cabinet system of teaching bookkeeping and business practise; when used in connection with the Cabinet of transactions provides a full course of instructions in bookkeeping and office practise; for use in commercial schools; rev. ed. 1910. 255p. 29cm. (Learn by doing ser.)

—Guide to Ellis system of teaching bookkeeping and business practise; when used in connection with the Business directions provides a full course of instruction in bookkeeping and office practise; rev. ed. [c1917] 92p. 29cm. (Learn by doing ser.)

Another ed. [c1919] 127p. 28½cm. (Learn by doing ser.)

—Guide to accompany the Ellis tablet method of teaching bookkeeping . . . [c1919] 2v. 28½cm.

Contents.—Elementary course.—Intermediate course.

—Student's tablet of transactions; the tablet method of teaching bookkeeping and business training . . . c1919. 2v. 29½cm. (Learn by doing ser.)

In tablet form.

Contents.—Elementary course.—Intermediate course.

JAMISON, Thomas Worth, 1853–1924.

A short course of double entry book-keeping. Balt. Strohm print. co. 1892. 131+[1]p. 21cm.

KEELER, Joseph Brigham, 1855–

The student's guide to book-keeping, double and single entry; for

use in business colleges, normal schools, academies, district schools, and for self-instruction. Provo, Utah, Skelton, 1892.
209p. 23cm.

LANING, J. F.
A synthetic course in book-keeping: a text book for schools and colleges unfolding the science in an easy and progressive manner; single and double entry taught without any sensible distinction . . . Norwalk, Ohio, Laning print. co. c1892.
118+[1]p. 19cm.

OSHAY, Franklin John.
A complete treatise on modern mercantile book-keeping by double and single entry; designed for use in academies, high and graded schools, and is especially prepared for self instruction . . . Rockford, Ill. Rockford stationery & print. co. 1892. 129p. 26½cm.
The title of this work was deposited for copyright, 1891.

SHAW, Judson Wade, 1833–1905.
A practice book in business forms and elementary book-keeping; including the keeping and posting of simple accounts, the writing of business letters, etc. Bost. Heath, 1892.
The title of this work was deposited for copyright, 1892.
—An elementary book-keeping with business forms; embracing systematic and applied training in keeping and posting simple accounts . . . Bost. Heath, 1894.
This work, evidently based upon the one copyrighted, 1892, was copyrighted, 1894.
Other eds. 1897; 1900. 110p. 25½cm.
—Busy man's bookkeeping and business forms . . . Bost. Heath, 1901.
The title of this work was deposited for copyright, 1901. It is probably based upon the above title.

SMITH, Osborn Levi.
Smith's practical single entry book-keeping; explaining and exhibiting the day-book and ledger; also the auxiliary books . . . for practical teaching. Richmond, E. Waddey, 1892.
98p. 21cm.

SOULÉ, George, 1834–1926.
Manual of auditing; suggestions to auditors, receivers and liquidators, and points on higher and expert accounting. N.O. 1892.
28p. 28 x 19½cm.

2d ed.	1893.	32p. 28 x 19½cm.
3d ed.	1893.	
4th ed.	1900.	24p. 27½cm.
6th ed.	1905.	24p. 26½cm.

SOUTHARD, Alexander L.

Normal book-keeping: a new system, modern, practical, abbreviated; single and double entry . . . for self-instruction and individual or private instruction . . . and adapted for use in business colleges, universities, public schools and private schools . . . [Cleveland, W. M. Bayne print. house] 1892.
223p. 29½ x 24½cm.

The preface states: "This book contains the original blackboard system . . . The system has been tested by the author for many years and by other teachers since its publication in 1885. The author of this book is the originator of such a system."

No copyright record of Southard's work published in 1885 exists. It is possible that J. C. Steiner, who, as author and proprietor of the copyright, deposited in 1885 "The blackboard and abbreviated book-keeping," might be a pseudonym for A. L. Southard. See 1885, Steiner, J. C.

Another ed. 1892. 223+40p. 29½ x 24½cm.
Contents as in entry above with the addition of second appendix: Bank book-keeping.

—First lessons in double entry book-keeping . . . c1893.

This title, deposited by the author for copyright, 1893, was probably based upon "Normal book-keeping . . . "

WATSON, William T.

Watson's accountant: a treatise on practical book-keeping; as applied in theory and practice by all modern book-keepers . . . and many useful rules valuable to a business man. Memphis, S. C Toof, 1892. 118p. 23½cm.

School edition.

Another ed. 1893. 221p. 23½cm.
Complete edition.

1893

BRIERLEY, John Thomas, 1854–1917.

Book-keeping at a glance: a simple and concise method of practical book-keeping . . . N. Y. Excelsior pub. house [c1893] 141p. 13cm.

Another ed. 1896. 141p. 13cm.
Another ed. N. Y. Nourse, 1920. 135p. 13cm.

BROWN, Pierre S., 1855?–1922.

Double entry book-keeping; part 1 in six sets; for teachers and self-instruction. [Kansas City, Mo. S. F. Woody print. co.] 1893. 42p. 21½cm.

EMMONS, Marcus A., 1837–1892.
Expert book-keeping and "100 helpful hints:" a concise, practical, and original manual on the art of accountancy; designed for all who desire to become expert book-keepers. Detroit, Book-keeper pub. co. 1893. 200p. 26½cm.
Another ed. 1897. 190p. 26cm.

GILBERT, Adelbert Lorenzo, 1851–1907.
Gilbert's manual of business book-keeping: a new and logical exposition of the science and practice of accounting; for the use of students, book-keepers and business men. Milw. 1893. 288+32p. 26cm.
Another ed. 1895. 104p. 26cm.
Part 1, revised.

GOOD, J. Dobson, 1845–
The auditor; plain suggestions for the guidance of trustees, directors and others, as to the auditing of books and accounts of stock companies, corporations, building associations and mercantile firms. [Cin. S. Rosenthal] 1893. 90p. 18½cm.

LAWRENCE, Wilber E.
Manual of the national B. & L. system of accounting. [Chic. c1893] 50p. 17cm.

McCAFFERTY, H. W., and FOWLER, Frank W.
The voucher system of bookkeeping . . . [East Liverpool, Ohio] East Liverpool tribune print [c1893] 16p. 20 x 23½cm.

SEAVY, Manson, 1838–1896.
Practical business book-keeping by double entry; for grammar, high, and commercial schools, academies, and for self-instruction. Bost. Heath, 1893. 238p. 26 x 20½cm.
Another ed. 1894. 238p. 26 x 20½cm.
—A manual of business transactions to accompany the author's "Practical business book-keeping," or for use without a text-book. Bost. Heath, 1893. 260p. 18cm.
Other eds. 1896; 1899. 260p. 18cm.

SHINN, William L., 1863–1897.
A revolution in the science of accounts; accounts kept with and without books: Shinn's short method of bookkeeping.
The title and two copies of this work were deposited for copyright, 1893.
"Shinn's short method of bookkeeping" was also deposited for copyright, 1893, and two copies were deposited, 1895. Both are forerunners of Shinn's work, published in 1896.

SHINN (continued)

—A brief explanation of Shinn's short method of bookkeeping. Phil. The author [c1895] 8p. 15cm.

—Shinn's short method of bookkeeping . . . [Bridgeton, N. J. Pub. by the author, c1896] 32p. 23½cm.

"Part 1, advanced sheets of a projected work."

The complete work was evidently not published before his death in 1897.

1894

ATKINSON, Edmund Clement, 1837–1911.

Modern methods in bookkeeping: a comprehensive business manual containing labor-saving forms for accounts, practical instruction in the composition of all kinds of papers used in ordinary business transactions, and a compilation of the laws appertaining thereto; for use in business colleges, high schools, and for self instruction. Sacramento, Calif. [Pub. by the author] 1894. 159+[1]p. 24½cm.

The title of this work was deposited for copyright, 1893.

2d ed. [1902] 160p. 26cm.

BALTES, Frank William, 1860–

The cost of printing: a system in practical operation; with forms and books especially adapted to large and small printing concerns. Portland, Or. Baltes, 1894. 74p. 17½ x 25cm.

CATON, Martin Jennings, 1863–

The actual business guide: a practical text-book for use in actual business departments of business colleges; and also adapted to use in commercial schools whose course begins with actual business. Cleveland, Progressive school bk. co. 1894. 75p. 30cm.

EATON, Seymour, 1859–1916.

Business forms, customs and accounts; for schools and colleges. [Phil.] Pub. by the author [c1894] 111p. 19½cm.

Another ed. N.Y. Amer. bk. co. 1895.

FOSTER, Horatio Alvah, 1858–1913.

Central station bookkeeping and suggested forms; with an appendix for street railways. N.Y. W.J. Johnston, 1894. 139p. 24cm.

Another ed. 1896. 139p. 24cm.

HARMON, Alta A.

Book-keeping for teachers' institutes. Omaha, J. L. Gideon, 1894. 54p. 18½cm.

The title of this work was deposited for copyright, 1893.

KEISTER, David Armel.

Expert and stock company accounting and auditing . . . Cleveland [c1894] 291p. 23½cm.

—Keister's corporation accounting and auditing: a practical treatise on higher accounting . . . with an introduction by Hon. H. C. White. Cleveland, Burrows bros. 1896. 525p. 23½cm.

4th ed. 1897. 525p. 23½cm.
7th ed. 1899. 525p. 23½cm.
8th ed. 1901. 525p. 23½cm.
9th ed. 1901. 525p. 23½cm.
10th ed. 1903. 525p. 23½cm.
11th ed. 1905. 569p. 23½cm.
12th ed. 1907. 569p. 23½cm.
13th ed. 1909. 569p. 23½cm.
14th ed. 1912. 569p. 23½cm.
15th ed. 1915. 569p. 23½cm.
16th ed. 1920. 569p. 23½cm.
16th ed. 1923. 569p. 23½cm.
17th ed. 1924. 569p. 23½cm.

LOOMIS, Henry Thomas, 1856–1918, BRYANT, James H., and STEVENS, Charles E.

Complete practical bookkeeping: a text-book on modern methods of accounting; including an appendix of useful information and helpful hints for bookkeepers and office men. Cleveland, Practical text bk. co. 1894. 308p. 27½cm.

The title and two copies of this work and the two listed below were deposited for copyright, 1893.

The title-page of this work does not contain the names of the authors.

"Bank bookkeeping" contained in "Complete practical bookkeeping" was separately published.

Another ed. 1898. 308p. 28cm.
Another ed. [n. d.] 308p. 27½cm.

—Mercantile practical bookkeeping; prepared for use in . . . schools and commercial colleges. Cleveland, Practical text bk. co. 1894. 192p. 28cm.

The first 192 pages of "Complete practical bookkeeping . . ."

Another ed. [c1898] 168p. 27½cm.

—Progressive practical bookkeeping . . . Cleveland, Practical text bk. co. 1894. 96p. 28½cm.

The first ninety-six pages of "Complete practical bookkeeping . . ."

Other eds. 1908; 1921. 96p. 28cm.

RICHARDSON, I. E.

The F. N. U. [Fayette normal university] book-keeping. Fayette, Ohio, Pub. by the author, 1894. 108p. 24cm.

RICHARDSON (continued)

The preface indicates that the book was prepared for use in the theory department of business colleges, public schools, and for private students.

ROBERTSON, Powhatan Wyndham, 1865–

A condensed treatise on progressive book-keeping; elucidating the principles and practice of double entry and the modern methods of arranging practical accounts. Wash. National pub. co. [c1894] 135p. 25cm.

—Bookkeeping and the science of accounts; elucidating the principles and practice of double entry . . . 1895. 176p. 24½cm.

A revised edition.

3d ed. Wash. The author, 1897. 183p. 24½cm.

4th ed. 1901. 183p. 24½cm.

—Code of business transactions to accompany the author's "Robertson's bookkeeping and science of accounts" . . . or for use with any text book.

The title of this work was deposited for copyright, 1899.

SADLER, Warren H., 1841–1909, ROWE, Harry Marc, 1860–1926, and BRYANT, James H.

Sadler's business book-keeping and practice; school ed. Balt. Sadler, 1894. 156p. 30cm.

The first edition is the only one which includes the name of James H. Bryant on the title-page.

2d ed. 1895. 156p. 30cm.
School edition.

10th ed. 1897. 181+[3]p. 30cm.

25th ed. Balt. Sadler-Rowe, 1899. 199+[2]p. 30cm.
In the 20th century H. M. Rowe was the publisher of this work which was reprinted many times.

Another ed. [n. d.] 92p. 30cm.
Abridged edition.

—Sadler's bookkeepers and office practice; supplementary to Sadler's business bookkeeping and practice. Balt. Sadler, 1895. 237 numb. l. 21 x 24½cm.

The title of this work was deposited for copyright three times in 1895. The first two titles deposited contained the word "business" instead of "office."

SANDY, William Charles, 1849–1926.

The American accountant: a new and practical treatise on double entry book-keeping; designed for use in high schools, business colleges, and as a book of reference in the counting-room [part one] [Newark, N. J.] 1894. 96p. 24cm.

The title of this work was deposited for copyright, 1885. Two copies were not deposited until 1894. It is doubtful that the book was published before 1894.

Another ed. [c1895] 272p. 24cm.
Two parts in one volume.

Another ed. N.Y. Univ. pub. co. 1895. 272p. 24cm.

Another ed. 1896. 298p. 24cm.

Another ed. 1904. 118p. 23½cm.
Part 1, revised.

WALDEN, Lee Roy, and WALDEN, Charles E.
Walden's manual of practical book-keeping; prepared for use in Walden's Texas business college . . . and for high schools, academies, normal schools and self-instruction. Austin, Tex. L. R. & C. E. Walden, 1894. 76p. 23cm.

1895

BROOK, William Henry.
Brook's lawyers' bookkeeping by double entry on the Kain triple column system . . . Detroit, Brook [c1895] 26p. 19cm.

BYRNE, Henry Edward, 1870–
The companion for students, teachers, bookkeepers, business men and expert accountants. Chillicothe, Mo. Printed by the Good way pub. co. [1895] 42p. 17cm.

CANADAY, W. F., and MAUPIN, L. L.
The Canaday-Maupin system of bookkeeping and business practice. Chillicothe, Mo. Moore pub. co. [c1895] 156p. 28cm.

DRAUGHON, John Franklin, 1863–1921.
Draughon's progressive bookkeeping and legal adviser . . . Nashville, Draughon's practical business college [c1895] 182+[1]p. 22½cm.

This is really a new work, though part of it is based on the third edition of "Draughon's new system of book-keeping . . ." published in 1894, the first edition of which was published in 1889.

Other eds. 1896; 1899; 1909. 241+[3]p. 22½cm.

—Draughon's progressive bookkeeping and business manual. Nashville, Draughon text-bk. co. [c1917] 2v. 26½cm.

A complete revision of "Draughon's progressive bookkeeping and legal adviser . . ."

Another ed. [c1919] 2v. 26½cm.

HUDSON, Lycurgus Leonidas, 1857–1911.
Hudson's bookkeeping instructor and accountants' hand-book; especially designed for self instruction, the accountant's desk and school room use. [Columbus, Ohio, Franklin print. co.] 1895. 209+[1]p. 28½ x 24cm.

LANTMAN, Edgar G., 1861–
The Werner bookkeeping: a six-column journal system of double-entry bookkeeping for grammar schools and high schools. Chic. Werner co. [c1895] 68p. 27½cm.

PACKARD, Silas Sadler, 1826–1898.
Advance sheets of Packard's revised manual of book-keeping . . . [N.Y. c1895] 48p. 26cm.
The first forty-eight pages of "The Packard method of teaching book-keeping," 1896.
—The Packard method of teaching book-keeping; advanced course; for use in business colleges and commercial departments of high schools. N.Y. Packard, 1896. 138p. 26cm.
Another ed. N.Y. Peoria, Ill. Packard [c1896] 138p. 26cm.
On cover: Advanced course.
Contents as in entry above.

PERRY, Caleb S.
Perry's practical bookkeeping: a comprehensive treatise on modern accounting; designed for use in public schools, business colleges . . . especially arranged as a self instructor . . . [Winfield, Kan. T.C. Copeland, printer] c1895. 115+[2]p. 24cm.

PINE, Charles C.
A safety system of bank bookkeeping, by the winner of the "Evening-telegram" prize for the best plan to prevent dishonesty in banks . . . N.Y. Pine [c1895] 103p. 21cm.

RENDELL, Charles H., and PINNEY, Edwin S., 1851–1916.
Rendell & Pinney's society and commercial book-keeping by double entry; for beginners, secretaries, and accountants . . . [Greeley, Col. Greeley tribune press, c1895] 199p. 18cm.

WOOD, George W., 1866–
The voucher system of book-keeping: a complete exposition of the subject is here presented for the first time. Pittsburgh, Wood, 1895. 29p. 21 x 28cm.
Another ed. Pittsburgh, Record co. 1896. 26p. 21 x 28cm.

WOODLOCK, Thomas Francis, 1866–
The anatomy of a railroad report. N.Y. U.S. bk. co. [c1895] 72p. 22cm.
Another ed. N.Y. S.A. Nelson [c1901] 121p. 17½cm. (Nelson's Wall street library, v.2)

1896

BENTON, Charles William, 1858–1932.
Practical bookkeeping; designed for the use of high schools, normal schools, business colleges and private study. Valparaiso, Ind. M.E. Bogarte, 1896. 216p. 27½cm.
Another ed. 1897. 216p. 27½cm.
Another ed. Chic. Chicago college of commerce, 1898.
Another ed. Valparaiso, Ind. M. E. Bogarte, 1901. 216p. 27½cm.
Another ed. 1910. 222p. 27½cm.

CRAWFORD, James M., 1854–1926, and FOOTE, William H., 1855–1926.
The Cleveland accountant: a treatise on the theory and practice of book-keeping by double entry . . . especially adapted to the use of schools, academies, colleges and private learners; also as a work of reference for the counting-room. Cleveland, F. W. Roberts, 1896. 155p. 24cm.

HAVEN, Curtis, 1854–1915.
Haven's actual bookkeeping; presenting the whole art in twelve easy lessons; for school use or home study . . . Phil. The author, 1896. [51]p. 28½cm.

JONES, T. H., and WOODS, H. H.
The eureka system of book-keeping and commercial science. Palestine, Tex. Semi-weekly times print, 1896. 36p. 23½cm.

POWERS, Orville Marcellus, 1852–
First lessons in book-keeping; designed for the use of public schools and private study . . . Chic. Powers, 1896. 89p.+p.27–33, 28cm.
Another ed. Chic. Powers & Lyons, 1900. 89p.+p.5–71, 28cm.

—Memoranda of business practice; for use in the practical department of all schools where the science of accounts is taught. Chic. Powers, 1896. 24p. 28cm.
With this is bound his Treatise on business practice; or, How business is done. Chic. 1897.

SWEET, James Sylvester, 1853–1930.
Bookkeeping by actual business practice: a thorough treatise in modern and practical methods of accounting; for the use of business colleges, business universities, commercial schools, high schools . . . Santa Rosa, Calif. Sweet, 1896. 108p. 27½cm.
Public school edition.
Another ed. [c1896] 128p. 27½cm.
Business college edition.

WELLS, Charles R.
The practice system of business training and bookkeeping; first course — complete. Rochester, N.Y. Williams & Rogers, c1896. 136p. 12½ x 33cm.
The second course was published in 1897.

1897

BROAKER, Frank, and CHAPMAN, Richard Marvin.
The American accountants' manual; volume 1. Examination questions prepared by the state board of examiners of expert public accountants appointed by the board of regents of the University of the State of New York . . . Subjects: theory of accounts; practical accounting; auditing; commercial law; together with answers in concise form, further elucidated by author's commentaries upon the technique and expression of modern accountancy. N.Y. Broaker & Chapman [c1897] 210p. 23cm.
"Volume 1" on the title-page.
No more published.
Another ed. N.Y. Broaker [c1915] 210p. 23cm.

BUCHANAN, William, 1853–
The latest improved system of book-keeping . . . [adapted to the use of students in high schools, normal schools . . . and business colleges] Cleveland, Cleveland bk. bindery [c1897–1902] 2v. 27cm.
Vol. 2 has title: "Appendix: the latest improved system of book-keeping; part third . . ." Cleveland, Cleveland legal blank & bk. binding co.
The author deposited for copyright, 1894: "The latest improved system of book-keeping; adaptable to any business." This work, not found to exist, is probably a preliminary edition of the work copyrighted in 1897.

DRAUGHON, John Franklin, 1863–1921.
Draughon's practical bookkeeping; illustrated for self-instruction by home study, and for use in literary and business colleges. [Nashville] c1897. 81p. 23cm.

The title of this work was first deposited for copyright, 1894. It was probably a preliminary edition.

GROVER, Preston Henry, 1854–1912.
Corporation book-keeping in a nut-shell; with an appendix containing a chapter on the treatment of manufacturing accounts; the latest and most approved rules for averaging accounts; the shortest and best rules for computing interest; rules for locating errors in trial balances . . . Detroit, Book-keeper co. 1897.
94p. 25½cm.
Another ed. Detroit, Book-keeper pub. co. 1902.
52p. 25cm.

KELLER, P. H., and LONGAKER, A. D.
Keller and Longaker's actual practice in expert accounting . . . for use in business colleges . . . Pottstown, Pa. 1897.
68p. 24½cm.
The title of this work was deposited for copyright, October 14, 1896, and March 25, 1897.
An "Illustrated key to Keller and Longaker's actual practice in expert accounting and book of reference for systems of book-keeping . . ." was deposited for copyright, October 8, 1897, and July 3, 1899.

KITTREDGE, Anson Oliver, 1848–1903, and BROWN, John F.
The self-proving accounting system . . . with special application made to the instalment business: a manual for business men, accountants and auditors. N. Y. Self-proving account-bk. co. 1897. 328p. 24½cm.

MONTGOMERY, James Louis.
Modern book-keeping; single and double entry. N. Y. Maynard, Merrill, 1897. 240p. 21cm.
Part 1, single entry, also published separately.
Other eds. 1898; 1899; 1900; 1901; 1905. 240p. 20cm.
Another ed. N. Y. C. E. Merrill [1906] 240p. 20cm.
—Modern book-keeping and business practice. N. Y. Maynard, Merrill, 1906. 381p. 21cm.
Contains supplementary material.

PACKARD, Silas Sadler, 1826–1898, publisher.
Bank book-keeping: a text-book for business schools and for private students. N. Y. Packard [c1897] 67p. 30cm.
S. S. Packard is named on the title-page as author. Mr. Edgar M. Barber wrote and signed a statement on the title-page of the New York public library copy as follows:
"With the exception of the publisher's statement, this work was written entirely by Edgar M. Barber, then in Mr. Packard's em-

PACKARD (continued)

ploy, with the assistance primarily of Mr. Herbert H. Swasey and, incidentally, of Mr. James G. Cannon, as stated in the publisher's statement. A chapter on the clearing house etc. was added in 1898 by E. M. B. and the work bound complete."—Edgar M. Barber, May 1, 1913.

Another ed. [c1898] 88p. 28cm.
Contents as in entry above with the addition of a chapter on the clearing house.

SCHWARTZ, George W., 1871–

Office routine and bookkeeping: a method of teaching the science of accounts and of illustrating the routine in business offices; for use in business colleges and commercial departments; script illustrations by E. C. Mills. Rochester, N. Y. Williams & Rogers, 1897. 120p. 26cm.

On cover: Commercial school edition.

Introductory course.

This work was reprinted many times.

Another ed. N. Y. Amer. bk. co. [n. d.] 120p. 26cm.
Introductory course.

—Office routine and bookkeeping . . . complete course. Rochester, N. Y. Williams & Rogers, 1898. 251p. 26cm.

Another ed. 1900. 251p. 26cm.

Another ed. N. Y. Amer. bk. co. [n. d.] 251p. 26cm.

STEVENSON, William C., 1865–1909.

Stevenson's introductory bookkeeping: a text-book on accounting; for public schools, academies, normal schools, and teachers' institutes. Topeka, Kan. J. S. Parks, 1897. 148p. 28cm.

2d ed. 1899. 148p. 28cm.

STOW, Carl B.

Stow's self-instructor of practical double-entry book-keeping: a thorough . . . treatise of the science . . . designed for the public schools. Chic. Donohue, Henneberry [c1897] 79p. 23cm.

WELLS, Charles R.

The practice system of business training and bookkeeping; second course — complete. Rochester, N. Y. Williams & Rogers, c1897. [142]p. 12½ x 33cm.

The first course was published in 1896.

1898

CLARKE, Edward W.

Brewery bookkeeping: a practical treatise on brewery accounts and office management. Chic. H. S. Rich, 1898. 181p. 31cm.

The title of this work was first deposited for copyright, 1897.

CRAWFORD, James M., 1854–1926.
The Cleveland accountant: a work designed for experienced bookkeepers on opening and closing the books of joint-stock companies; also, a complete manual of forms for organizing and managing all kinds of companies and associations, including partnership settlements and partnership changes; auditors,—their duties and responsibilities; also points on higher and expert accounting; and a practical treatise on banking. Cleveland, Pub. by the author, 1898. 390p. 26½cm.
Though the preliminary matter is the same as that in the "The Cleveland accountant," published in 1896, the treatise is different.

HALL, Marshall Parker, 1838–1896.
The art of accounts: an elementary treatise on bookkeeping and the nature and use of money. Bost. Silver, Burdett [c1898] 120p. 21 x 25½cm.
At head of title: Bookkeeping for grammar and high school grades.
[2d ed.] [c1913] 86p. 21 x 25½cm.
At head of title: Bookkeeping for grammar and high school grades.

PACKARD, Silas Sadler, 1826–1898.
Commission business; exhibiting the material and forms for a complete record thereof; adapted to schools and private learners. N.Y. Packard [c1898] 24p. 26cm.

PRACTICAL TEXT BOOK COMPANY, Cleveland.
Twentieth century business practice and practical accounting from vouchers. [Cleveland, Practical text bk. co. c1898] 5v. 23 x 22½cm.
Contents.—pt.1. Flour and feed.—pt.2. Boots and shoes.—pt.3. Groceries.—pt.4. General store.—pt.5. Commission.

WHINYATES, John W., 1841–1920.
Bookkeeping with or without a master . . . with specimens of books used in both single and double entry; for the use of students, clerks, tradesmen, and merchants. Salt Lake City, The author [c1898] 62p. 24cm.
Another ed. Chic. M. A. Donohue [c1903] 73p. 23½cm.

1899

BARRETT, Charles R.
Bookkeeping, single and double entry. [Chic.] 1899. 179p. 28cm.

BROWN, George Wycoff, 1845–1918, and REA, James, 1863–
The Packard method of teaching bookkeeping by single and double entry; short course; for use in commercial departments of public and private schools, theory departments of business colleges, night schools, and by private learners; accompanied by Packard's business practice tests; script illustrations by G. E. Nettleton.
N. Y. Peoria, Ill. Packard, 1899. 96p. 26cm.
This work was also published with no author named on the title-page. S. S. Packard is named as publisher of this edition and L. H. Packard copyrighted the work in 1899.
No record of the publication of this work before 1899 was found, although the work was advertised in "The Packard method of teaching book-keeping; advanced course . . ." first published in 1895.
"Packard's progressive business practice tests" designed to accompany this work was separately copyrighted.

HOFFMAN, John V., 1868–
Bookkeeping as it is practiced in large business houses; a book for business college graduates . . . [Balt. 1899] 78p. 24cm.
Although the author's name has two "n's" on the title-page, the author signed his name in 1931 with one "n" only.

MARTIN, William R., 1842–1918.
The keystone system of bookkeeping and commercial training. [Balt. c1899] 13+[1]p. 23½cm.

NEAL, E. Virgil.
Modern banking and bank accounting; containing a complete exposition of the most approved methods of bank accounting; designed as a text book for schools and private students and a handbook of reference for bankers; script illustrations by E. C. Mills. Rochester, N. Y. Williams & Rogers [c1899] 227p. 26cm.

POWERS, Orville Marcellus, 1852–
Single entry bookkeeping for grammar schools. Chic. Powers, 1899. 59p. 23½cm.

RAHILL, John Joseph.
Corporation accounting and corporation law: a complete exposition of the science of corporation accounting both in theory and practice; with a digest of the corporation laws of all the states and a valuable treatise on stock exchanges . . . Fresno, Calif. Rahill, 1899. 192p. 26cm.
[2d ed.] 1906. 443+[9]p. 22½cm.
"The old work has been more than revised. It has been rewritten . . . the size has been more than doubled." — Pref.

Contains an appendix on California examinations for C. P. A. certificates; with a full set of questions and answers, by Alfred G. Platt.

Another ed. N. Y. Continental audit co. 1907. 443+[9]p. 22½cm.

ROWE, Harry Marc, 1860–1926.

Commercial and industrial bookkeeping; an educational method for teaching the principles and laws of accounts . . . specially designed for use in high schools, commercial departments and bookkeeping classes in public schools. Balt. Sadler-Rowe [1899] 96p. 21½cm.

"Commercial and industrial bookkeeping" consists of the above title known as Reference book no.100, and five sets, each separate and distinct, with its own set of blank books and business papers.

The titles of the sets follow:

Inductive set; budget no.101. c1900. 106p. 21½cm.

Wholesale and retail set; budget no.102. c1901. p.107–200.

Jobbing and commission set; budget no.103. c1902. p.201–264.

Manufacturing set; double entry voucher system; no.1A. 1902.

Banking set; nos. 56; 57; 58; 59. 1901.

Another ed. Balt. Rowe [c1899] 96p. 21½cm. (Reference book no.100)

SKAGGS, Eli Harrison.

The cosmos accountant and business self instructor; containing all the practical variations of the science of recording mercantile transactions . . . San Antonio, San Antonio print. co. 1899. 68p. 21cm.

SPENCER, Enos, 1851–1920.

The art of modern bookkeeping. Louisville, Ky. Spencerian business college co. 1899. 231p. 26½cm.

The title of this work was deposited for copyright, 1896, but two copies were not deposited until 1899. It is doubtful that it was published for general distribution before 1899.

2d ed. 1907. 443p. 26cm.

3d ed. 1909. 444+[2]p. 26cm.

VYE, John Alexander, 1867–

Creamery accounting. Delano, Minn. The author, 1899. 42p. 24 x 31½cm.

1900

ARNOLD, Horace Lucian, d. 1915, compiler.
The complete cost-keeper: some original systems of shop cost-keeping or factory accounting; together with an exposition of the advantages of account keeping by means of cards instead of books, and a description of various mechanical aids to factory accounting; now comp. for the first time by Horace Lucian Arnold (Henry Roland) N.Y. Engin. mag. press, 1900. 408p. 25cm.
The title of this work was deposited for copyright, 1899.
Other eds. 1903; 1904; 1907; 1912. 408p. 24cm.

BOOK-KEEPER PUBLISHING COMPANY, LTD., Detroit.
Accounting for department stores . . . Detroit, Book-keeper pub. co. 1900. 56p. 23cm.

—Factory cost accounting: a text book for those who require "complete comparative records" of the cost of every article manufactured; so that any increase or decrease in items of cost may be instantly detected . . . Detroit, Book-keeper pub. co. 1900. 32p. 24cm.

DEAN, W. F.
Bookkeeping for retail stores. Phil. E. Stern, 1900. 67p. 19cm.

EATON, James Shirley, 1868–
Railroad operations; how to know them from a study of the accounts and statistics. N.Y. Railroad gazette, 1900. 313p. 19cm.

GARDNER, Elmer Elsworth, 1868–
Fireside accounting and business training: a plain, practical, actual business method of keeping accounts; designed especially for self-instruction; including also rapid calculation, business ethics, letter writing, and commercial law. Battle Creek, Mich. Fireside accounting pub. co. [c1900] 130p. 26½cm.

—New card system of bookkeeping and business practice: a clear, comprehensive, and practical method of accounting; designed for use in public, parochial, and private schools. Lansing, Mich. Hammond pub. co. 1900.
Instructions, sample blanks, and forms in envelopes.
—Reference book to the New card system of bookkeeping and business practice. Battle Creek, Mich. Gregory pub. co. 1900.

MARSHALL, Carl Coran, 1852–
Bookkeeping and business training. Cedar Rapids, Ia. Goodyear-Marshall pub. co. [c1900] 115p. 28cm.
Other eds. 1901; 1904; 1910; 1915. 115p. 28cm.

MAYNE, Dexter Dwight, editor.
Office methods and practical bookkeeping; combining instruction in approved methods of business practice with modern accounting and commercial law; arranged for business colleges, high schools . . . Chic. Powers & Lyons, 1900. 96+9p. 27cm.
Interleaved with various kinds of business forms.
Another ed. [c1900] 136+10+[1]p. 28cm.
Interleaved with various kinds of business forms, dated 1905.
No author or editor for this edition is given on the title-page.

MESERVEY, Atwood Bond, 1831–1901.
Manual of bookkeeping and banking. Bost. Thompson, Brown, 1900. 288p. 22½cm.

NATIONAL ELECTRIC LIGHT ASSOCIATION.
System of accounts for hydraulic power companies. [N.Y. 1900?] 59p. 23½cm.

NEAL, E. Virgil, and CRAGIN, Charles Thompson.
Modern illustrative bookkeeping; designed as a text-book for all schools giving a course in business training; introductory course; script illustrations by E. C. Mills. N.Y. Williams & Rogers, c1900. 146p. 25½cm. (Williams & Rogers ser.)
Another ed. 1901. 208p. 25½cm.
(Williams & Rogers ser.)
—Modern illustrative bookkeeping; designed as a text-book for all schools giving a course in business training; advanced course; script illustrations by E. C. Mills. N.Y. Amer. bk. co. [c1901] p.134–274, 25½cm. (Williams & Rogers ser.)
—Modern illustrative bookkeeping; designed as a text-book for all schools giving a course in business training . . . complete course; script illustrations by E. C. Mills. N.Y. Amer. bk. co. [c1901] 273+[1]p. 25½cm. (Williams & Rogers ser.)
—Modern illustrative bookkeeping . . . introductory course; rev. and enl. by D. D. Mueller. N.Y. Amer. bk. co. [c1909] 160p. 25½cm. (Williams & Rogers ser.)
—Modern illustrative bookkeeping . . . advanced course; rev. and enl. by J. E. King; script illustrations by E. C. Mills. N.Y. Amer. bk. co. [1911] p.[149]–324, 25cm. (Williams & Rogers ser.)
—Modern illustrative bookkeeping; complete course; rev. and enl. by D. D. Mueller and J. E. King; script illustrations by E. C. Mills. N.Y. Amer. bk. co. [c1911] 324p. 25½cm.
(Williams & Rogers ser.)

NEAL (continued)
—New modern illustrative bookkeeping; introductory course by Charles F[orest] Rittenhouse; script by Edward C. Mills. N.Y. Amer. bk. co. [c1918] 152p. 25½cm.
(Williams & Rogers ser.)
—New modern illustrative bookkeeping; advanced course; based upon the Neal & Cragin edition of Modern illustrative bookkeeping, advanced course; with revised classification of accounts and financial statements by Charles F[orest] Rittenhouse . . . to conform to the procedure followed in New modern illustrative bookkeeping; introductory course . . . N.Y. Amer. bk. co. [c1919] p.153–324, 25cm. (Williams & Rogers ser.)
—New modern illustrative bookkeeping; complete course; script by E. C. Mills. N.Y. Amer. bk. co. [c1919] 326p. 25½cm.
(Williams & Rogers ser.)
—New modern illustrative bookkeeping; elementary course, journal method [rev. by Ralph Ernest Rogers] based upon New modern illustrative bookkeeping; introductory course by Charles F[orest] Rittenhouse; script by Edward C. Mills and Charles E. Leslie. N.Y. Amer. bk. co. [c1923] 152p. 25½cm.
(Williams & Rogers ser.)
Another ed. [c1931] 152p. 25½cm.
(Williams & Rogers ser.)

NICHOLS, William G.
Methods of cost finding in cotton mills; a full description of methods used in accurate cost finding for cloth or yarn mills; fully illustrated by blanks and tables; adapted to mills with a wide variety of product. Waltham, Mass. E. L. Barry, 1900.
70p. 25½cm.

STEVENS, Louis V.
Stevens' true method of actual business; systematically arranged for use in business colleges, schools of business, high schools, etc. . . [Buffalo?] 1900. 67+[1]p. 17½cm.

YORK, John.
Questions and answers on bookkeeping, commercial papers, and commercial law; together with a vocabulary of mercantile terms and abbreviations. Stockton, Calif. L. S. Atwood, 1900.
73p. 19½cm.
The title of this work was deposited for copyright, 1899.

PART TWO

PART TWO

A classification of the works listed in Part One, except those which would be classified as works on the general principles of bookkeeping theory and practice.

INTRODUCTION

PRIOR to 1901 the works on accounting by American authors were chiefly treatises on the general principles of bookkeeping theory and practice. Since the titles of these works, listed chronologically in Part One, are self-explanatory they are not classified in this chapter.

Of the 392 titles listed in Part One, 336 are general treatises, and 56 are works devoted principally to some one subject in advanced accounting or to accounting for some one business, profession, or service. Each one of these specialized treatises is classified in Part Two under the specific subject or subjects to which the work relates. Six are listed under two separate headings. Brief treatises and sets on specialized accounting subjects contained in general bookkeeping texts are not included in this classification.

The pioneer works presented in this chapter trace the growth of specialization in accounting literature in the 19th century.

The items are listed chronologically under each subject according to the bibliographical technique used in Part One.

SUBJECTS IN ADVANCED ACCOUNTING

CORPORATIONS

1884

CARNES, Andrew J., 1836–1889.

Carnes' manual on opening and closing the books of joint stock companies: a work designed for experienced book-keepers . . . Cin. Carnes, 1884. 42p. 23cm.

2d ed. 1888. 42p. 23cm.

3d ed. Balt. [J. Murphy & co. printers] 1891. 42p. 22½cm.

1892

CRAIGE, A. S.

Organization and management of private corporations; with notes on corporation bookkeeping. Chic. Bankers' stationery supply co. 1892. 128p. 20cm.

Practically one half of this work is devoted to accounting.

1897

GROVER, Preston Henry, 1854–1912.

Corporation book-keeping in a nut-shell; with an appendix containing a chapter on the treatment of manufacturing accounts; the latest and most approved rules for averaging accounts; the shortest and best rules for computing interest; rules for locating errors in trial balances . . . Detroit, Book-keeper co. 1897. 94p. 25½cm.

Another ed. Detroit, Book-keeper pub. co. 1902. 52p. 25cm.

1899

RAHILL, John Joseph.

Corporation accounting and corporation law: a complete exposition of the science of corporation accounting both in theory and practice; with a digest of the corporation laws of all the states and a valuable treatise on stock exchanges . . . Fresno, Calif. Rahill, 1899. 192p. 26cm.

[2d ed.] 1906. 443+[9]p. 22½cm.

"The old work has been more than revised. It

RAHILL (continued)

has been rewritten . . . the size has been more than doubled." — Pref.

Contains an appendix on California examinations for C. P. A. certificates; with a full set of questions and answers, by Alfred G. Platt.

Another ed. N. Y. Continental audit co. 1907. 443+[9]p. 22½cm.

VOUCHER SYSTEM

1893

MCCAFFERTY, H. W., and FOWLER, Frank W.

The voucher system of bookkeeping . . . [East Liverpool, Ohio] East Liverpool tribune print [c1893] 16p. 20 x 23½cm.

1895

WOOD, George W., 1866–

The voucher system of book-keeping: a complete exposition of the subject is here presented for the first time. Pittsburgh, Wood, 1895. 29p. 21 x 28cm.

Another ed. Pittsburgh, Record co. 1896. 26p. 21 x 28cm.

COST ACCOUNTING

1885

METCALFE, Henry, 1847–1927.

The cost of manufactures and the administration of workshops, public and private. N. Y. Wiley, 1885. 322p. 24cm.

2d ed. 1890. 322p. 24cm.
3d ed. 1894.
Another ed. 1907. 366p.

1887

CHILD, Frederick W.

Elements of cost and methods of accounting in steam engine works. N. Y. Office co. 1887. 20p. 18½cm.

A paper read before the Institute of accounts.

1894

Baltes, Frank William, 1860–
The cost of printing: a system in practical operation; with forms and books especially adapted to large and small printing concerns. Portland, Or. Baltes, 1894. 74p. 17½ x 25cm.

1900

Arnold, Horace Lucian, d. 1915, compiler.
The complete cost-keeper: some original systems of shop cost-keeping or factory accounting; together with an exposition of the advantages of account keeping by means of cards instead of books, and a description of various mechanical aids to factory accounting; now comp. for the first time by Horace Lucian Arnold (Henry Roland) N. Y. Engin. mag. press, 1900. 408p. 25cm.
The title of this work was deposited for copyright, 1899.
Other eds. 1903; 1904; 1907; 1912. 408p. 24cm.

Book-keeper publishing company, ltd., Detroit.
Factory cost accounting: a text book for those who require "complete comparative records" of the cost of every article manufactured; so that any increase or decrease in items of cost may be instantly detected . . . Detroit, Book-keeper pub. co. 1900. 32p. 24cm.

Nichols, William G.
Methods of cost finding in cotton mills; a full description of methods used in accurate cost finding for cloth or yarn mills; fully illustrated by blanks and tables; adapted to mills with a wide variety of product. Waltham, Mass. E. L. Barry, 1900. 70p. 25½cm.

AUDITING

1892

Soulé, George, 1834–1926.
Manual of auditing; suggestions to auditors, receivers and liquidators, and points on higher and expert accounting. N. O. 1892. 28p. 28 x 19½cm.

2d ed.	1893.	32p. 28 x 19½cm.
3d ed.	1893.	
4th ed.	1900.	24p. 27½cm.
6th ed.	1905.	24p. 26½cm.

1893

Good, J. Dobson, 1845–
The auditor; plain suggestions for the guidance of trustees, directors and others, as to the auditing of books and accounts of stock companies, corporations, building associations and mercantile firms. [Cin. S. Rosenthal] 1893. 90p. 18½cm.

1894

Keister, David Armel.
Expert and stock company accounting and auditing . . . Cleveland [c1894] 291p. 23½cm.
—Keister's corporation accounting and auditing: a practical treatise on higher accounting . . . with an introduction by Hon. H. C. White. Cleveland, Burrows bros. 1896. 525p. 23½cm.

4th ed. 1897. 525p. 23½cm.
7th ed. 1899. 525p. 23½cm.
8th ed. 1901. 525p. 23½cm.
9th ed. 1901. 525p. 23½cm.
10th ed. 1903. 525p. 23½cm.
11th ed. 1905. 569p. 23½cm.
12th ed. 1907. 569p. 23½cm.
13th ed. 1909. 569p. 23½cm.
14th ed. 1912. 569p. 23½cm.
15th ed. 1915. 569p. 23½cm.
16th ed. 1920. 569p. 23½cm.
16th ed. 1923. 569p. 23½cm.
17th ed. 1924. 569p. 23½cm.

C. P. A. EXAMINATION QUESTIONS AND ANSWERS

1897

Broaker, Frank, and Chapman, Richard Marvin.
The American accountants' manual; volume 1. Examination questions prepared by the state board of examiners of expert public accountants appointed by the board of regents of the University of the State of New York . . . Subjects: theory of accounts; practical accounting; auditing; commercial law; together with answers in concise form, further elucidated by author's commentaries upon the technique and expression of modern accountancy. N. Y. Broaker & Chapman [c1897] 210p. 23cm.
"Volume 1" on the title-page.
No more published.
Another ed. N. Y. Broaker [c1915] 210p. 23cm.

ACCOUNTING FOR BUSINESSES, PROFESSIONS, OR SERVICES

AGRICULTURE

1858

COCHRAN, William D.
Agricultural book-keeping; being a concise and scientific system of keeping farm accounts; divested of all technical terms, and accompanied with blank books ruled and adapted to the system. Detroit, Daily advertiser steam presses, 1858. 67+[1]p. 24½cm.
The title of this work was deposited for copyright (District of Michigan) November 28, 1857.

1892

ATKESON, Thomas Clark, 1852–
Bookkeeping for farmers: a treatise on farm accounts; to which is added the Stockbridge system accounts; ed. by Herbert Myrick. N.Y. Judd, 1892. 40p. 19cm.
Other eds. 1905; 1920. 40p. 19cm.

BANKS (National, State, and Private)

1856

MARSH, Christopher Columbus, 1806–1884.
The theory and practice of bank book-keeping and joint stock accounts; exemplified and elucidated in a complete set of bank account books; arranged in accordance with the principles of double entry; embracing the routine of business from the organization of a company to the declaration of a dividend; with all the forms and details and an original diagram. N.Y. D. Appleton & co. 1856. 292p. 31cm.

Other eds. 1859; 1863. 292p. 31cm.
4th ed. 1864. 292p. 31cm.
5th ed. 1866. 292p. 31cm.
7th ed. 1875. 300p. 31cm.
The seventh edition contains a supplement: Examples of entries in opening books of joint stock companies under different organizations.
Another ed. 1884. 292p. 31cm.

1868

DUFF, Peter, 1802–1869.

Duff's book-keeping by single and double entry; practically illustrating merchants', manufacturers', private bankers', railroad and national bank accounts; 20th ed. enl. & rev. N.Y. Harper & bros. 1868. 398p. 25½cm.

Cover-title: Mercantile, bank, and railroad bookkeeping.

The title of this work was deposited for copyright (Western District of Pennsylvania) 1867.

Based upon Duff's North American accountant and called 20th edition enlarged and revised.

The fourth part, p.227–383, is devoted entirely to railroad and bank bookkeeping.

It is practically a new work.

Other eds. 1869; 1870; 1871; 1873; 1876; 1882; 1896. 400p. 25½cm.

This work is listed in part one under 1848.

1885

SMITH, William H.

A manual of bank book-keeping; designed for the use of schools and private study . . . N.Y. Smith, 1885. 93+[2]p. 23cm.

The title of this work was deposited for copyright, 1884.

1895

PINE, Charles C.

A safety system of bank bookkeeping, by the winner of the "Evening-telegram" prize for the best plan to prevent dishonesty in banks . . . N.Y. Pine [c1895] 103p. 21cm.

1897

PACKARD, Silas Sadler, 1826–1898, publisher.

Bank book-keeping: a text-book for business schools and for private students. N.Y. Packard [c1897] 67p. 30cm.

S. S. Packard is named on the title-page as author. Mr. Edgar M. Barber wrote and signed a statement on the title-page of the New York public library copy as follows: "With the exception of the publisher's statement, this work was written entirely by Edgar M. Barber, then in Mr. Packard's employ, with the assistance primarily of Mr. Herbert H. Swasey and, incidentally, of Mr. James G. Cannon, as stated in the publisher's statement. A chapter on the clearing house etc. was added in 1898 by E. M. B. and the work bound complete." — Edgar M. Barber, May 1, 1913.

Another ed. [c1898] 88p. 28cm.

Contents as in entry above with the addition of a chapter on the clearing house.

1899

NEAL, E. Virgil.

Modern banking and bank accounting; containing a complete exposition of the most approved methods of bank accounting; designed as a text book for schools and private students and a handbook of reference for bankers; script illustrations by E. C. Mills. Rochester, N. Y. Williams & Rogers [c1899] 227p. 26cm.

BREWERIES

1898

CLARKE, Edward W.

Brewery bookkeeping: a practical treatise on brewery accounts and office management. Chic. H. S. Rich, 1898. 181p. 31cm.

The title of this work was first deposited for copyright, 1897.

BUILDING AND LOAN ASSOCIATIONS

1889

HART, Walter.

Hart's precise system for building and loan associations. N. Y. Press of H. J. Ronalds [c1889] 28p. 16cm.

1893

LAWRENCE, Wilber E.

Manual of the national B. & L. system of accounting. [Chic. c1893] 50p. 17cm.

CLERGY

1885

HARKINS, Francis A.
Bookkeeping by single and double entry: a business manual specially adapted to the wants of the Catholic clergy. Balt. Foley bros. 1885. 191p. 20cm.
The title of this work was deposited for copyright, 1882.

COMMISSION MERCHANTS

1817

GERISHER, Charles, 1773–1832.
Modern book-keeping by double entry; adapted to commission business as it is conducted in the United States of America; designed for mercantile young men. N.Y. Printed by E. Conrad, 1817. [158]p. 24cm.

1898

PACKARD, Silas Sadler, 1826–1898.
Commission business; exhibiting the material and forms for a complete record thereof; adapted to schools and private learners. N.Y. Packard [c1898] 24p. 26cm.

COTTON MILLS

1900

NICHOLS, William G.
Methods of cost finding in cotton mills; a full description of methods used in accurate cost finding for cloth or yarn mills; fully illustrated by blanks and tables; adapted to mills with a wide variety of product. Waltham, Mass. E.L. Barry, 1900. 70p. 25½cm.

CREAMERIES

1899

VYE, John Alexander, 1867–
Creamery accounting. Delano, Minn. The author, 1899. 42p. 24 x 31½cm.

DEPARTMENT STORES

1900

BOOK-KEEPER PUBLISHING COMPANY, LTD., Detroit.
Accounting for department stores . . . Detroit, Book-keeper pub. co. 1900. 56p. 23cm.

ELECTRIC LIGHT COMPANIES

1894

FOSTER, Horatio Alvah, 1858–1913.
Central station bookkeeping and suggested forms; with an appendix for street railways. N.Y. W.J. Johnston, 1894. 139p. 24cm.
Another ed. 1896. 139p. 24cm.

1900

NATIONAL ELECTRIC LIGHT ASSOCIATION.
System of accounts for hydraulic power companies. [N.Y. 1900?] 59p. 23½cm.

GAS LIGHT COMPANIES

1869

FODELL, William P., 1833–1906.
A system for keeping the histories and accounts of gas-light com-

FODELL (continued)
panies; with forms, etc. usual for such companies. Phil. Printed by W. K. Bellows; N. Y. M. L. Callender & co. 1869. 43p. 23cm.

HYDRAULIC POWER

1900

NATIONAL ELECTRIC LIGHT ASSOCIATION.
System of accounts for hydraulic power companies. [N. Y. 1900?] 59p. 23½cm.

INSTALMENT HOUSES

1897

KITTREDGE, Anson Oliver, 1848–1903, and BROWN, John F.
The self-proving accounting system . . . with special application made to the instalment business: a manual for business men, accountants and auditors. N. Y. Self-proving account-bk. co. 1897. 328p. 24½cm.

LAWYERS

1895

BROOK, William Henry.
Brook's lawyers' bookkeeping by double entry on the Kain triple column system . . . Detroit, Brook [c1895] 26p. 19cm.

MINING

1883

KAUFFMAN, Luther S., 1846–
Kauffman's manual for book-keepers; with special forms and in-

structions for keeping books of mining and other stock companies; also for keeping books of private firms in general business. Greeley, Col. Kauffman, c1883. 240p. 15½cm.

MUNICIPAL

1878

MILLS, E. S.
Public accounts; with practical suggestions for keeping them, and for making examinations, settlements, annual financial statements, and official reports. St. Paul, Pioneer press co. 1878. 27p. 23cm.

PRINTING

1894

BALTES, Frank William, 1860–
The cost of printing: a system in practical operation; with forms and books especially adapted to large and small printing concerns. Portland, Or. Baltes, 1894. 74p. 17½ x 25cm.

RAILROADS

1858

HILL, John J.
A concise method of keeping the accounts and stock transfers of railroads and other corporate agencies in the city of New York. N.Y. N. Lane & co. 1858. 92p. 23½cm.

1868

DUFF, Peter, 1802–1869.
Duff's book-keeping by single and double entry; practically illustrating merchants', manufacturers', private bankers', railroad and national bank accounts; 20th ed. enl. & rev. N.Y. Harper & bros. 1868. 398p. 25½cm.

DUFF (continued)

Cover-title: Mercantile, bank, and railroad bookkeeping.

The title of this work was deposited for copyright (Western District of Pennsylvania) 1867.

Based upon Duff's North American accountant and called 20th edition enlarged and revised.

The fourth part, p.227–383, is devoted entirely to railroad and bank bookkeeping.

It is practically a new work.

Other eds. 1869; 1870; 1871; 1873; 1876; 1882; 1896. 400p. 25½cm.

This work is listed in part one under 1848.

1875

FINK, Albert, 1827–1897.

Cost of railroad transportation, railroad accounts, and governmental regulation of railroad tariffs . . . extract from the annual report of the Louisville and Nashville railroad co. for the year ending June 30, 1874. Louisville [Ky.] Printed by J. P. Morton & co. 1875. [48]p. 23½cm.

Popularly known as "The Fink report" and "The famous twenty-third annual report of the Louisville and Nashville."

2d ed. N. Y. Railroad gazette [187–?] p.[51]–95+p.[19]–48, 23½cm. This work was reprinted several times.

1877

KIRKMAN, Marshall Monroe, 1842–1921.

Railway disbursements and the accounts into which they are naturally divided. N. Y. Railroad gazette, 1877. 264p. 18½cm.

"A revised and enlarged edition of a small volume published in January last [1876] for private distribution." — p.[iii]

—Railway revenue and its collection; containing rules and regulations necessary to ensure faithful accounting, and explaining, generally, the object and extent of railway accounts and the necessity of their being organized upon scientific principles. N. Y. Railroad gazette, 1877. 499p. 18½cm.

2d ed. 1879. 595p. 18½cm.

1880

KIRKMAN, Marshall Monroe, 1842–1921.

Railway expenditures; their extent, object and economy . . . Chic. Railway age pub. co. [1880] 2v. 18½cm.

1881

KIRKMAN, Marshall Monroe, 1842–1921.
Hand book of railway expenditures; explaining in the form of specific rules how the labor, material, fuel, and other items of expenditure should be kept . . . Chic. Railway age pub. co. [1881] 111+[62]p. 19cm.

1882

KIRKMAN, Marshall Monroe, 1842–1921.
The track accounts of railroads and how they should be kept . . . Chic. C. N. Trivess, printer, 1882. 45p. 23cm.
[2d ed.] 1889. 50+[2]p. 19½cm.

1886

KIRKMAN, Marshall Monroe, 1842–1921.
Division of railway expenses and earnings, and the limitation of accounts in connection therewith. Chic. C. N. Trivess, printer [1886] 75p. 23½cm.

1889

CAMPBELL, Edward P.
System of freight accounts; reporting, auditing, and settlements between railroads, of revenue on through way-bills; with samples of blanks, etc. [N. Y. M. B. Brown, 1889] 51p. 23½cm.

1890

KIRKMAN, Marshall Monroe, 1842–1921.
Hand book of freight accounts . . . Chic. C. N. Trivess, printer, 1890. 157+[52]p. 18½cm.

—Hand book of passenger traffic and accounts . . . Chic. C. N. Trivess, printer, 1890. 170+[3]p. 18cm.

1895

WOODLOCK, Thomas Francis, 1866–
The anatomy of a railroad report. N. Y. U. S. bk. co. [c1895] 72p. 22cm.

WOODLOCK (continued)

Another ed. N.Y. S.A. Nelson [c1901] 121p. 17½cm. (Nelson's Wall street library, v.2)

1900

EATON, James Shirley, 1868–

Railroad operations; how to know them from a study of the accounts and statistics. N.Y. Railroad gazette, 1900. 313p. 19cm.

SHIPMASTERS

1840

CLARKE, Francis Gedney, 1792–1843.

A synthetic and inductive system of book-keeping by double entry; designed particularly for schools and academies and as a reference for the young accountant . . . also directions and illustrations for the ship master in arranging ship accounts . . . Portland [Me.] S.H. Colesworthy; Bost. B.B. Mussey, 1840. 82p. 19cm.

At head of title: Clarke's book-keeping.

On cover: Directions for Clarke's book-keeping.

—A synthetic and inductive system of book-keeping by double entry . . . to which is appended two complete sets of waste book entries . . . with a full set of ship masters' accounts; with explanations . . . Portland [Me.] S.H. Colesworthy; Bost. B.B. Mussey, 1841. 150p. 24cm.

This work is part 2 of "Clarke's book-keeping."

In 1830 the author published "The seaman's manual" which contains a section devoted to shipmaster's accounts. This work includes more bookkeeping for shipmasters than does his general bookkeeping text listed above.

STEAM ENGINE WORKS

1887

CHILD, Frederick W.

Elements of cost and methods of accounting in steam engine works. N.Y. Office co. 1887. 20p. 18½cm.

A paper read before the Institute of accounts.

STEAMBOATS

1839

STONE, Eli.

The steam boat clerk: a complete systematic and concise manual of accounts; for the use of steam boats. Cin. E. Lucas & co. 1839. 24p. 26½cm.

1845

FLEMING, John.

The national system of book-keeping; containing the art and science thereof . . . applicable to all kinds of business . . . exemplified in two sets of books kept by double entry . . .

The title of this work was deposited for copyright (Western District of Pennsylvania) February 6, 1845. This work is in later editions referred to as the first edition.

Another ed. Pittsburgh, M'Donald & Elliott, 1846. 117p. 26cm. The title varies slightly from the 1845 edition. This edition contains an appendix with separate title-page: The steam-boat book-keeper's assistant . . . Pittsburgh, M'Donald & Elliott, 1846.

3d ed. Cin. B. Davenport; Pittsburgh, M'Donald & Beesom, 1848. 141p. 25cm.

—Fleming's book-keeping by double entry; in five sets . . . with an appendix; containing a complete system of steamboat book-keeping, as now practiced on western rivers; together with many useful rules and calculations in equation of payments, partnerships &c.; designed for the use of schools and colleges, and a very useful companion in the counting-house. Pittsburgh, W. S. Haven; Phil. Cowperthwait, Desilver & Butler, 1854. 209p. 25½cm.

"This work is an expansion of the author's 'National system of book-keeping . . . ' published in 1845 and now in its fifth edition." — Pref.

The author introduced four short sets and omitted the set for retailers. It contains the same introductory and preliminary matter as the 1846 edition. It is practically a new work. Appendix has separate title-page: The steamboat book-keeper's assistant . . . 5th ed. Pittsburgh, W. S. Haven; Phil. Cowperthwait, Desilver & Butler, 1854.

1846

DUFF, Peter, 1802–1869.

The western steamboat accountant: a new and complete system of

Duff (continued)
book keeping; arranged and practically adapted for the use of steamers navigating the great western rivers and lakes; exemplified in one set of books kept by double entry . . . designed for the use of schools, book keepers, steamboat masters and owners. Pittsburgh, Pub. by the author, 1846. 63p. 26cm.
Another ed. N. Y. Pub. by the author, 1847. 63p. 28cm.
This edition was published under the title: "The steamboat accountant . . ."

STREET RAILWAYS

1894

Foster, Horatio Alvah, 1858–1913.
Central station bookkeeping and suggested forms; with an appendix for street railways. N. Y. W. J. Johnston, 1894. 139p. 24cm.
Another ed. 1896. 139p. 24cm.

PART THREE

PART THREE

A chronological bibliography of copyright works on accounting by American authors, published prior to 1901 for restricted use in some one school or correspondence course. At least one edition of each work is known to exist. Additional reprints and editions are recorded insofar as they have been verified.

INTRODUCTION

CONSIDERABLE time was spent to determine definitely the copyright works which were issued exclusively for students in some one school or correspondence course. Though they were restricted in their sale and use, they must be considered as part of the accounting literature of the 19th century. At least one edition of each work in Part Three was found in one or more libraries. They are listed separately for the convenience of collectors, bibliographers, and school historians.

The total number of titles in Part Three is eighty-four. The total number of authors, including joint authors, is seventy-four. Fifty-five of this number are not in either Part One or Part Two.

The items are listed in this chapter according to the bibliographical technique used in Part One.

1853

Comer, George Nixon, 1816–1877.
A record of the transactions of a merchant, named Accurate Accountant, during three months' business: a device for the better illustrating and understanding of double-entry; designed for the use of the compiler's own students. Bost. [Printed by Damrell & Moore] 1853. 31+[1]p. 21cm.

1858

Gundry, John, 1822?–1875.
Double-entry book-keeping: a new, original and progressive series of exercises in journalising; with rules and elucidations and an exposition of the science of double-entry . . . for use of Gundry's mercantile college. Cin. Spiller & bros. printers, 1858. 12 numb. l.+[4]p. 39 x 29½cm.

1863

Bartlett, Robert Montgomery, 1807–1891.
R. M. Bartlett's manuscript system of teaching double entry book-keeping; written (1847) expressly for the purpose of developing a clear and complete knowledge of the art of making historical day-book entries . . . Cin. C. Clark, 1863. 62p. 23cm.

Cover-title varies.

With this is bound "James . . Watters original manuscript (written in 1860) system of teaching double entry book-keeping as applied to steamboats, insurance, and banking companies, wholesale and retail business, commission and forwarding business . . ." p.15–62.

This work was separately copyrighted.

1864

Eastman national business college, Poughkeepsie, N. Y.
The student's guide to the junior department of actual business in Eastman national business college. Poughkeepsie [N. Y.] Printed by Platt & Schram, 1864. 16p. 22½cm.

This work was prepared by Thomas H. Stevens.

—The student's guide through the theoretical departmant of Eastman national business college . . .

The title of this work was deposited for copyright (Southern District of New York) May 19, 1864, by Harvey Gridley East-

EASTMAN NATIONAL BUSINESS COLLEGE (continued)
man (1838–1878) and Thomas H. Stevens, proprietors of the copyright.

Another ed.	1865.
Another ed.	Poughkeepsie [N.Y.] Pub. by the college [c1871] 127p. 22cm.
10th ed.	Poughkeepsie, N.Y. Haight & Dudley, printers, 1887.
14th ed.	1891. 122+[6]p. 23½cm.
16th ed.	Poughkeepsie, N.Y. A.V. Haight, printer, 1898. 122+6p. 23½cm. H. G. Eastman's name appears on the title-page as author.

JENKINS, Friend W., 1825?–1888, and SMITH, John Coley, 1823–1883.
Introduction to the science of book-keeping; being the preliminary course of study pursued in the Iron City commercial college, Pittsburgh, Pa. Pittsburgh, Printed by W. S. Haven, 1864. 144p. 23cm.

1865

HARRISON, Edward.
The student's guide to a complete knowledge of the science of accounts; as taught at Great western business college, Mount Pleasant, Iowa. Springfield, Ohio, News & republic steam print, 1865. 43p. 21cm.

1866

BURNHAM, Louis W.
Book-keeping; its rule and reasons [for use in Claverack commercial college] [n.p.] 1866. 16p. 23cm.

MAYHEW, Ira, 1814–1894.
Albion commercial college, Albion, Michigan: Rules for journalizing the opening and closing entries of consignments, shipments, merchandise co's, shipment co's, and adventure co's, and for treating them generally; prepared for use in the theory and actual business departments of that institution. [Albion? Mich.] c1866. 10p. 14½cm.

1867

SPALDING, James Franklin, 1835–1916.
Manual of rules and instructions to be used in writing up the

manuscript work of the theory and actual business departments of Spalding's commercial college . . . Kansas City, Mo. 1867.

Another ed. 1871.

Another ed. Kansas City, Mo. Press of Ramsey, Millett & Hudson, 1878. 40p. 18cm. Title varies.

4th ed. 1885. 40p. 18cm.

THOMAS, William M.
Theory department of Thomas' great national business college, city of Flint, Mich.; the day-book, comprising six sets . . . Flint, Mich. F. H. Rankin, printer, 1867. 76p. 20½cm.

1870

LAUDEN, Martin K.
Manual for the theoretical department of the Pacific business college, San Francisco. San Fran. B. F. Sterett, printer, 1870. 24p. 22½cm.

1871

EASTMAN, Almon R., 1841–(?)
Eastman's practical book-keeping by single and double entry; for the theoretical department of Eastman business college, Atlanta, Ga. Poughkeepsie [N. Y.] Platt & sons, 1871. 94p. 21½cm.

—The merchant's guide for the practice of bookkeeping in the actual business department of Eastman business college . . . Atlanta, J. J. Toon, 1871. 10p. 21cm.

1872

DYHRENFURTH BUSINESS COLLEGE, Chicago.
Actual business department of the Dyhrenfurth college of Chicago. [Chic. 1872?] 10 numb. l. 21 x 35½cm.

1873

HOWE, Granville L., and MUSSELMAN, De Lafayette, 1842–1910.
A systematic exposition of the science of accounts; embracing a thorough and comprehensive treatise of all branches of book-keeping in the different departments of manufacture, agriculture, navigation, trade and commerce . . . in single and double entry; prepared . . . for the . . . Gem city business college. Quincy, Ill. Herald print. co. 1873. 244p. 26cm.

Moore, Benjamin F.
Practical book-keeping; prepared expressly for the students of Moore's southern business university, Atlanta, Georgia. Atlanta, Economical bk. & job print. house, 1873. 24p. 23cm.
Another ed. 1876.

1874

Nelson, Horatio, and Kelley, H. P.
The student's assistant; being a text book containing questions and answers on the science of book-keeping . . . designed for use of the students of Nelson's college. Cin. Nelson & Kelley, 1874. 80+[2]p. 23cm.
Another ed. Cin. Nelson & Kelley, 1875. 135p. 22cm.

—Routine of Nelson's actual business college, Cincinnati . . . Cin. Cincinnati monthly print. works, 1874. 9+[1]p. 23cm.

1875

Moore, Benjamin F.
The actual business guide of Moore's southern business university, Atlanta, Georgia. Atlanta, 1875. 11p. 22½cm.

Slack, John R.
A treatise on the rationale and practice of bookkeeping; designed to impart a knowledge of the methods of the art . . . prepared for use of the advanced class in Decorah business college. Decorah, Ia. E. W. Wood, printer, 1875. 92p. 23½cm.

1876

Bryant, Thomas J.
Complete chart of book-keeping by double entry . . . Bryant's business college. St. Joseph, Mo. 1876. 8p. 21cm.

Faber, Henry A.
Faber's manual: a programme of exercises for the students of the Queen city commercial college. Cin. Queen city commercial college [c1876] 80p. 25½cm.
The author was assisted by R. H. Langdale in the preparation of this work.
Another ed. c1879. 88p. 24cm.
R. H. Langdale appears on the title-page as author. The content of this work is practically the same as that of Faber's work published in 1876.

MARTIN, Thomas.
Martin's manual: a programme of exercises for the students of Martin's Queen city business college. Cin. T. Martin & son business college co. [c1876]
4th ed. c1887. 101p. 25cm.

SANTA ROSA, CALIF. CHRISTIAN COLLEGE.
Business manual; for the commercial department of Christian college, Santa Rosa. Santa Rosa [Calif.] Sonoma Democrat print. house, 1876. 48+[2]p. 22½cm.

1878

CURTISS, Charles Carroll.
Manual of theory and practice in double entry book-keeping; prepared for use in high schools, normal schools, and business colleges. Minneapolis, Johnson, Smith & Harrison, 1878.
31p. 22cm.
The first and fifth editions are the only ones which appear to have been prepared for unrestricted use and these editions were intended primarily for the Curtiss business college.
The cover-title of the first edition: Elementary course in the theory and practice of double entry book-keeping as taught in the Minneapolis business college.
—Manual of the theory and practice of accounts; prepared for use in the Curtiss business college . . . Minneapolis, The author, 1880. 73p. 21½cm.
Contents as in entry above with additional sets and forms.
Part 2 and part 3 of the Manual were published separately in 1881.
Supplementary exercises prepared to supplement the practice sets in the Manual were also published separately.
3d ed. 1883. 80p. 22½cm.
4th ed. 1887. 64p. 26½cm.
On cover: Advanced sheets, Curtiss manual of book-keeping.
5th ed. [Minneapolis, Tribune job print co.] 1889. 112p. 26cm.

1879

PARSONS, W. F.
Parsons' practical book-keeping, penmanship, commercial law, business forms, etc. Kalamazoo, Mich. [Parsons' business college, 1879?] 126p. 23½cm.
Pages at end missing.

1880

NELSON, Horatio, and MOORE, Benjamin F.
The student's assistant; being a text-book, containing questions and answers on the science of book-keeping . . . designed for the use of students at Moore's business university. Atlanta, Moore's business univ. 1880. 95p. 22½cm.

PEIRCE, Thomas May, 1837–1896.
Manual for the student-traders in the business department of Peirce's union business college . . . [Phil.] Peirce, 1880. 16p. 18½cm.

SPRAGUE, Levi L., 1844–
Student's guide; through single-entry book-keeping. Wilkes-Barre, Pa. E. B. Yordy, printer, 1880. 74p. 23cm.
—Student's guide; theoretical and actual business departments of Wyoming commercial college. Wilkes-Barre, Pa. E. B. Yordy, 1880. 212+20p. 23cm.
Many later editions were published for the exclusive use of Wyoming seminary. In the 20th century they were revised by Willis Leonard Dean.

1881

CANNON, Gordon Clark, 1853–1916.
The complete course in book-keeping; as taught at Cannon's commercial college, Lawrence, Mass. . . Lawrence [Mass.] Pub. by the college, 1881. 48p. 23½cm.

COLEMAN, Henry, 1838–1903.
The student's guide in the theoretical department of Coleman's national "B. & S." business college . . . Newark, N. J. Pub. by the college, 1881. 80p. 22½cm.

EASTMAN NATIONAL BUSINESS COLLEGE, Poughkeepsie, N. Y.
The student's hand-book . . . [Poughkeepsie, N. Y.] 1881. 106p. 14½ x 11½cm.
Authorship of this work has been attributed to Ezra White (1838?–1903).
Other eds. 1884; 1891. 158p. 23cm.

TONG, Lucius G., 1842–1908.
Practical book-keeping [as taught in the commercial course at University of Notre Dame, Indiana] South Bend, Ind. Register print. co. 1881. 47p. 19½cm.

1882

BACKUS, L. C.
Large manuscript of the business department of the Fayette normal, music, and business college . . . Fayette, Ohio, Record bk. & job off. 1882. [16]p. 23½cm.

MESERVEY, Atwood Bond, 1831–1901.
Manual designed to be used in the New Hampton commercial college . . . Bristol [N.H.] Enterprise job print. off. 1882. 23p. 21½cm.

ROYALL, John Price, 1831–(?)
Elements of book-keeping: a reference book for accountants . . . prepared especially for use of students in the commercial department of Missouri state university. Columbia, Mo. Herald bk. & job print, 1882. 28p. 19½cm.
—Manual of the elements of book-keeping . . . Columbia, Mo. Herald print. house, 1884. 82p. 18cm.
Another edition of "Elements of book-keeping," with additional exercises.

1883

EASTMAN NATIONAL BUSINESS COLLEGE, Poughkeepsie, N.Y.
Students' guide to the office and banking department of Eastman national business college . . . Poughkeepsie, N.Y. A.V. Haight, printer, 1883. 41p. 22½cm.
Another ed. 1883. 46p. 22cm.

RECKERS, John, 1837–1911.
A text book on modern book-keeping and commercial computations; compiled expressly for the students of Reckers & Bradford's commercial school . . . part I. Bost. Reckers & Bradford [c1883] 136+77p. 21cm.

1884

NIHART, Benjamin Franklin, 1854–
A treatise on book-keeping and commercial law; designed as a text-book for the Kansas state agricultural college. [Manhattan, Kan.] College press, 1884. 102p. 22cm.

SPALDING, James Franklin, 1835–1916.
Final examination work; prepared expressly for use in writing up the commercial course of Spalding's commercial college, Kansas City, Mo. Kansas City, Mo. Ramsey, Millett & Hudson, 1884. 38p. 17½cm.
Other eds. 1887; 1890. 38p. 18cm.

SPALDING (continued)

—Sales set; prepared expressly for use in the actual business department of Spalding's commercial college, Kansas City, Mo. in connection with the Lamson cash railway. Kansas City, Mo. c1884. 4p. 30cm.

1885

EASTMAN NATIONAL BUSINESS COLLEGE, Poughkeepsie, N. Y.
Merchant's guide for the practical departments of Eastman national business college . . . Poughkeepsie [N. Y.] Pub. by the college, 1885. 31p. 22cm.

PALMS, Theodore W.
Guide for the theoretical department of the Palms business college. [Phil. c1885]
Later editions were written and copyrighted by Theodore W. Palms and Daniel D. Miller.

SPAULDING, Samuel S., and CLARK, Harold Chauncey, 1856–
Actual business guide for the practical exchange of Clark's business college, Erie, Pa. Erie, Pa. H. C. Clark, 1885. 26p. 22½cm.

WARREN, Emanuel Frank, 1857–1898.
A class-book guide in theoretical and practical book-keeping. [Cin. Elm street print. co.] c1885. 16p. 23cm.

1886

COMER, Charles Evelyn, 1858–1918.
Comer's new book-keeping; an exponent of the best modern methods of keeping accounts. Bost. Comer's commercial college, 1886. 180p. 21cm.

HILL, Robert H., 1852–1919.
Practical treatise on book-keeping for the department of theory in Hill's practical business college . . . Waco, Tex. W. Lambdin, printer, 1886. 70p. 21cm.

MOOAR, J. F.
The student's manual of double entry book-keeping and practical business forms. Bost. H. E. Hibbard, 1886. 183p. 24cm.
On cover: Bryant & Stratton commercial school, Boston.
Other eds. 1894; 1904; 1905. 183p. 23½cm.

STOWELL, Theodore B., 1847–1916.
The essentials of book-keeping. Providence, J. A. & R. A. Reid, printers, 1886. 56p. 23½cm.
Bryant & Stratton business college, Providence.
Another ed. 1888. 72+[14]p. 23½cm.

1887

DEVLIN, Cyrus H.
Devlin's manual of double entry book keeping and students hand book of rules, definitions, and forms of business paper. Bay City [Mich. Devlin's business college] 1887. [23]p. 20cm.

DEVON, William H., 1847–1889.
Hand-book of book-keeping, commercial paper, business forms, and correspondence; prepared expressly for use in Sadler's Bryant and Stratton business college. Balt. W. H. Sadler, 1887. 131p. 24cm.

JENNINGS, Alfred C., and CHAPMAN,—
Manual of the Iowa business college course in the science of accounts and theoretical business training. Des Moines, Iowa print. co. 1887. 170p. 25cm.

MARTYN, Francis Galatea.
Text book for the practical department of Martyn's commercial college, Washington, D. C. Wash. Pub. by the college, 1887. 30p. 22cm.

MARVIN, Charles.
Two hundred business actions with directions, explanations, suggestions for the practical department. Elmira, N. Y. Pub. by the school, 1887. 47p. 22½cm.
At head of title: Elmira school of commerce.

SMITHDEAL, George Michael, 1855–1912.
Students' guide in the theory department of Smithdeal practical business colleges, Greensboro, N. C. and Richmond, Va.; 2d ed. Richmond, Johns & co. printers, 1887. 80p. 22½cm.
The second edition was the only edition copyrighted.

1888

EMERSON, James C.
Science of accounts . . . Minard commercial college; no.1 National banks; no.2 Day-book, journal; no.3 Wholesale business. [N. Y. Munn, c1888–89] 3v. 20½cm.

JAMISON, Thomas Worth, 1853–1924.
A short course of double entry book-keeping. Balt. Papyrograph print. co. 1888. 34p. 26 x 20cm.
Maryland institute, commercial department.

LEVY, Max.
The Max Levy system of teaching book-keeping by correspondence; double and single entry. San Fran. Bacon & co. printers, 1888. 37p. 22½cm.

MULVEY, Martin, 1850–
All actual business course of accounts; especially compiled and arranged from the best business sources for the students of the Newark business college; embracing double and single entry . . . rev. ed. Newark, N. J. A. Pierson & co. printers, 1888. 58p. 23cm.
3d ed. Newark, N. J. Grover bros. 1898.

PEIRCE, Thomas May, 1837–1896.
Exercises in book-keeping; Peirce college of business . . . [Phil. Burk & McFetridge, printers, c1888] 141p. 25½cm.
Another ed. 1890. 120p. 25½cm.
—Peirce manual of bookkeeping. Phil. Peirce, 1895. 145p. 26cm.
This work is a revised edition of "Exercises in book-keeping" listed above.
5th ed. 1897. 145p. 26cm.
6th ed. 1899.
8th ed. Phil. Peirce school, 1908. 175p. 26cm.
Louis Burdelle Moffett (1874–) appears on the title-page as author.

YERINGTON, Charles William, 1856–
Actual business manuscript of the commercial department of Alma college. Alma, Mich. Alma news presses, 1888. 13p. 22½cm.

1889

CATON, William E.
Valley city commercial college and short hand institute text book of practical business book-keeping. [Grand Rapids, Daily democrat print] 1889. 96p. 22cm.
—Detroit college of commerce . . . text book of practical business book-keeping; 2d ed. Detroit, J. H. Stone, 1897. 96p. 21½cm.

KENWORTHY, Joseph W., 1859–1922.
Bookkeeping; educational department, Young men's Christian association . . . [lesson no.1–6] [Phil. c1889–90] 6v. 25cm.

The author also deposited for copyright several lessons on book-keeping in 1891, 1892, and 1893.

WARREN, Emanuel Frank, 1857–1898.
Students' guide through the practical departments of Western college of commerce, Toledo, Iowa. Toledo, Ia. Lee & Wilson, printers [c1889] 15p. 23cm.

WELLS, Charles R.
Practical lessons in book-keeping; for the exclusive use of students in the Chautauqua school of business; lesson no.1 . . . [n.p. c1889] [8]p. 23½cm.

1890

VALPARAISO, IND. NORTHERN INDIANA NORMAL SCHOOL AND BUSINESS COLLEGE.
General instructions and memoranda of the Northern-Indiana business college, Valparaiso, Ind. [Valparaiso, c1890] 52p. 21cm.
This work was copyrighted by Charles William Benton.
Another ed. [c1898] 40p. 21½cm.
Another ed. [c1899]

1891

BRYANT & STRATTON BUSINESS COLLEGE, Louisville, Ky.
Theory of book-keeping; arranged especially for use in the business department of the Louisville college. Louisville, Ky. 1891. 7v. 23cm.

SPENCERIAN BUSINESS COLLEGE, Milwaukee.
Manual of business and book-keeping; for use in the Spencerian business college. Milw. 1891. 104p. 24cm.

1892

SPENCER, Enos, 1851–1920.
Spencerian book-keeping manual. Louisville [Ky.] Spencerian business college co. 1892. 97+[1]p. 22½cm.

1893

JACKSON, L. H.
Practice guide for use in the business exchange department of the Charlotte commercial college, Charlotte, N. C. [Charlotte, N. C. The Blakey print. house, c1893] 49p. 22cm.

Rearick, C. C.
Business practice manual; arranged expressly for use in the Actual business department of the N. I. N. S. and Dixon business college . . . Dixon, Ill. Evening star print, 1893.
59p.+1 l. 22cm.
Northern Illinois normal school and Dixon business college, inc., Dixon, Ill.

Sweet, James Sylvester, 1853–1930.
Instruction book to Sweet's system of actual business practice. Santa Rosa, Calif. 1893. 46p. 18 x 22½cm.

1896

Call, Z. G.
Call's double entry bookkeeping and desk practice. [Pittsburgh, c1896] 145 l. 27½ x 21cm.
The Curry business college.

Massey, Richard Walter, 1868–
Massey's modern book keeping taught by actual transactions. Atlanta, Foote & Davies co. 1896. 168p. 22cm.
Eight revised editions of this work were published for the exclusive use of Massey's practical business college between 1896 and 1912.
Titles vary.

1897

International correspondence schools, Scranton.
Single-entry bookkeeping; double-entry bookkeeping; opening, closing, and changing books. Scranton, Colliery engineer co. c1897–99.
The Colliery engineer company copyrighted and published various question papers and instruction papers on single entry bookkeeping, double entry bookkeeping, and opening, closing, and changing books; prepared for the use of students enrolled in the courses offered by the International correspondence schools, 1897–1899. These papers were revised frequently.
In 1899 the Colliery engineer company copyrighted and published treatises on bookkeeping based upon the question papers and instruction papers. They were bound in various volumes of the International correspondence schools business course.

Spalding, James Franklin, 1835–1916.
Spalding's practical and progressive book-keeping by double and single entry; prepared expressly for use in the commercial department of Spalding's commercial college, Kansas City, Mo. . .

Kansas City, Mo. Spalding print. and pub. co. [c1897] 171+[41]p. 30½cm.

A reprint of the first forty-three pages was published in 1897.

Von Deylen, Henry.

Von Deylen's double entry bookkeeping: tuition letters. Brooklyn, Von Deylen's business school, 1897–1900.

Between 1897 and 1900, inclusive, the author copyrighted and published a series of "tuition letters" for students enrolled in his correspondence course of instruction in bookkeeping.

1898

Van Matre, Nelson B.

Business practice manual; arranged expressly for use in the actual business department of the La Salle Township high school . . . La Salle, Ill. H. E. Wickham, printer, 1898. 43p. 21cm.

1899

Brady, Frederick Barzillai

The bookkeeping guide of actual business practice. Chillicothe, Mo. Brady-Moore pub. co. [c1899] 175p. 27cm.

Chillicothe normal school. Actual business institute.

1900

Browne, Thomas Robert, 1834–1912.

First book-keeping course. Brooklyn, Browne's Brooklyn business college [c1900] 84p. 23cm.

3d ed. 1905. 163p. 23½cm.
4th ed. 1908. 119p. 23½cm.

Comer, Charles Evelyn, 1858–1918.

Book-keeping and office work. Bost. Comer's commercial college, 1900. 235p. 21½cm.

Eastman national business college, Poughkeepsie, N. Y.

The Eastman system of teaching bookkeeping; presenting a complete course of business training . . . Poughkeepsie, N. Y. The author, 1900. 151+[1]p. 24½cm.

Authorship of this work has been attributed to Clement Carrington Gaines (1857–) who copyrighted the work in 1900.

Stouffer, G. R.

Inter-communication: business practice manual. Los Angeles, 1900. 18p. 22½cm.

PART FOUR

PART FOUR

A chronological bibliography of works on accounting by American authors, copyrighted prior to 1901 but not known to exist in any library and about which there is no complete bibliographical information available.

INTRODUCTION

PART Four consists of three classes of works on accounting in one chronological list: (1) titles which it is impossible to determine ever existed as published works; (2) titles of published works which are credited with having been deposited for copyright but which cannot now be located in the Library of Congress or in any other library; (3) titles of published works known to have been in one or more libraries but which cannot now be located in any library. No complete bibliographical information for these titles exists. Such information as is available was gleaned almost entirely from an examination of the records of copyright, a detailed explanation of which is given in the Introductory Chapter.

Since none of the works listed in Part Four was examined, it was necessary to make an arbitrary decision from a perusal of the title that each one was a "work on accounting" as defined in the preface. It is well known that during the 19th century many "books" were copyrighted which consisted only of blank books, that is, of ruled forms, such as ledgers, journals, cash books, sales books, payroll books, trial balance books, etc., in spite of the fact that several court decisions held that such articles were not subject to copyright. By reason of the copyright law which provided for registration of the printed title before the deposit of the published work many articles were copyrighted as "books" which were not properly subject to copyright according to law. Approximately twelve hundred titles of this nature were found in the copyright record books and were arbitrarily eliminated from this supplementary bibliography.

Since it is impossible to determine definitely which titles were intended for general use and which were intended for exclusive use, all were included in one chronological list.

The author's name is given as it was found in the copyright record book unless his name is given in fuller form in Part One.

The place given after the title is the residence of the copyright owner. This information is in most cases the only indication of the place in which the work may have been published. Only a few title entries recorded the place of publication and the publisher.

The year and month of copyright and the district court in which the title was deposited are given for those titles copyrighted prior to July 8, 1870. The year of copyright is given for the titles deposited for copyright in the Library of Congress between July 8, 1870, and December 31, 1900. Note of the deposit of copies of the published work is given when it is recorded in the copyright record book.

STATISTICS

NUMBER OF TITLES LISTED IN PART IV

By Decades

1801–1810	4
1811–1820	4
1821–1830	2
1831–1840	7
1841–1850	7
1851–1860	25
1861–1870	12
1871–1880	27
1881–1890	46
1891–1900	114
Total number of titles listed in Part IV	248

The total number of authors, including joint authors, listed in Part IV is 236. Of this number, 196 are not in Parts I, II, and III.

Part Four

Supplementary Bibliography

1804

WALSH, Michael, 1763–1840.
A new system of book-keeping; adapted to various concerns.
Title deposited, January 24, 1804, District of Massachusetts.

1806

GEAREY, Ebenezer.
A new American system of book keeping; including domestic, foreign, and speculative trade; wherein the origin, nature, relation, proportion and connection are clearly explained, as well as the theory of the art; and reduced to practice with rules and methods entirely new in a comprehensive manner in several sets of books; the whole is accompanied with philosophical principles and mathematical demonstrations . . .
Title deposited, February 28, 1806, District of New York.

1808

THRESHER, George.
An epitome of book-keeping; showing at one view by single or by double entry the proper manner of keeping the various accounts of merchants either by wholesale or retail.
Title deposited, January 15, 1808, District of New York.

—Thresher's book-keeper's assistant and young man's introduction to trade and business; showing the most plain and easy method of keeping the various accounts of merchants and retail dealers; to which will be added a variety of miscellaneous questions relating to mercantile business and bank accounts; also an epitome of book-keeping; shewing at one view by single and double entry the method of keeping accounts wholesale or retail; with rules for reducing the different currencies, &c.
The title of this work which evidently included the contents of the work copyrighted in 1808 was deposited for copyright, December 4, 1809, District of New York.
To the title entry was added this note:
"This work will be comprised in one octavo volume of upwards of 300 pages . . . price to subscribers $1.50. Geo. Thresher, professor of writing, accompts, ec. No.10 Gold St., New York."

1816

SHAIN, Benjamin Jones.

Book-keeping: practical book-keeping illustrated in the form of debtor and creditor; comprised in three systems; the first and second by single entry and the third by double entry; completely adapted to the trade of the mechanic and shop keeper of every description as well as that of the merchant.

Title deposited, August 12, 1816, District of Pennsylvania.

1819

BECKER, Christian.

The teacher's magazine of arithmetic and book-keeping in which the application of the arithmetical rules consist of mechanic's, farmer's and storekeeper's book accounts; by means of which arrangement a teacher is not only enabled to teach all his scholars the book-keeping of that trade which they intend to learn but also to teach them all by the use of one book only.

Title deposited, August 7, 1819, Eastern District of Pennsylvania.

HANDS, William G.

Elementary and practical treatise on book-keeping by double and single entry . . .

This work was advertised in the Baltimore city directory, 1819.

1820

BENNET, James Arlington, 1788–1863.

A pack of conversation cards; exemplifying the journalizing, posting, and balancing of a set of merchants' books of accounts; comprehending a complete system of book-keeping by double entry; by the playing of which, in addition to the amusement, each person becomes a teacher of the art.

Title deposited, October 11, 1820, Southern District of New York.

A printed title-page of this "work" was used as the copyright title entry.

Though this is not a "work on accounting," it is listed because of the remarkable method of presenting the subject.

1827

GREENE, Roscoe Goddard.

Questions on the science of book keeping by double and single entry; adapted to Bennet's system; with explanations of technical words and phrases; accompanied with short methods of calculation, notes, observations, ec. Portland [Me.] A. Shirley, printer, 1827.

Title deposited, August 28, 1827, District of Maine, by Arthur Shirley, proprietor of the copyright.

A printed title-page of this work is located in the rare book department of the Library of Congress.

1830

McNevin, John.

The American accountant; or, Merchant's and mechanic's text book; containing lectures on book keeping wherein the theory and practice of the science are demonstrated in a familiar manner; with a variety of examples and rules perfectly suited to the accountant, man of business, academies, schools and young gentlemen desirous of becoming proficient in accounts.

Title deposited, March 20, 1830, Western District of Pennsylvania.

1832

Dubayle, P. B.

Treble entry book-keeping in a single book and half the writing hitherto employed in book-keeping.

Title deposited, May 18, 1832, Eastern District of Louisiana.

"Book since publication (if published at all) has not been deposited in clerk's office agreeably to law."—List of printed titles sent to the Department of State by the clerk of the Eastern District of Louisiana.

1833

Mackay, George W. S.

The juvenile accountant; or, An introduction to arithmetic and book-keeping; containing all the arithmetical knowledge absolutely necessary for the farmer or mechanic; and particularly adapted to the use of young ladies and gentlemen.

Title deposited, September 3, 1833, Southern District of New York.

This work is recorded as deposited in the clerk's office of the Southern District of New York and forwarded to the Department of State but no record of the deposit of the copy in the Department of State could be found.

Elias Gates, bookseller and stationer, offered for sale: "Winslow, Bucklin, Preston, Bennett and Mackay's book-keeping."—Advertisement in Winslow's "System of book-keeping . . ." 2d ed., 1836.

1834

WARREN, Orlando, 1796–1871.

The mercantile catechism and book-keeper's guide; being a series of lectures by which the art and science of book-keeping by double entry are simplified; intended to impart a thorough knowledge of the system to the learner and as a guide to the clerk.

Title deposited, November 1, 1834, Southern District of New York.

This work is listed by Nixon in his bibliography of American works on bookkeeping. (Nixon, James. Rudiments of book-keeping. N.Y. 1854. p.165–167)

1835

SUTHERLAND, Hector.

A concise and improved system of steam boat book-keeping . . . with approved forms of the principal and auxiliary books; the necessary instructions for systematically conducting, recording, and closing the business transactions of each trip . . .

Title deposited, April 28, 1835, Western District of Pennsylvania.

1836

EDWARDS, William.

The application of a new method of book keeping by double entry; by which three fourths of the writing usually required is dispensed with, and a balance sheet of every month's transactions is shown by continual additions upon title columns in the journal.

Title deposited, January 12, 1836, Southern District of New York.

Record of deposit of copy found in the Department of State index of copyright deposits, 1831–1841.

FINN, Matthew D.

The book keeper's assistant in journalizing, posting and closing accounts from rules laid down; forms for drawing and bills, notes, and sets of exchanges; showing how the same are entered in bill books; introduced with equation of payments and other useful matter; addressed to students.

Title deposited, November 26, 1836, Southern District of New York.

1840

O'CONNOR, Henry.

Exercises in practical book-keeping; adapted to O'Connor's system of teaching that important art: a system approved and recommended by some of the most respectable commercial houses of the city.

Title deposited, November 6, 1840, Eastern District of Pennsylvania.

The title entry for "The clerk's pocket companion," August 26, 1842, Eastern District of Pennsylvania, records the fact that Henry O'Connor was a private teacher of bookkeeping and mercantile correspondence and author of "A treatise on bookkeeping in theory and practice." The title entry for the latter title could not be located.

1841

THOMAS, Sidney Adolphus, 1805?–1865.

First lessons in book-keeping for common schools; in three successive parts; each part forming a separate book; containing transactions, explanations, and rules, and the necessary ruled paper.

Title deposited, November 15, 1841, District of Connecticut.

The same title was again deposited, January 3, 1844, District of Connecticut.

—A key to First lessons in book-keeping; containing all the books complete as they should be written by the learner; with explanations and directions for the use of teachers. New Haven, S. Babcock; N.Y. Clark & Austin [c1843]

[73]p. 13½ x 10½cm.

The title was deposited, January 3, 1844, District of Connecticut, but the book bears the copyright date 1843.

Another ed. New Haven, Peck, White & Peck [n.d.]
[73]p. 13½ x 10½cm.

1842

SEXTON, A. I.

An introduction to single entry book-keeping; or, Book-keeping simplified on the oral and productive system; adapted to the use of academies and common schools . . . in three parts.

Title deposited, June 11, 1842, Southern District of New York.

The author may be A. Jones Sexton who copyrighted another school textbook in 1840. The "I" may be an error in the record book.

The contents of this work as they are given in the title entry are as follows:

Part 1. Introduction to book-keeping simplified. — Part 2. Designed for females to instruct them in keeping their domestic accounts . . . — Part 3. Book-keeping by double entry.

1844

CRITTENDEN, A. F.

The productive system of book-keeping; founded in reason as deduced from the definition of debtor and creditor, and applied to transactions in the form of a general rule . . . used as an index for composing the journal; being an entirely new plan; the whole familiarly illustrated in twelve sets of books practically opened, conducted and closed by double entry . . . designed as a text book for individuals, schools and practical accountants; to which is added a set of steam boat books . . .

Title deposited, April 9, 1844, Western District of Tennessee.

1846

BRANIGAN, William.

The book-keeper's manual; containing the necessary directions for opening books, recording transactions in the day book, journalizing and posting; together with the definitions and closing rules for thirty four accounts; engaged to close any set of books that can be produced. Detroit, Pub. by the author, 1846.

27p. D.

Title deposited, District of Michigan, August 20, 1846.

Imprint information and paging found in Register of copyrights received from the Department of State by the Patent office.

The "pamphlet" was recorded as transmitted to the Department of State and transferred to the Patent office.

In 1865 the author deposited for copyright (Eastern District of Michigan) "The key of book-keeping; prepared for the accountant, teacher, and student."

1847

JOHNSTON, A. P.

A system of book-keeping.

Title deposited, March 9, 1847, District of South Carolina.

"No copies were deposited."—District of South Carolina. List of copyrights from 1845 to 1856.

THOMAS, Sidney Adolphus, 1805?–1865.

First lessons in book-keeping by double entry; for schools, containing day book, journal, ledger, invoice book, and sales book.

Title deposited, July 12, 1847, District of Connecticut.

—A key to First lessons in book-keeping by double entry; for schools . . . New Haven, Peck, White & Peck [n. d.]

61p. 13½ x 10½cm.

1849

Tucker, T. T.

A new treatise on the practice and theory of book-keeping by single and double entry; explained in an easy and familiar manner and adapted to the comprehension of anyone; designed particularly for the use of those desirous of entering into mercantile wholesale and retail stores. Balt. Pub. by Sherwood & co. 1849. 47p. 8vo.

Title deposited, July 6, 1849, District of Maryland.

Record of deposit of copy found in List of copyright deposits in Smithsonian institution; Register of copyright deposits received from the Department of State by the Patent office; and Register of copyrights received by the Library of Congress.

1852

Jones, Thomas, 1804–1889.

The scholar's system of book-keeping; exhibiting in dollars and cents the profits and losses in separate accounts kept by himself . . . forming a complete set of books by double entry; thus combining an effective system of rewards and punishments with practical instruction in the principles of book-keeping.

Title deposited, April 20, 1852, Southern District of New York. Another title with almost the same wording was deposited, September 8, 1852, Southern District of New York, by Thomas Jones. This work is recorded as deposited in the clerk's office, Southern District of New York, February 26, 1853.

1854

Smith, Ephraim Waldo, 1820–1895.

Smith's counting room synopsis; adapted to all kinds of business; showing at one view the whole business transactions of each day, week, month and year . . . accompanied with a day book which is applicable to the most extensive wholesale or retail business.

Title deposited, March 4, 1854, District of Ohio.

1855

Cochran, William D.

A system of book-keeping according to which the student is furnished with a simple statement of each transaction or the original documents as they are presented to the book-keeper in actual business; and from which he is required to originate his own day-book entries and construct all auxiliary books; the system is adapted to

Cochran (continued)
every form of single and double entry; embracing commission, jobbing, banking, steam-boat and railroad books. Detroit.
Title deposited, August 15, 1855, District of Michigan.

Smith, Ephraim Waldo, 1820–1895.
Smith's book-keeping for ladies by double and single entry; containing also a variety of forms for receipts, notes, and bills.
Title deposited, May 19, 1855, Southern District of Ohio.

Strong, W. O., and Frost, George S.
Improved system of book-keeping by double entry without the use of auxiliary cash books, day books, or blotters.
Title deposited, November 24, 1855, District of Michigan.

1856

Bell, Digby V.
Railroading: a systematic method of practical railroad book-keeping; with the most approved auxiliary books in the various departments; designed for instruction in Bell's commercial college and for practical use. Chicago, 1856.
Title deposited, April 21, 1856, District of Illinois.

Bryant, Henry Beadman, 1824–1892, and Stratton, Henry Dwight, 1824–1867.
Bryant and Stratton's sett [sic] of commission; designed for the use of their mercantile colleges and for practical use; consisting of six books; day book, receiving book, sales book, journal, cash book, and ledger.
Title deposited, May 23, 1856, Northern District of Ohio.

—Bryant and Stratton's sett [sic] of practical banking; designed for the use of their mercantile colleges and for practical use; consisting of twelve books; dr. journal, cr. journal, discount register, collection register, domestic tickler, foreign tickler, cash book, statement book, domestic exchange, general ledger, deposit ledger, stock ledger, and individual liabilities.
Title deposited, May 23, 1856, Northern District of Ohio.

—Bryant and Stratton's sett [sic] of practical manufacturing books; designed for the use of their mercantile colleges and for practical use; consisting of fifteen books, viz. day book, cash book, journal, general ledger, stock ledger, consignment book, pay roll, sorting book, time book, wool book, weaving book, quality book, abstract book, finishing book.
Title deposited, June 25, 1856, Northern District of Ohio.
Fourteen books only were listed in the title entry.

HAMMOND, William Pool, 1827–1901, and ALVORD, C. M.
A course of practice in accounts; being a simple method of keeping books by single entry; improved by a proof or trial balance with the same set changed to double entry; being one of the sets embraced in the course of book-keeping as taught by the authors at the Providence commercial academy.
Title deposited, December 30, 1856, District of Rhode Island.

PHILIPP, Joseph.
Self-instruction in the art of book-keeping by double entry; prepared and arranged by Joseph Philipp. Jackson, Miss. Printed at the True witness bk. & job off. 1856.
Title deposited, March 10, 1856, District of Mississippi.

1857

FOLSOM, Ezekiel Gilman, 1821–1897.
Folsom's mercantile bank: complete set on banking; the course of instruction embraces the system of bank accounts; including all the books used in our largest banking institutions, such as ledger, journal, discount and collection registers, domestic and foreign bill books, ticklers, liability, cash, and statement books; and illustrating clearly and fully every kind of transaction and its proper record that is known in banking operations.
Title deposited, March 24, 1857, Northern District of Ohio.

HARDER, William W.
Railroad set; designed for the use of mercantile and commercial colleges in teaching the science of accounts as pertaining to railroading; comprising a day-book in three forms, journal, ledger, treasurer's cash book, auditor's book, stock register, and stock ledger.
Title deposited, March 17, 1857, Northern District of Ohio.
This work is recorded as deposited in the clerk's office of the Northern District of Ohio, August 25, 1857.

1858

BELL, Digby V.
A complete system of railroad accounts as taught at Bell's commercial college.
Title deposited, February 22, 1858, District of Illinois.

—A complete system of steam boat accounts as taught at Bell's commercial college.
Title deposited, February 22, 1858, District of Illinois.

MOONEY, Patrick J.

The whole art of book keeping simplified by a subject and an entry for every transaction that can occur in the whole course of merchant's dealing.

Title deposited, May 17, 1858, Southern District of Alabama.

O'CONNOR, Henry H.

Book keeping in theory and practice: a treatise containing an inductive and philosophical exhibition of its principles; together with a new and infallible method of acquiring in schools the practice of that valuable and important art . . .

Title deposited, July 7, 1858, Southern District of New York.

"Formerly an accountant and for several years a teacher of arithmetic and book keeping and mercantile correspondence."—Title entry.

The author, no doubt, is the same as "Henry O'Connor" listed under 1840.

RICE, E. B.

Exercises for teaching book keeping by single or double entry; arranged by E. B. Rice, practical accountant and teacher of penmanship and mercantile book keeping; no.1.

Title deposited, November 3, 1858, Northern District of New York, by Elias Gates, proprietor of the copyright.

1859

BACON, R. S.

Bacon's new method of keeping books by double entry; combining day book, journal, cash book, invoice book and sales book in one book; also complete sets of books for railroads, steamboat, insurance, commission and banking business.

Title deposited, February 8, 1859, Southern District of Ohio.

CHURCH, A. B.

The art of double-entry book-keeping simplified in an entirely new form; arranged particularly for easy instruction to learners, and for ease, clearness and expedition in practical business; with other useful matter to those engaged in mercantile and trading operations . . . school ed.

Title deposited, March 23, 1859, Southern District of Ohio.

1860

BEHM, Jeremiah.

A practical treatise on the science of book-keeping.

Title deposited, March 9, 1860, District of Indiana.

BOZORTH, B. D.
The mammoth book-keeping; designed for schools and colleges; containing two sets by single entry, one set by double entry, and a set of western steamboat books . . .
Title deposited, February 27, 1860, Eastern District of Pennsylvania.

HOIT, Daniel.
Book-keeping.
Title deposited, September 10, 1860, District of Minnesota.
A printed title-page was used as the copyright title entry.

—Book-keeping by single and double entry.
Title deposited, October 8, 1860, District of Minnesota.
A printed title-page was used as the copyright title entry.
In 1865 Daniel Hoit "attorney at law and accountant" deposited for copyright (District of Minnesota) another title: "Book-keeping."
These titles may be based upon Hoit's work published in Boston in 1859.

PURDY, William.
A new and practical elementary treatise on book keeping by double entry; designed expressly for Purdy's mercantile college, Richmond, Indiana.
Title deposited, September 5, 1860, District of Indiana.

1862

DUNNING, Jacob.
Dunning's new form of double entry book-keeping; a practical, simple, and self-instructive method. N. Y. Hosford & Ketcham, 1862.
Title deposited, July 11, 1862, Southern District of New York.
Imprint information found in the Register of copyrights deposited in the Patent office, 1860–66.
Record of deposit of copy found in the Register . . . 1863.

POLLOCK, T. H.
A treatise on book keeping; embracing an analytical comparison between the single and double entry systems; showing wherein they agree and wherein they differ and wherein the latter is superior to the former by a plain, practical elucidation of both systems; to which is added a variety of business calculations.
Title deposited, November 22, 1862, Eastern District of Pennsylvania.
"T. H. Pollock, principal of the Lancaster mercantile college."—Title entry.

1864

MOONEY, P. J.
The universal accountant.
Title deposited, September 15, 1864, Eastern District of Pennsylvania.

1865

CALKINS, Storrs Seabury.
The accountant's assistant; or, Instruction for commercial students.
Title deposited, January 5, 1865, Northern District of Ohio.

EATON, William H.
A book for self-instruction in book-keeping, penmanship, and business arithmetic . . .
Title deposited, February 1, 1865, District of Massachusetts.
Record of deposit of copy found in the Register of copyrights deposited in the Patent office, 1860–66.

MILLS, T. B.
The student's guide through the theoretical department of the Kansas state and national business college, Topeka, Kansas . . . Topeka, Kan. Printed at the State record off. 1865.
Title deposited, December 15, 1865, District of Kansas.

1866

HOLLINGSWORTH, A., and PARSHALL, A.
Exercises for journalizing and posting and rules for closing the ledger.
Title deposited, June 4, 1866, Southern District of Ohio.
This work is recorded as deposited in the clerk's office of the Southern District of Ohio, June 27, 1866.

MCVICAR, Malcolm, 1829–1904, and PAYSON, Jesse Wentworth, 1815–1889.
Payson, Dunton and Scribner's national system of book keeping . . .
Title deposited, December 12, 1866, District of Massachusetts, by Crosby and Ainsworth, proprietors of the copyright.
This work may be based upon Hanaford and Payson's work, copyrighted, 1858.

1868

HARRISON, Edward.
The student's guide to a complete knowledge of the science of

accounts as taught at Frederick city commercial college; in two parts.

Title deposited, July 3, 1868, District of Maryland.

This work may be the same as the work by Edward Harrison published for the exclusive use of Great western business college, Mount Pleasant, Iowa, in 1865.

The author also deposited for copyright, January 20, 1869 (District of Maryland) "The accountant's key to successful trial balance."

1869

DRIESSLEIN, Charles L.

Double entry book-keeping simplified; for the use of commission merchants; time and labor saved and great accuracy secured by using my printed forms of produce receiving book, produce sales book and produce sales journal; with directions for their use. Chicago.

Title deposited, October 27, 1869, District of Illinois.

The title of each book of accounts was also deposited for copyright in 1869.

FAERBER, Emanuel, 1844–1887, and STEINBRINK, B. B.

A new and improved system of double entry book-keeping; dispensing with a journal and trial balance; proving the correctness of the books without the use of either and simplifying the entire system of book-keeping; particularly adapted for book-keepers and business men in general; 1st ed.

Title deposited, March 5, 1869, Southern District of New York.

1870

PIATT, Isaiah.

Piatt's system of book-keeping. Lagrange, Ind.

Record of deposit of copy found in Register of copyrights received by the Library of Congress. The work was received, January 3, 1870.

The original copyright title entry in the record books of the District of Indiana could not be found.

1871

BRYANT, H. Goulding.

A short treatise on practical book-keeping; embracing the elementary principles of the "art of business" . . . Buffalo, Haas & Kelley, 1871.

Title and two copies deposited, 1871.

PHELAN, John.
General questions and answers on the system of book-keeping by double entry as taught by John Phelan. Charlotte, N.C. 1871. 32p.
Title and two copies deposited, 1871.

SPALDING, James Franklin, 1835–1916.
Spalding's full commercial course in book-keeping by single and double entry; in five parts. Kansas City, Mo.
Title deposited, 1871.
It is not known whether this work is an edition of one of the works listed in part three.
In 1894 the author deposited another title with almost the same wording as the title listed above.

1872

BOUCHET, M.
Principles of book keeping; adapted to the use of churches, schools, etc. Louisville, Ky. Webb & Breeding, 1872.
Title deposited, 1872.

1873

BARTLETT, Robert Montgomery, 1807–1891.
R. M. Bartlett's complete self business instructor in eight parts; seven sets each: the science of double-entry book-keeping and business calculations combined and the art of imparting business knowledge perfected . . . Cin. R. M. Bartlett & co. 1873.
Title deposited, 1873.

FAERBER, Emanuel, and LONG, Marshal.
Faerber and Long's book-keeping: a time and labor-saving system; proving the correctness of a double entry set of books, while entirely dispensing with the tedious work of a trial balance and avoiding a possibility of error . . . designed for merchants, book-keepers and students. New York.
Title deposited, 1873.

KNOWLTON, Charles B.
Practical lessons in book-keeping. Buffalo.
Title deposited, 1873.

LYTE, Eliphalet Oram, 1842–1913.
Definitions, forms, etc. of single entry book-keeping; designed for the use of classes at the state normal school, Millersville, Pa. Lancaster, Pa.
Title deposited, 1873.

1874

Bailey, William K., and Bailey, J. K.
Bailey's method of book-keeping and form of books. Helena, Ark.
Title and two copies deposited, 1874.

Hyde, J. F.
The science of accounts on the inductive plan; including single and double entry in three parts; consisting of twelve distinct sets of books; to which is added a variety of labor-saving forms . . . and an original diagram. Lincoln, Ill.
Title deposited, 1874.

Morison, A. W.
Treatise on book-keeping. Memphis, Southern Baptist publication soc. 1874.
Title deposited, 1874.

Simpson, W. W.
Simpson's new method of book-keeping by double entry. Chattanooga.
Title deposited, 1874.

1875

Natkanson, M.
Self instructor in double entry bookkeeping. New York.
Title deposited, 1875.

1876

Baird, John W.
The practical book-keeper; being a short, plain system of keeping accounts, thorough and concise in all its parts; comprising a complete theoretical training, at the same time being a guide and book of reference; together with forms of business papers. Indianapolis.
Title deposited, 1876.

Choguill, F. M.
The book-keeper's guide; or, Analysis of accounts: a complete exposition of the art and science of book-keeping; designed, illustrated and arranged for the use of schools, colleges, private study, and the counting room. Zanesville, Ohio.
Title deposited, 1876.

Goodwin, J. Henry (probably Joseph Henry Goodwin, 1854–1912)
Goodwin's new system of practical book-keeping; with its complete explanation and simplicity of comprehension, all are enabled

GOODWIN (continued)
to master the art of book-keeping without a teacher. Davenport, Ia.
Title deposited, 1876.
(See I:1881, Goodwin, J. H.)

ROBERTSON, R.
Robertson's bank book-keeping. New York.
Title deposited, 1876.

1877

LANDON, Alson.
The Al Sono system of book-keeping: a system of single and double entry book-keeping combined; with practical forms illustrating by examples the principles of the system. San Francisco.
Title deposited, 1877.

SILSBEE, J.
Routine of Silsbee's commercial course for the Janesville commercial college. Janesville, Wis.
Title deposited, 1877.

1878

CRITTENTON, Harlow M.
Crittenton's national system of compound double entry book-keeping. Chicago.
Title deposited, 1878.

GRIER, S. J., and GRIER, W. L.
The commercial accountant; containing a complete course of business computation and accountantship according to modern methods of practice; comprising an improved plan of instruction . . . the complete work is arranged in five parts with an appendix. St. Louis.
Title deposited, 1878.

JOHNSON, Thomas Richard.
A key to the mysteries of book-keeping; or, Double entry made easy as taught in six lessons only by the author.
Title deposited, 1878.

KOHN, D.
The new era of book keeping in double entry. Philadelphia.
Title and two copies deposited, 1878.

MILLS, E. S.
A treatise on accounts; comprising in part a new system of book-keeping by the use of memorandums in connection with accounts . . . Bigelow, Minn.
Title and two copies deposited, 1878.

STRONG, William E.
W. E. Strong's special course in book-keeping. Miami, Mo.
Title deposited, 1878.

1880

GARRETT, L. G.
The accountant's practical assistant. Pittsburgh.
Title deposited, 1880.

WILSON, J. M.
Exercises in single entry book-keeping; and forms for business papers; for use in the common schools. Terre Haute, Ind.
Title deposited, 1880.

1881

BARTLETT, Robert Montgomery, 1807–1891.
Double-entry book-keeping crystallized; school ed. . . with blank and auxiliary books designed and ruled expressly to suit both teacher and pupil.
—Inductive self-business instructor . . . embracing the science of double-entry book-keeping . . . Cincinnati.
The above entries were entered as one title, 1881.
Two copies deposited, 1888.

BRIGGS, Benjamin F.
Common sense book-keeping. Seattle.
Title deposited, 1881.

DUNCAN, John M.
The sentinel book-keeping by single and double entry: a new system of single and double entry book-keeping by which the proprietor or proprietors can know the amount of stock on hand without taking an inventory of stock after doing business one month . . . also several other practical styles of book-keeping. Industry, Pa.
Title deposited, 1881.

JONES, T. H.
T. H. Jones' book-keeping in three entries. Crockett, Tex.
Title deposited, 1881.
Two copies deposited, 1882.

RITNER, P.
A guide to a knowledge of double entry book-keeping; containing the definitions, principles and steps by which this science may be acquired. St. Joseph, Mo.
Title deposited, 1881.

1882

Baker, C. E.
Baker's science of accounts; embracing theory and practice; arranged upon a new and original plan for use in the Evergreen city business college. Bloomington, Ill.
Title deposited, 1882.

Carrie, W. W.
Carrie's improved, simplified, and labor saving system of accounting; adapted to all classes of merchandising and manufacturing; with special features for retail business.
Title deposited, 1882.

Cleveland, George B.
Cleveland's method of double entry book-keeping. Mobile, Ala.
Title and two copies deposited, 1882.

Harshaw, George L.
A course of business training for the theoretical and practical departments of a business college. Savoy, Tex.
Title deposited, 1882.

Hartwick, Charles M.
A concise and improved system of double entry book-keeping; also an exposition of the science of accounts; including complete sets of books for merchandising, banking, exchange, stock brokerage, forwarding, commission and settlement of estates. Minneapolis.
Title deposited, 1882.

Miller, A. D.
Miller's daily abstract and balance sheet; with rules and instructions on book-keeping. Canton, Ohio.
Title and two copies deposited, 1882.

Woodward, W. W.
Triple-entry book-keeping: a simple and condensed system of keeping accounts in a labor-saving form; adapted to self-instruction.
Title deposited, 1882, by Curtis Haven, proprietor of the copyright.
Two copies deposited, 1882.

1883

Holbrook, Josiah.
Book-keeping rules. Lebanon, Ohio.
Title and two copies deposited, 1883.

MEUSER, Bernhard.
Bernhard Meuser's complete bookkeeper. Chicago.
Title and two copies deposited, 1883.

1884

ELLIOTT, George W., 1843–1913.
Outline of practical work in book-keeping. Burlington, Ia.
Title deposited, 1884.
The same title was deposited for copyright, 1893.

KRUG, John B.
Krug's omnibus ledger, double or single entry; book-keeping made easy; errors avoided and time saved: a complete system of book-keeping for all persons and purposes; day-book, cash-book, and ledger. Battle Creek, Mich.
Title and two copies deposited, 1884.
The same title was again deposited in 1884.
Two copies of this title were deposited, 1885.

PLUMB, Charles M.
Book keeping in a nut shell: a new and complete system of double entry book keeping in six easy lessons. New York.
Title deposited, 1884.

1885

CARPENTER, W. M.
Rules for journalizing. St. Louis.
Title and two copies deposited, 1885.

HAINES, Augustin S.
Journal of the combined text and blank books for book-keeping; designed for common and high schools: a thorough course in single and double entry book-keeping; complete in two sets. Nashville, Ia.
Title deposited, 1885.
The "cash book," "day book," and "ledger" were copyrighted separately.

HOWARD, Frederick F.
Howard's system of book keeping, single and double entry; being a condensed arrangement of commercial transactions . . . Washington, D. C.
Title deposited, 1885.

PALMER, James Henry, 1836–1886.
Debit and credit: the elements of book-keeping for schools or home study. Jacksonville, Ill.
Title deposited, 1885.
An advertisement in the author's other work (See I:1885) states that this work listed above was in preparation. It probably was not published before the author's death in 1886.

WELLS, Charles R.
Book-keeping: a lesson for beginners.
Title deposited, 1885.

WOODS, N. E.
Business forms and book-keeping; teaching to do by doing. Chicago.
Title and two copies deposited, 1885.

1886

ARMSTRONG, J. Hagood.
Book-keeping consolidated: a treatise on double entry book-keeping; with special reference to and in explanation of Armstrong's consolidated account forms. Marion, Ala.
Title deposited, 1886.

BLISS, Fred H.
Bliss' compendium for self-instruction in double entry book-keeping in twelve parts; part first. Saginaw, Mich.
Title deposited, 1886.

MURFEE, James T.
Intellectual and written book-keeping; for schools, colleges and business houses. Marion, Ala.
Title deposited, 1886.
The same title was deposited, 1893.

RATH, A. B.
Practical system of book-keeping. Burr Oak, Kan.
Title deposited, 1886.
The author deposited for copyright, 1887, the following: journal book, cash book, ledger, and book of accounts.

STONER, Philip.
Stoner's new practical, popular and progressive principles of book keeping; the only book of original entry being a double entry journal cash book; intended for self instruction. San Francisco.
Title deposited, 1886.

1887

BURKE, Hugh.
The complete account book; embracing theory and practice; containing a thorough explanation of the principles and practice of single and double entry book-keeping and giving a full illustration of modern business forms . . . Gouldsboro, Pa.
Title deposited, 1887.

JOHNSON, PERRIN, and OSBORN.
Actual business book keeping; double and single entry: a text book for use wherever the subject of book keeping is taught. Buffalo.
Title deposited, 1887.
The proprietors of the copyright were listed as above. "Perrin" is probably Charles O. Perrin (See I:1891, Dudley, A. W.) and "Osborn" may be Frank E. Osborn (See I:1890, Osborn, F. E.).

SPENCERIAN BUSINESS COLLEGE, Milwaukee.
Book-keeping . . . Milw. C. N. Caspar, 1887.
Listed in the American catalogue.

1888

ALBERT, E. T.
E. T. Albert's mercantile guide: the difficult science of book-keeping reduced to simplicity; double entry book-keeping side-tracked . . . Alvarado, Tex.
Title and two copies deposited, 1888.

GRIM, Washington S., 1830–1902.
Grim's new method of book-keeping. Springfield, Ohio.
Title and two copies deposited, 1888.

KING, Isaac R.
Aids for the teaching and study of double entry book-keeping. Hibernia, N. J.
Title and two copies deposited, 1888.

SEAVY, Manson, 1838–1896.
Book-keeping manual. Bost. Rockwell & Churchill, 1888.
Title deposited, 1888.

1889

BECK, F. E.
Bank book keeping; designed and arranged to meet the requirements of an interior bank. 2v. San Francisco.
The title of each volume was deposited separately, 1889.

SADLER, Warren H., 1841–1909, and WHITNEY, M. E.
Introduction to accounts; prepared expressly for use in Sadler's Bryant and Stratton business college. Balt. 1889.
Title deposited, 1889.

1890

AGNEW, Samuel.
The peerless guide to book-keeping; or, Book-keeping at a glance; showing principles of posting and balancing according to the most improved system by a diagram and epitome which explain in a simple manner any difficulties that may occur.
Title and two copies deposited, 1890.

CAMPBELL, James B.
Campbell's complete self-instructing book-keeping. Chic. 1890.
Title deposited, 1890.

CHOGUILL, F. M.
Elements of business and book-keeping. Los Angeles.
Title deposited, 1890.

HORNE, John W.
Safeguard system of accounts; improved method of bookkeeping. Boston.
Title deposited, 1890.

NELSON, Horatio.
Accounts and business for the use of book-keepers, schools and colleges. Cincinnati.
Title and two copies deposited, 1890.

PARISH, Aaron S., and MARTIN, Harry R.
Railroad book-keeping; containing a general exposition of railroad accounts; arranged in conformity with the latest construction and development of inter-state commerce law; and adapted to meet the requirements of railroads from 50 to 2,000 miles or more in length . . . Grand Rapids.
Title deposited, 1890.

ROBINSON, George J.
Common sense book-keeping; designed to make the learner's work clear, short and simple; especially adapted to the use of teachers and to self-instruction and as a text book for schools, law offices and private libraries. Alpena, Mich. 1890.
Title deposited, 1890.

TURNER, Charles L., and TURNER, G. T.
A short cut to practical double entry book-keeping: a new method of practical double entry book-keeping; showing the entire transactions for a day, month or year; requiring the use of but two books.
Title deposited, 1890.

WALTON, George O.
Walton's improved system of book-keeping. Easton, Pa.
Title deposited, 1890.

1891

EASTMAN, Adelbert L.
Eastman's accountant. New York.
Title deposited, 1891.

FALES, Ellis Copeland.
Fales' new method of book-keeping. Brockton, Mass.
Title and two copies deposited, 1891.

FERRIS, Sherman W.
Practical book-keeping. Lexington, Ky.
Title and two copies deposited, 1891.

IRISH, William Carlton.
Cosmon ledger system of book-keeping. Salt Lake City.
Title deposited, 1891.

KELLY, Alfred.
Kelly's short, easy, accurate book-keeping; demonstrating the only true common sense system of double entry; nicely arranged for use in business colleges, common schools, etc.; volume first. Portland, Mich.
Title deposited, 1891.

ROBINSON, John L.
John L. Robinson's practical suggestions in relation to a simple system of accounts by double entry; derived from an experience of forty-nine years, thirteen of which have been in expert work. Boston.
Title deposited, 1891.

1892

BUCHANAN, Robert J.
Hints to beginners in book-keeping. Pittsburgh.
Title deposited, 1892.
—Hints to beginners in book-keeping; 2d ed. Pittsburgh.
Title deposited, 1893.

CARNELL, John R., and GUTCHESS, —
New practical book-keeping by single and double entry; complete ed.; for use in business colleges, short-hand schools, high schools, academies, and home instruction. Albany.
Title deposited, 1892.

CONSTABLE, Henry B.
Debit and credit: book-keeping, its rules, forms, entries, calculations, tables and explanations; for the use of merchants, accountants, teachers and students. Norfolk, Va.
Title deposited, 1892.

CURTISS, Charles Carroll.
The new and complete course in the theory and practice of book-keeping by double and single entry; for use in commercial colleges, public and private schools, academies, and for self instruction. Minneapolis.
Title deposited, 1892.
It is not known whether this work is an edition of the work by Curtiss listed in part three.

HAINER, Daniel H.
A new and brief method of book-keeping; or, The accountant's handy book. Pittsburgh.
Title deposited, 1892.

HENDRYX, F. H.
Hendryx' compendium of book-keeping and business forms; instruction book. Bath, N. Y.
Title and two copies deposited, 1892.
—Hendryx' compendium of book-keeping and business forms; for self instruction.
Title and two copies deposited, 1892.
Listed in the American catalogue.
Probably the former work serves as a guide to the latter.

HOOD, John H.
Hood's simple system of double entry book-keeping. Litchfield, Ill.
Title deposited, 1892.
Two copies deposited, 1893.

LEDYARD, John T.
Ledyard's book-keeping: a theoretical and practical treatise on the science of accounts; containing the principle of double entry and modern practical forms used in business. Chicago.
Title deposited, 1892.

MARSDEN, Nicholas, and MEHAN, John M.
Joint stock [company] bookkeeping. Des Moines.
Title deposited, 1892.
Another title with almost the same wording was deposited, 1894.

PERRINE, B. F.
Instructions for single entry. Valparaiso, Ind.
Title deposited, 1892.

—Instructions for the lumber set. Valparaiso, Ind.
Title deposited, 1892.

PHILLIPS, John Edwin.
Lessons 1, 2, 3: day book; book-keeping made easy. Syracuse, N. Y.
Title and two copies deposited, 1892.

—Lessons 4, 5, 6: journal; book-keeping made easy. Syracuse, N. Y.
Title and two copies deposited, 1892.

WARD, James Murphy.
Ward's office bookkeeping and manual of business education; designed especially for young bookkeepers and those graduating from business colleges. Centralia, Wash.
Title deposited, 1892.

YOUNG, Charles W.
Bankers' short method of book-keeping, and reference book . . . Charleston, W. Va.
Title deposited, 1892.

1893

ADAMS, Allston.
Complete double entry book-keeping. Selkirk, N. Y.
Title deposited, 1893.
—A rule that will cover all entries in the entry book. Albany.
Title deposited, 1894.
—The rule of complete double entry book-keeping.
Title deposited, 1894.
The above three titles are probably separately copyrighted parts of one work.

BAINE, William Connell.
Easy lessons in the science of accounts; by an expert. Chicago.
Title and two copies deposited, 1893.

ERHARD, Charles Thomas.
Erhard's peerless system of double entry bookkeeping. Brooklyn.
Title deposited, 1893.

KUGLER, Joseph L.
Instructions for correctly closing the ledger. Trenton.
Title deposited, 1893.

MCCHESNEY, A. S.
Accountants' favorite system: the most practical, accurate, concise, brief and satisfactory system of book-keeping now in use. Brownwood, Tex.
Title and two copies deposited, 1893.

ULMER, H. C.
Guide to accompany the practical book-keeping; adapted to any business; farmers' ed. for the public schools. Lancaster, Pa.
Title and one copy deposited, 1893.
A separately published treatise on bookkeeping by Ulmer was not found but the author published " Lessons in business . . . " [c1893] which included a section on bookkeeping.

1894

BENNETT, A. M.
A simple rule for an accountant to use in journalizing. Elmira, N. Y.
Title deposited, 1894.

COBURN, Byron.
Practical double and single entry book-keeping on playing cards. Le Roy, N. Y.
Title deposited, 1894.

COLEMAN, Mary F.
Coleman's hand book of business methods and principles of book-keeping; for the student, teacher and business man. Gloversville, N. Y. Collins & Leaning, 1894. 57p.
Title and two copies deposited, 1894.
Card, noting imprint and paging, is in the Library of Congress old official catalog but the work is missing.

COMER, Charles Evelyn, 1858–1918.
Business and book-keeping. Bost. Comer's commercial college.
Title deposited, 1894.

FARR, John Wesley.
Farrian system of book-keeping; for use in common schools, high schools . . . Downs [Kan.] Kansas bk. co. 1894.
Title deposited, 1894.
Imprint information found in the American catalogue. The work was not located. The contents of this work may be part

of the "Farrian complete system of penmanship, correspondence, business forms, and book-keeping" published in 1894. The part on bookkeeping was probably published separately.

FOLLETT, Lewis.
The Follett account book: a cash book, journal and sales book; combined into one for double-entry book-keeping; adapted as a text book for schools and colleges. Cleveland.
Title deposited, 1894.
Two copies deposited, 1895.

FRANK, William.
Frank's shortened system of book-keeping; also a short method of obtaining inventory or balance of property on hand and unsold at closing.
Title deposited, 1894.

HEALD'S BUSINESS COLLEGE, San Francisco.
Business manual of the practical department of Heald's business college. San Francisco.
Title deposited, 1894.
In 1897 Heald's business college copyrighted and deposited two copies of a "Manual of the business practice department . . ." by J. M. Davis. This work may be based upon the "Business manual . . ." entered above and also Davis's work listed in part one, 1892.

HESTON, J. H.
Experts' exchange system of double entry book-keeping. Marietta, Ohio, 1894.
Title and two copies deposited, 1894.

LE JEUNE, Capel Ellis.
Accounting systems; their organization for financial and commercial corporations and large business establishments; with brief notes. New York. 31p.
Title and two copies deposited, 1894.
The second edition was copyrighted, 1895. Two copies deposited, 1896.

MATHISON, John S.
Double entry book-keeping practically illustrated. San Francisco.
Title and two copies deposited, 1894.

ROBERTS, W.
Double entry book-keeping made easy by a new system. Abilene, Tex.
Title deposited, 1894.

Smith, I. L., and Smith, Amos W.
Smith's annual business guide to book-keeping; for use in business colleges. Warren, Pa. Smith's business college.
Title and one copy deposited, 1894.

Staples, John R.
Short and accurate system of accounts. Cincinnati.
Title and two copies deposited, 1894.
—Staples' quick, simple, accurate and comprehensive system of book-keeping; or, Universal and practical method of accounts; accompanied with key. Cin. Pub. by the author.
Title and two copies deposited, 1895.
This work is probably an enlargement of the work first copyrighted.

Tarkington, J. H.
Prospectus of exhibit accounting: a system of ascertaining trial balances, making out balance sheets in advance of the general ledger, and locating errors in posting; exemplified in a set of joint stock company books; double entry. Rosemark, Tenn.
Title and two copies deposited, 1894.
—A synopsis of exhibit accounting. Rosemark, Tenn.
Title deposited, 1894.
This is probably a part of the work listed above, separately copyrighted.

Ulmer, George Gabriel.
American science of standard book-keeping. New York.
Title deposited, 1894.

Vaile, E. O.
Vaile's single entry book-keeping. Chicago.
Title deposited, 1894.

Whitehead, T. P.
Whitehead's short method of bookkeeping and common sense ledger. Shreveport, La.
Title deposited, 1894.
Two copies deposited, 1895.

1895

Bansil, William Andruss.
The student's and business man's self-instructor in the principles of accounts; both single and double entry book-keeping fully illustrated. Marianna, Fla.
Title deposited, 1895.

BENNETT, M. Eugene.
Modern book-keeping; initiatory; volume one. Johnstown, Pa.
Title deposited, 1895.

CAMPBELL, Thomas F.
San Jose business college: directions for actual business practice. San Jose, Calif.
Title deposited, 1895.
—Campbell's commercial course; comprising outlines of actual business practice; rev. and improved.
Title deposited, 1896.
This work is probably a revised edition of the one listed above.

COBURN, Byron.
Algebraic book-keeping ledger; with instruction, balance and proof columns. Le Roy, N. Y.
Title deposited, 1895.
Two copies deposited, 1897.
A note says that the work was published in 1896.
One copy of a 1900 edition was received, 1900.

FRYE, Ulysses S.
Actual business memoranda, single and double entry; for use in business colleges. Chicago.
Title and two copies deposited, 1895.

HOWE, William L.
Practical book keeping for joint stock companies and corporations; with illustrated examples for opening and closing; also complete specimen set. Quincy, Ill.
Title and two copies deposited, 1895.

MEREDITH, Reuben Leslie.
Guide at book-keeping and the science of accounts: a complete and practical exposition of the science of accounts and the recording of business transactions as applied by expert accountants; arranged for use in business colleges, high schools and academies. Sandusky, Ohio.
Title and one mimeographed copy deposited, 1895.
"Not published, December, 1896."—Title entry.

SNYDER, Carrie.
The universal system of practical book-keeping. Chicago.
Title deposited, 1895.

1896

CATLIN, Frank E.
Catlin's improved system of bookkeeping. Mason, Wis.
Title deposited, 1896.

Eye, J. L.
Eye's condensed system of auditing. Chicago.
Title deposited, 1896.

Hoskins, Benjamin.
Hoskins' "up to date" accounting applied to hotels. Chicago.
Title deposited, 1896.

Kittredge, Anson Oliver, 1848–1903, and Brown, John F.
Accounting for the instalment business or retail credit sales.
Title deposited, 1896.
Two copies deposited, 1897.

Lundberg, John, jr.
John Lundberg's instructions for a new system of bookkeeping. Litchfield, Minn.
Title and two copies deposited, 1896.

Meredith, Reuben Leslie.
Business and accounting; a scientific development of the theory of accounts and the forms of record for double-entry book-keeping; also a presentation of business calculations, negotiable paper and mercantile correspondence. Zanesville, Ohio.
Title deposited, 1896.

Roach, Thomas Watson.
Double entry book-keeping made easy; containing the "seven sets" as taught at the Kansas Wesleyan business college, Salina, Kan. Salina, Kan.
Title and two copies deposited, 1896.

Schwartz, George W., 1871–
The daily balance system of bookkeeping. Rochester, N. Y.
Title deposited, 1896.

Ziegler, P. W., and company, Philadelphia.
Second course in book-keeping; set no. 1, wholesale dry goods; set no. 2, wholesale carpets; set no. 3, wholesale groceries. Philadelphia.
Each set was deposited separately, 1896. Two copies of each set were deposited, 1897.

1897

Abell, Evaline.
Business practice; adapted to the use of commercial schools; with instructions for the teacher.
Title deposited, 1897.

BRAAM, Jacob W.
An introduction to bookkeeping: an exposition of the essential principles of the art. Chicago.
Title deposited, 1897.

CAMPBELL, Thomas F.
Manual and practice outlines for instruction in book-keeping in the Gas city business college, Stockton, Calif. Stockton, Calif.
Title and two copies deposited, 1897.

COX, J. O.
The book-keeper's vade mecum. Memphis.
Title deposited, 1897.

FRYE, Ulysses S.
Set 1: practical book-keeping in which the duties of the practical book-keeper [are] shown by doing actual business from the beginning; for use in commercial colleges, high schools and academies. Chicago.
Title and two copies deposited, 1897.

HOFFMAN, Henry Charles.
Hoffman's ledger proof book-keeping and actual business training; for private instruction by mail; part 1. Black River Falls, Wis.
Title deposited, 1897.

JONES, Charles F.
The bookkeeping of department stores. New York.
Title deposited, 1897, by the Accountics association.
Two copies deposited, 1898.

THE JOURNAL PRINTING COMPANY, Minneapolis.
The Journal school of business: a winter's course in book-keeping at home; with rules and suggestions for doing business in a business-like way. Minneapolis.
Several titles with almost the same wording were deposited in 1897 and 1898. They undoubtedly were part of a correspondence course in bookkeeping.

KITTREDGE, Anson Oliver, 1848–1903.
Balance-sheet accounting. New York.
Title deposited, 1897.

—Branch house auditing. New York.
Title deposited, 1897.
Two copies deposited, 1898.

—Credits and accountancy. New York.
Title deposited, 1897.

KITTREDGE (continued)
—Up-to-date business methods and the balance sheet system of accounts. New York.
Title deposited, 1897.

RITNER, P.
Budget for teaching book-keeping. St. Louis.
Title and two copies deposited, 1897.

SMITH, W. Fitzgerald.
Series no.3: bookkeeping. Providence.
Title deposited, 1897, by Jason Rogers, proprietor of the copyright.

STOUT, Rufus S.
Stout's practical business guide. Hot Springs, Ark.
Title and two copies deposited, 1897.

TAYLOR, Arthur J., 1870–
20th century book-keeping: a series of articles on the art of bookkeeping; embodying newest methods. Indianapolis.
Title deposited, 1897.

TODD, J. W. L.
Modernized book-keeping and business practice; for students, book-keepers, and business men. San Antonio.
"Lesson no.1" and "Lesson no.2" were deposited, 1897.
Two copies of "Lesson no.1" were deposited, 1897.

UNION COLLEGE OF BUSINESS, Philadelphia.
First lesson sheet of the Union college system of bookkeeping by correspondence. Philadelphia.
Title deposited, 1897.

1898

DANE, S.
A progressive and practical course of book-keeping taught by actual transactions. New York.
Title deposited, 1898.

DARLING, W. C.
Darling's practical business method of teaching book-keeping by mail. Carrollton, Ky.
Title and two copies deposited, 1898.

FRYE, Ulysses S.
Elements of business and practical bookkeeping: a new work illustrating modern methods of accounting by the actual performance of the duties of the practical bookkeeper from the start;

teachable in all grades of schools; fully illustrated. Chic. Practical bookkeeping co.
Title deposited, 1898.

HYDE, Joseph Eldridge Sherman.
Reference book to the supply and demand system of teaching bookkeeping. Denver.
Title and two copies deposited, 1898.

KELLY, F. L.
Kelly's practical work on book-keeping. Hannibal, Mo. Hannibal commercial college, 1898.
Title deposited, 1898.

KELLY, George.
A practical course in bookkeeping. Malone, N. Y.
Title and two copies deposited, 1898.

LIPPINCOTT, J. B., AND COMPANY, Philadelphia.
Lesson no.1 : course in bookkeeping.
Title and two copies deposited, 1898.
Lessons 5 and 6 were also deposited, 1898.

SAWHILL, A. F.
The short cut accounting system. Allegheny City, Pa.
Title and two copies deposited, 1898.

VAN OMMEREN, John.
Van Ommeren's complete comparative business records covering a period of twelve years: a new and improved system of keeping perfect records of a business . . . with a scientific treatise of the freight, discount, insurance, and expense accounts. Evanston, Ill.
Title deposited, 1898.

VORIES, Hervey D.
Vories' laboratory method of book keeping. Indianapolis.
Title and two copies deposited, 1898.

1899

BAZE, Jessie Kindrick.
Common sense bookkeeping; or, Bookkeeping simplified. Hext, Tex.
Title deposited, 1899.

BECK, Charles Edgar.
Beck's easy-rule book-keeping; initiatory sets. Piqua, Ohio.
Title deposited, 1899.

Broaker, Frank, and Chapman, Richard Marvin.
A treatise upon the keeping of hotel accounts; with hints and suggestions relative to clubs, apartment houses and the like. New York.
Title deposited, 1899.

Hailman, J. W.
Bookkeeping rules, etc. Kansas City, Mo.
Title and two copies deposited, 1899.

Hooper, John E.
D. Q. Sellers; or, Double entry simplified: kinetescope system of teaching book-keeping. Columbia, S. C.
Title deposited, 1899.

Hutchison, John R.
Hutchison's auditing system of actual business from start to finish. Salt Lake City.
Title deposited, 1899.

Kingsbury, George B.
Manual of book-keeping. Brockton, Mass.
Title deposited, 1899.

Lindeman, M. H.
Every-day bookkeeping. Brooklyn.
Title deposited, 1899.

Magly, William S.
Magly's teaching of practical bookkeeping; abridged. Cincinnati.
Title deposited, 1899.
Two copies deposited, 1900.

Motter, Harry L.
How to audit; published solely in the interest of bank directors, and for the protection of bank depositors. York, Pa.
Title and two copies deposited, 1899.

Rathbun, G. R.
A short and practical course in double-entry bookkeeping; designed for use in high schools, academies and Y. M. C. A. associations; this course is calculated to complete the first year in the high school. Omaha.
Title deposited, 1899.

1900

Beck, Charles Edgar.
Beck's easy-rule bookkeeping; advanced sets. Dayton, Ohio.
Title deposited, 1900.

COHN, Max.
Cohn's auto-bookkeeping. Milwaukee.
Title deposited, 1900.

PERSHITZ, Nathan.
Practical and theoretical bookkeeping and factory accounts. New York.
Title deposited, 1900.

PHELPS, H. G.
A short course in practical book-keeping; consisting of fourteen plates designed for business men and private students. Bozeman, Mont.
Title deposited, 1900.

RIGG, S. A.
The plain way of teaching the science and art of bookkeeping; first week; prepared for the Central correspondence college.
Palmyra, Ill.
Title deposited, 1900.

STENOGRAPHERS AID ASSOCIATION.
Simplified business bookkeeping by single and double entry on an entirely new plan; embracing banks, stocks, corporations; with practical business forms. New York.
Title deposited, 1900.

WEINBERG, Abraham I.
The improved department system of bookkeeping for department stores. Baltimore.
Title deposited, 1900.

WILLIAMS, D. B.
The Chicago method of teaching bookkeeping; actual business from the start. Chicago.
Title deposited, 1900.

AUTHOR INDEX

AUTHOR INDEX

THIS index is an alphabetical author index to Parts One, Two, Three, and Four. The parts are designated by the Roman numerals I, II, III, and IV. Each date given is the first date of publication of an author's work. For example, Thomas Jones published two separate works in the 19th century which are indexed as follows: Jones, Thomas. I:1841; 1849.

BIBLIOGRAPHY

OF

WORKS ON ACCOUNTING BY AMERICAN AUTHORS

BY

HARRY C. BENTLEY

AND

RUTH S. LEONARD

TWO VOLUMES IN ONE

VOLUME II

1901-1934

[1934]

REPRINTS OF ECONOMIC CLASSICS

AUGUSTUS M. KELLEY · PUBLISHERS

NEW YORK 1970

PREFACE

THIS bibliography of works on accounting by American authors covers the period from January 1, 1901, to January 1, 1935, and may be called the *20th century bibliography* to distinguish it from Volume I, the *19th century bibliography,* published in October, 1934.

In addition to its historical interest, this volume has practical value as a source of reference for accountants, teachers, students, librarians, and others interested in the accounting literature of the 20th century.

Part One is a chronological list of works on accounting by American authors which were published for general distribution during the 20th century. It traces the growth of accounting literature and makes it possible to determine at a glance the first editions in any one year. An adequate bibliographical record is given for each title published.

Part Two classifies the works listed in Part One as follows:

1. Works on bookkeeping intended primarily for use in high schools and private business schools
2. Works on elementary and advanced accounting intended primarily for students of college grade or for general reference purposes
3. Works dealing with the preparation and interpretation of financial statements
4. Cost accounting and system building:
   (a) Works dealing chiefly or wholly with general principles and practice
   (b) Treatises applicable to specific businesses and professions
5. Auditing:
   (a) Works dealing chiefly or wholly with general principles and procedure
   (b) Treatises applicable to specific businesses and professions
6. C.P.A. examination questions and answers
7. Encyclopedias, handbooks, etc.

The Supplement to this bibliography was compiled for the benefit of those interested in what has been done toward uniformity in accounting practice and procedure by trade associations, professional and industrial organizations, government bureaus, and federal and state government regulatory bodies. It includes (1) an alphabetical list of the businesses and professions for which uniform accounting systems, or some phase of uniformity in accounting practice and procedure, have been sponsored, with the names of the sponsors listed alphabetically under each heading, and (2) an alphabetical list of the various public utility industries for which uniform systems or uniform classifications of accounts have been prescribed, with the names of the federal or state government regulatory bodies listed alphabetically under each heading.

The Appendix contains a selected alphabetical list of the publishers of works on accounting published during the last decade, national associations of accountants, office managers, comptrollers, etc., with the names of the periodicals which they sponsor, histories and bibliographies of accounting, and miscellaneous sources of reference of aid to the accountant.

The Author Index directs the reader to each author included in Part One, the chronological list, Part Two, the classified list, and the reference sources in the Appendix.

The Subject Index is an alphabetical index to the specific lines of business classified in Part Two and in the Supplement.

One of the major problems in compiling this bibliography was that of fixing the boundaries of its content. In the absence of adequate precedents to serve as a guide in solving this problem, it was necessary to make arbitrary definitions and restrictions.

American authors, for the purpose of this bibliography, include all authors of works on accounting, adapted to American practice, who resided in the United States at the time their works were first published, regardless of whether or not they were citizens of this country and regardless of whether or not they continued to reside in the United States thereafter.

Works on accounting, for the purpose of this bibliography, consist of books and pamphlets of more than twenty-five pages devoted chiefly or wholly to accounting and offered for general rather than restricted distribution.

Probably no two persons would agree on what should be included and what should not be included in a bibliography of "works on accounting." Confusion exists because many fail to distinguish between the subject matter involved in the *work of accountants* and in *works on accounting.* In an effort to clarify this distinction the following classification of the major subjects included in the work of accountants is submitted:

1. *Accounting*
    - Recordative accounting (bookkeeping)
        - Financial accounting
        - Compilation of financial statements and statistics
        - Cost accounting
        - Compilation of cost statements and statistics
    - Constructive accounting (system building)
        - Designing accounting systems and methods
        - Installation
    - Inspective and interpretative accounting (auditing)
        - Audits
        - Investigations
        - Interpretation of financial data
2. Budgeting
3. Taxes
4. Payroll methods and bonus systems
5. Inventory methods and practice
6. Insurance
7. Corporate organization and finance
8. Investments
9. Business mathematics
10. Business law
11. Machines and other mechanical aids
12. Office organization and management

These twelve subjects represent approximately the scope of the work directly relating to the department of Accounting and Finance in an industrial organization. "Accounting" represents only one division of an accountant's work and it is "accounting" to which this bibliography is devoted. Each of the other eleven subjects should have its own bibliography.

The department of Accounting and Finance is, in turn, but one of the major departments of an industrial organization. In a like manner, the subjects involved in the functioning of each of the other departments, such as Purchasing, Production, Publicity, Selling, Credits, Traffic, Personnel, and General management, should have their own bibliographies.

Many books treat of subjects relating to more than one department. In classifying, for bibliographical purposes, the works pertaining to business administration it is necessary to determine not only the content of the work but the author's intent. Was it written for the credit manager or for the accountant? A book dealing with the analysis and interpretation of financial statements as a basis for granting credit should be classified under Credits rather than Accounting. Was it written for the production manager or for the accountant? A work on factory organization and administration may contain a treatise on cost accounting, but if written primarily from the standpoint of plant management, it should be assigned to Production rather than Accounting.

In addition, works on such subjects as banking, domestic economy, school management, law, engineering, etc. which contain some "accounting" are omitted.

In brief, many books in which some space is given to accounting in its relation to the major subject treated are not included in this bibliography because they were not intended to be works on accounting, and also because accounting is treated as incidental to the main subject. These books add nothing which is new or unique to the literature of *accounting per se*.

Works dealing with statistics, statistical methods, cost estimating, depreciation theory, principles of valuation, production, operating and distribution cost studies and reports, and annuity studies, are often aids to the accountant but cannot properly be termed "works on accounting."

The following classes of works are arbitrarily eliminated from the bibliography:

1. Works issued for restricted distribution, such as textbooks and practice material published for the exclusive use of some one private business school, university school of business, correspondence school, state extension course, etc.; manuals of accounting practice and procedure published for the exclusive use of federal, state, or municipal government departments; classifications of accounts and manuals of accounting procedure published for the exclusive use of some one corporation or private organization, such as a railroad, public utility company, or business corporation; printed addresses, bulletins, mimeographed material, etc. published exclusively or primarily for distribution among members of associations and societies; handbooks, keys, tests, and solutions published for teachers only; and doctoral dissertations and masters' theses (unless they were reprinted for general distribution).
2. Blank books, such as account books for farmers, merchants, professional men, housekeepers, etc.; various units for "actual busi-

ness practice" including outgoing papers, ledgers, vouchers, etc.; drill books and manuals; miscellaneous forms for keeping financial records; and charts and diagrams.

3. The study and teaching of accounting.
4. Individual C.P.A. examinations published annually or semi-annually by the American Institute of Accountants, the American Society of Certified Public Accountants, and by various state boards of accountancy; and the laws, rules, and regulations relating to the issuance of certified public accountant certificates.
5. Articles on accounting contained in magazines, bulletins, journals, year books, proceedings, reports, etc.

The decision to omit all works on accounting of less than twenty-five pages was made rather than burden this bibliography with nearly one hundred pamphlets ranging in number of pages from two to twenty-four which have little or no value as "works on accounting."

The decision to segregate in the Supplement works on accounting sponsored by trade associations, professional and industrial organizations, and government bureaus, and classifications of accounts prescribed by government regulatory bodies was made rather than burden the main bibliography with many works which have little general reference value.

It will thus be seen that this bibliography is not an index to every book, pamphlet, or article dealing with accounting. It is restricted to (1) separately bound works of twenty-five pages or more, (2) by American authors, (3) intended as contributions to the literature of accounting, and (4) published in the United States between January 1, 1901, and January 1, 1935, for unrestricted distribution.

The cooperation of many librarians and other individuals who have aided in the compilation of Volume II is acknowledged with appreciation.

Harry C. Bentley

May, 1935.

TABLE OF CONTENTS

PART ONE

PART ONE

Chronological bibliography of works on accounting by American authors which were published for general distribution from January 1, 1901, to January 1, 1935.

INTRODUCTION

THE growth of accounting literature in the 20th century is traced by the use of the chronological method. Under each consecutive year, beginning with 1901, are listed alphabetically the names of authors of first editions published during the year, and under each author's name is the descriptive title of his first edition, place of publication, number of pages, and size in centimeters. Then follows a record of the reprints or revised editions which could be verified. No attempt was made to distinguish between reprints and editions. Each reprint is called "another edition" unless it is numbered.

The title is given in the fullness necessary to identify and explain the content and purpose of the work. Three dots, . . . , indicate an omission on the title-page.

The following cities are so well known that they are given without appended state designation. (In some cases abbreviations only are given.)

Albany (Alb.)
Atlanta

Baltimore (Balt.)
Boston (Bost.)
Brooklyn
Buffalo

Chattanooga
Chicago (Chic.)
Cincinnati (Cin.)
Cleveland

Dallas
Denver
Des Moines
Detroit

Fort Wayne

Grand Rapids

Hartford

Indianapolis

Los Angeles

Memphis
Milwaukee (Milw.)
Minneapolis

Nashville
New Haven
New Orleans (N. O.)
New York (N. Y.)

Omaha

Philadelphia (Phil.)
Pittsburgh
Providence

Richmond

St. Louis (St. L.)
St. Paul
Salt Lake City
San Antonio
San Francisco (San Fran.)
Savannah
Scranton
Seattle
Spokane

Tacoma
Toledo
Trenton

Washington, D. C. (Wash.)

In general, only the surnames of well-known firms are given (e.g. Harper). Both surnames are given if they are hyphenated in the firm name (e.g. Bobbs-Merrill).

In the case of personal firms, the words "publishing company" and "and company" are omitted.

If the publisher is the author, the surname only is repeated.

If unchanged, the place of publication and the name of the publisher are not repeated for each reprint or edition; but if one or both change, both are repeated.

Brackets, [], are used when (1) the date is not on the title-page; (2) the pages are not numbered; and (3) the insertion does not appear on the title-page.

Common abbreviations are used throughout. The letter "c" before a date signifies "copyrighted." The letter "l" signifies leaves, meaning that the work was printed on one side of leaf only. The abbreviation "cm." signifies centimeters.

STATISTICS

NUMBER OF TITLES LISTED IN PART I

By Years

1901– 8	1911–16	1921–32	1931–19
1902–12	1912–21	1922–49	1932–22
1903–12	1913–30	1923–51	1933–23
1904–12	1914–29	1924–52	1934–24
1905–20	1915–25	1925–36	
1906–13	1916–25	1926–38	
1907–15	1917–33	1927–30	
1908–20	1918–27	1928–25	
1909–22	1919–11	1929–39	
1910–24	1920–20	1930–39	

By Decades

1901–1910	158
1911–1920	237
1921–1930	391
1931–1934	88
Total number of titles listed in Part I	874

The total number of authors, including joint authors and subordinate authors or editors, listed in Part I is 741.

Part One

Chronological Bibliography

1901

BEACH, Elmer Henry, 1861–1914, and THORNE, William Winter, 1870– , compilers.
The American business and accounting encyclopaedia: a standard reference book for accountants and business men; profusely illustrated with hundreds of special forms and tables . . . 3d ed. Detroit, Book-keeping pub. co. 1901. 1090p. 28cm.
Various parts of the encyclopaedia had appeared in the Home study course of the Book-keeper publishing company in 1900.
An advertisement in the third edition states that the first and second editions published in 1901 were exhausted in only six weeks.
Another ed. 1904. 4v.
Another ed. [c1908–09] 6v. 27½cm.

BLANCHARD, Isaac H.
Actual costs in printing and how to discover and reckon them . . . N. Y. Blanchard, 1901. 58p.

DANDO, J. Clifford.
Fundamental principles of ascertaining cost of manufacturing; applied to manufacturing printing; applicable to all other kinds of manufacturing. Phil. Dando print. & pub. co. 1901. 81+[1]p. 32cm.
3d ed. 1901. 81p. 32cm.

FIELD, Millard Lincoln.
Outlines in book-keeping . . . Topeka, Kan. Crane, 1901. 64p. 19cm.

INGERSON, Carlos Ira, 1853–
A normal method in double entry bookkeeping. Chic. Inter-state bk. co. [1901] 88p. 20cm.

MACPHERSON, Frank Herbert, 1861–
Municipal accounting: a comprehensive treatise on the subject of municipal accounts; illustrated by specimens of improved forms of books and reports . . . Detroit, Book-keeper pub. co. 1901. 47p. 24cm.

MULLER, S. F.
A graded system of book-keeping; embracing single and double entry; adapted to the use of the common schools, high schools, etc. [Balt. c1901] 155p. 21cm.

TANNER, Henry T., 1842–1918.
Practical business instructor; giving complete definitions, explanations, and rules for opening, conducting, and closing all kinds of account-books; with full instructions for doing business generally . . . Cleveland, Burrows bros. 1901. 151p. 27½cm.
Another ed. Akron, Ohio, Saalfield pub. co. [c1907] 151p. 28cm.

1902

BARRETT, Albert Reed, 1841–
Modern banking methods and practical bank bookkeeping; illustrated with over two hundred forms of bank books, records, and blanks. N. Y. B. Rhodes, 1902. 325p. 26½cm.
Another ed. N. Y. Bankers pub. co. 1903. 325p. 26½cm.
5th ed. 1907. 325p. 26½cm.

CURTISS, Charles Carroll.
The American standard bookkeeping; high school ed. N. Y. Amer. bk. co. [1902] 192p. 24½cm.

GILBERT, Adelbert Lorenzo, 1851–1907.
Modern business bookkeeping; arranged as a textbook for schools and colleges. Indianapolis, Bowen-Merrill, 1902. 215p. 25½cm. (Bowen-Merrill ser.)
Other eds. Indianapolis, Bobbs-Merrill, 1911; 1912. 216p. 25½cm.
—Twenty lessons in bookkeeping: a complete course for eighth grade pupils . . . with voucher practice by T. F. Campbell. Indianapolis, Bobbs-Merrill, 1911. 100p. 15½cm.
From the author's larger work "Modern business bookkeeping," 1902.
Another ed. 1915. 100p. 15½cm.
—Business practice for Twenty lessons in bookkeeping, by T. F. Campbell. Indianapolis, Bobbs-Merrill, 1915.
(Campbell, Thomas Findley, 1860–)

GOTTSBERGER, Francis.
Accountant's guide for executors, administrators, assignees, receivers, and trustees. N. Y. G. G. Peck [1902] 196p. 26cm.

McKinney, W. J.
The ideal self-instructor in double entry book-keeping. Pittsburg, Kan. The author, 1902. [110]p. 21cm.

Marshall, Carl Coran, 1852–
Marshall's corporation and voucher accounting. Cedar Rapids, Ia. Goodyear-Marshall pub. co. 1902. 67+[1]p. 27½cm.
Another ed. 1907. 67+[1]p. 27½cm.

Moore, John Henry, 1874–1909, and Miner, George Washington, 1860–
Accounting and business practice; for use in all schools where bookkeeping is taught. Bost. Ginn, 1902. 400p. 24cm.
—Accounting and business practice; shorter course. Bost. Ginn, 1903. 266p. 24cm.
From the authors' larger work "Accounting and business practice; for use in all schools where bookkeeping is taught," 1902.
—Accounting and business practice; corporation accounting and banking. Bost. Ginn, 1903. p.253–400, 24cm.
From the authors' larger work "Accounting and business practice; for use in all schools where bookkeeping is taught," 1902.

Read, Frederick H.
Bookkeeping, business arithmetic, and correspondence. Phil. P. W. Ziegler [c1902] 262p. 23½cm. (Success in business, v.1)
"Theoretical and practical bookkeeping": part 1, p.11–119.

Snyder, Carrie, 1866– , and Thurston, Ernest Lawton, 1873–
The universal system of practical bookkeeping. N. Y. Amer. bk. co. [c1902] 192p. 28½cm.
Another ed. Chic. Snyder, 1915. 192p. 27½cm.

Sweetland, Charles Augustus, 1854–
The science of loose leaf book-keeping and accounting. St. L. Sweetland [1902] 238p. 19½cm.
Another ed. [1904] 239p. 19½cm.
4th ed. Chic. System co. 1905. 239p. 21cm.

Tipson, Frederick Samson, 1858–
The theory of accounts. N. Y. Tipson [1902] 134p. 17½cm.
"This volume contains all questions set in the Theory of accounts paper at the New York state semi-annual examinations of certified public accountants from December, 1896 (the first examination held), to June, 1902, inclusive, with full answers and explanations."—Pref.

TIPSON (continued)
Another ed. 1912. 134p. 19½cm.
2d ed. N. Y. Mendoza bk. co. 1913. 216p. 19½cm.
3d ed. 1921. 271p. 19½cm.
Another ed. 1922. 271p. 19½cm.

WATTS, Charles J.
The cost of production. Muskegon, Mich. Shaw-Walker [c1902] 64p. 20cm.

1903

ARNOLD, Horace Lucian, d. 1915, compiler.
The factory manager and accountant; some examples of the latest American factory practice; collected and arranged by Horace Lucian Arnold (Henry Roland) N. Y. Engin. mag. 1903. 431p. 24½cm.
Another ed. 1905. 431p. 24½cm.

BAKER, James William, 1873–
Reference book: 20th century bookkeeping and office practice: a treatise on modern accounting and business customs as illustrated in the "Business transactions" which accompany this work. Knoxville, Tenn. Southern pub. co. 1903. 116p. 28cm.
Nine editions, all similar, published in rapid succession.
9th ed. Cin. South-western pub. co. 1911. 183p. 26½cm.
—20th century bookkeeping and accounting: a treatise on modern bookkeeping, accounting, and business customs; as illustrated in the "Business transactions" which accompany this work . . . Cin. South-western pub. co. 1912. 304p. 27cm.
A complete revision of "20th century bookkeeping and office practice . . ." listed above.
The second edition through the sixth edition followed with minor changes.
7th ed. 1917. 308p. 24½cm.
A complete revision of the first edition.
The eighth edition and ninth edition followed with minor changes.
10th ed. 1920. 308p. 24½cm.
A complete revision.
The eleventh edition through the fourteenth edition followed with minor changes.
—Bookkeeping exercises; developing the principles of debits and credits . . . 1921. 148p. 24½cm.
"Preliminary printing of the fifteenth edition. These exercises were printed in pamphlet form and tried out in a number of

schools before the fifteenth edition was published."—South-western publishing company.

—20th century bookkeeping and accounting: a treatise on the principles of accounting and bookkeeping practice applied by modern bookkeepers and accountants; 15th ed.; for use in all schools that teach bookkeeping and accounting . . . 1922. 384p. 24½cm.

A complete revision.

"For all of these editions books were available in different divisions. The text contained four parts. Each part was usually bound separately. There were also different combinations of the parts. For example, parts 1 and 2 were frequently combined as were parts 3 and 4."

"A practice set was available for each part with each edition. These sets were known as part 1, part 2, part 3, and part 4."—South-western publishing company.

—and PRICKETT, Alva Le Roy, 1890–

20th century bookkeeping and accounting; 16th ed. 1928. 490p. 24½cm.

A complete revision; edited by Earl Glen Blackstone.

"The sixteenth edition is not divided into parts like the previous editions and therefore the practice sets are not designated as parts. The sixteenth edition contains five practice sets which are numbered consecutively and are known by their numbers. For this edition there are also various work books."—South-western publishing company.

—Cost accounting; rev. ed.: a treatise on the principles of cost accounting applied by modern bookkeepers and accountants. [c1928] 139p. 24½cm.

"Up to the fourteenth edition '20th century cost accounting' was part 4 of '20th century bookkeeping and accounting.' With the publication of the fifteenth edition 'Cost accounting' was taken out of the regular bookkeeping text and was made a separate text. This separate text listed above is a revision of part 4 of the old editions of '20th century bookkeeping and accounting.' "—South-western publishing company.

—20th century accounting; college ed.; ed. by John F. Sherwood. [c1929] 364p. 24½cm.

"Four practice sets are available; one for each of the four parts of the text. Work books for each of the four parts have also been published."—South-western publishing company.

BEACH, Elmer Henry, 1861–1914, and THORNE, William Winter, 1870–

The science and practice of auditing. Detroit, Book-keeper pub. co. 1903. 76p. 25½cm.

This work was not copyrighted until 1906.

FOELLER, Joseph Paul, 1860–

A short and practical illustration of double entry book-keeping;

FOELLER (continued)
general country store, milling, and the modern method of division of ledger, general and personal . . . Belleville, Ill. [c1903] 35p. 21x17cm.

GOODWIN, Phillip C.
Bookkeeping self-taught . . . including accounts in illustration, exercises for practice, and a glossary of commercial terms. Chic. F. J. Drake [1903] 127p. 20cm.

HASKINS, Charles Waldo, 1852–1903.
How to keep household accounts: a manual of family finance. N. Y. Harper, 1903. 116+[1]p. 17½cm.

HIRSCH, Adolph.
The science of commercial bookkeeping; explanation of the various systems, their principles and practical application; with special reference to condensed bookkeeping and many practical devices for the use of bookkeepers, business-men, and instructors. [N. Y. The author, c1903] 139p. 21cm.
Another ed. N. Y. J. S. Ogilvie, 1910. 139p. 21cm.

KIRKMAN, Marshall Monroe, 1842–1921.
Surplus material and track accounts; the collection of scrap and surplus articles and an effective method for keeping the accounts of track material, tools, labor, etc., and making returns thereof; supplement to The science of railways . . . N. Y. World railway pub. co. 1903. 67p. 19cm.
Another ed. 1904. 67p. 20cm.

—Track accounts and returns; supplement to The science of railways. N. Y. World railway pub. co. 1903. 39p. 19½cm.

MARSHALL, Carl Coran, 1852–
Marshall's double entry drills: a course of practice exercises in journalizing and in opening and closing double entry accounts. Cedar Rapids, Ia. Goodyear-Marshall pub. co. 1903. 60p. 27½cm.
6th ed. 1911. 60p. 27½cm.
9th ed. 1920. 60p. 27½cm.

ROBERTS, Isaac Phillips, 1833–
The farmer's business handbook: a manual of simple farm accounts and of brief advice on rural law. N. Y. Macmillan, 1903. 300p. 18cm. (Rural science ser.)
Rural law, by H. D. Mason.
4th ed. 1911. 300p. 19½cm.
6th ed. 1913. 300p. 19½cm.

UNTERBRINK, John Roman, 1869–
The bookkeeping owl; or, Practical bookkeeping explained; designed for the use of the general reader. Valparaiso, Ind. Wade & Wise, 1903. 102p. 15½cm.

1904

BROAKER, Frank.
The technique of accountics; lessons 1–20. [N. Y. c1904] 262p. 33½x20cm.
Twenty parts in one volume.
Contains examination questions taken from the New York C.P.A. examinations.

BRYANT, Henry Willis, 1855–
Bryant's practical book-keeping: a new work on the theory and practice of accountancy; for the use of business colleges, graded, normal, and high schools. [Chic. Bryant & Stratton business college] 1904. 116p. 23½cm.
Other eds. 1906; 1907. 116p. 23½cm.
Other eds. 1910; 1913; 1920. 110p. 23½cm.

DRAUGHON, James William.
Draughon's practical accountant and commercial law: a system of actual business from the start . . . [Fort Worth, Tex. Speer print. co. 1904] 176+[2]p. 22cm.

FROST, Edward Allin, and TALBERT, Joseph T.
System of accounts for receivers of national banks, 1904: a handbook of general and technical information relating to the books and accounts to be kept by receivers of national banks; 1st ed. Chic. Lawyer's co-operative pub. co. [1904] 63p. 22½cm.

HALL, Harry Lovinas Cephas, 1866–
Manufacturing cost. Detroit, Book-keeper pub. co. 1904. 191p. 20½cm. (Office library)
Another ed. Detroit, Business man's pub. co. 1907. 191p. 20½cm. (Office library)

HOOKLAND, Seibert S., 1864– , and HAYWARD, William Richart, 1868–
Inductive bookkeeping and business practice; for use in public and private schools; introductory course. Phil. Hookland & Hayward [1904] 147p. 28½cm.

MEREDITH, Reuben Leslie.
Practical exercises in higher accounting; for advanced students in commercial high schools, business colleges, and for the practical book-keeper; part 1. [Zanesville, Ohio] c1904. 59p. 22½cm.
Cover-title: Exercises in accounting.

MILLER, O. L.
Miller's system of bookkeeping and business; a student's manual of instruction; a young bookkeepers' ready reference; a teachers' assistant . . . Seattle, Acme text-bk. co. 1904.
179+[2]p. 27½cm.
Another ed. Seattle, Seattle business college, 1907.
108p. 31cm.
Abridged edition.

MOORE, John C.
Moore's modern methods; containing . . . valuable information on the science of bookkeeping and loose leaf accounting. Rochester, N. Y. Moore [1904?] 80p. 22cm.

STRAYER, S. Irving, 1867–
Modern bookkeeping: a drill book containing a complete course of lessons in bookkeeping and a large amount of carefully selected practice work; designed especially for use in business colleges, high schools, normal schools, academies, and the higher grades of public and private schools; also for use as a reference book. Balt. Modern text-bk. co. 1904. 164p. 27x20½cm.

THORNE, William Winter, 1870–
Thorne's twentieth century book-keeping and business practice. Detroit, Book-keeper pub. co. 1904. 384p. 27½cm.
Another ed. Detroit, Business man's pub. co. 1910.
384p. 27½cm.
Published under the title: "The international accountants' manual; or, Twentieth century bookkeeping and business practice." It is a reprint without Thorne's name on the title-page.

TIPSON, Frederick Samson, 1858–
Auditing. N. Y. Tipson [c1904] 129p. 17½cm.
"This volume contains all questions set in the Auditing paper at the New York state semi-annual examinations for certified public accountants from December, 1896 (the date of the first examination held), to June, 1902, inclusive, with full answers and explanations."—Pref.

1905

BEAN, Burt Clifford, 1874– , editor.
The cost of production: the principles of the science of costs; with illustrative examples by cost experts for various lines of manufacturing industry; collected and ed. by B. C. Bean; enl. ed. Chic. System co. 1905. 198p. 21cm. (Business man's library, v.3)
Contents.—pt.1. The science of costs: utility of a cost system. Development of the science of costs. Elements of the science of costs. Selling price, the factors composing it. Material. Labor. Burden. Indirect labor. Minor burden elements. Depreciation, upkeep, and other factors. Selling expense. The factors of selling expense. Profit.—pt.2. Illustrative cost systems: a factory cost system [by] E. C. Warren. Regarding factory costs [by] L. A. Ely. The cost of wood working. Ascertaining the cost of production [by] E. J. Hathaway. How factory costs are found [by] N. W. Charles. The cost of production [by] Charles J. Watts.
Other eds. 1907; 1908; 1909; 1910; 1913; 1916.
196p. 21½cm. (Business man's library, v.3)
Contents vary.

BOGLE, Artemas Melvin, 1860–
Comprehensive bookkeeping; a first book . . . N. Y. Macmillan, 1905. 142p. 24cm. (Macmillan's commercial ser.)
Other eds. 1908; 1911; 1919. 142p. 24cm.

BOOK-KEEPER PUBLISHING COMPANY, LTD., Detroit.
Improved balance system of cost accounting. Detroit, Bookkeeper pub. co. c1905. 48p.

BUCHANAN, William, 1853–
The journal dictionary and bookkeepers' proof book; based on laws and principles of commercial science; designed for use in the counting room and business office, high school, and college. Cleveland, W. D. Browning, 1905. 534p. 23cm. (Buchanan's commercial ser.)

BYRNE, Henry Edward, 1870–
Byrne practical bookkeeping; 5th ed. Tyler, Tex. Byrne pub. co. [c1905] 90p. 22½cm.
This work may be a revised edition of the work published in 1895.

CLEARY, P. Roger.
Study and practice of business bookkeeping and accounting: a complete system of commercial training for business colleges, high schools, and private use. Ypsilanti, Mich. Cleary pub. co. [c1905] 216p. 27½cm.

DARBY, Willis W., and RAGLAND, Alphonso.
Darby & Ragland's practical bookkeeping: a complete text book on the latest methods of practical accounting; containing invaluable information for students, bookkeepers, and office men. [Dallas, Darby & Ragland, c1905] 203p. 27cm.

EATON, Abijah H., 1840–1917, STALEY, H. N., and DIXON, J. W.
Corporation bookkeeping; rev. and enl.; embodying not only all of the details from the organization of a joint stock co. to the declaration of dividend, but embracing the voucher system of accounting, illustrating the voucher and voucher register for mercantile and manufacturing business; 2d ed. Balt. Eaton, 1905. 72p. 26cm.
On cover: Corporation and voucher bookkeeping.
The first edition could not be found.

HYANS, Edward Malcolm, 1878–
Theory of accounts for accountant students. N. Y. Universal business institute, c1905. 144p. 22½cm.
Other eds. 1908; 1909; 1916; 1918. 208p. 22cm.

INTERNATIONAL TEXTBOOK COMPANY, Scranton.
Single-entry bookkeeping; double-entry bookkeeping; opening, closing, and changing books; corporation organization and bookkeeping; elements of cost accounting; bank bookkeeping. Scranton, International textbk. co. [c1904–05] Various pagings, 23cm. (International library of technology, v.59)
This work is v.59 of the series of volumes comprising the "International library of technology" issued for general distribution. Each volume was printed from the plates used in printing the texts for the exclusive use of students enrolled in the International correspondence schools. The books were not issued simultaneously. The first volume of the series appeared in 1902; the first on accounting was issued in 1905. There were many revisions of each work and portions of some texts appeared combined with new text matter on accounting under new titles and volume numbers. It is impossible to keep track of all the revisions.
Some of the text matter in the "International library of technology" was also used in the new series called the Blue book series, titles of which appear in this bibliography in 1922, 1923, 1924, 1926, and 1931.

LYONS, James A., 1861–1920.
Wholesale accounting; being a comprehensive, scientific, and teachable presentation of a method of bookkeeping; adapted to wholesaling in general and to the grocery business in particular; to be worked in connection with the vouchers of the transaction. [Chic.] Powers & Lyons [c1905] 37p. 26½cm.
—and SMITH, Oliver Saxton, 1881–

Wholesale accounting . . . [rev. ed.] Chic. Lyons & Carnahan [c1920] 51p.+forms, 35cm.

LYONS, James A., 1861–1920, and WHIGAM, Wallace Hugh, 1860–
Modern accountant; designed for the use of schools and for private study. Chic. Powers & Lyons [c1905] 130p. 25cm.
"The work of 'Modern accountant' is elementary. It brings the student up to the point where he is ready for 'Wholesale accounting.' "

LYONS, James A., 1861–1920, and READ, Walter L.
Modern accountant; rev. Chic. J. A. Lyons [c1911] 168p. 25½cm.
"A complete revision of the old 'Modern accountant.' It is not a revision in the common acceptation of the word for the text has been entirely rewritten. The method of presentation and general plan of development . . . has been retained."

MOULL, John.
Auditing for accountant students. N. Y. Universal business institute, 1905. 71p. 22cm.
Other eds. 1908; 1918. 140p. 22½cm.

MULHALL, John Francis Joseph, 1862–
Quasi-public corporation accounting and management. Bost. Corporation pub. co. [c1905] 198p.+3 l. 24½cm.

RENN, George Benton, 1862–
Practical auditing: a working manual for auditors; describing the details of a commercial audit in progressive steps from the proper point of beginning through to completion; with general notes on auditing. Chic. Renn [c1905] 32p. 23cm.
2d ed. [c1907] 130p. 23cm.
3d ed. [c1907] 130p. 23cm.
3d ed. [c1909] 130p. 23cm.

RYAN, George Weiser, 1875–
Bookkeeping for the plumber. Pittsburgh, Standard sanitary mfg. co. 1905. 60+[2]p. 20cm.
"Published in Modern sanitation from September, 1904, to April, 1905, inclusive."
2d ed. 1909. 58p. 19½cm.
2d ed. 1910. 58p. 20cm.

SNYDER, William Thomas.
A brief exposition of the fundamental principles of bookkeeping; with a complete guide to corporation bookkeeping. Charlottes-

SNYDER (continued)
ville, Va. [Conway print. co.] 1905. 51p. 22cm.
Cover-title: Guide to bookkeeping.

STEINER, Harry Lee, 1865–
How to keep farm accounts; a practical book for the practical farmer. Toledo, Steiner, 1905. 148+[2]p. 26½cm.
2d ed. 1908. 150+[2]p. 26½cm.
3d ed. 1909. 152+[2]p. 24cm.

STUART, Eden Burroughs, 1876–
A money-making system for the employing printer: a book describing a simple, economical, yet practical system for ascertaining the cost of producing printing. Marshall, Mich. Statesman print. & pub. co. 1905. 99p. 18cm.

WOLFF, Arthur, 1870–
Practical accounting; problems for accountant students. N. Y. Universal business institute, 1905. 66p. 22cm.
Other eds. 1908; 1910; 1918. 167p. 22½cm.

1906

BROCKWAY, Walter Belding, 1870–
Electric railway accounting; the monthly report, the accounting department, and the accountant. N. Y. McGraw, 1906. 84p. 20½cm.

COOK, Charles Bannister, 1875–
Factory management. Detroit, Book-keeper pub. co. 1906. 215p. 20cm.

DELAY, David W.
DeLay's manual of bookkeeping, up-to-date, practical, theoretical; a vade-mecum for the business man and clerk; containing many short and valuable methods. Mattoon, Ill. Gazette print. co. c1906. 98p. 23cm.

GOODYEAR, Lloyd Earnest, 1867–
Goodyear's bank accounting; tablet method. Cedar Rapids, Ia. Goodyear-Marshall pub. co. 1906. 68p. 27½cm.

KING, Thomas.
Expert King's double entry bookkeeping manual; business pointers and the secret of success . . . [N. Y.] 1906. 113p. 19½cm.

KIRKMAN, Marshall Monroe, 1842–1921.
Collection of revenue and other fiscal affairs . . . forming one of the series of volumes comprised in the Revised and enlarged edition of The science of railways; edition 1906. N. Y. World railway pub. co. 1906. 470p. 20cm.
Another ed. 1907. 470p. 20cm.

—General accounts and cash and how handled at headquarters . . . forming one of the series of volumes comprised in the Revised and enlarged edition of The science of railways; edition 1906. N. Y. World railway pub. co. 1906. 395p. 20cm.
Another ed. 1907. 395p. 20cm.

—Passenger train traffic and accounts . . . forming one of the series of volumes comprised in the Revised and enlarged edition of The science of railways; edition 1906. N. Y. World railway pub. co. 1906. 616p. 20cm.
Another ed. 1907. 616p. 20cm.

—Safeguarding railway expenditures . . . forming one of the series of volumes comprised in the Revised and enlarged edition of The science of railways; edition 1906. N. Y. World railway pub. co. 1906. 551p. 20cm.
Another ed. 1907. 551p. 20cm.

PRINCE, William Layphayette, 1874–
New practical bookkeeping and short system of double entry: a text book for the million. Huntingdon, Tenn. Southern pub. co. 1906. 109+[1]p. 24cm.

THOMPSON-BROWN COMPANY, Boston.
The forms of hospital financial reports . . . Bost. Thompson-Brown, 1906.
A copy of the first edition was not located.
—The forms of hospital financial reports and statistics outlined on the following pages, showing desirable forms to work to if uniformity in such matters is to be obtained, are recommended to other hospitals by the New York hospital, the Presbyterian hospital, the Roosevelt hospital, etc., in New York City, and by the Massachusetts general hospital, Boston, and Christ hospital, Jersey City, N. J.; rev. August, 1908. Bost. Thompson-Brown [1908] 78p. 24cm.
Cover-title: Hospital accounting and statistics.
—Hospital accounting and statistics; 3d ed.; comp. and arranged by William V. S. THORNE. N. Y. E. P. Dutton, 1916. 93p. 24cm.
(THORNE, William Van Schoonhoven, 1865–1920, compiler)

THOMPSON-BROWN COMPANY (continued)

"The third edition differs slightly from the previous August, 1908, edition."—Pref.

4th ed. 1918. 119p. 24cm.

(Thorne, William Van Schoonhoven, 1865–1920, compiler)

THORNE, William Winter, 1870–

The abolition of the trial balance; together with twelve studies in book-keeping and accounting . . . Detroit, Book-keeper pub. co. [c1906] 168p. 24cm.

VYE, John Alexander, 1867–

Farm accounts: a manual for farmers and those desiring a simple method of keeping accounts; prepared for the classes of the School of agriculture, University of Minnesota; and adapted to high schools and business colleges. St. Paul, The author [c1906] 141p. 23½cm.

2d ed. 1910. 141p. 24cm.

1907

BOOTH, W. Vernon, and others.

Accounting and office methods; the organization and functions of the various departments of an office—modern accounting systems—how reports may be made to show the executive all details—reports on the condition of a business—how to arrange an office for greatest efficiency—the cost of office work [by] W. Vernon Booth, Marshall D. Wilber, Eugene M. Elliott, William E. Wilson, and other contributors. Chic. System co. 1907. 136+45p. 22½cm. (Business man's library, v.10)

CLARENBACH, Ernst, 1875– , and WILLY, John.

Clarenbach system of hotel accounting: hotel monthly patented room rack-ledger system, by John Willy; Clarenbach system of hotel accounting, by Ernst Clarenbach; specially ruled hotel blank books, by John Willy. Chic. Hotel monthly, c1907. 46p. 30½cm.

Another ed. 1911. 46p. 30½cm.

Another ed. [c1930] 66p. 31cm.

CLEARY, P. Roger.

Student's guide to the Cleary system of business, bookkeeping, accounting, and auditing; for every school and college where bookkeeping is taught; part 1 [and part 2] Ypsilanti, Mich. Cleary [c1907–08] 2v. 25cm.

Part 2 published also in separate sections.

Another ed. [c1909] 2v. 24½cm.

CROXTON, Oscar Charles, 1873–
Short cuts to practical bookkeeping. Columbia, S. C. State co. 1907. 44p. 16½cm.

DEYO, Willet Abram, 1874–
A manual for actual business practise in high schools . . . Kewanna, Ind. [c1907] 43p. 21cm.

ELLIS, Carlos Bent, 1860–1935.
Practical bookkeeping; with illustrations of the principal features of office practice. Bost. Allyn & Bacon [c1907] 252p. 23½cm.
Another ed. 1908. 252p. 23½cm.
—Reference book for use with Ellis's Practical bookkeeping. Bost. Allyn & Bacon [c1908] 149p. 18cm.

GOODYEAR, Samuel Horatio, and GOODYEAR, Lloyd Earnest, 1867–
Goodyear's higher accounting; a reference book for accountants and commercial teachers; a text book for students in advanced accounting methods. Cedar Rapids, Ia. Goodyear-Marshall pub. co. 1907. 112p. 28cm.
The contents of this work include Commission, Real estate and insurance, Banking, Corporation, Factory, and Railway accounting sets. Some of these sets published separately and reprinted several times.
Another ed. 1908. 112p. 28cm.
2d ed. 1909. 131+[1]p. 27½cm.
Another ed. [n.d.] 107p. 27½cm.
Another ed. [n.d.] 121p. 22cm.

—Wholesale accounting; with routine for office training. Cedar Rapids, Ia. Goodyear-Marshall pub. co. 1907. 26p. 27cm.

—and MARSHALL, Carl Coran, 1852–
Modern inductive bookkeeping; with business practice by office and tablet methods. Cedar Rapids, Ia. Goodyear-Marshall pub. co. 1907. 158p.+1 l. 28cm.
The text is published in two general editions, each of which is divided into parts 1 and 2. In the *regular edition,* part 1 consists of textbook drills in elementary and standard accounting forms and a business practice set arranged for either the office or tablet method. In the *actual business edition,* part 1 introduces business practice at the start, arranged for either the office or tablet method. Part 2 is the same in the two editions. It contains two sets of business practice.
Each part is also bound separately. Part 1 of the regular edition is called "The elements of bookkeeping." Part 1 of the actual business edition is called "New practical accounting." Part 2

GOODYEAR (continued)
of both editions, when bound in a separate volume, is called "Modern inductive bookkeeping—part 2."

ILLINOIS. UNIVERSITY.
Questions set at the examinations of candidates for the certificate of certified public accountant in Illinois, 1903–07. [Urbana, Ill. Univ. of Illinois, 1907] 65p. 20cm. (Bulletin, v.4, no.26)
—Questions set at the examinations of candidates for the certificate of certified public accountant in Illinois, 1903–12. [Urbana, Ill. Univ. of Illinois, 1912]
—Questions set at the examinations of candidates for the certificate of certified public accountant in Illinois, 1903–18. [Urbana, Ill. Univ. of Illinois, 1920] [247]p. 20cm.
Published also in the University of Illinois bulletin, v.18, no.22, 1921.

MCKINNEY, Winfield S.
Mercantile accounting: an advanced bookkeeping set with which modern forms are used and the latest practices are followed. Chic. Powers & Lyons [c1907] 59p. 25cm.

MURRAY, George Stanley, 1873–
Elements of accounts. Emporia, Kan. Murray, 1907. 92p. 24cm.

RISQUE, Ferdinand William, 1850–
Loose leaf books and systems for general business. St. L. Press of R. P. Studley, 1907. 174p. 22½x18cm.

VAN CLEVE, Charles McKinstry, 1852–
Theory of double-entry bookkeeping. [N. Y. J. Kempster print. co. c1907] 59+[1]p. 23cm.

WEBER, Fred Charles, 1873–
Introductory bookkeeping; arranged for use in the classes of the commercial department of the Los Angeles polytechnic high school. Los Angeles, The author, 1907. 66p. 22½cm.
This work was copyrighted, 1906.
2d ed. 1909. 58p. 22½cm.
Arranged for use in the classes of high school commercial departments and private commercial schools.
3d ed. 1911. 69p. 22cm.
—Bookkeeping and accountancy . . . arranged for use in the classes of high schools, intermediate schools, and private commercial schools; 5th ed. 1916. [257]p. 24½cm.
In five parts; each part has a special title-page.
6th ed. 1920. 275p. 24½cm.

1908

BENTLEY, Harry Clark, 1877–
Corporate finance and accounting; treating of the corporate finances and securities, the corporate books of account, reports, negotiable instruments, and the powers, duties, and relations of the corporation treasurer; with forms; legal notes by Thomas Conyngton. N. Y. Ronald, 1908. 525p. 24cm.
Another ed. 1911. 525p. 24cm.

BYRNE, Henry Edward, 1870–
Byrne bookkeeping for business colleges, high schools, and self instructions. Dallas, Byrne pub. co. 1908. 110p. 22½cm.
Other eds. 1914; 1918. 110p. 22½cm.
4th ed. 1923. 163p. 22cm.

CHURCH, Alexander Hamilton, 1866–
The proper distribution of expense burden. N. Y. Engin. mag. 1908. 116p. 20cm. (Works management library)
"The contents of this book appeared originally in the Engineering magazine as a series of articles."—Pref.
Another ed. 1908. 144p. 19½cm. (Industrial management library)
Other eds. 1912; 1913; 1916; 1921. 144p. 19cm. (Industrial management library)

COLE, William Morse, 1866–
Accounts; their construction and interpretation; for business men and students of affairs. Bost. Houghton Mifflin [1908] 345+[1]p. 23cm.
Another ed. [1908] 345+[1]p. 23cm.
Another ed. [c1915] 445+[1]p. 23cm.

CORNEIL, George Russel, 1872–
A text-book in bookkeeping for use in the common schools; arranged expressly for use in the common schools of the states following the 1907 Illinois state course of study. Litchfield, Ill. E. B. Lewis [1908] 79p. 23cm.

DAVIS, Walter, 1863–
Simple mine accounting. N. Y. Hill pub. co. 1908. 63p. 24cm.
Issued under the author's pseudonym, David Wallace.
2d ed. 1909. 63p. 24cm.
2d ed. N. Y. McGraw-Hill, 1909. 78p. 24cm.
Second edition with added material.

Day, Clarence Munro, 1870–
Accounting practice. N. Y. Appleton, 1908. 318p. 24½cm.
Other eds. 1915; 1920; 1924. 318p. 24½cm.

Forse, William Harry, 1876–
Electric railway auditing and accounting. N. Y. McGraw, 1908. 157p. 24½cm.

Lamb, Henry Grant, 1879–
Farm book-keeping: a practical book of instruction written particularly for use on the farm. N. Y. Thomas press, 1908. 69p. 19½cm.

Lyons, James A., 1861–1920.
Modern corporation accounting (voucher system) including instruction in corporate organization, methods of transacting business, and bookkeeping. Chic. Powers & Lyons [c1908] 80p. 25cm.

—The new complete accountant; designed for the use of schools and for private study. Chic. Powers & Lyons [c1908] 222p. 25cm.

Mayer, Clarence.
Telephone construction methods and cost . . . Chic. M. C. Clark, 1908. 281p. 23½cm.
Presents a simple, comprehensive, and practical system for collecting, analyzing, and recording telephone costs. *cf.* Pref.

Nelson, Richard James, 1858–
Nelson's new book-keeping: a text-book for schools and colleges and a book of reference for accountants; 1st ed. Cin. Cincinnati & Springfield pub. co. 1908. 330p. 27cm.

Pennsylvania. State board of examiners of public accountants.
Examination questions set at each examination from November, 1899, to November, 1907, inclusive; including also copy of the Pennsylvania C.P.A. act and the rules of the board of examiners. Phil. G. H. Buchanan, 1908. 158p.

Porte, Roy Trewin.
The practical cost system for printing offices. 1908.
This work was not located.
The foreword to the 1925 edition states: "The original edition of this 'Practical cost system' was the very first attempt ever made to put cost-finding for printing offices into book form. The first edition was prepared in 1908."

Another ed. Minneapolis, Minnesota cost system co. [19–?] 28p. 23½cm.
Another ed. Salt Lake City, Porte pub. co. c1920. 94p. 19½cm.
Another ed. [c1924] 159p. 19cm.
Another ed. [c1925] 159p. 19cm.

PRICE, WATERHOUSE & co., New York.
Treatment of maintenance and depreciation accounts in the new classification of accounts prescribed for railroads by the Interstate commerce commission; being a reprint of communications submitted to the Interstate commerce commission. N. Y. Price, Waterhouse [1908] 27p. 22cm.

SPEAR, Raymond Herbert, 1886– , editor.
The Commercial world encyclopedia of accounting; for bookkeepers, accountants, auditors, and business men; containing practical working forms and tables. Detroit, Commercial world pub. co. 1908. 2v. 28cm.
2d ed. [c1911] 2v. 24½cm.

SPRAGUE, Charles Ezra, 1842–1912.
The philosophy of accounts. N. Y. The author, 1908. 161p. 23½cm.
2d ed. 1908. 161p. 23½cm.
3d ed. 1910. 161p. 23½cm.
4th ed. 1913. 161p. 22cm.
4th ed. 1917. 161p. 22cm.
4th ed. 1918. 161p. 22cm.
4th ed. 1919. 161p. 22cm.
5th ed. 1922. 183p. 22cm.
5th ed. 1923. 183p. 22cm.

WOODS, Clinton Edgar.
Practical cost accounting for accountant students. N. Y. Universal business institute, 1908. 2v. 22cm.
Another ed. 1918. 2v. 22cm.

—Woods' reports on industrial organization, systematization, and accounting. N. Y. Woods pub. co. [c1908] 12 pamphlets, each 31½cm.
This work consists of twelve reports, each published separately, totalling 344 pages.
Charts and forms added to each report.
Other eds. 1909; 1914. 12 pamphlets, each 31½cm.

1909

Allen, George, 1833–1912.
The science of accounts made clear and simple: a text-book for use in the public schools; embracing single entry and double entry bookkeeping. Raleigh, N. C. Edwards & Broughton, 1909.
136p. 23cm.
High school edition.
Another ed. 1909. 65p. 23cm.
Graded school edition.

Barnett, Samuel.
Life insurance accounting. Louisville, Ky. Insurance field [c1909]
112p. 26cm.

Beversdorf, Allen A.
The self-instructing book-keeper . . . St. L. The author, 1909.
112p. 18cm.

Bexell, John Andrew, 1867–
The business side of farming; part 1, farm records: a text-book for students in agriculture and a manual for home-study. Corvallis, Or. Oregon agricultural college press, 1909. 71p. 23cm.
2d ed. 1911. 53p. 22½cm. (Oregon agricultural college bulletin, ser.1, no.33)

Bishop, William George, 1863–
A short course in business training; for normal schools, high schools, common schools, teachers, and independent students. Lincoln, Neb. Univ. pub. co. 1909. 85p. 22½cm.
Another ed. 1911. 124p. 22½cm.
Other eds. 1912; 1914. 149p. 22½cm.

Cleveland, Frederick Albert, 1865–
Chapters on municipal administration and accounting. N. Y. Longmans, Green, 1909. 361p. 20½cm.

Cooley, Morgan L.
American audit record [with blank forms] N. Y. Accountancy pub. co. [c1909] 72p.

Ellis publishing company, Battle Creek, Mich.
Bookkeeping outlines. Battle Creek, Mich. Ellis pub. co. [c1909]
56p. 29½cm.

GARRISON, Elisha Ely, 1871–
Accounting every business man should know. N. Y. Doubleday, Page, 1909. 188p. 19cm.
Other eds. 1910; 1912; 1915; 1919. 188p. 19cm.
Other eds. 1919; 1920. 214p. 19½cm.
—Principles of business accounting and business letters. [Garden City, N. Y.] Doubleday, Page, for the International business institute, 1925. 272p. 19½cm.

GILLETTE, Halbert Powers, 1869– , and DANA, Richard Turner, 1876–
Cost keeping and management engineering: a treatise for engineers, contractors, and superintendents engaged in the management of engineering construction. N. Y. M. C. Clark, 1909. 346p. 21½cm.
Another ed. 1916. 346p. 21½cm.
—Construction cost keeping and management . . . N. Y. McGraw-Hill, 1922. 572p. 21cm.
A revision with additions of the authors' "Cost keeping and management engineering" published in 1909 and reprinted in 1916. *cf.* Pref.

GOODYEAR, Samuel Horatio.
Goodyear's advanced accounting; with business practice by office and tablet methods. Cedar Rapids, Ia. Goodyear-Marshall pub. co. 1909. 114p. 28cm.
The contents of this work include three sets: Lumber accounting, Business practice in jobbing, and Special column books. These sets separately published and reprinted several times.

GREENDLINGER, Leo, 1879–
Accountancy problems with solutions; with introduction by John R. Loomis. N. Y. Accountancy pub. co. 1909–[c11] 2v. 23½cm.
v.1, 1909, 1st ed.; v.2, 1911, 1st ed.
"This treatise is the result of contributions made by the author and a number of other accountants to the Journal of accountancy."—Pref.
Vol.2 has title: "Accountancy problems with solutions . . . by Leo Greendlinger [and] legal notes by Charles W. Gerstenberg." N. Y. Business bk. bur. [c1911]
Another ed. N. Y. Business bk. bur. 1910–11. 2v. 24cm.
v.1, 1910, 2d ed.; v.2, 1911, 1st ed.
Another ed. 1911–13. 2v. 23½cm.
v.1, 1911, 3d ed.; v.2, 1913, 2d ed.

HATFIELD, Henry Rand, 1866–
Modern accounting; its principles and some of its problems. N. Y. Appleton, 1909. 367p. 20cm.

HATFIELD (continued)

Other eds. 1911; 1912; 1914; 1916; 1918; 1919; 1921; 1922; 1923. 367p. 20cm.

—Accounting; its principles and problems. N. Y. Appleton, 1927. 548p. 21cm.

A revised edition of "Modern accounting . . ." first published in 1909.

Other eds. 1928; 1929; 1930. 548p. 21cm.

LYONS, James A., 1861–1920, and READ, Walter L.

Bookkeeping from vouchers: a course in bookkeeping for beginners in which the transactions are based upon business papers. Chic. Lyons [c1909] 189p. 25cm.

—Lyons' bookkeeping: a course for beginners; parts 1 and 2. Chic. Lyons [c1909–10] 205+xixp. 25cm.

Parts 1 and 2 also published separately.

Another ed. Chic. Lyons & Carnahan [c1913] 216+xixp. 25cm.

MUSSELMAN, De Lafayette, 1879–

Musselman's bookkeeping for business colleges, schools, and private instructions. Quincy, Ill. Musselman [c1909] 73p. 27cm.

Another ed. [c1911] 111p. 27cm.
College edition.
Contents as in entry above; with additional sets.

Another ed. [c1911] 143p. 27cm.
Complete edition.
Contents as in entry above; with additional sets.

NICHOLSON, Jerome Lee, 1863–

Nicholson on factory organization and costs. N. Y. Kohl technical pub. co. 1909. 410p. 29cm.

Another ed. 1911. 410p. 29cm.

PENNSYLVANIA. STATE BOARD OF EXAMINERS OF PUBLIC ACCOUNTANTS.

Examination questions set at each examination from November, 1908, to November, 1909, inclusive; including also copy of the Pennsylvania C.P.A. act. Phil. G. H. Buchanan, 1909. 50p.

STEPHENS, John Rittenhouse, 1858–

Principles of accounting. Kansas City, Mo. Stephens, 1909. 91p. 21cm.

TUTT, R. G.

Telephone accounting. St. L. 1909. [27]p. 35x24½cm.

UNCKLESS, Leslie.
How to find manufacturing costs and selling costs. Detroit, Modern methods pub. co. [c1909] 90p. 20cm.

WEBER, Fred Charles, 1873–
Corporation bookkeeping: a text book for high schools and private commercial schools. Los Angeles, The author, 1909. 41p. 22½cm.

WIGHTMAN, William W., compiler.
Student's guide to the principles of bookkeeping. Battle Creek, Mich. Ellis pub. co. [c1909] 116p. 29½cm.
—Student's guide to the principles of bookkeeping in chart-form; 2d ed. 1909. 38p. 29½cm.

1910

AMERICAN SCHOOL OF CORRESPONDENCE, Chicago.
Cyclopedia of commerce, accountancy, business administration . . . prepared by a corps of auditors, accountants, attorneys, and specialists in business methods and management; illustrated with over two thousand engravings . . . Chic. Amer. school of correspondence, 1910. 10v. 25cm.
Such authors as Arthur Lowes Dickinson, James Bray Griffith, Charles E. Hathaway, E. C. Landis, William M. Lybrand, Frank Herbert Macpherson, Robert Hiester Montgomery, Jessie M. Shepherd, Charles Augustus Sweetland, and Hugh Wright wrote instruction papers and were, therefore, contributors to the cyclopedia.
Vol.2 and v.4–10 contain material which appeared originally in 1909 as instruction papers for the American school of correspondence students.
—Cyclopedia of practical accounting: a general reference work on accounting, bookkeeping, banking, office records, cost keeping, systematizing, etc.; prepared by accountants and specialists in business methods and management . . . Chic. Amer. technical soc. 1912. 4v. 25cm.
Reprinted from the "Cyclopedia of commerce, accountancy, business administration" issued by the American school of correspondence, Chicago, 1910.
—Accountancy and business management . . . prepared by a corps of auditors, accountants, attorneys, and specialists in business methods and management; illustrated with over fifteen hundred engravings . . . Chic. Amer. technical soc. 1920. 7v. 21½cm.
Vol.2 and v.4 contain material on accounting based on the material in v.4 and v.6 of the "Cyclopedia of commerce, accountancy, business administration . . ." published in 1910.

BAUGH, Frederick Henry, 1879– , and SCHMEISSER, William Christian.
Theory and practice of estate accounting for accountants, lawyers, executors, administrators, and trustees. Balt. M. Curlander, 1910. 321p. 23½cm.
Other eds. 1917; 1925. 321p. 23½cm.

CARNEGIE FOUNDATION FOR THE ADVANCEMENT OF TEACHING.
Standard forms for financial reports of colleges, universities, and technical schools . . . N. Y. [1910] 37p. 25½cm. (Bulletin no.3)
2d ed. [Bost. Merrymount press, 1921] 37p. 25½cm. (Bulletin no.3; 2d ed.)

CHASE, William Arthur, and others.
Auditing and cost accounting. Chic. LaSalle extension univ. 1910. 517p. 23½cm. (Business administration text-books)
Published also as v.2 of "Higher accountancy; principles and practice," under the supervision of William Arthur Chase and the managing editor, Samuel MacClintock, in 1911 and 1914.

CHURCH, Alexander Hamilton, 1866–
Production factors in cost accounting and works management. N. Y. Engin. mag. 1910. 187p. 19½cm. (Works management library)
First published in the Engineering magazine, Oct. 1909, to Apr. 1910. *cf.* Introd.
Another ed. 1919. 187p. 19½cm. (Works management library)

COLE, William Morse, 1866–
Accounting and auditing. Minneapolis, Cree pub. co. 1910. 479p. 24½cm.
At head of title: Business, commerce, and finance.
Another ed. 1912. 479p. 24½cm.
—Bookkeeping, accounting, and auditing. Chic. Washington institute [c1914] 479p. 24½cm.
At head of title: Business, commerce, and finance.
—Accounting and auditing. Chic. Home study pub. co. [c1915] 479p. 24cm.
At head of title: The concise business course.
—Bookkeeping, accounting, and auditing. Chic. National institute of business [c1915] 479p. 23cm.
At head of title: International business library.
Another ed. Chic. Lincoln institute of business [c1921] 479p. 23cm.
Lettered on cover: Business library. Lincoln institute of business.

DEWHIRST, John Mark, 1875–
Elements of bookkeeping; designed for class instruction . . . Galesburg, Ill. Wagoner print. co. 1910. 63p. 28cm.

GOODWIN, Frank Elbert, 1867–
Cost accounting pathfinder. St. L. Midland pub. co. 1910. 128p. 17½cm.
7th ed. 1910. 267p. 19½cm.

GOODYEAR, Lloyd Earnest, 1867–
Progressive business accounting: an elementary course in bookkeeping business practice, forms, and usages; for commercial schools and individual reference. Waterloo, Ia. Waterloo systems co. [1910] 148+[6]p.+1 l. 26cm.
Another ed. Cedar Rapids, Ia. Goodyear-Marshall pub. co. [c1912] 146+[8]p. 26cm.

GRIFFITH, James Bray, 1871–
Corporation accounts and voucher system: a working handbook of approved methods of corporation accounting; with special reference to records of stock issues, manufacturers' accounts, and the use of the voucher system; part 1—Corporation accounts; part 2—Voucher system accounting charts. Chic. Amer. school of correspondence, 1910. 76+51+vp. 25cm. (American accountants' library)
Each part was published in 1909 as an instruction paper for the American school of correspondence students.
Another ed. 1914. 76+51+vp. 25cm. (American accountants' library)
Other eds. Chic. Amer. technical soc. 1918; 1919. 76+51+vp. 21½cm. (American accountants' library)

—Practical bookkeeping: a working handbook of elementary bookkeeping and approved modern methods of accounting; including single proprietorship, partnership, wholesale, commission, storage, and brokerage accounts. Chic. Amer. school of correspondence, 1910. 288p. 25cm. (American accountants' library)
The contents of this work appeared in 1909 as instruction papers for the American school of correspondence students.
Other eds. 1913; 1914. 287p. 24cm. (American accountants' library)
Another ed. Chic. Amer. technical soc. 1916. 284p. 24½cm. (American accountants' library)
Other eds. 1917; 1918; 1919. [264]p. 21½cm. (American accountants' library)

HATHAWAY, Charles E., and GRIFFITH, James Bray, 1871–
Factory accounts: a working handbook of departmental organization and methods as applied to factories; with special reference to purchase, stores, labor records, manufacturing orders, general expense distribution, and cost accounts . . . Chic. Amer. school of correspondence, 1910. 207p. 25cm. (American accountants' library)
The contents of this work appeared in 1909 as instruction papers for the American school of correspondence students.
Another ed. 1913. 207p. 25cm. (American accountants' library)

HEITMANN, Henry.
A course in the theory and practice of higher accounting; prepared for students of Eastman college. Poughkeepsie, N. Y. Eastman college, 1910. 240p. 22cm.
This work was also issued for general distribution.

INTERNATIONAL TEXTBOOK COMPANY, Scranton.
The bookkeeper's handbook: a convenient reference book for bookkeepers and business men. Scranton, International textbk. co. 1910. 302p. 14cm.
Another ed. 1911. 302p. 14cm.
2d ed. 1920. 302p. 14cm.

KAIB, Daniel Joseph, 1869–
Bookkeeping for parish priests: a treatise on accounting, business forms, and business laws; designed for the use of the Catholic clergy and as a text-book in seminaries. Milw. M. H. Wiltzius, 1910. 129p. 20½cm.
2d ed. Cin. Mountel press, 1916. 137p. 21½cm.
3d ed. Latrobe, Pa. Archabbey press, 1931. 154p. 21cm.

LOUGHRY, James Cooper, 1868–
How to install a foundry cost system. N. Y. W. W. White mfg. co. c1910. 41p. 19½x24½cm.
Complete set of practical foundry cost records also copyrighted in 1906 and published in 1907.

ROWE, Harry Marc, 1860–1926.
Bookkeeping and accountancy; presenting the art of bookkeeping in accordance with the principles of modern accountancy [with] script by C. P. Zaner. Balt. Rowe [c1910] 263p. 23½cm.
The text is accompanied by four practice sets: Elementary set, Wholesale set, Corporation set, and Cost accountancy for manu-

facturers, each consisting of a budget, blank books, and outgoing papers. "Advanced text" contained in this work separately published.

Other eds. 1911; 1918; 1920; 1921; 1927. 264p. 23cm. Practice sets designed to accompany each edition of this work.

—Bookkeeping and accountancy . . . Balt. Sadler-Rowe [c1910] 190p. 23½cm.

Abridged text.

RUSSELL, Thomas Herbert, 1862– , and JACKMAN, William James, 1850–

Bookkeeping, accounting, and auditing. Minneapolis, International law & business institute [c1910] 409+[6]p. 24½cm. (International business library . . . v.12)

Another ed. Chic. National institute of business [c1911] 409+[6]p. 24½cm. (Practical business library . . . v.12)

Other eds. 1912; 1916. 409+[6]p. 24½cm.

SWEETLAND, Charles Augustus, 1854–

Bank bookkeeping: a working handbook of bookkeeping and accounting methods in use in modern banks; including departmental organization and the duties of officers and clerks. Chic. Amer. school of correspondence, 1910. 140p. 25cm. (American accountants' library)

The content of this work appeared in 1909 as an instruction paper for the American school of correspondence students.

Other eds. 1912; 1914. 140p. 25cm. (American accountants' library)

This work is also contained in v.9 of "Practical business administration," an encyclopedia published by the American technical society in 1927, 1929, 1932, and 1934.

—Department store accounts: a working handbook of retail accounting methods; including the best simple account systems for the small retailer, bookkeeping for general stores, and methods of management of the largest department stores; part 1—Department store accounts; part 2—Retailers' accounts. Chic. Amer. school of correspondence, 1910. 118+61+viiip. 25cm. (American accountants' library)

Each part published in 1909 as an instruction paper for the American school of correspondence students.

Another ed. 1913. 118+61+viiip. 25cm. (American accountants' library)

SWEETLAND (continued)
—Insurance and real estate accounts: a working handbook of modern methods of accounting and office routine as used in the offices and agencies of insurance companies and by dealers in real estate; part 1—Insurance accounts; part 2—Real estate accounting. Chic. Amer. school of correspondence, 1910. 154+46+viiip. 25cm. (American accountants' library)
Each part published in 1909 as an instruction paper for the American school of correspondence students.

WHIGAM, Wallace Hugh, 1860– , and FREDERICK, Oliver Detwiler, 1864–
Bookkeeping and business practice. Bost. Heath, 1910. 142p. 23½cm.

WILLIS, Henry Parker, 1874– , and others.
Accounting theory and practice. Chic. LaSalle extension univ. 1910. 545p. 23½cm. (Business administration text-books)
Published also as v.2 of "Higher accountancy; principles and practice," under the supervision of William Arthur Chase and the managing editor, Samuel MacClintock, in 1911 and 1914.

WOLFE, Samuel Herbert, 1874–
The examination of insurance companies; a series of talks to the members of his office staff. N. Y. Insurance press, 1910. 248p. 24cm.

1911

BENTLEY, Harry Clark, 1877–
The science of accounts: a presentation of the underlying principles of modern accounting; designed as a work of reference for accountants and as a text book for advanced students of accountancy. N. Y. Ronald, 1911. 393p. 23½cm.
Another ed. 1913. 393p. 23½cm.

BEXELL, John Andrew, 1867–
Farm accounting and business methods . . . Springfield, Mass. Home correspondence school, 1911. 161p. 23cm.

BLUIM, J. M.
The accounting system of an ice company. [Cleveland, Press of the J. B. Savage co.] c1911. 104p. 28½cm.

BUNNELL, Sterling Haight, 1871–
Cost-keeping for manufacturing plants. N. Y. Appleton, 1911. 232p. 24½cm.

CAMPBELL, Thomas Findley, 1860–
Campbell's actual accounting; an apprenticeship in business; the modern method of instruction in elementary and advanced accounting, business forms, and business customs. Indianapolis, Bobbs-Merrill, 1911. 135p. 29cm.
Another ed. [c1912] 267p. 28½cm.

CHASE, William Arthur.
C.P.A. examinations and how to pass them; also examination questions as set by various state boards of examiners; this treatise forms part of a course in higher accountancy, under supervision of William Arthur Chase . . . managing editor, Samuel MacClintock. Chic. LaSalle extension univ. [c1911] 89p. 23cm.
Another ed. 1915. 93p. 23½cm.

COUNTY, Albert John, 1871–
Railway accounts and statistics. Chic. LaSalle extension univ. [c1911] 67p. 22½cm.

DENHAM, Robert Scudder, 1871–
The science of cost-finding applied to factories making products to special or shop orders. Cleveland, Denham costfinding co. [1911] 104p. 15½cm.
Another ed. 1914. 104p. 15½cm.

EVANS, Holden A.
Cost keeping and scientific management. N. Y. McGraw-Hill, 1911. 252p. 24cm.

FREEMAN, Charles Edmund, 1855–
Adjustments through elimination; including a detailed explanation of why trial balance totals vary. Indianapolis, Freeman [c1911] [49]p. 21cm.

GOODYEAR, Lloyd Earnest, 1867–
Farm accounting for the practical farmer. Cedar Rapids, Ia. Goodyear-Marshall pub. co. 1911. 36p. 27½cm.

LOCKYEAR, Melvin H.
An introductory course: Lockyear's bookkeeping [with] script il-

LOCKYEAR (continued)
lustrations by F. B. Courtney. N. Y. Gregg [c1911] 105p. 22½cm.
This work was first copyrighted in 1907 by Lockyear.
Another ed. 1931. 105p. 22½cm.

PRIOR, Frank Samuel, 1882–
Office methods for the plumber: a model text book dealing with office management for the plumber. [Akron, Ohio, Commercial print. co. c1911] 47p. 23cm.

SEITZ, Jacob Charles, 1878–
A system and accounting for a life insurance company. N. Y. Spectator co. 1911. 112p. 24x31½cm.
2d ed. 1931. 190p. 33x24cm.

WEBNER, Frank Erastus, 1865–
Factory costs: a work of reference for cost accountants and factory managers. N. Y. Ronald, 1911. 611p. 23½cm.

WILDMAN, John Raymond, 1878–
Cost accounting. N. Y. Accountancy pub. co. 1911. 106p. 19½cm.
—Principles of cost accounting. N. Y. N. Y. univ. press, 1914. 96p. 23½cm.
Revised edition of "Cost accounting."
Another ed. 1916. 96p. 23½cm.

1912

BENNETT, Robert Joseph, 1871–
Bookkeeping and accounting exercises . . . N. Y. Amer. bk. co. [c1912] 2v. 20½cm.

BLISS, Fred H., 1861–1912.
Bliss system of bookkeeping and office practice [with] script by E. C. Mills. Saginaw, Mich. Bliss [c1912] 154p. 27½cm.
Book of forms to be used with the Bliss system . . . separately published.
Other eds. 1913; 1920. 188p. 27½cm.

BROTHERS OF THE CHRISTIAN SCHOOLS.
First steps in bookkeeping. Glencoe, Mo. LaSalle institute, 1912. 68p. 25½cm.

CAROLINA PUBLIC SERVICE COMPANY, Columbia, S. C.
Classification of accounts, Carolina public service company, Columbia, South Carolina. [Atlanta, La Hatte print. co. 1912] 46p. 23cm.

CHARLTON, William Hurst, 1875–
American mine accounting . . . N. Y. McGraw-Hill [c1912] 367p. 23cm.
Other eds. 1912; 1913. 367p. 24cm.

DAVENPORT, Reginald Arthur, 1879–
The railroad traveling auditor's work and methods, theory and practice; treats fully and authoritatively upon the subject of auditing station accounts at stations. [San Fran. H. S. Crocker] 1912. 66 numb. l. 16cm.
Leaves printed on rectos only; versos ruled for notes.

DAY, Clarence Munro, 1870–
Silk mill costs. N. Y. Day, 1912. 70p. 19½cm.

ELLIS PUBLISHING COMPANY, Battle Creek, Mich.
Business directions used in connection with Ellis industrial bookkeeping; a direct didactic method of presenting mercantile, manufacturing, and corporation bookkeeping and business methods . . . Battle Creek, Mich. Ellis pub. co. [c1912] 75p. 23½cm.
Other eds. 1919; 1920. 75p. 23½cm.

JOBSON, Walter Paxton, 1886–
An accounting system for printing concerns. Louisville, Ky. Press of Jobson print. co. [c1912] 76p. 25cm.
Another ed. [c1914] 106p. 24cm.

JOYCE, Bryan Pope, 1885–
The Joyce system of cost keeping; designed for the use of contractors, architects, and engineers. [Kansas City, Mo. Walkenhorst & Park print. co.] c1912. [29]p. 43cm.

LYONS, James A., 1861–1920.
The Lyons accounting; series A. Chic. Powers & Lyons, 1912.
The publishers have bound in one cover the following four books which were previously issued separately:
1. Modern accountant; rev. 1911.
2. Wholesale accounting. 1905.
3. Mercantile accounting. 1907.
4. Modern corporation accounting. 1908.

LYONS (continued)

—The Lyons accounting; series B. Chic. Powers & Lyons, 1912.

The publishers have bound in one cover the following four books which were previously issued separately:

1. Lyons' bookkeeping; part 1. 1909.
2. Lyons' bookkeeping; part 2. 1910.
3. Wholesale accounting. 1905.
4. Modern corporation accounting. 1908.

MEREDITH, Arthur John, 1874–

Meservey's new bookkeeping and manual of business forms. Bost. Thompson, Brown, 1912. 276p. 23½cm.

"The material used has come from two sources: Meservey's 'Bookkeeping, single and double entry,' his 'Manual of bookkeeping and banking,' and also from the writer's experiences as a teacher of the subject."—Pref.

MINER, George Washington, 1860–

Bookkeeping; introductory course. Bost. Ginn [c1912] 126p. 24cm. (Moore and Miner ser.)

—Bookkeeping; introductory course and intermediate course. Bost. Ginn [c1912] 248+xxxp. 24cm. (Moore and Miner ser.)

Another ed. [c1916] 248+xxxp. 24cm. (Moore and Miner ser.)

—Bookkeeping; intermediate and advanced courses. Bost. Ginn [c1912] 218p. 24cm. (Moore and Miner ser.)

Another ed. [c1916] 218+xxxviiip. 24cm. (Moore and Miner ser.

—Bookkeeping; complete course. Bost. Ginn [c1912] 334p. 24cm. (Moore and Miner ser.)

Another ed. [1916] 334p. 24cm. (Moore and Miner ser.)

MONTGOMERY, Robert Hiester, 1872–

Auditing theory and practice. N. Y. Ronald, 1912. 673p. 23½cm.

Another ed. 1913. 673p. 24cm.

2d ed. 1916. 889p. 22cm.

Other eds. 1917; 1919; 1920. 781p. 22cm.
Appendix on the Federal income tax excluded.

3d ed. 1921–22. 2v. 22cm.
"In many respects this is a new book rather than a new edition. In rewriting the part relating to general principles, I have retained much of the old text, because it is not obsolete. There are about two hundred pages of new text . . . In

the first volume general principles are discussed; the second volume is devoted to audit procedures that are applicable to various classes of business."—Pref.

4th ed. [c1927] 859p. 22cm.
5th ed. [c1934] 772p. 22cm.

—Auditing theory and practice; student's ed. N. Y. Ronald, 1915. 542p. 22½cm.
(Auditing syllabus and instructor's guide, by David E. Boyce; for use in connection with Auditing theory and practice (student's ed.) by Robert H. Montgomery. N. Y. Ronald, 1915. 48p. 21½cm.)
Other eds. 1916; 1918; 1920. 542p. 22½cm.

—and Staub, Walter Adolph, 1881–
Auditing principles: a textbook. N. Y. Ronald, 1923. 494p. 22cm.
"Based on 'Auditing theory and practice.'"—Pref.
(The following practice set is closely articulated with "Auditing principles," but it can be used with other text books: Auditing practice set, by Paul E. Bacas. N. Y. Ronald [c1923] 8 parts in 1v. 29½x23cm.)
Another ed. 1924. 494p. 22cm.

Moody, John, 1868–
How to analyze railroad reports. N. Y. Analyses pub. co. 1912. 224p. 17½cm.
2d ed. 1912. 218p. 17½cm.
3d ed. 1913. 218p. 17½cm.
4th ed. N. Y. Moody's investors service, 1916. 218p. 17½cm.
5th ed. 1919. 218p. 17½cm.

Rogers, C. S., and Rogers, O. L.
Personal bookkeeping: an exposition of the art of bookkeeping as applied to private accounting. Fort Wayne, Fort Wayne print. co. 1912. 62p. 20cm.

Spear, Raymond Herbert, 1886–
Scientific auditing. Detroit, Commercial world pub. co. [c1912] 63p. 23cm.

Stockwell, Herbert Grant, 1866–
Net worth and the balance sheet. N. Y. Ronald, 1912. 206p. 18½cm.

Vaughan, L. Brent.
Complete course in bookkeeping, double and single entry; devised

VAUGHAN (continued)
and arranged especially for home study; an entirely new method of instruction which makes a teacher or correspondence unnecessary; including business forms. Chic. Civil service pub. co. 1912. 91p. 17½x24½cm.

VIERLING, Frederick.
Fiduciary accounting. Chic. LaSalle extension univ. [c1912] 47p. 23½cm.
Other eds. 1918; 1920; 1923; 1931. 49p. 23½cm.

1913

BARNETT, Samuel.
The statements of a life insurance company; including the gain and loss exhibit. [Louisville, Ky. Courier journal job print. co.] c1913. 57p. 25½cm.

BENNETT, Robert Joseph, 1871–
Pennsylvania C.P.A. examinations for 1912; with answers and solutions. Phil. Pub. by the author [1913] 72p. 23½cm.
Reprinted from the Journal of accountancy, Mar. Apr. and May, 1913.

BEXELL, John Andrew, 1867– , and NICHOLS, Frederick George, 1878–
Principles of bookkeeping and farm accounts [with] script illustrations by E. C. Mills. N. Y. Amer. bk. co. [c1913] 184p. 22½cm.
Another ed. [c1927] 180p. 22cm.

BORDWELL, George Otis, 1882–
Modern banking methods as applied to the tellers and bookkeepers. San Fran. Hicks-Judd co. [c1913] 122p.+1 l. 23½cm.

BRIERLEY, John Thomas, 1854–1917.
Manufacturing cost accounts; being a manual of instruction for bookkeepers and managers in factory cost accounting. Brooklyn, The author [c1913] 42p. 17½cm.

BROWN, Michael J.
"Tally"; or, Every debit has its credit. Phil. The author, 1913. 40p. 22cm.

BUREAU OF MUNICIPAL RESEARCH, New York. Metz fund.
Handbook of municipal accounting; prepared by the Metz fund from descriptive and critical data collected and constructive recommendations made by the Bureau of municipal research. N. Y. Appleton, 1913. 318p. 19cm. (Metz fund handbooks of city business methods . . .)

COLE, William Morse, 1866–
Cost accounting for institutions. N. Y. Ronald, 1913. 248p. 22½cm. (Ronald accounting ser.)
Another ed. 1920. 248p. 22½cm.

EATON, James Shirley, 1868–
Handbook of railroad expenses. N. Y. McGraw-Hill, 1913. 559p. 19cm.

FRANKLIN, Benjamin Alvey, 1869–
Cost reports for executives as a means of plant control. N. Y. Engin. mag. 1913. 149p. 22cm.
"A series of articles originally prepared by Mr. Franklin for appearance in the Engineering magazine, and published in its issues from January to August, 1912."—Introd.

GOODYEAR, Lloyd Earnest, 1867–
Principles of accountancy . . . Cedar Rapids, Ia. Goodyear-Marshall pub. co. [c1913] 189p. 19½cm. (American bookkeeping ser.)
The American bookkeeping series consists of the "Principles . . ." published as a textbook and various practice sets or units, each complete in itself and issued under various titles and editions. These sets or units are not listed separately.
—Principles, rules, and definitions for bookkeeping. Cedar Rapids, Ia. Goodyear-Marshall pub. co. [c1915] 189p. 19½cm. (American bookkeeping ser.)
Contents as in entry above. It is the same work, with a changed title.
5th ed. 1916. 208p. 19½cm. (American bookkeeping ser.)
6th ed. 1918. 232p. 19½cm. (American bookkeeping ser.)
8th ed. 1924. 238p. 19½cm. (American bookkeeping ser.)

HERTZ, Joseph Emmett.
Secrets of accounting: a practical treatise on how to conduct general audits and ascertain working capital. [Portland, Me. Jewett print. co. c1913] 37p. 20cm.

KLEIN, Joseph Jerome, 1884–
Elements of accounting theory and practice. N. Y. Appleton [c1913] 422p. 20cm.
Other eds. [c1915] 1917; 1920; 1926; 1927. 422p. 20cm.
—Student's handbook of accounting; solutions to questions in theory of accounts, practical accounting, and auditing contained in Elements of accounting; for the use of teachers, students, and practicing accountants. N. Y. Appleton [c1915] 136p. 18½cm.

MACFARLAND, George Arthur, 1887– , and ROSSHEIM, Irving David, 1887–
A first year in bookkeeping and accounting. N. Y. Appleton [c1913] 227p. 23cm.

MINER, George Washington, 1860–
Bookkeeping: banking. Bost. Ginn [c1913] 104p. 24cm. (Moore and Miner ser.)

MOXEY, Edward Preston, 1881–
Principles of factory cost keeping. N. Y. Ronald, 1913. 102p. 18cm.
Published also with thesis note: Ph.D.—University of Pennsylvania, 1909.
Other eds. 1918; 1920. 102p. 18½cm.

—and others.
Practical accounting methods: a description of systems appropriate to various kinds of business. N. Y. Key pub. co. [1913] 502p. 23½cm.
"The authors are Edward P. Moxey, jr. . . Harold Dudley Greeley . . . Howard McNayr Jefferson . . . Otto A. Grundman . . ."—Pref.

NEWELL, George Griffiths, 1863–
"Department store auditing": a practical text book on modern systems and methods of protection in accounting for sales . . . Chic. Amer. audit systems co. c1913. 103 numb. l. 27cm.

NICHOLSON, Jerome Lee, 1863–
Cost accounting theory and practice. N. Y. Ronald, 1913. 341p. 22½cm. (Ronald accounting ser.)
Forms also separately published.
Other eds. 1915; 1917. 341p. 22½cm.
—Cost accounting syllabus; for use in connection with Cost accounting theory and practice (student's ed.) N. Y. The author, 1916. 2v. 29cm. (v.2: 35cm.)

POWERS, Orville Marcellus, 1852–
Theory of bookkeeping. Chic. Metropolitan text bk. co. [c1913] 125p. 24cm. (Metropolitan ser.)

RACINE, Samuel Frederick, 1882–
Accounting principles. [Seattle, Western institute of accountancy, commerce & finance] 1913. 280p. 20cm. (Accounting students' ser.)
Another ed. 1917. 320p. 21½cm. (Accounting students' ser.)

ROBY, James J., 1865–
A treatise on cost accounting as applied to coal mining. [Cleveland, Calvert-Hatch co.] c1913. [16]p. 28cm.
Another ed. N. Y. 1914. 32p. 23½cm.
Reprinted from the Coal age, 1914.

SMITH, Chester William, 1852– , and THOMAS, S. M.
Farm accounts. Phil. Laurel bk. co. 1913. 82p. 19½cm.

STEWART, Ethelbert.
Tannery production costs and methods of accounting. Bost. Rogers & Atwood, 1913. 39p. 23½cm.

SWEET, James Sylvester, 1853–1930.
Business practice bookkeeping: a thorough treatise on modern and practical methods of accounting; for the use of business and commercial schools and colleges, commercial high schools, technical schools, and commercial departments in other educational institutions. Santa Rosa, Calif. Sweet [c1913] 192p. 27cm.

TATLOW, Herbert Johnson, 1862–
Institute of railway accounting: text-book of inter-line freight accounts . . . Chic. c1913. 86p. 20cm.

THORNTON, Frank Weldon, 1863–
Brewery accounts. N. Y. Ronald, 1913. 102p. 22½cm. (Ronald accounting ser.)

VAN CLEVE, Charles McKinstry, 1852–
Principles of double-entry bookkeeping. N. Y. J. Kempster print. co. 1913. 210p. 20cm.

WHIGAM, Wallace Hugh, 1860– , and FREDERICK, Oliver Detwiler, 1864–

WHIGAM (continued)
Household accounting. N. Y. A. N. Palmer, 1913. 47p. 23cm. (Palmer ser. of commercial text-books)
Book of forms separately published.

WINCHELL, Samuel Dixon, 1877–
The model system of bookkeeping and cost finding; prepared especially for the printing and allied industries. [Phil. T. A. Winchell] c1913. [36]p. 35½cm.

1914

ALLEN, Leslie Herbert, 1881–
Cost accounting on construction work; with a description of the system used by the Aberthaw construction company. Bost. Aberthaw construction co. 1914. 46p. 24cm.
2d ed. 1915. 46p. 24cm.

BENNETT, Robert Joseph, 1871– , and MORTON, Frederick W., 1871–
C.P.A. questions and answers. Detroit, International accountants' soc. 1914. 310p. 27cm.

BENTLEY, Harry Clark, 1877– , compiler.
C.P.A. auditing questions to January 1, 1914; comprising all the available examination questions in auditing that have been set by C.P.A. examining boards up to and including December 31, 1913. N. Y. Ronald, 1914. 247p. 22½cm.

DAVIS, Albert Eugene, 1864–
How to find costs in printing. N. Y. Oswald pub. co. 1914. 120p. 19½cm.

DETROIT SCHOOL OF ACCOUNTS AND COMMERCE.
Book-keeping in six lessons . . . Detroit, Detroit school of accounts & commerce [c1914] [94]p. 21cm.

DICKINSON, Arthur Lowes, 1859–1935.
Accounting practice and procedure. N. Y. Ronald, 1914 [c1913] 315p. 22cm.
Another ed. 1914. 315p. 22cm.
2d printing.
Other eds. 1918; 1919; 1922. 309p. 22cm.

DUDLEY, George Osgood.
Corporation accounting; including exercises in special accounting problems of the large corporation. [Saginaw, Mich. F. H. Bliss] c1914. 86p. 26½cm.

EDWARDS, Henry Moore, 1860–
Electric light accounts and their significance. N. Y. McGraw-Hill, 1914. 172p. 19cm.

EGGLESTON, De Witt Carl, 1881–
Municipal accounting. N. Y. Ronald, 1914. 456p. 22½cm. (Ronald accounting ser.)
Another ed. 1922. 456p. 22cm. (Ronald accounting ser.)

ESQUERRÉ, Paul Joseph, 1872–1934.
The applied theory of accounts. N. Y. Ronald, 1914. 519p. 22cm.
Other eds. 1917; 1918. 519p. 22cm.
Other eds. 1919; 1921; 1923; 1924; 1926. 575p. 22cm.
—Problems involving the application of the theory of accounts; prepared or selected by Paul-Joseph Esquerré . . . for use . . . with "The applied theory of accounts" . . . N. Y. Ronald, 1915. 69p. 21½cm.

HUTCHINSON, J. Howard, 1883–
School costs and school accounting. N. Y. Teachers college, Columbia univ. 1914. 151p.+1 l. 24½cm. (Teachers college, Columbia university. Contributions to education, no.62)
Published also as thesis (Ph.D.)—Columbia university, 1913.

JACKSON, Harry Albert, 1870–
Better store system and department accounting: a system for departmentizing a store, or for department stores. Grinnell, Ia. [Grinnell herald pub. co. 1914] 73+[1]p. 21cm.
Portfolio of forms separately published.

JONES, Arthur Francis, 1873–
Lumber manufacturing accounts. N. Y. Ronald, 1914. 112p. 22½cm. (Ronald accounting ser.)
Another ed. 1919. 112p. 21½cm. (Ronald accounting ser.)

JONES, E. Horton.
Unit construction costs from the new smelter of the Arizona copper co. ltd. . . N. Y. McGraw-Hill, 1914. p.[1497]–1649, 23½cm.

JONES (continued)

Reprinted from the Bulletin of the American institute of mining engineers, July, 1914.

This work was also printed by McGraw-Hill under the title: "Smelter construction costs."

MCINTOSH, Robert James, 1871–

Reference book of accounts for manufacturing and mercantile companies. Toledo, McIntosh [c1914] 299+[1]p. 23½cm.

2d ed. Chic. Metropolitan text bk. co. 1923. 299+[1]p. 23½cm.

MANKATO COMMERCIAL COLLEGE, Mankato, Minn.

Student's guide to accompany the Brandrup & Nettleton system of teaching bookkeeping and business practice; when used in connection with the outline of transactions provides a full course of instructions in bookkeeping and office practice. Mankato, Minn. Mankato commercial college, 1914. 255p. 29cm.

—Business directions used in connection with Brandrup & Nettleton system of teaching bookkeeping and business practice: a direct didactic method of presenting mercantile, manufacturing, and corporation bookkeeping and business methods. Mankato, Minn. Mankato commercial college, 1914. 65p. 23½cm.

Both titles copyrighted by the Ellis publishing company, Battle Creek, Mich.

MANN, Jasper Dalton.

Mann's agricultural bookkeeping instructor; designed for self-instruction and school room use. [Columbus, Ohio, Schmitt print. co.] c1914. 55p. 30½cm.

Fifty ruled leaves at end.

METAL WORKER, PLUMBER AND STEAM FITTER.

Estimating, cost keeping, and profit making in the plumbing, heating, and sheet metal trades; comp. from articles which have appeared in Metal worker, plumber and steam fitter; descriptive of the methods in practical use by some of the leading and most successful merchant mechanics in these trades. N. Y. D. Williams [c1914] 380p. 23cm.

PECK, Roscoe H., and READ, Harlan Eugene, 1880–

Peck and Read's bookkeeping . . . course in bookkeeping taught in the Brown's business colleges. St. L. Peck & Read [c1914] 2v. 25cm.

PORTE, Roy Trewin.

How to figure costs in printing offices . . . Minneapolis, Minne-

sota cost system co. [c1914] 134p. 19cm.
Another ed. 1921. 143p. 19cm.
Another ed. Salt Lake City, Porte pub. co. [c1924] 181p. 19cm.

RACINE, Samuel Frederick, 1882–
Graded corporation problems. [Seattle, Western institute of accountancy, commerce & finance, c1914] 54 l. 27½cm. (Accounting students' ser.)

—Guide to the study of accounting. [Seattle, Western institute of accountancy, commerce & finance] 1914. 76p. 19½cm. (Accounting students' ser.)
Arranged in question form to accompany "Applied theory of accounts," by Paul-Joseph Esquerré; "Modern accounting," by Henry Rand Hatfield; "Accounting practice and procedure," by Arthur Lowes Dickinson; "Cost accounting theory and practice," by Jerome Lee Nicholson; "Cost accounts," by L. Whitten Hawkins.
Another ed. 1916. 91p. 19½cm. (Accounting students' ser.)

—Guide to the study of auditing. [Seattle, Western institute of accountancy, commerce & finance] 1914. 63p. 19cm. (Accounting students' ser.)
Arranged in question form to accompany "Auditing theory and practice," by Robert H. Montgomery, 1912.
2d ed. 1916. 74p. 19½cm. (Accounting students' ser.)

SHAW, A. W., company, Chicago.
Accounting and office methods; organizing the office, accounting principles and systems, office work, and record keeping. Chic. Shaw [c1914] 200p. 21½cm. (Students' business book ser.)
Also issued as v.9 of the Library of business practice.
The content of this work differs from the work of the same title published in 1907. (See 1907, Booth, W. Vernon, and others)
Other eds. 1915; 1917. 200p. 21½cm.
Published under the title: "Office methods and accounting."

—Costs and statistics; basic cost principles, mapping out the cost system, graphs and statistics, expense control. Chic. Shaw [c1914] 200p. 21½cm. (Students' business book ser.)
Also issued as v.10 of the Library of business practice.

SHAW (continued)
Another ed. 1917. 200p. 21½cm.
Issued as v.2 of the Library of office management.
Another ed. 1920. 216p. 21½cm.

SHEAFFER, William Adam, 1876–
Metropolitan system of bookkeeping; embracing theory and practice of bookkeeping and accounting; for high schools, parochial schools, academies, and all other schools teaching the subject [in four parts] Chic. Metropolitan text bk. co. 1914–[15]
2v. 25x19½cm. (Metropolitan ser.)
Another ed. 1916. 382+xixp. 25x20cm. (Metropolitan ser.)
Parts 1 to 4 published in one volume.
Other eds. 1920; 1921; 1922. 208+xviiip. 25x20cm.
Parts 1 and 2 published in one volume.

SMALL, Frederic Lincoln, 1866–
Treatise on comprehensive accounting methods; adapted to shoe manufacturing and other industries. Bost. L. & S. print. co. [c1914] 227p. 24cm.

TIMKEN, Frank Herrmann, 1866–
General factory accounting; designed as a practical guide for the use of manufacturers and their employees . . . Chic. Trade periodical co. 1914. 171p. 23½cm.

WILDMAN, John Raymond, 1878–
Elementary accounting problems. Brooklyn, W. G. Hewitt press, 1914. 218p. 23½cm.
Another ed. N. Y. N. Y. univ. press, 1918. 218p. 23½cm.

1915

ARMSTRONG, Augustus, 1855–
Double entry bookkeeping up to date: a valuable reference book for students, bookkeepers, accountants, business men, and others; showing how to open, keep, close, and audit a set of books . . . N. Y. Armstrong [c1915] 64p. 22½cm.

BAILLET, Henry F.
Overhead expense and percentage methods: a lecture on the cost of doing business; explaining how to find it and what to do with it when found; with practical examples of its use taken from actual business experiences. N. Y. D. Williams, 1915. 128p. 18cm.

BAUGH, Frederick Henry, 1879–
Principles and practice of cost accounting; for accountants, manufacturers, mechanical engineers, teachers, and students. Balt. Baugh, 1915. 194p. 22½cm.

BELDING, Albert G., 1870–
Accounts and accounting practice. N. Y. Amer. bk. co. [c1915] 224p. 22cm.
Another ed. [c1918] 224p. 22cm.

BONNER, Joseph Claybaugh, 1855–
Farm cost system. Toledo, Bonner, c1915. 58p.
Work book and forms to be used with this system separately published.

BRADLEY, Carolyn H.
Suggestive exercises in bookkeeping for grammar schools. [San Jose, Calif.] Calif. state print. off. 1915. 30p. 23cm.

BROAKER, Frank.
Post graduate expert accountancy course; special teacher's course . . . comprehending theory—practical accounting—auditing—commercial law; qualifying for private and public practice and C.P.A. exams. N. Y. Broaker [c1915] 2v. 25½cm.

COLE, William Morse, 1866–
Problems in the principles of accounting. Cambridge [Mass.] Harvard univ. press, 1915. 102p. 22½cm.
Other eds. 1919; 1924; 1927. 102p. 22½cm.

HOLLISTER, Horace Edward.
Practical garage accounting: a complete system of general and cost records for the garage. Rockford, Ill. c1915. 57 numb. l. 28cm.
2d ed. Rockford, Ill. Garage systems co. 1916. 173p. 22cm.

HOOPER, William Everett, 1883–
Railroad accounting. N. Y. Appleton, 1915. 461p. 21½cm. (Appleton's railway ser.)

INTERNATIONAL TEXTBOOK COMPANY, Scranton.
Corporation organization and accounting; partnerships; auditing. Scranton, International textbk. co. [1915] Various pagings, 23cm. (International library of technology, v.132)
Various parts of this work copyrighted in 1913 and 1914.
"Corporation organization and accounting," by Robert J. Bennett published in 1924 as v.132D of the International library of technology.
(See 1905, International textbook company, Scranton)

INTERNATIONAL TEXTBOOK COMPANY (continued)

—Cost accounting; analysis of accounts; insolvent and decedents' estates. Scranton, International textbk. co. [1915] Various pagings, 23cm. (International library of technology, v.133)

Various parts of this work copyrighted in 1913 and 1914.

"That part of this volume comprised under the title 'Cost accounting' was prepared by J. Lee Nicholson, C.P.A."

"Cost accounting; insolvent and decedents' estates; analysis of accounts; elements of cost accounting" published in 1922 as v.133C of the International library of technology.

(See 1905, International textbook company, Scranton)

—Railroad agency accounting; railroad general-office accounting. Scranton, International textbk. co. 1915. Various pagings, 23cm. (International library of technology, v.129)

Various parts of this work copyrighted in 1913 and 1914.

(See 1905, International textbook company, Scranton)

MELCHIOR, Roger Logan, 1887–

Hints on bookkeeping. Toledo, Melchior, c1915. 60p. 23½cm.

MICHIGAN. STATE BOARD OF ACCOUNTANCY.

Michigan C. P. A. manual, 1915; comp. by Durand W. Springer, secretary-treasurer . . . [Ann Arbor, Mich. Ann Arbor press, c1915] 183p. 23½cm.

—Michigan C. P. A. manual, 1920; comp. by Durand W. Springer, secretary-treasurer . . . [Ann Arbor, Mich. Ann Arbor press, c1920] 260p. 23½cm.

"Second edition."

NICHOLS, Henry Wyman, 1872–

A method of determining costs in a cotton mill. New Bedford, Mass. E. Anthony & sons, 1915. 115p. 23½cm.

OTIS, Daniel Henry.

Farm accounts simplified: a simplified system of farm accounts that requires no posting, the minimum of descriptions and additions, and sufficiently itemized to determine the cost of production. N. Y. Judd, 1915. 42p. 35½cm.

2d ed. [1915] 42p. 36cm.
3d ed. 1917. 42p. 36cm.
6th ed. 1918. 40p. 35cm.

THE RONALD PRESS COMPANY, New York.

1914 C. P. A. problems and solutions . . . N. Y. Ronald, 1915. 2v. 22cm.

Contents.—v.1. Presenting problems with solutions for the following examinations: Pennsylvania, Nov. 1913; New York, Jan. 1914; Illinois, May, 1913; Colorado, Dec. 1913.—v.2. Presenting problems with solutions for the following examinations: Missouri, Dec. 1913; Ohio, Nov. 1913; New York, June, 1914; Massachusetts, Oct. 1914.

—C. P. A. problems with solutions, 1915 . . . N. Y. Ronald, 1915–[16] 2v. 22cm.
v.1, 1915; v.2, 1916.
Contents.—v.1. Presenting problems with solutions for the following examinations: Wisconsin, April, 1914; Ohio, Nov. 1914; New York, Jan. 1915; Pennsylvania, Nov. 1914.—v.2. Presenting problems with solutions for the following examinations: Missouri, Dec. 1914; Illinois, May, 1914; Massachusetts, Oct. 1915; New York, June, 1915.

SALIERS, Earl Adolphus, 1884–
Depreciation in theory and practice. Chic. LaSalle extension univ. [1915] 27p. 23cm.
Other eds. 1918; 1921; 1927; 1932. 28p. 23cm.

—Principles of depreciation. N. Y. Ronald, 1915. 200p. 22½cm. (Ronald accounting ser.)
Another ed. 1916. 200p. 21½cm.
—Depreciation; principles and applications. N. Y. Ronald, 1922. 590p. 22cm.
Reconstruction and broad expansion of the earlier work.
Another ed. 1923. 590p. 22cm.

SHAW, A. W., company, Chicago.
Operation and costs; bringing factory production up to capacity—scheduling and dispatching work—maintaining quality—cost keeping methods and systems—cost cutting and plant control. Chic. Shaw [c1915] 216p. 22½cm. (Factory management ser.)
Also issued as v.5 of the Library of factory management.

SOBEL, Joseph.
Practical accounting . . . comp. arranged and classified. [Brooklyn, Brows print. co.] 1915. 7v. 22½cm.
This work consists of seven pamphlets totalling 124 pages.

SULLIVAN, Frank Joseph, 1874–
System of accounts for county government. [Salt Lake City, Rose print. co. c1915] 72p. 24½cm.
"Installed in Salt Lake County, state of Utah, January 1st, 1916."

TIMKEN, Frank Herrmann, 1866–
Accounting in the furniture and woodworking industries; designed in combination with General factory accounting by the same author to afford a definite standard of practice in the industries referred to in the title . . . Chic. Trade periodical co. 1915. 118p. 23½cm.

1916

BENNETT, Robert Joseph, 1871–
Corporation accounting. N.Y. Ronald, 1916. 563p. 22½cm. (Ronald accounting ser.)
Other eds. 1917; 1918; 1919; 1920; 1922. 563p. 22½cm. (Ronald accounting ser.)
(See also 1922, Conyngton, Thomas)

BLACHLY, Frederick Frank, 1880–
The accounting and reporting methods of the state of New York. [N.Y. 1916] 151p. 22½cm.
Thesis (Ph.D.)—Columbia university, 1916.
Published also by the Bureau of municipal research, New York, as parts 1–2 of Municipal research no. 74, June, 1916.

CONSOLIDATED GAS COMPANY OF NEW YORK.
In re theoretical depreciation: a discussion of the subject with an analysis of a paper by Dr. Weber, statistician of the Public service commission for the first district, state of New York, entitled "Accounting for depreciation"; presented for the consideration of the Public service commission for the first district, state of New York, by the Consolidated gas co. of New York . . . prepared by James E. Allison. St. L. Buxton & Skinner, printers [1916?] 155p. 25½cm.

COX, Henry Clay, 1845– , compiler.
Classified C.P.A. problems and solutions, 1915; covering the more important questions given in the 1915 examinations of the following states: Arkansas, Delaware, Florida, Kansas, Louisiana, Maine, Maryland, Massachusetts, Michigan, Minnesota, Missouri, Nebraska, Nevada, New York, Ohio, Oregon, Pennsylvania, South Carolina, Washington, Wisconsin. N.Y. Ronald, 1916. 414p. 22½cm.

DALE, Samuel Sherman, 1859–
Cost finding for textile mills; cotton, woolen, worsted, hosiery, underwear [2d ed.] Bost. Textiles [c1916] 32p. 22½cm.

GILMAN, Stephen, 1887–
Principles of accounting. Chic. LaSalle extension univ. 1916. 415p. 21½cm. (Business administration text-books)
Other eds. 1917; 1918; 1920. 415p. 21½cm.

HAWORTH, Smith Gordon, 1880– , and ASHBY, William Silas, 1869–
Cotton seed oil mill bookkeeping; illustrating the use of the voucher system. Battle Creek, Mich. Ellis pub. co. 1916. 55p. 29cm.

HOFFMAN, George Lawrence, 1884–
Simplified bookkeeping [with] script work by H. A. Roush. [McKeesport, Pa.] Hoffman [c1916] 58+[2]p. 28cm.

HUNTER, Joel, 1870–1928.
Thinking in figures; commerce, finance and accounts, business systems, and short cuts. Atlanta, Hunter [c1916] 234p. 22½cm.

LARSON, Carl William, 1881–
Milk production cost accounts; principles and methods. N. Y. Columbia univ. press, 1916. 60p.+1 l. 23cm.
Thesis (Ph.D.)—Columbia university, 1916.
Published also without thesis note.

MOXEY, Louis White, 1877–
The electrical contractor: principles of cost-keeping and estimating, wiring and illumination calculations, and other technical problems of the business. N. Y. McGraw-Hill, 1916. 86p. 23½cm.
"Much of the material has already appeared in the Electrical world."

PARKHURST, Frederic Augustus, 1877–
The predetermination of true costs and relatively true selling prices. N. Y. Wiley, 1916. 96p. 23½cm.

PATON, William Andrew, 1889– , and STEVENSON, Russell Alger, 1890–
Principles of accounting. Ann Arbor, Mich. [Ann Arbor press] 1916. 222p. 24cm.
Another ed. Ann Arbor, Mich. G. Wahr, 1917. 373p. 23cm.
Other eds. N. Y. Macmillan, 1918; 1920; 1921; 1922; 1928. 685p. 22½cm.
—Problems and exercises in accounting. Ann Arbor, Mich. G. Wahr, 1917. 163p. 21½cm.

PATON (continued)

"To accompany the authors' 'Principles of accounting.' "—Note.

2d ed. 1920. 195p. 22cm.
3d ed. 1920. 195p. 22cm.
4th ed. 1921. 329p. 22cm.

RACINE, Samuel Frederick, 1882–

Practical problems graded; series "A." [Seattle, Western institute of accountancy, commerce & finance, c1916] [116] l. 27½cm. (Accounting students' ser.)

Printed on versos only.

Other eds. 1920; 1926. 162p. 22½cm. (Accounting students' ser.)

RATIONAL BUSINESS SYSTEM, Cedar Rapids, Ia.

The rational business system; for use in the common schools and business colleges. Cedar Rapids, Ia. Rational business system, 1916. 95p. 23½cm.

Introduction signed "W. W. Webber" who was William Wilson Webber, 1866– His name does not appear on the title-page. The work is called "Manual I."

SCOVELL, Clinton Homer, 1876–1926.

Cost accounting and burden application. N. Y. Appleton, 1916. 328p. 20½cm.

Other eds. 1917; 1920. 328p. 20½cm.

TANNER, John B.

C.P.A. examinations and how to prepare for them. Chic. LaSalle extension univ. [c1916] 70p. 23cm.

THOMPSON, Clarence Bertrand, 1882–

How to find factory costs; illustrated with fifty-one charts, seven diagrams, and one table. Chic. A. W. Shaw [c1916] 191p. 25cm.

This work reprinted seven times between 1916 and 1920.

—A report: factory costs as an aid to greater profits. Chic. A. W. Shaw, 1925. 208p. 25cm.

No author named on the title-page.

This work is the first revised edition of "How to find factory costs . . ." by C. B. Thompson, published in 1916.

THORNTON, Frank Weldon, 1863–

Memorandum on moving picture accounts, July 10, 1916. N. Y. Price, Waterhouse [c1916] 54p. 23½cm.

TODMAN, Frederick Simson.
Brokerage accounts: a treatise on the business of brokerage; its accounting books and records. N. Y. Ronald, 1916.
338p. 22½cm. (Ronald accounting ser.)
—Wall street accounting: a description of the business of brokerage; its accounting records and procedure. N. Y. Ronald, 1921.
352p. 22cm.
"An enlargement and fundamental revision of the author's 'Brokerage accounts' published in 1916."

U. S. FEDERAL TRADE COMMISSION.
Fundamentals of a cost system for manufacturers, July 1, 1916. Wash. Govt. print. off. 1916. 31p. 24½cm.
At head of title: Federal trade commission.
Prepared by Robert E. Belt, chief accountant, and R. W. Gardiner, assistant.
Another ed. 1922. 31p. 23cm.

WALKER, Frank Rabold, 1888–
Practical cost keeping for contractors: a book giving a system of accurate cost keeping and the methods used for adapting it to all classes of construction work. Chic. Walker, 1916. 273p. 18cm.
2d ed. 1918. 275p. 17cm.

WALKER, James Cree, 1867–
Retail accounting and store management. Cin. South-western pub. co. [c1916] 91p. 22½cm. (20th century bookkeeping ser.)

WILDMAN, John Raymond, 1878–
Principles of auditing. Brooklyn, W. G. Hewitt press, 1916. 196p. 23½cm.
Another ed. N. Y. N. Y. univ. bk. store, 1923. 196p. 23½cm.
—Auditing studies. Brooklyn, W. G. Hewitt press, 1917. 26p. 23cm.
Supplements the theory contained in "Principles of auditing."

WOLFF, Mark, 1888–
Interpretation of water-works accounts. Balt. 1916.
p.529–556, 23½cm.
Reprinted from the Journal of the American water works association, 1916, v.3, no.2.

1917

ANDERSEN, Arthur, HIMMELBLAU, David, 1889– , and KOHLER, Eric Louis, 1892–
Complete accounting course. N. Y. Ronald, 1917–21. 3v. 29x24½cm.
v.1, c1917; v.2, c1919; v.3, c1921.

BENINGTON, Harold.
The detection of frauds: an interesting summary of the chief methods of frauds . . . suggests methods of prevention and detection. Chic. LaSalle extension univ. c1917. 30p. 23cm.
Other eds. 1918; 1921. 32p. 22cm.

BOGLE, Artemas Melvin, 1860–
Everyday bookkeeping. N. Y. Macmillan, 1917. 126p. 24cm. (Macmillan's commercial ser.)
Another ed. 1918. 126p. 24cm.

BOOKMAN, Clarence Monroe, 1882– , and BLUE, Franz Sigel, 1879–
First steps in bookkeeping: a practical introduction to bookkeeping; containing an abundance of drill work in arithmetic; arranged to accompany Bookman's Business arithmetic or any other modern arithmetic in eighth or ninth grade work. Cin. [Printed by Powell & White] c1917. 86p. 26x17½cm.
p. 45–86: ledger blanks.

CHURCH, Alexander Hamilton, 1866–
Manufacturing costs and accounts. N. Y. McGraw-Hill, 1917. 452p. 24cm.
Another ed. 1917. 452p. 24cm.
2d ed. 1929. 516p. 23½cm.

CRANDELL, John Chester, 1887– , and CRANDELL, Mercy Frye.
A manual of household accounts; including complete instructions, illustrative figures, and forms for actual use covering three years. Bost. Whitcomb & Barrows, 1917. 24p.+68 forms, 28cm.

DWORAK, E. A., compiler.
The Corey & McKenzie complete accounting system and record for national farm loan associations; prepared and comp. by E. A. Dworak . . . under the direction of the Federal land bank of Omaha; containing complete records for organization, directors' meetings, and by-laws; with complete illustrations of accounting records and full description of the accounts. Omaha, Corey & McKenzie print. co. c1917. 49p. 17x26½cm.

EATON, Abijah H., 1840–1917.
The Eaton and Burnett revised and improved bookkeeping, corporation, voucher, and cost accounting; embracing all modern and scientific methods used in business. Balt. Eaton & Burnett business college, 1917. 261p. 24½cm.
The content of this work differs from "Eaton and Burnett's bookkeeping . . ." published in 1881.
Another ed. 1918. 261p. 23½cm.
—The learner's guide in the study of Eaton and Burnett's bookkeeping. Balt. 1917. 15p. 16cm.

FICKER, Nicholas Thiel, 1885–
Industrial cost-finding. N. Y. Industrial extension institute [c1917] 511p. 19½cm. (Factory management course, v.10)
Another ed. [c1922] 511p. 19cm. (Factory management course, v.5)

—Shop expense analysis and control. N. Y. Engin. mag. 1917. 236p. 22cm. (Industrial management library)
"The first eight chapters of this book appeared originally in the Engineering magazine."—Introd.

HARPMAN, Charles Andrew, 1875–
Home bookkeeping for the thrifty. Balt. Rowe [c1917] 98p. 19½cm.

HATTON, Linius Monroe, 1870– , and PROWINSKY, Joseph Albert, 1879–
The H. and P. practical bookkeeping . . . designed as a text book for teaching theoretical and practical bookkeeping and accountancy by the most modern and approved methods; for use in business colleges, commercial departments of colleges and high schools, and by private learners. [Tampa, Fla.] Tampa business college, c1917. 47+[1]p. 31cm.
3d ed. c1920. 52p. 27cm.

HAYES, Pryor Lee.
The bookkeeping teacher: a treatise on the science of double entry bookkeeping. [Chic. R. R. Donnelley] 1917. 126p. 23½cm.

HERZ, Eugene, 1883–
Controlling profits; simplified efficiency methods in store record keeping. Chic. Laird & Lee [c1917] 103p. 23cm.

KESTER, Roy Bernard, 1882–
Accounting theory and practice . . . N. Y. Ronald, 1917–21. 3v. 22cm.

KESTER (continued)

v.1, 1917; v.2, 1918; v.3, 1921.

Vol.1, a first-year text now known as "Principles of accounting," was first published in 1916 for Kester's classes at Columbia university. The 1917 edition was reprinted several times.

Vol.2, a second-year text now known as "Advanced accounting," was reprinted several times.

Vol.3, a third-year text now known as "Accounting applications to various forms of industry," was written by Kester and many collaborators and reprinted several times. It has not been revised.

2d ed. 1922–25. 2v. 22cm.
v.1, 2d ed., 1922; v.2, 2d ed., 1925.

3d ed. 1930–33. 2v. 22cm.
v.1, 3d ed., 1930; v.2, 3d ed., 1933.
Practice problems for v.1 known as the "1930 problem book" separately published.
Another series of problems prepared to accompany v.1 published in 1934.
Practice problems for v.2 separately published.

—A study in valuation of the commercial balance sheet (comprising chapters iv to xxvii inclusive of this volume) [Accounting theory and practice, v.2] N. Y. Ronald, 1918. 796p. 22cm.

Thesis (Ph.D.)—Columbia university, 1919.

KLEIN, Joseph Jerome, 1884–

Bookkeeping and accounting. N. Y. Appleton, 1917. 453p. 23cm. (College of the city of New York ser. in commerce, civics, and technology)

Complete course.

Other eds. 1918; 1919; 1923; 1924; 1926; 1929.
453p. 23cm.
Complete course.

—Bookkeeping and accounting; advanced course. N. Y. Appleton, 1918. 247p. 22½cm. (College of the city of New York ser. in commerce, civics, and technology)

The advanced course includes all the material contained in the complete course not incorporated in the introductory course.

—Bookkeeping and accounting; introductory course. N. Y. Appleton, 1918. 226p. 23cm. (College of the city of New York ser. in commerce, civics, and technology)

Another ed. 1922. 226p. 23cm.

MAY, Irville Augustus.

Street railway accounting: a manual of operating practice for electric railways. N. Y. Ronald, 1917. 454p. 22cm.

MORTON, Davis Walter, 1880–
Banking and bank accounting: an advanced set on the individual business practice plan. (Chic. Lyons & Carnahan [c1917] 112p. 25cm.
—and Cox, John Henry, 1876–
Banking and bank accounting; theory and practice. [c1933] 112p. 23½cm.
This work is a revised edition of the one published in 1917.
Forms separately published.

MUCKLOW, Walter, 1864–
Real estate accounts; treating of the proper classification, construction, and operation of accounts for the real estate business; including forms. N. Y. Ronald, 1917. 357p. 22½cm.
Other eds. 1921; 1924. 357p. 22½cm.

RITTENHOUSE, Charles Forest, 1881– , and CLAPP, Philip Francis, 1879–
Advanced accounting problems; with explanatory notes. N. Y. Assn. press, 1917. 96p. 28cm.

—Exercises in accounting. N. Y. Assn. press, 1917. 117p. 28cm.
Other eds. 1918; 1920. 114p. 28cm.

—Notes on accounting theory and practice. N. Y. Assn. press, 1917. 85p. 18cm.

ROSS, George Edward, 1880–
Cost keeping and construction accounting; adapted to any work consisting of numerous items, departments, or divisions on which detailed unit costs are desired. [Salem, Or.] c1917. 59p. 19½cm.
[2d ed.] Salem, Or. Ross system co. c1919. 171p. 21cm.

ROWE, Harry Marc, 1860–1926.
Junior arithmetic-bookkeeping; for junior high schools, advanced grades, and such other schools as desire to give an intensely practical training course in the arithmetic of bookkeeping and in the bookkeeping of everyday business affairs that is graded to suit elementary students. Balt. Rowe [c1917–18] 2v. 23cm.
v.1, 1917; v.2, 1918.

SHEAFFER, William Adam, 1876–
Household accounting and economics. N. Y. Macmillan, 1917. 161p. 19½cm.

SIKES, Clarence Steven, 1868–
Railway accounting. Chic. LaSalle extension univ. [c1917] 2v. 23½cm.
Another ed. 1920–[21] 2v. 22½cm.
v.1, 1920; v.2, 1921.

STOREY, Eugene Wilfred, 1871–
Monthly cost accounting for varnish plants; fully illustrated by tables and forms . . . prepared by special request of the National varnish manufacturers' association. [Phil. Philadelphia print. & pub. co.] c1917. 51p. 23cm.

U. S. FEDERAL RESERVE BOARD.
Uniform accounting: a tentative proposal submitted by the Federal reserve board, Washington, for the consideration of banks, bankers, and banking associations; merchants, manufacturers, and associations of manufacturers; auditors, accountants, and associations of accountants; reprinted from Federal reserve bulletin, April, 1917. Wash. Govt. print. off. 1917. 25p. 27cm.
—Approved methods for the preparation of balance sheet statements: a tentative proposal submitted by the Federal reserve board, Washington . . . Wash. Govt. print. off. 1918. 25p. 26cm.
Running title: Preparation of balance sheet statements.
The content of this work is the same as the one listed above issued with a different title.
—Verification of financial statements (rev.): a method of procedure submitted by the Federal reserve board, Washington, for the consideration of bankers, merchants, manufacturers, auditors, and accountants; a revision by the American institute of accountants, of suggestions for the preparation of balance-sheet statements printed in the April, 1917, issue of the Federal reserve bulletin and reprinted in pamphlet form in 1918 for general distribution under the title "Approved methods for the preparation of balance-sheet statements." Wash. Govt. print. off. 1929. 26p. 24½cm.
On cover: . . . Revised May, 1929.
The American institute of accountants also published this revision in 1929.

WEBNER, Frank Erastus, 1865–
Factory accounting. Chic. LaSalle extension univ. 1917. 345p. 24½cm.
Another ed. 1918. 345p. 24½cm.

WIHLFAHRT, Julius Emil.
Treatise on increasing bakery efficiency; specimens for figuring costs, expenses, and results. [N. Y. R. A. Haag, printer] c1917. [12]p.+26 l. of forms, 21½x36cm.

Another ed. [c1923] 19p.+26 l. of forms, 21½x36cm.
Another ed. [1927] 19p.+26 l. of forms, 21½x35cm.

WINSPEAR, Clara Schmudde, 1876–
Winspear's 1917 bookkeeping manual; containing fundamental and comprehensive rules for applying debit and credit entries. [Cin. Methodist bk. concern, c1917] 40p. 18cm.

WOLFF, Mark, 1888–
Bookkeeper and accountant civil service examination instruction; 250 ques. and ans. including problems and solutions & 500 specimen ques. . . Board of education questions for license to teach bookkeeping in high schools and evening schools, N. Y. city; digest of uniform accounting systems prescribed by the Public service commission, First district, New York; certified public accountant, answers to New York state examination questions; practice questions and answers on bookkeeping, commercial practice, and terms. N. Y. Civil service chronicle, c1917. 108p. 25cm.
Another ed. 1918. 108p. 25cm.

WOODS, Clinton Edgar.
Unified accounting methods for industrials. N. Y. Ronald, 1917. 484p. 22½cm.
Another ed. 1919. 484p. 22½cm.

1918

ADAMS, Henry Carter, 1851–1921.
American railway accounting: a commentary. N. Y. Holt, 1918. 465p. 21cm.

ALCORN, Edgar Greenville, 1876–
The Alcorn system of modern bank book-keeping and accounting: a plain, practical method by which the student issues, handles, and records all the papers and documents that pass through a bank in the ordinary course of business; giving actual practice in every department of bank work; for use in connection with the Alcorn banking set. Columbus, Ohio, Amer. school of banking [c1918] 3v. 15½x23cm.

BASSET, William Rupert, 1883–
Accounting as an aid to business profits. Chic. A. W. Shaw [c1918] 316p. 25cm.
"Chart showing basic method for linking factory costs with general books": 1 sheet folded and laid in.
Other eds. 1921; 1924; 1925. 316p. 25cm.

BASSET (continued)

Another ed. [Chic.] Shaw management service, c1926. 315p. 29½cm.
"Third revised edition . . . February, 1926."
No author named on title-page of this edition.

CASTENHOLZ, William Burtis, 1879–

Auditing procedure. Chic. LaSalle extension univ. 1918. 342p. 24½cm.

Other eds. 1919; 1920. 342p. 24½cm.
2d ed. 1927. 430p.+5 l.+50 forms, 21½cm.
"Illustrative audit working papers": five leaves, fifty forms at end.
Another ed. 1932. 430p. 21½cm.

—Auditing procedure assignments, by F. J. Rothing, Ennes C. Rayson, L. E. Terry, H. C. Beck, and William Rodney Thompson: a series of fifteen coordinated assignments based upon Auditing procedure . . . prepared . . . in cooperation with LaSalle extension university . . . Chic. LaSalle extension univ. 1923. 288p. 23cm.

Complete practical solutions are available.
Other eds. 1924; 1926; 1927; 1929; 1930; 1931; 1932. 288p. 23cm.

—and MOREY, Lloyd, 1886–

C.P.A. problems and solutions; selected problems from American institute and state C.P.A. examinations . . . Chic. LaSalle extension univ. 1918. 457p. 27½cm.

Other eds. 1921; 1926; 1928; 1932. 457p. 27½cm.

CLEARY, P. Roger.

How to figure profit: a comprehensive reference book for business men, teachers, and students. Ypsilanti, Mich. Cleary [c1918] 265p. 21½cm.

DALE, Samuel Sherman, 1859–

Cost finding in woolen and worsted mills. Bost. Textiles [c1918] 49p. 21cm.

DENHAM, Robert Scudder, 1871–

Fundamentals of cost and profit calculation; a vigorous discussion of the vital elements of business. Cleveland, Cost engineer pub. co. 1918. 120p. 19½cm.

Another ed. 1919. 126p. 19cm.

EGGLESTON, De Witt Carl, 1881–

Problems in cost accounting. N. Y. Appleton, 1918.

349p. 23cm. (College of the city of New York ser. in commerce, civics, and technology)

FINK, Wesley Albert, 1870–
Bookkeeping and cost-finding for the plumber. Chic. Domestic engineering [c1918] 128p. 17cm.

JEFFERSON, Howard McNayr.
Accrued interest receivable and payable; an accurate daily statement. N. Y. Bankers pub. co. 1918. 93p. 17½cm. (Bank department ser.2)

KENT, William, 1851–1918.
Bookkeeping and cost accounting for factories. N. Y. Wiley, 1918. 261p. 28½cm.

KRACH, Edward Tingey, 1884– , compiler.
Standardized accounting system for country clubs . . . Chic. Glennon & Kern [c1918] [32]p. 28cm.

McCORMACK, Charles Thomas, 1877–
The bookkeeper's ready reference manual. [Fort Worth, Tex. Smith print. co.] c1918. 80p. 22cm.

MINER, George Washington, 1860– , and ELWELL, Fayette Herbert, 1885–
Principles of bookkeeping; first course; illustrating the journal method of closing the ledger. Bost. Ginn [c1918] 192p. 24cm. (Miner and Elwell ser.)
Published with slight alterations under title: "Principles of bookkeeping; brief course."
—Principles of bookkeeping; introductory course . . . Bost. Ginn [c1918] 256+xxp. 23½cm. (Miner and Elwell ser.)
Published with slight alterations under title: "Principles of bookkeeping; elementary course."
—Principles of bookkeeping; intermediate course. Bost. Ginn [c1918] p.257–368+xviiip. 23cm. (Miner and Elwell ser.)
—Principles of bookkeeping; advanced course. Bost. Ginn [c1918] p.365–500, 23cm. (Miner and Elwell ser.)
—Principles of bookkeeping; intermediate and advanced courses. Bost. Ginn [c1918] p.167–416+xviiip. 23½cm. (Miner and Elwell ser.)
Published also with slight alterations as chapters xiv–xxxii of the authors' "Principles of bookkeeping; combined course."
—Principles of bookkeeping; corporation and voucher accounting. Bost. Ginn [c1918] p.417–500, 23cm. (Miner and Elwell ser.)

MINER (continued)

—Principles of bookkeeping; combined course; illustrating the direct method of closing the ledger . . . Bost. Ginn [c1918] 416p. 23½cm. (Miner and Elwell ser.)

Published with slight alterations under title: "Principles of bookkeeping; complete course."

—Principles of bookkeeping; single-entry set. Bost. Ginn [c1918] 10p. 23cm. (Miner and Elwell ser.)

(Manual for teachers of bookkeeping, by Karl F[ranklin] McMurry. Bost. Ginn [c1923] 151p. 19cm.

"This manual is intended to be especially helpful to those who are using Miner and Elwell's 'Principles of bookkeeping.'"—Pref.)

NICHOLS, Frederick George, 1878–

Elementary bookkeeping; exercises for class drill. Rochester, N. Y. Scrantom, Wetmore [c1918] 115p. 20½cm.

Another ed. N. Y. Amer. bk. co. [c1922] 156p. 16cm.

PRICE, Isaac.

Questions in advanced bookkeeping for drill, test, and review. N. Y. Hinds, Hayden & Eldredge [c1918] 80p.+3 l. +p.107–210, 17cm. (Progressive ser.; regents question and answer books)

"Answers in advanced bookkeeping for drill, test, and review" (3 l.+p.107–210) has special title-page.

Published also without answers.

—Questions in elementary bookkeeping for drill, test, and review. N. Y. Hinds, Hayden & Eldredge [c1918] 68p.+3 l.+p.107–220, 17cm. (Progressive ser.; regents question and answer books)

"Answers in elementary bookkeeping for drill, test, and review" (3 l. +p.107–220) has special title-page.

RACINE, Samuel Frederick, 1882–

Syllabus of bookkeeping. [Seattle, Western institute of accountancy, commerce & finance] 1918. 26 numb. l. 30½cm. (Accounting students' ser.)

Another ed. 1920. 86 numb. l. 27½cm. (Accounting students' ser.)

REYNOLDS, Ward Burham, and THORNTON, Frank Weldon, 1863–

Duties of the junior accountant. N. Y. Endowment fund of the Amer. institute of accountants, 1918. 102p. 18½cm.

"The text . . . consists of matter which appeared in three articles in the Journal of accountancy of September, October, and

November, 1917, and additional matter supplied later by the authors."

2d ed. 1919. 107p. 18½cm.
3d ed. 1920. 107p. 18½cm.
Other eds. 1922; 1923; 1929. 107p. 18½cm.

RITTENHOUSE, Charles Forest, 1881–
Elements of accounts for individuals, professional men, and institutions. N. Y. McGraw-Hill, 1918. 264p. 23½cm.
The original edition published in 1915 was a private edition for use in the author's own classes.

—and CLAPP, Philip Francis, 1879–
Accounting theory and practice. N. Y. McGraw-Hill, 1918. 2v. 23½cm.
v.1, unit 1, elementary accounting; v.2, unit 2, advanced accounting.
Vol.1 reprinted several times. Latest date of printing, 1933.
2d ed. 1919. 186p. 23½cm.
Vol.2 revised in 1919 and reprinted several times. Latest date of printing, 1929.

—Practice set. N. Y. McGraw-Hill, 1918. 56p. 23½cm.
At head of title: Unit 2, practice set.

SCOVILL, Hiram Thompson, 1885–
Farm accounting. N. Y. Appleton, 1918. 429p. 19½cm.
Another ed. 1921. 429p. 19cm.

SHAW, A. W., company, Chicago.
Accounting and costs; finding bank costs—how to check profit leaks—simple cost systems that pay—making every account profitable—tested ways to reduce costs. Chic. Shaw [c1918] 225+[4]p. 21½cm. (Shaw banking ser.)

STRAYER, S. Irving, 1867– , and WRIGHT, H. Winfield.
Modern bookkeeping, accounting, and business practice . . . prepared for the use of students attending business colleges, high schools, normal schools, academies . . . Phil. Modern text bk. co. 1918. 258p. 27½cm.

WILSON, Richard Patrick, 1890– , and CARPENTER, Harry James, 1886–
Analysis of financial statements. Chic. LaSalle extension univ. [c1918] 38p. 23cm.
Other eds. 1920; 1921; 1923; 1927; 1931. 38p. 23cm.

WISCONSIN. STATE BOARD OF ACCOUNTANCY.
Governmental accounting questions and answers; 1914, 1915, 1916, 1917, 1918. Madison, Wis. State board of accountancy [1918] 50p. 23cm.
—Governmental accounting questions and answers; 1914, 1915, 1916, 1917; 1918; 1919; 1920; 1921. Madison, Wis. State board of accountancy [1922] 87p. 23cm.
This work includes questions prepared for C.P.A. examinations with unofficial answers.

1919

ADAMS, William James, 1878–
Up-to-date regents questions in bookkeeping. Syracuse, N.Y. C.W. Bardeen, c1919. 49p. 17cm.
Another ed. 1919. 57p. 17cm.

BARTHOLOMEW, Wallace Edgar, 1877–
Bookkeeping exercises. N.Y. Gregg [c1919] 2v. 19cm.
Contents.—pt.1. Elementary bookkeeping.—pt.2. Advanced bookkeeping.
Vol.1 reprinted in 1923; v.2, in 1932.

BASSET, William Rupert, 1883–
How to audit: a manual of instruction originally prepared for the staff of and under the supervision of a certified public accountant and member of the American institute of accountants. N.Y. McArdle press [c1919] 112p. 24cm.

BELT, Robert E.
Foundry cost accounting practice and procedure. [Cleveland, Penton press] 1919. 271p. 22cm.
2d ed. 1926. 267p. 23½cm.

BENDER, George De Witt, 1884–
Accounting and business secrets: a ready reference book of accounting principles, forms, charts, rules, outlines, and other information; for business men, executives, office managers, accountants, bookkeepers, and clerks. Seattle [Metropolitan press] 1919. 64p. 21cm.

BEXELL, John Andrew, 1867– , and SCUDDER, H. D.
The standard farm accounts and records; 4th ed. Corvallis, Or. Oregon agricultural college [1919] 72p. 28cm.
This work is not a later edition of either of Bexell's earlier works. The early editions of this work could not be found.

DENHAM, Robert Scudder, 1871–
The A-B-C of cost engineering. Cleveland, Denham cost-finding co. [c1919] 105p. 15½cm.
Another ed. [c1922] 109p. 15½cm.

LEMOWITZ, Nathan H.
Bookkeeping made easy. N. Y. E. J. Clode [c1919] 193p. 19cm. (Made easy ser.)

LITTLETON, Ananias Charles, 1886–
An introduction to elementary accounting; with a program of study and practice assignments. [Champaign, Ill. Flannigan Pearson] c1919. 64p. 23½cm.
Another ed. Cin. South-western pub. co. 1920. 64p. 23cm.

NICHOLSON, Jerome Lee, 1863– , and ROHRBACH, John Francis Deems, 1889–
Cost accounting. N. Y. Ronald, 1919. 576p. 22cm.
Other eds. 1920; 1922; 1923. 576p. 22cm.

VINCENT, John P.
Cost accountancy and profit figuring; presenting the art and principles of cost figuring from all angles; coupled with practical profit sharing and disposition. Cin. Campbell commercial school [c1919] 68p. 23cm.
—Results to Cost accountancy and profit figuring. Cin. Hamilton school [n.d.] 40p. 23cm.

1920

BENNETT, George Edward, 1889–
Accounting principles and practice. N. Y. Biddle business publications, 1920–21. 2v. 22cm.
v.1, 1920; v.2, 1921.
2d ed. N. Y. Gregg, 1923. 2v. 22cm.

BERNDT, Irving A.
Costs; their compilation and use in management. Chic. H. P. Gould [c1920] 235p. 24cm.
First published, in part, in the 100% magazine.

CARTHAGE, Philip I.
Retail organization and accounting control. N. Y. Appleton, 1920. 349p. 19½cm.
Another ed. Scranton, International textbk. co. 1924. 349p. 23cm.

CUNNINGHAM, Earle H., 1888–
Bookkeeping and elementary accounting. Portland, Me. [c1920] [409]p. 23cm.

FOOTE, Lewis A.
The Adap-table system; a practical and economic solution of the accrual accounting problem. N. Y. Thrift systems co. c1920. 2v. 23½cm. (v.2: 28½x29½cm.)
Contents.—v.1. Text book.—v.2. Graphics.

GREELEY, Harold Dudley, 1882– , editor.
Business accounting . . . N. Y. Ronald, 1920. 5v. 22cm.
Contents.—v.1. Theory of accounts, by Harold Dudley Greeley.—v.2. Constructive accounting, by George Edward Bennett.—v.3. Cost and accounting, by De Witt Carl Eggleston.—v.4. Advanced and analytical accounting, by Henry Clay Cox.—v.5. Illustrative accounting problems, by Charles Forest Rittenhouse and Harold Dudley Greeley.
(Reading guide, by Arthur H[enry] Rosenkampff and Gould L[each] Harris. N. Y. Ronald [c1920] 199p. 19½cm.)

HODGE, Albert Claire, and MCKINSEY, James Oscar, 1889–
Principles of accounting. Chic. Univ. of Chic. press [1920] 389p. 23cm.
Other eds. 1920; 1921; 1927. 394p. 22cm.

HOOVER, Simon Robert, 1867–
Bookkeeping and accounting practice; the Hoover system of modern bookkeeping—easy to learn and practical to use. Chic. A. W. Shaw [c1920] 301p. 24½cm. (Shaw educational ser.)
Other eds. 1923; 1927. 309p. 24½cm.

JORDAN, John Packard, 1877–1932, and HARRIS, Gould Leach, 1892–
Cost accounting principles and practice. N. Y. Ronald, 1920. 529p. 22cm.
Other eds. 1921; 1923. 543p. 22cm.
2d ed. [c1925] 562p. 22cm.
—Problem appendix for Cost accounting . . . N. Y. Ronald, 1921. p.481–512, 21½cm.
Special imprint of the appendix to the larger work "Cost accounting . . ." 1920, by the same authors.

KIRK, John George, 1881– , and STREET, James Layman, 1879–
Bookkeeping for modern business [with] script by René Guillard. Phil. Winston [c1920] 236p. 25½cm.
Elementary course.
Advanced course published in 1921.

LYNAUGH, Matthew Edmund, 1894– , and THOMPSON, Clyde Ordell, 1874–
Practice exercises in bookkeeping. N. Y. Amer. bk. co. [c1920] 144p. 19cm.

LYONS, James A., 1861–1920, and SMITH, Oliver Saxton, 1881–
Lyons' bookkeeping and accounting. Chic. Lyons & Carnahan, c1920. 240p. 25cm.
This work also published in two parts.
Another ed. 1922. 240p. 24½cm.
Cover-title: Bookkeeping and accounting; complete.

McGARRAUGH, Robert.
Mine bookkeeping: a comprehensive system of records and accounts for mining operations of moderate dimensions. N. Y. McGraw-Hill, 1920. 118p. 23½cm.

McKINSEY, James Oscar, 1889–
Bookkeeping and accounting [series A] Cin. South-western pub. co. [c1920] 2v. 23½cm.
Practice sets separately published.
2d ed. [c1926] 2v. 23½cm.
3d ed. [c1931–33] 2v. 23½cm.
v.1, 1931; v.2, 1933.
—Bookkeeping and accounting [series B] Cin. South-western pub. co. [c1920] 3v. 23½cm.
The content of the two volumes of series A is the same as that of the three volumes of series B.
Practice sets separately published.
2d ed. [c1926–27] 3v. 23½cm.
3d ed. [c1931–32] 2v. 22½cm.
Vol.3 has not been revised.

PARSONS, Theodore C.
Parsons' [insurance] accounting system. [Chic. Gunthorp-Warren print. co. c1920] 26p. 23cm.

RACINE, Samuel Frederick, 1882–
Practical problems graded; series "C." [Seattle, Western institute of accountancy, commerce & finance, c1920] 96 l. 27cm. (Accounting students' ser.)
Other eds. 1925; 1926. 143p. 23cm. (Accounting students' ser.)

SALIERS, Earl Adolphus, 1884–
Accounts in theory and practice; principles. N. Y. McGraw-Hill, 1920. 301p. 23½cm.

SHERWOOD, John F., 1890–
Public accounting and auditing. Cin. South-western pub. co. [c1920–21] 2v. 23½cm.
v.1, 1920; v.2, 1921.
3d ed. [c1922] 2v. 23½cm.

THOMPSON, Alfred J.
Supplementary exercises for schools of accountancy and business administration. N.Y. Assn. press, 1920. 68p. 28cm.

VAN DE WALKER, Frank C., and ROWE, Harry Marc, 1887–
Logging and lumber manufacturing set. Balt. Rowe [c1920] 68p. 23cm.

1921

ALGER, Francis Russell.
Actual business bookkeeping and accounting; part 1 [with] script illustrations by E.C. Mills. Saginaw, Mich. Bliss pub. co. [c1921] 78p. 28cm.
—Bliss & Alger bookkeeping and accounting theory and practice, complete: a textbook in bookkeeping and accounting; for high schools, business schools, and all institutions conducting commercial courses. Saginaw, Mich. Bliss pub. co. [c1923] 175+[2]p. 28cm.
The complete edition in which part 1 entered above is incorporated.
Bliss, referred to above, is Fred H. Bliss, author of a work published in 1912.
Another ed. [c1928] 175+[2]p. 27½cm.
Another ed. [c1930] 214+[3]p. 27½cm.
Alger was assisted in this revision by William Francis Robins.

AMERICAN INSTITUTE OF ACCOUNTANTS. Board of examiners.
Examination questions prepared by the Board of examiners of the American institute of accountants for the examinations conducted from June, 1917, to May, 1921, inclusive. N.Y. Amer. institute of accountants, 1921. 204p. 18½cm.
[2d ed.] 1924. 359p. 18½cm.
Contents include examinations conducted from June, 1917, to May, 1924, inclusive.
[3d ed.] 1928. 555p. 18½cm.
Contents include examinations conducted from June, 1917, to Nov. 1927, inclusive.
(See 1932, American institute of accountants. Board of examiners, for examinations conducted from May, 1927, to Nov. 1931, inclusive)

ARMSTRONG, George Simpson.
Essentials of industrial costing. N.Y. Appleton, 1921. 297p. 22½cm.

BEACH, Frank Loomis, 1894–
Twenty twenty-minute lessons in bookkeeping. N.Y. Ronald, 1921. 124p. 19½cm.
Another ed. [c1921] 124p. 18½cm.

BELL, Spurgeon, 1880–
Accounting principles; their use in business management. N.Y. Macmillan, 1921. 482p. 20½cm.
Practice sets separately published.

BELL, William Hansell, 1883–
Accountants' reports. N.Y. Ronald, 1921. 247 numb. l. 28cm.
Another ed. 1922. 247 numb. l. 27cm.
2d ed. [c1925] 386p. 22cm.
3d ed. [c1934] 397p. 22cm.

BLOCK, Milton D.
C.P.A. examinations and how to prepare for them. Chic. LaSalle extension univ. 1921. 76p. 23cm.
The preliminary matter is similar to that contained in Tanner's work published in 1916.
Another ed. 1922. 76p. 23cm.

BOURNE, Clifford Norman.
A special course in accounting and commercial law; for the student, business man and woman; the picturit system of study. [Syracuse, N.Y. Press of John Single paper co. c1921] 125p. 23½cm.

COLE, William Morse, 1866– , and GEDDES, Anne Elizabeth.
The fundamentals of accounting. Bost. Houghton Mifflin [c1921] 434p. 22½cm.

CONNOR, W. N.
Construction costs. Bost. 1921. p.157–197, 23½cm.
Reprinted from the Journal of the Boston society of civil engineers, May, 1921, v.8, no.5.

CONYNGTON, Thomas, 1855– , KNAPP, Harold C., and PINKERTON, Paul Whittier, 1887–
Wills, estates, and trusts: a manual of law, accounting, and procedure; for executors, administrators, and trustees. N.Y. Ronald,

CONYNGTON (continued)
1921. 2v. 22cm.
Another ed. 1922. 2v. 22cm.

DUDLEY, A. W.
Modern commercial bookkeeping: a logical, teachable, scientific presentation of accounting as practiced in progressive business institutions; designed for use in high schools, commercial colleges, academies, colleges, and for private learners. Des Moines, Accredited schools supply co. [c1921] 200p. 27cm.

EGGLESTON, De Witt Carl, 1881– , and ROBINSON, Frederick Bertrand, 1883–
Business costs. N. Y. Appleton, 1921. 587p. 23cm. (College of the city of New York ser. in commerce, civics, and technology)

ESQUERRÉ, Paul Joseph, 1872–1934.
Practical accounting problems; theory, discussion, and solutions. N. Y. Ronald, 1921–22. 2v. 28cm.
v.1, 1921; v.2, 1922.
Autographed from typewritten copy.

GARBER, Osborne.
20th century bank accounting: a treatise on modern banking as illustrated in the business transactions which accompany this text. Cin. South-western pub. co. 1921. 79p. 23½cm.
Practice set separately published.
2d ed. 1922. 79p. 23½cm.

GOGGIN, Walter John, 1882–
Cost accounting. N. Y. La Fayette institute [c1921] 86p. 25½cm.
Another ed. [Phil.] c1930. 86+[2]p. 25½cm. Foreword and addenda by Frederick Wells Woodbridge.

HARRISON, George Charter, 1881–
Cost accounting to aid production: a practical study of scientific cost accounting. N. Y. Engin. mag. 1921. 234p. 23½cm.
This work is a compilation of the author's articles which appeared in "Industrial management" from Oct. 1918, to June, 1919. It appeared in unbound form in 1919 but the book was not copyrighted until 1921.
Another ed. 1921. 231p. 22½cm. (Industrial management library)
2d ed. 1924. 234p. 23cm.

KIRK, John George, 1881– , and STREET, James Layman, 1879–
Bookkeeping for modern business; advanced course. Phil. Winston [c1921] 118p. 24½cm.
Elementary course published in 1920.

KOOPMAN, Sietse Bernard, 1876– , and KESTER, Roy Bernard, 1882–
Fundamentals of accounting; principles and practice of bookkeeping. N. Y. Ronald, 1921–23. 2v. 22cm.
v.1, 1921; v.2, 1923.
Another ed. 1922–24. 2v. 22cm.
v.1, 1922; v.2, 1924.
—Fundamentals of bookkeeping and accounting. N. Y. Ronald, 1930. 404p. 22cm.
v.1, 2d ed.

MCGRATH, Thomas Orrin, 1883–
Mine accounting and cost principles. N. Y. McGraw-Hill, 1921. 257p. 23½cm.

MINSTER, Leopold.
Retail profits, turnover, and net worth; simple methods of determining gross profit, expense, and net profit in any size store; with concise forms for approximating stock on hand any month, week, or day and finding average stock and turnover. N. Y. U.P.C. bk. co. [c1921] 48p. 24cm.
Reprinted from Atlantic coast merchant.

MUSICK, William L., 1860–
Practical bookkeeping and accounting: a system of modern bookkeeping and accounting logically developed; with forms and statements amply illustrated . . . contains a system of accounts for retail merchants . . . Chic. Universal text bk. co. [c1921] 242+[6]p. 25cm.

NEWLOVE, George Hillis, 1893–
C.P.A. accounting; theory, questions, and problems . . . N. Y. Assn. press, 1921–22. 3v. 22cm.
v.1, 1921; v.2, 1921; v.3, 1922 (contains solutions)
Preliminary edition entitled "C.P.A. accounting; theory, auditing, and problems" contained all questions and problems in all C.P.A. examination papers obtainable, 284 in number. This work published by Appleton in 1920 consisted of 416 pages.
Another ed. Wash. White press, 1923. 3v. 22cm.
2d printing.
2d ed. 1926. 3v. 23cm.

NEWLOVE (continued)

2d ed.	1927. 3v. 23cm. 2d printing.
3d ed.	1928. 4v. 23½cm.
3d ed.	1930. 4v. 23½cm. 2d printing. The 1930 edition is entitled "C.P.A. accounting; theory, auditing, and problems."

—and PRATT, Lester Amos, 1892–
Industrial accounting; with C.P.A. questions and problems. N. Y. Appleton, 1921. 266p. 22cm.

OAKEY, Francis.
Principles of government accounting and reporting. N. Y. Appleton, 1921. 561p. 22½cm. (Institute for government research. Principles of administration)

RACINE, Samuel Frederick, 1882–
Cost accounts. [Seattle, Western institute of accountancy, commerce & finance] 1921. 183p. 23cm. (Accounting students' ser.)

—Practical problems graded; series "B." [Seattle, Western institute of accountancy, commerce & finance, c1921] [93] l. 27½cm. (Accounting students' ser.)
Printed on versos only.

SALIERS, Earl Adolphus, 1884–
Principles of accounting. [N. Y.] La Fayette institute, c1921. 72p. 25x20cm.

Another ed.	[Phil.] La Fayette institute, c1930. 76p. 26cm. Foreword and addenda by Frederick Wells Woodbridge.

SAXTON, Lynn Mateer, 1874–
Auditing. [N. Y.] c1921. 88 numb. l. 33cm.
Autographed from typewritten copy.

SMITH, W. J.
Modern commercial banking; presenting the science and art of bank bookkeeping with complete explanations and comprehensive memoranda for practice. Des Moines, Accredited schools supply co. [c1921] 47p. 26½cm.

TONER, James B.
Auditing. N. Y. La Fayette institute [c1921] 45p. 25½cm.

WALKER, Edmund.
Newspaper accounting and federal taxation. N. Y. Walker [1921] 27p. 23cm.

1922

AMERICAN SYSTEM COMPANY, Roanoke, Va.
American agency accounting system; its methods of accounting and record keeping for insurance agents and brokers. Roanoke, Va. Amer. system co. c1922. 27+[1]p. 28cm.
Another ed. c1924. 31p. 28cm.

ARNETT, Trevor, 1870–
College and university finance. N. Y. Gen. educ. bd. 1922. 212p. 22cm.

BASSET, William Rupert, 1883– , and HEYWOOD, Johnson.
Production engineering and cost keeping for machine shops. N. Y. McGraw-Hill, 1922. 311p. 23½cm.

BELL, Spurgeon, 1880–
Theory and practice of accounting; use in managerial control. Chic. Amer. technical soc. [c1922] 2v. 21½cm. (Business management ser.)
The necessary preliminary survey and detailed working outline were made by George Enfield Frazer.
Vol.1 was reprinted in 1927 under the title: "Practical accounting; its use in managerial control."
Vol.2 contains "Managerial accounting," p.441–532, by H. W. Quaintance, editor-in-chief of the Business management series.
This work was reprinted as part of the "Business management series" in 1925 and 1929.
Vol.1 was reprinted in 1927, 1929, and 1932 as v.7 and in 1934 as v.5 of the encyclopedia "Practical business administration" copyrighted by the American technical society.
Vol.2 was reprinted in 1927, 1929, and 1932 as v.8 and in 1934 as v.6 of the encyclopedia "Practical business administration." "Managerial accounting" by H. W. Quaintance contained in v.2 was revised by E. Roscoe Jones in the 1934 edition.

BENNETT, George Edward, 1889–
Advanced accounting. N. Y. McGraw-Hill, 1922. 661p. 23½cm.

BIENVENU, Emile, 1873–
Accounting and business dictionary: an encyclopedia of accounting, financial, commercial law, and general business terms. N. O. Poynton press, 1922. 314p. 21½cm.

BORSODI, Ralph.
The new accounting; bookkeeping without books of original entry by the use of a natural system of double entry bookkeeping. N. Y. Dodd, Mead, 1922. 127p. 22cm.

BOSTON. CHAMBER OF COMMERCE. Bureau of commercial and industrial affairs.
Balance sheets and profit and loss statements analyzed and defined for business executives . . . [Bost. Boston Chamber of commerce, c1922] 36p. 22½cm.
Another ed. [c1923] 36p. 23cm.

—Classification and definitions of ledger accounts . . . [Bost. Boston Chamber of commerce, 1922] 34p. 23cm.
"Prepared by the Chamber's Committee on industrial accounting and executive reports."

BOSTON. CHAMBER OF COMMERCE. Retail trade board.
Retail inventory shortages and remedies . . . Bost. Boston Chamber of commerce, c1922. 47+[1]p. 23cm.
The Committee of the Retail trade board of the Boston Chamber of commerce also acting as a committee with similar assignment from the Controllers' congress of the National retail dry goods association prepared the report listed above. This work was also printed by the Controllers' congress of the National retail dry goods association. In 1923 another committee composed of members of the Controllers' congress published a revised edition of "Retail inventory shortages and remedies."
A new study published in 1931 entitled "Stock shortage control manual" consists of eight pages and is not included in this bibliography.

CASTENHOLZ, William Burtis, 1879–
Cost accounting procedure [with] charts by Ennes C. Rayson. Chic. LaSalle extension univ. 1922. 333p. 23½cm.
Other eds. 1924; 1929; 1932. 359p. 22cm.
—Cost accounting assignments, by Ennes C. Rayson in cooperation with LaSalle . . . staff: a series of fifteen coordinated assignments based upon Cost accounting procedure . . . Chic. LaSalle extension univ. 1923. 220p. 23cm.
Solutions and special working forms separately published.
Other eds. 1931; 1932. 220p. 23cm.

CHAMBER OF COMMERCE OF THE UNITED STATES OF AMERICA. Dept. of manufacture.
Perpetual inventory or stores control. Wash. Chamber of commerce [1922] 30p. 24cm.
Other eds. 1924; 1925; 1926; 1928; 1929. 26p. 23cm.

CONYNGTON, Thomas, 1855– , BENNETT, Robert Joseph, 1871– , and PINKERTON, Paul Whittier, 1887–
Corporation procedure; law, finance, accounting; ed. by Hugh R. Conyngton. N.Y. Ronald, 1922. 1689p. 22cm.
This work is based upon three volumes: "Corporate management" and "Corporate organization," by Thomas Conyngton, not included in this bibliography, and "Corporation accounting," by Robert Joseph Bennett, listed in 1916.
Another ed. [c1927] 1479p. 22cm.
Pinkerton's name does not appear on the title-page of the revised edition.

FINNEY, Harry Anson, 1886–
Consolidated statements for holding company and subsidiaries. N.Y. Prentice-Hall, 1922. 229p. 23½cm.
Supplement, consisting of solutions and answers to problems and exercises, separately published.
2d ed. 1922. 229p. 23½cm.
The first edition published in June; second edition, in September.
Another ed. 1923. 229p. 23½cm.
3d printing.
Another ed. 1923. 164p. 24cm.
Appendices which give the answers omitted in this edition.
Another ed. 1924. 229p. 23½cm.
4th printing.

GILES, John Henry.
Farm-ranch bookkeeping. San Antonio, Lodovic print. co. c1922. 45 numb. l. 28cm.

GRANT, Harris Denison, 1864–
Practical accounting for general contractors. N.Y. McGraw-Hill, 1922. 254p. 23½cm.
2d ed. 1925. 329p. 23½cm.

HADLEY, Charles R., company, Los Angeles.
Exhibit and book of instructions of Hadley's pathfinder bookkeeping system for contractors and builders. Los Angeles, Hadley, c1922. 36 numb. l.+forms, 28x36cm.
Another ed. 1931. 36 numb. l.+forms, 28½x38cm.

HAFNER, George W., 1882–
The dealers' handy cost book; containing the Building supply news' adaptable uniform cost accounting system for every building supply, lumber, and coal retail merchant; with graphs and illustrations and a facsimile of all necessary forms . . . [Chic. Building supply news] c1922. 158p. 18½cm.
Supplement (1 sheet, 126½x67½cm. folded to 17x13cm.) laid in.

HAYWARD, William Richart, 1868– , and PRICE, Isaac.
Progressive problems in bookkeeping and accountancy. N. Y. Macmillan, 1922. 149p. 19½cm.

HIBBS, Weston J.
Cost system of the U. G. I. [United gas improvement] contracting co. [Phil. c1922] 62+[1]p. 24cm.

INTERNATIONAL TEXTBOOK COMPANY, Scranton.
Audit procedure and reports. Scranton, International textbk. co. c1922. 131p. 19½cm. (International library of technology. Blue book ser. v.54)
(See 1905; 1925, International textbook company, Scranton)

—Bank accounting; financial calculations. Scranton, International textbk. co. c1922. 158p. 19½cm. (International library of technology. Blue book ser. v.58)

KILBURN, Florence M.
Bookkeeping exercises . . . [Brooklyn, Guide print. & pub. co.] c1922. 32p. 22cm.
At head of title: Bushwick high school, Brooklyn, N. Y.
"These exercises are to be used in connection with Unit I of the New York city syllabus."
Another ed. c1923. 47p. 22½cm.

KOEHLER, Theodore, and KOEHLER, Theodora, 1879–
The accounting mentor of theory and practice . . . N. Y. Tri-service accounting corp. 1922. 2v. 23½cm. (Study and service ser.)

—The accounting quiz-answerer . . . an untechnical reading, study, and working course on the technique of accounting practice and procedure . . . N. Y. Tri-service accounting corp. 1922–23. 12v. 23½cm. (Earn and learn ser.)
—The encyclopedic index to The accounting quiz-answerer . . . designed to meet . . . the specific requirements of all classes of readers according to the Tri-service accounting utility of the entire work . . . N. Y. Tri-service accounting corp. 1923. 331p. 23½cm. (Earn and learn ser.)

LYBRAND, William M., MACPHERSON, Frank Herbert, 1861– , and DICKINSON, Arthur Lowes, 1859–1935.
Accounting for modern corporations; prepared especially for the instruction and training of students of the American school. Chic. Amer. technical soc. [c1922] 87+[4]p. 21½cm.
Earlier editions published by the American school of correspondence, Chicago, in 1909 and 1919 were not issued for general distribution.

NATIONAL RETAIL DRY GOODS ASSOCIATION. Controllers' congress.
A standard method of accounting for retail stores; financial statements, operating statements, classification and distribution of expense, classification of merchandise . . . N. Y. Controllers' congress of the National retail dry goods assn. c1922. 2v. 22 charts (part fold.) 29½cm.
"Amplifying and revising 'The classification and distribution of expense in retail stores' issued by the National retail dry goods association in 1917."
Contents.—v.1. Descriptive text.—v.2. Charts.

NEWLOVE, George Hillis, 1893–
Cost accounts; preliminary ed. Wash. White press, 1922. 124+A42p. 21½cm.
Autographed from typewritten copy.
3d ed. 1923. 183p. 22cm.
—Practice set to be used with Cost accounts. Wash. White press, 1922. 2v. 27½cm.
Part 1, journals; part 2, ledgers.
2d ed. 1923. 2v. 27½cm.
—Solutions to Cost accounts. Wash. White press, 1922. [34]p. 27cm.
2d ed. 1923. 70p. 23cm.

PATON, William Andrew, 1889–
Accounting theory; with special reference to the corporate enterprise. N. Y. Ronald, 1922. 508p. 22cm.

PIPER, Clarence Brett, 1882–
Manual explaining the use of an accounting system; designed for chapters of college fraternities. [Belmont? Mass.] c1922. 159 l.+forms, 28½cm.
Autographed from typewritten copy.

PORTE, Roy Trewin.
John Smith's bookkeeping. Salt Lake City, Porte pub. co. [c1922] 168p. 19½cm.
This work is a treatise on accounting for printers.
Another ed. [c1924] 187p. 19½cm.

RACINE, Samuel Frederick, 1882–
Practical problems graded; series "D." [Seattle, Racine, c1922] 89 l. 27½cm. (Accounting students' ser.)
Printed on versos only.

REED, William Blose, 1874–
Bituminous coal mine accounting. N. Y. McGraw-Hill, 1922. 221p. 23½cm.
First published in part in the Coal review under title "Cost accounting in the bituminous industry."

RICHARDSON, Franklin Whittemore.
The check list method of auditing & bookkeeping [2d ed.] N. Y. [W. H. Rich print. co.] 1922. 63+[1]p. 15cm.

3d ed.	1923.	100p.	15cm.
4th ed.	1924.	100p.	15cm.
5th ed.	1925.	100p.	15cm.
6th ed.	1927.	100p.	15cm.

RISQUE, Ferdinand William, 1850–
Risque's bookkeeping and business management . . . N. Y. U. P. C. bk. co. [c1922] 189p. 25½cm.

RITTENHOUSE, Charles Forest, 1881– , and PERCY, Atlee Lane, 1880–
Accounting problems; intermediate. N. Y. McGraw-Hill, 1922. 429p. 23½cm.
2d ed. 1931. 460p. 23½cm.

ROBERT MORRIS ASSOCIATES.
The financial audit as viewed by bankers; statement analysis; suggested methods for a credit index: publications of the Robert Morris associates condensed, rearranged, and commented on by Scovell, Wellington & company. [Bost. c1922] 56p. 23cm.

ROWE, Harry Marc, 1860–1926, and ROWE, Harry Marc, 1887–
Accountancy and business management . . . part 1 [with] script by the late C. P. Zaner and E. A. Lupfer. Balt. Rowe [c1922] 132p. 23½cm.
—Accountancy and business management . . . Balt. Rowe [c1923] 268p. 23½cm.
The complete edition in which part 1 entered above is incorporated.
"The course of study provided in 'Accountancy and business management' is based to some extent upon the author's previous work, 'Rowe's bookkeeping and accountancy.' However, a number of important changes in the selection and arrangement

of subject matter make the present course of study substantially a new and original work."

Two laboratory units accompany the text.

Another ed. 1924.

Another ed. [c1925] 268+[2]p. 23cm.

The textbook with the laboratory sets which accompany the text is sometimes referred to as the "Star combination course in accountancy, business management, corporation, and cost accounting."

SCHULZ, Arthur Karl.

Bank bookkeeping. N. Y. Amer. institute of banking [c1922] 189p. 20cm.

SHEPHERD, Jessie M.

Practical accounting problems; prepared especially for the instruction and training of students of the American school. Chic. Amer. technical soc. [c1922] 88+[6]p. 21½cm.

Earlier editions published by the American school of correspondence, Chicago, in 1909 and 1920 were not issued for general distribution.

SHURICK, Adam Thomas, 1883–

Coal mining costs. N. Y. McGraw-Hill, 1922. 515p. 23½cm.

SZEPESI, Eugene.

Cost control and accounting for textile mills. N. Y. Bragdon, Lord & Nagle [c1922] 441p. 22cm.

THEISS, Edwin Leodgar.

Elements of accounting practice: a series of thirty coordinated texts covering elementary accounting and double entry bookkeeping. Chic. LaSalle extension univ. 1922. 30 pamphlets, each 23cm.

Texts available singly or in a complete set with solutions to practice problems.

Titles of the texts follow:

1. The balance sheet. c1922; 1926; 1928; 1932. 22p. 23cm.
2. The profit and loss statement. c1922; 1930. 15p. 23cm.
3. The general ledger. c1922; 1925; 1930. 16p. 23cm.
4. Closing the ledger. c1922; 1930. 18p. 23cm.
5. The journal. c1922; 1927; 1932. 11p. 23cm.
6. Closing the ledger by journal entries. c1922; 1931. 9p. 23cm.
7. The cash journal. c1922; 1928. 11p. 23cm.
8. Merchandise records. c1922; 1927; 1931. 20p. 23cm.
9. Subdivision of the ledger. c1922; 1931. 22p. 23cm.

THEISS (continued)

10. Columnization. c1922; 1930. 16p. 23cm.
11. Accounting procedure for promissory notes. c1922; 1930. 24p. 23cm.
12. Drafts, trade acceptances, and bills of lading. c1922; 1931. 14p. 23cm.
13. Auxiliary cash records. c1922; 1930. 17p. 23cm.
14. Sundry auxiliary books and business records. c1922; 1931. 16p. 23cm.
15. Finding, correcting, and preventing errors. c1922; 1931. 20p. 23cm.
16. Periodic adjustments for accrued and deferred items. c1922; 1926; 1930. 16p. 23cm.
17. Periodical adjustments for depreciation and uncollectible accounts. c1922; 1925; 1930. 17p. 23cm.
18. Partnership accounting; formation and operation. c1922; 1927; 1931. 19p. 23cm.
19. Partnership accounting . . . dissolution problems . . . joint ventures. c1922; 1927; 1932. 21p. 23cm.
20. Corporation accounting; formation and operation. c1922; 1930. 19p. 23cm.
21. Corporation accounting; reorganizations and mergers. c1922; 1930; 1931; 1932. 15p. 23cm.
22. The voucher system. c1922; 1925; 1927; 1931. 28p. 23cm.
23. Factory accounting. c1922; 1925; 1930; 1931. 18p. 23cm.
24. Factory accounting; the perpetual inventory. c1922; 1931. 22p. 23cm.
25. Classification of accounts. c1922; 1930. 24p. 23cm.
26. Single entry. c1922; 1927; 1931. 16p. 23cm.
27. Accounting for non-trading concerns. c1922; 1930. 19p. 23cm.
28. Agency accounts; branches, consignments. c1922; 1927; 1932. 28p. 23cm.
29. Comparative statements. c1922; 1927. 26p. 23cm.
30. Analysis of financial statements. c1922; 1931. 21p. 23cm.

WALKER, Ross Graham.
A classified selection of problems in accounting. Ann Arbor, Mich. G. Wahr [c1922] 181p. 22½cm.

WERMUTH, Charles E.
Classification of accounts for sugar estates. N. O. [c1922] 30p. 23cm.

WILDMAN, John Raymond, 1878–
Principles of accounting. N. Y. N. Y. univ. press, 1922. 310p. 23½cm.
Previous editions not available for general distribution. The author's unrevised copies were copyrighted in 1912. An edition of 360 pages was copyrighted in 1913.

WILLARD, Raymond Delmar, 1884–
System building and constructive accounting. N. Y. McGraw-Hill, 1922. 307p. 23½cm.
Appendix containing problems copyrighted and published separately, 1923.
2d ed. 1924. 361p. 23½cm.
Problems included.

WILLARD, Rex Ethan, 1883–
Simple farm accounts: a text book and guide. Fargo, N. D. The author [c1922] 106p. 23½cm.
2d ed. [c1924] 107p. 23½cm.
4th ed. [c1930] 102p. 23½cm.

WOODS, Clinton Edgar.
Analytical balance sheets for industrials. [Phil. c1922] 31+[1]p. 20½cm.

1923

ATKINS, Paul Moody, 1892–
Industrial cost accounting for executives. N. Y. McGraw-Hill, 1923. 322p. 24cm.
—Textbook of industrial cost accounting. N. Y. McGraw-Hill, 1924. 396p. 23½cm.
"To an extent the material presented in this book was offered in the author's volume 'Industrial cost accounting for executives.'"

BARUCH, Alfred.
Standard costs for sheet metal workers. N. Y. U. P. C. bk. co. 1923. 298p. 23½cm.
First published in the Sheet metal worker in 1921 and 1922. The articles were completely rewritten and brought up to date.

BEASLEY, Leonard.
An outline of municipal accounts. N. Y. Loomis, Suffern & Fernald [c1923] 48p. 23cm.

Bliss, James Harris, 1889–
Financial and operating ratios in management. N. Y. Ronald, 1923. 396p. 22cm.

Borton, E. J., 1891–
Cost accounting principles and methods. Chic. Lyons & Carnahan [c1923] 243p. 20½cm.

Boston. Chamber of commerce. Bureau of commercial and industrial affairs.
Financial reports for industrial executives. [Bost. Boston Chamber of commerce [c1923] 42p. 23cm.
"Prepared by the Chamber's Committee on industrial accounting and executive reports."

Carey, Thomas Joseph.
Vest pocket bookkeeper and short cuts in figures: a simple and concise method of practical bookkeeping; with complete instructions for the correct keeping of books of accounts . . . N. Y. The author, 1923. 160p.

Cowles, Clarence E.
Elements of bookkeeping . . . N. Y. Merrill [c1923–25] 2v. 22½cm.
v.1, 1st unit, 1923; v.2, 2d unit, 1925.
Second unit by Clarence E. Cowles and Warren Lafayette Starkey.
Another ed. [c1926] 2v. 22½cm.
v.1, 1st unit; v.2, 2d unit.
Second unit by Clarence E. Cowles and Warren Lafayette Starkey.

Eggleston, De Witt Carl, 1881–
Principles of accounting practice: a series of fifteen coordinated texts covering advanced accounting theory and practice. Chic. LaSalle extension univ. c1923. 15 pamphlets, each 23cm.
Texts available singly or in a complete set with solutions to practice problems.
Titles of the texts follow:
1. Capital and revenue expenditures. c1923; 1925; 1926; 1930. 28p. 23cm.
2. Assets and their valuation. c1923; 1925; 1930. 31p. 23cm.
3. Methods of depreciation and depletion. c1923; 1925; 1929; 1931. 32p. 23cm.
4. Liabilities and their determination. c1923; 1925; 1930. 31p. 23cm.

5. Sinking funds and reserves. c1923; 1925; 1927; 1930. 26p. 23cm.
6. Bond investments and amortization. c1923; 1926; 1930. 27p. 23cm.
7. Capital stock and its value. c1923; 1930. 28p. 23cm.
8. Surplus and reserves. c1923; 1928; 1930. 17p. 23cm.
9. Insurance and fire loss adjustments. c1923; 1928; 1931. 20p. 23cm.
10. Corporate combinations. c1923; 1929. 23p. 23cm.
11. Holding companies. c1923; 1927; 1930. 29p. 23cm.
12. Bankruptcy accounting. c1923; 1928; 1931. 23p. 23cm.
13. Estate accounting. c1923; 1928; 1934. 38p. 23cm.
14. Public utility accounting. c1923; 1929. 28p. 23cm.
15. Municipal accounting. c1923; 1927; 1934. 33p. 23cm.

ELLIS, Carlos Bent, 1860–1935.
Elementary bookkeeping; with some suggestions for personal uses. Bost. Allyn & Bacon [c1923] 142p. 23½cm.
"While it covers the same ground as the first part of the author's 'Practical bookkeeping' it is distinctly a new book."—Pref.

ELLMORE, D. Carroll.
Audit program and specimen audit; comprising audit program, working papers, "working sheet," exhibits and schedules, instruction for audit report; with explanatory comments. Sheboygan, Wis. Ellmore-Schaafs co. [c1923] 72 numb. l.

EVERITT, Frank, and HEYWOOD, Johnson.
Cost control for foundries; ed. by William R. Basset. N.Y. McGraw-Hill, 1923. 226p. 23½cm.

FILFUS, Nathaniel, and ROBINSON, Nathaniel.
Graded exercises in bookkeeping and accounting. N.Y. Oxford bk. co. [c1923–24] 3v. 20½cm.
v.1, 1923; v.2, 1923; v.3, 1924.

FINNEY, Harry Anson, 1886–
Principles of accounting. N.Y. Prentice-Hall, 1923. 2v. 23½cm.
Regular edition.
v.1, intermediate accounting; v.2, advanced accounting.
"Loose-leaf solutions have been offered for general distribution on this edition of 'Principles of accounting.'"—Publishers.
Other eds. v.1: 1924; 1925; 1926; 1927; 1929.
Other eds. v.2: 1924; 1926; 1927; 1930.
These are reprints. There were two printings in 1927.
The "regular edition" has not been revised.

FINNEY (continued)

—Principles of accounting; rev. ed. N. Y. Prentice-Hall, 1928. 2v. 23½cm.

School edition.

v.1, intermediate accounting; v.2, advanced accounting.

The text matter is the same as that of the regular edition with a different set of problems.

"No solutions were offered for general distribution on this edition."—Publishers.

Other eds. 1929; 1930; 1931; 1932. 2v. 23½cm.
These are reprints of the 1928 "school edition."
There were two printings in 1929.

Another ed. 1934. 2v. 23½cm.
Revised edition.
Vol.1, intermediate, and v.2, advanced, have been completely revised and published both with and without "personal progress tests."

FRITCH, Edouard Henri, 1857–1930.

Simplified bookkeeping; arranged as a simplified textbook of present time methods for schools and colleges. St. L. Fritch [c1923] 219p. 25½cm.

GOODYEAR, Samuel Horatio.

New inductive accounting. Cedar Rapids, Ia. Metropolitan supply co. 1923. 142p. 24cm.

GORDON, Stephen Robbins, 1888–

Cost finding in knitting mills . . . N. Y. Bragdon, Lord & Nagle [c1923] 204p. 23½cm.

GREENWOOD, G. W.

Accounting simplified. Chic. [1923] 48p. 30½x23cm.

Reprinted from the Brick and clay record.

A system of accounting for the brick and clay industry is described.

HADLEY, Charles R., company, Los Angeles.

Exhibit and book of instructions of Hadley's pathfinder bookkeeping system, double entry; for wholesale and retail merchandising establishments. Los Angeles, Hadley, c1923. 36 numb. l. +forms, 28x28cm.

Other eds. 1928; 1930. 36 numb. l. +forms, 28x28cm.

—Exhibit and book of instructions of Hadley's pathfinder bookkeeping system for automobile dealers. Los Angeles, Hadley [c1923] 67 numb. l. +forms, 28x36cm.

—Supplement . . . [c1925] 17 numb. l. +forms, 28x36cm.

—Exhibit and book of instructions of Hadley's pathfinder building trades bookkeeping system; for plumbers, electrical contractors and dealers, tinners, roofers, sheet metal workers, plasterers, painters and other lines of busines selling labor and material. Los Angeles, Hadley, c1923. 58 numb. l. +forms, 28x28cm.
Another ed. 1931. 84 numb. l. +forms, 28x28cm.

—Exhibit and book of instructions of Hadley's pathfinder personal accounting system, double entry. Los Angeles, Hadley, c1923. 26 numb. l. +forms, 18x28cm.
Another ed. 1928. 26 numb. l. +forms, 18x28cm.
Another ed. c1934. 38 numb. l. +forms, 18x28cm.

—Exhibit and book of instructions of Hadley's pathfinder "straight line" bookkeeping system. Los Angeles, Hadley, c1923. 31 numb. l. +forms, 28x28cm.
Another ed. 1928. 31 numb. l. +forms, 28x28cm.

HAFNER, George W.
An accounting system for retailers. [Chic. Amer. lumberman] c1923. 45+[4]p. 20x27½cm.
Reprinted from a series of articles in the American lumberman during 1922.

INTERNATIONAL TEXTBOOK COMPANY, Scranton.
Public-utility accounting practices. Scranton, International textbk. co. c1923. 85p. 19½cm. (International library of technology. Blue book ser. v.61)
(See 1905; 1925, International textbook company, Scranton)

—Reserves and the balance sheet. Scranton, International textbk. co. c1923. 81p. 19½cm. (International library of technology. Blue book ser. v.48)

—Theory of accounts. Scranton, International textbk. co. c1923. 118p. 19½cm. (International library of technology. Blue book ser. v.47)
(See 1905; 1925, International textbook company, Scranton)

JACKSON, Jacob Hugh, 1891–
Audit working papers; their preparation and content. N.Y. Amer. institute of accountants foundation, 1923. 201p.+1 l. 24½cm.

KEMP, William S.
Departmental and standard costs. N.Y. National assn. of cost accountants [c1923] 85p. 26½cm.

KREBS, William Samuel, 1889–
Outlines of accounting. N. Y. Holt, 1923–27. 2v. 21cm. (American business ser.)
v.1, 1923; v.2, 1927.
Practice sets separately published.
—Accounting laboratory manual. N. Y. Holt [c1924] 132p. 21cm. (American business ser.)

—Valuation accounts. [St. L.] 1923. p.325–369, 28cm.
Reprinted from Washington university studies, Apr. 1923, v.10, no.2.

LEIDNER, Walter E., and RITTENHOUSE, Charles Forest, 1881–
Essential exercises in bookkeeping. Cin. South-western pub. co. 1923. 171p. 23cm.

MAHONY, J.
A practical accounting system for the sawmill operator. [Chic. Amer. lumberman, c1923] 61+[2]p. 20x27½cm.
Reprinted from a series of articles in the American lumberman from Apr. 1920, to June, 1922.

MORRIS, William F.
Motion picture theatre accounting. Phil. M.P.T. pub. co. c1923. [144]p. 28½cm.

NUESE, Marie A.
Elementary bookkeeping. Buffalo, W. H. Smith [c1923] 71+[45]p. 18½cm. (Smith's Regents review books)
This book contains the questions in elementary bookkeeping asked by the Board of regents of the State of New York since 1903.
(See 1930, Lee, E. B., compiler, for recent examinations)

PALMER, Leslie E., 1887– , and BELL, William Hansell, 1883–
Accountants' working papers. N. Y. Ronald, 1923. 194 numb. l. 28cm.
Another ed. [c1929] 313p. 22cm.

PUTNAM, Alonzo.
Putnam's practical principles of accounting; for the business man, office executive, accountant, and student. Bost. Practical business pub. co. c1923. 102p. 18cm.

RACINE, Samuel Frederick, 1882–
Elementary accounting. [Seattle, Western institute of account-

ancy, commerce & finance, c1923] 277p. 23cm. (Accounting students' ser.)
Preliminary edition issued in 1922.

—Introduction to accounting. [Seattle, Institute press] 1929. 288p. 23cm. (Accounting students' ser.)
This work is an expansion of the author's "Elementary accounting."

—Estate accounts. [Seattle, Western institute of accountancy, commerce & finance, c1923] 191p. 23cm.
Preliminary edition issued earlier in the same year.

ROSENKAMPFF, Arthur Henry, 1884– , and WALLACE, William Carroll.
Bookkeeping principles and practice; introductory course. N. Y. Prentice-Hall, 1923. 232p. 23½cm.
Advanced course published in 1929.
Other eds. 1924; 1929; 1930. 303p. 23½cm.
Another ed. 1932. 426p. 23½cm.

ROSS, Francis Ellsworth.
Elementary accounting; practice set; part one. Ann Arbor, Mich. G. Wahr [c1923] 30p. 26cm.

—and MASON, Perry.
Elementary accounting; practice set; part two. [c1924] 30+[1]p. 26cm.

SAKOLSKI, Aaron Morton, 1880–
The analysis of financial statements. N. Y. Putnam, 1923. 48p. 19½cm.
Folded table, with title: "Illustrative financial statements" selected and annotated to accompany "The analysis of financial statements," laid in.

SALIERS, Earl Adolphus, 1884– , editor.
Accountants' handbook. N. Y. Ronald, 1923. 1675p. 18½cm.
(For "Accountants' handbook; 2d ed." see 1932, Paton, William Andrew)
Another ed. 1924. 1675p. 18½cm.
Another ed. [n.d.] 1596p. 18½cm.

SANDERS, Thomas Henry, 1885–
Problems in industrial accounting. Chic. A. W. Shaw, 1923. 643p. 23½cm.

—and COFFMAN, Paul Brown.
Problems in industrial accounting; 2d ed. completely rev. N. Y. McGraw-Hill, 1930. 816p. 24cm.

SCHAAFS, Francis J.
Simplified parish accounting . . . Sheboygan, Wis. Ellmore-Schaafs co. 1923. [26]p. 29½cm.

SHEAFFER, William Adam, 1876– , and MCINTOSH, Robert James, 1871–
Common sense course in accounting; consists of texts, blanks, papers, checking results, reading guide; complete for home reading course. Chic. Metropolitan textbk. co. 1923. 740p.

SZEPESI INDUSTRIAL ORGANIZATION, Boston.
Cost and production standards; worsted men's wear. Bost. [c1923]
Portfolio of forms and charts, unpaged.

TABER, Clarence Wilbur, 1870– , and WARDALL, Ruth Aimee, 1877–
Economics of the family. Phil. Lippincott [c1923]
224p. 20½cm. (Lippincott's unit texts)

TODMAN, Frederick Simson.
The work of the cashier's cage. N. Y. Doubleday, Page, for Investment bankers' assn. of America, 1923. 77p. 18½cm.
Reprinted in part from the author's "Wall street accounting."

WIEGAND, William B.
Accounting for fire insurance companies; preparation of annual reports to state insurance departments. Chic. LaSalle extension univ. [c1923] 95p. 27½cm.
Thirty-one technical forms included.

YEO & LUKENS CO., Philadelphia.
Building and loan association accounting; the theory and practice of accounting for serial and non-serial building and loan associations; with proper forms of books and stationery; also instructions how to keep the accounts and use the forms; including complete illustrations of the annual report, profit and loss account, distribution of profits. Phil. Yeo & Lukens [1923] 54p. 24cm.

1924

AFFELDER, William Maurice, 1879–
Contractors' accounting practice; with procedure also for owners, architects, and engineers. N. Y. Ronald, 1924. 386p. 22cm.

ALTMAN, George T.
Cash records. N. Y. Ronald [c1924] 117p. 18½cm. (Ronograph library, no.20)

—Recording sales transactions. N. Y. Ronald [c1924] 92p. 18½cm. (Ronograph library, no. 23)

BELL, William Hansell, 1883– , and POWELSON, John Abrum, 1883–
Auditing, by William H. Bell [with] cases and questions . . . by John A. Powelson. N. Y. Prentice-Hall, 1924. 518p. 23½cm.
Solutions to cases and answers to questions based on "Auditing . . ." separately published.
Other eds. 1925; 1926; 1928; 1929; 1930. 518p. 23½cm.

BENNETT, Robert Joseph, 1871–
Accounting for building and loan associations. [Phil. Bennett accountancy institute, c1924] 45p. 23cm.

BERG, John, 1895–
Elementary accounting problems and solutions. Wash. White press, 1924. 43p. 22½cm.

BLISS, James Harris, 1889–
Management through accounts. N. Y. Ronald, 1924. 851p. 22cm.

COBB, Howard P.
Shoe factory accounting and cost keeping. Chic. Jacobsen pub. co. 1924. 392p. 23½cm.
First published in "Hide and leather" in 1923.

COUCHMAN, Charles Bennington, 1879–
The balance-sheet; its preparation, content, and interpretation. N. Y. Journal of accountancy, 1924. 288p. 24cm.

COWAN, Harold E., and LOKER, Harold W.
Exercises in bookkeeping and business problems. Bost. Ginn [c1924–25] 3v. 23cm.
v.1, 1924; v.2, 1925; v.3, 1925.

CURRIER, Edwin Lovejoy, 1887– , LENNES, Nels Johann, 1874– and MERRILL, Archibald Shepard, 1887–
Farm accounting. N. Y. Macmillan, 1924. 287p. 20½cm.

Curtis, Gay Waite, 1890–
Improved methods in hospital management: a treatise on the introduction of business methods in the management of modern hospitals. Santa Barbara, Calif. Hospital service exchange, 1924. 176p. 22cm.

Dingman, Charles Francis, 1885–
Accounting and business methods for contractors. N. Y. McGraw-Hill, 1924. 175p. 18cm.

Dohr, James Lewis, 1892–
Cost accounting theory and practice. N. Y. Ronald, 1924. 631p. 20½cm.

Finney, Harry Anson, 1886–
Accounting principles and bookkeeping methods. N. Y. Holt [c1924] 2v. 25cm.

Fisher, Everard Ellsworth, 1861–
Condensed practical bookkeeping and accounting; Fisher system. Wichita, Kan. Educational pub. co. [c1924] 33+[1]p. 30½cm.

Fowlkes, John Guy, 1898–
A handbook of financial accounting for schools (tentative edition) Eau Claire, Wis. Eau Claire bk. & stationery co. [c1924] 56p. 23½cm.

Gordon, William Duncan, 1892– , and Lockwood, Jeremiah, 1891–
Modern accounting systems. N. Y. Wiley, 1924. 464p. 23½cm. (Wiley accounting ser.)
Another ed. 1926. 464p. 23½cm. (Wiley accounting ser.)
2d ed. 1933. 481p. 23½cm. (Wiley accounting ser.)

Greeley, Harold Dudley, 1882–
Estate accounting. N. Y. Ronald [c1924] 110p. 18½cm. (Ronograph library, no. 24)
Another ed. [c1930] 114p. 19½cm.

Greer, Howard Clark, 1894–
Chain store accounting. N. Y. McGraw-Hill, 1924. 312p. 23½cm.

Hadley, Charles R., company, Los Angeles.
Pathfinder accounting manual for realtors and subdividers. Los Angeles, Hadley, c1924. 20 numb. l.+forms, 28x36cm.

HALSEY, STUART & CO., INC., New York.
Investment bond accounting. N. Y. [c1924] 40p. 28cm.
Another ed. 1926. 40p. 28cm.

HILSEE, Donald Ashcraft, 1897–
Auditing; making an audit. Phil. La Fayette institute [c1924] 53p. 25½cm.
Another ed. [c1930] 55p. 25½cm.
Foreword and addenda by Frederick Wells Woodbridge.

HIMMELBLAU, David, 1889– , editor.
Complete accounting course by members of the Department of accounting, Northwestern university, School of commerce. N. Y. Ronald, 1924–[34] 7v. 24½cm.
Contents.—v.1. Fundamentals of accounting, by David Himmelblau, c1924.—v.2. Principles of accounting, by David Himmelblau, c1924.—v.3. Intermediate accounting, by Earl Adolphus Saliers, c1925.—v.4. Auditing, by Ernest Coulter Davies, c1926. —v.5. Advanced accounting, by John V. Tinen, c1927.—v.6. Advanced auditing; financial investigations, by David Himmelblau, c1928.
v.1, rev. 1933; v.2, rev. 1934.
Vol.3, "Intermediate accounting," completely revised by Harry Altschuler and published in 1932, replaced Saliers' work as v.3 of the "Complete accounting course."
"Introductory cost accounting," by Cecil Merle Gillespie, published in 1932, is now (1934) referred to as v.4 of the "Complete accounting course."
Vols. 4, 5, 6, listed above, are now (1934) referred to as v.5, 6, and 7 of the "Complete accounting course."
Practice sets separately published for v.1, 2, and 4. (Practice set for v.4 written by Cecil Merle Gillespie and George A. Neff)
(See 1917, Andersen, Arthur E., for the first series of the "Complete accounting course")

INTERNATIONAL TEXTBOOK COMPANY, Scranton.
Insolvent and decedents' estates; accounting methods of banks; consignment, joint trading and branch office accounting; amalgamation and consolidated statements; departmental accounting and estimating inventories; financial calculations. Scranton, International textbk. co. 1924. Various pagings, 23cm. (International library of technology, v.379)
(See 1905; 1915, International textbook company, Scranton)

—Public-utility accounting principles. Scranton, International textbk. co. c1924. 107p. 19½cm. (International library of tech-

INTERNATIONAL TEXTBOOK COMPANY (continued)
nology. Blue book ser. v.60)
(See 1905; 1925, International textbook company, Scranton)

—Station agents' accounting for freight and passenger business . . . Scranton, International textbk. co. 1924. Various pagings, 23cm. (International library of technology, v.417)
(See 1905, International textbook company, Scranton)

KESTER, Roy Bernard, 1882–
Depreciation. N. Y. Ronald [c1924] 105p. 18½cm. (Ronograph library, no.28)

KILDUFF, Frederic W., 1892–
Auditing and accounting handbook. N. Y. McGraw-Hill, 1924. 813p. 23½cm.

KOHLER, Eric Louis, 1892– , and PETTENGILL, Paul W.
Principles of auditing. Chic. A. W. Shaw, 1924. 231p.+4 numb. l. 21cm.

Another ed.	1925.	231+96p.+4 numb. l. 21cm.
2d ed.	1927.	297p.+4 numb. l. 21½cm.
3d ed.	N. Y. McGraw-Hill, 1932.	298p. 21cm.
	The seven groups of forms and indexes not included in the paging of this edition.	

—Illustrative audit . . . Chic. A. W. Shaw, 1924. 115p. 21cm.
"The audit materials . . . are intended as a collateral problem to accompany the auditing text of the authors. It may be used independently or in connection with other texts."—Introd.

KONOPAK, Lothar Theodore, 1884–
The auditor's working guide. Toledo, Skadden pub. co. 1924. 86p. 26½cm.

—Cost accounting fundamentals from the standpoint of management. N. Y. Ronald, 1924. 235p. 22cm.

LUTZ, Werner, and GORDON, Stephen Robbins, 1888–
Cost accounting manual for the knitted outerwear industry. N. Y. National knitted outerwear assn. [c1924] 145p. 23cm.

MACDONALD, Ernest F.
Municipal accounting. Phil. Bennett accountancy institute [c1924] 59p. 23cm. (Bennett accountancy institute, Philadelphia. Accountancy, special course)

McKinsey, James Oscar, 1889–
Managerial accounting. Chic. Univ. of Chic. press [1924] 655p. 21½cm. (Materials for the study of business)
"Volume 1."
The second volume has not been published.
Another ed. [1925] 655p. 21cm. (Materials for the study of business)
v.1, 2d impression.

Manning, Anthony B., 1885–
Elements of cost accounting. N. Y. McGraw-Hill, 1924. 166p. 21cm.

Miller, Franklin & company, New York. (formerly Miller, Franklin, Basset & co.)
Cost control for knit underwear factories, published under the auspices of the Associated knit underwear manufacturers of America. N. Y. Ronald, 1924. 259p. 22cm.

Paton, William Andrew, 1889–
Accounting. N. Y. Macmillan, 1924. 894p. 22½cm.
Another ed. 1926. 894p. 22½cm.

Pinkerton, Paul Whittier, 1887–
Accounting for surplus. N. Y. Ronald [c1924] 120p. 18½cm. (Ronograph library, no.21)

Potter, Homer D., 1878–
Cost finding principles for furniture factories: a treatise on the principles which underlie all correct cost determination; with explanations as to means of securing more accurate and analytical knowledge of costs. Grand Rapids, Periodical pub. co. [c1924] 140p. 23½cm.

Read, Harlan Eugene, 1880– , and Harvey, Charles J.
Bookkeeping and accounting [with] script illustrations by E. C. Mills. N. Y. Macmillan, 1924. 207p. 25cm.
This work also published in two volumes.
Practice sets separately published.

Rittenhouse, Charles Forest, 1881– , and Percy, Atlee Lane, 1880–
Accounting problems; advanced. N. Y. McGraw-Hill, 1924. 402p. 23½cm.
"A companion volume to 'Accounting problems; intermediate,' published in 1922."

—Accounting problems; elementary. N. Y. McGraw-Hill, 1924. 266p. 23½cm.

SCOVELL, Clinton Homer, 1876–1926.
Interest as a cost. N. Y. Ronald, 1924. 254p. 19½cm.

SCOVILL, Hiram Thompson, 1885– , and BAILY, Henry Heaton.
Elementary accounting . . . Bost. Heath [c1924–26]
2v. 23cm.
v.1, part 1, 1924, by Hiram Thompson Scovill.
v.2, part 2, 1926: "Accounting procedure," by Hiram Thompson Scovill and Henry Heaton Baily.
—Illustrative problem in elementary accounting. Bost. Heath, 1931. 106p. 22½cm.
This problem prepared primarily for use with the authors' "Elementary accounting, part 2," but adaptable to any text of the same grade.

SEIDEMANN, Henry Peter, 1883–
Manual of governmental accounting. [Wash.] 1924.
229 numb. l. 28cm. (Institute for government research. Studies in administration)
—Manual of accounting and reporting for the operating services of the national government. Balt. Johns Hopkins press, 1926. 399p. 22½cm. (Institute for government research. Studies in administration)
This work is a revised and enlarged edition. It is now distributed by Brookings institution, Washington, D. C.

SWEENEY, Henry Whitcomb, 1898–
Bookkeeping and introductory accounting; prepared in the Extension division of the University of Wisconsin. N. Y. McGraw-Hill, 1924. 545p. 23½cm. (Commercial education ser.)
Practice set separately published.

SWINDELL, Walter B.
Newspaper accounting and cost finding. N. Y. Ronald, 1924. 87p. 18½cm. (Ronograph library, no.16)

WALKER, Frank Rabold, 1888–
Practical accounting and cost keeping for contractors; illustrating and describing in easy, understandable language bookkeeping and accounting systems for contractors; giving complete instructions and examples of the proper methods of keeping time and compiling costs on all classes of construction work. Chic. Walker, 1924. 169p. 29½cm.
Another ed. 1926. 169p. 29½cm.

WEBNER, Frank Erastus, 1865–
Factory overhead: a work of reference for factory managers, engi-

neers, cost accountants, and students. Wash. White press, 1924. 456p. 22cm.

WERMUTH, Charles E.
Railroad accounts and statistics. N. Y. Prentice-Hall, 1924. 349p. 23½cm.

WRIGHT, H. Winfield.
Cost accounting theory and practice. Phil. Bennett accountancy institute [c1924] 68p. 23cm. (Bennett accountancy institute, Philadelphia. Accountancy, special course)

1925

BENNETT, George Edward, 1889–
Auditing; an introduction to practice. N. Y. Macmillan, 1925. 377p. 22½cm.

—Basic accounting. N. Y. Gregg [c1925] 777p. 22½cm.
Another ed. 1928. 777p. 22½cm.

BERGER, J. A.
Foreign branch accounting. Chic. LaSalle extension univ. 1925. 43p. 23cm.
Another ed. 1931. 43p. 23cm.

BLANK, Rudolph.
Bookkeeping and elementary accounting for business men. N. Y. Blank audit co. [c1925] 210+[2]p. 19½cm. (I. S.-I. home study course and pocket guide)

BLOCK, Milton D., and ALLEN, Leslie Herbert, 1881–
Accounting for construction companies; principles, procedure, and special problems. Chic. LaSalle extension univ. [c1925] 75p. 28cm.

CHAMBER OF COMMERCE OF THE UNITED STATES OF AMERICA. Dept. of manufacture.
Cost accounting through the use of standards. Wash. Chamber of commerce [1925] 27p. 23cm.
Originally printed, June 3, 1925.
Another ed. 1925. 52p.+2 l. 23cm.
Revised, Nov. 30, 1925.
Another ed. 1926. 52p. 23cm.
Reprinted, May 6, 1926.
Another ed. 1933. 52p. 23cm.
Reprinted, Oct. 1933.

COMSTOCK, Lynn M.
Modern retail methods, records, and accounting. N. Y. U. S. corp. co. c1925. 522p. 26½cm.

FILFUS, Nathaniel, and ROBINSON, Nathaniel.
Bookkeeping and accounting; elementary course. N. Y. Oxford bk. co. [c1925] 130p. 22½cm.
—Fundamentals of bookkeeping and accounting. N. Y. Oxford bk. co. 1928. 2v. 23½cm.
Vol.1 published in 1925 under title: "Bookkeeping and accounting."
Contents.—[v.1] Elementary course.—[v.2] Advanced course.

GILMAN, Stephen, 1887–
Analyzing financial statements. N. Y. Ronald [c1925] 222p. 22cm.
Another ed. [c1934] 475p. 22cm.
"The general structure and plan of the older book has been followed in this volume, but in content it is an entirely new work."—Pref.

GLOVER, James Waterman, 1868– , and WIGHTMAN, Earl Charles, 1889–
Life insurance accounting: a study of the principles of accounting as applied to the life insurance business; including both a descriptive and a critical analysis of the annual statement blank prescribed for life insurance companies by the National convention of insurance commissioners. Ann Arbor, Mich. Edwards bros. 1925. 178p. 27½cm.

GUTHMANN, Harry George, 1896–
The analysis of financial statements. N. Y. Prentice-Hall, 1925. 454p. 23½cm.
Other eds. 1926; 1927; 1929; 1930. 454p. 23½cm.

HADLEY, Charles R., company, Los Angeles.
Exhibit and book of instructions; Hadley's pathfinder bookkeeping system for hotels. Los Angeles, Hadley, c1925.
82 numb. l. +forms, 28x36cm.
Another ed. c1928. 82 numb. l.+forms, 28x36cm.

—Exhibit and book of instructions of Hadley's pathfinder bookkeeping system for laundries. Los Angeles, Hadley, c1925.
47 numb. l.+forms, 28x36cm.
Another ed. 1929. 47 numb. l.+forms, 28x36cm.

—Hadley's pathfinder system for building and loan associations. Los Angeles, Hadley [1925] Various pagings, 28x36cm.

HAMMOND, W. M.
Accounting methods and procedure for electric, gas, and water utilities. Chic. LaSalle extension univ. [c1925] 412p. 28cm.

HODGE, Albert Claire.
Retail accounting and control. Chic. Univ. of Chic. press [c1925] 545p. 21cm. (Materials for the study of business)

INTERNATIONAL TEXTBOOK COMPANY, Scranton.
Auditing; auditing procedure; special accounting examinations and reports; graphs. Scranton, International textbk. co. 1925. Various pagings, 23cm. (International library of technology, v.377)
(See 1905; 1922, International textbook company, Scranton)

—Public utility accounting. Scranton, International textbk. co. 1925. Various pagings, 23cm. (International library of technology, v.358)
(See 1905; 1923, International textbook company, Scranton)

—Theory of accounts; operating on the New York stock exchange and stock brokerage accounting methods. Scranton, International textbk. co. 1925. Various pagings, 23cm. (International library of technology, v.378)
(See 1905; 1923, International textbook company, Scranton)

JONES, Edwin E., 1882– , and others.
American business accounting: a comprehensive, concise and practical course of instruction in accounting and business, and an extensive, cross-indexed, and practical reference library, by Edwin E. Jones . . . Ernest W. Ludlow . . . James M. Hayden . . . Samuel R[obertson] Winchell . . . and a corps of accountants, attorneys, and leading business men. Rockford, Ill. Amer. business bur. [c1925] 3v. 20cm.

KINMAN, James Irvin, 1887– , and MORRIS, Anthony William.
Kinman's bookkeeping and accounting; principles and practice. Spokane, Kinman [c1925] 156p. 23cm.
This work was first copyrighted, 1922.
Another ed. [c1925] 179p. 23½cm.
Another ed. Spokane, Kinman-Morris [c1930] 180p. 24cm.
"Revised—seventh printing."

LAWRENCE, William Beaty, 1882–
Cost accounting. N. Y. Prentice-Hall, 1925. 528p. 23½cm.
Practice sets separately published.
Other eds. 1926; 1927; 1928. 528p. 23½cm.
Another ed. 1930. 548p. 23½cm.
Revised questions and problems for Appendix I added. Text also published with "personal progress records" (supplementary sets of questions which follow most of the chapters).

LAZARUS, Arthur.
Stock control in department stores. N. Y. Dry goods economist [c1925] 77p. 20cm.

McCARTY, Wesley James, 1869–
Accounting elements. N. Y. Prentice-Hall, 1925. 375p. 23½cm.

McNAIR, Malcolm Perrine, 1894–
The retail method of inventory. Chic. A. W. Shaw, 1925. 143p. 21cm.

MORLAND, David F., and McKEE, Raymond W., 1894–
Accounting for the petroleum industry. N. Y. McGraw-Hill, 1925. 304p. 23½cm.

NEWLOVE, George Hillis, 1893– , and PRATT, Lester Amos, 1892–
Specialized accounting. N. Y. McGraw-Hill, 1925. 475p. 23½cm.
This work was called the first edition. The chapters were prepared and issued, however, in mimeographed form during 1921–1923.

PEEL, Arthur J.
Simplified school accounting. Milw. Bruce pub. co. [c1925] 118p. 19½cm.

SCOTT, D R, 1887–
Theory of accounts. N. Y. Holt [c1925] 284p. 22½cm. (American business ser.)
This work is called v.1.
(See Appendix, p.369, for v.2, "The cultural significance of accounts," c1931)

SHERWOOD, John F., 1890–
Accountancy; the theory and practice of accounting. Cin. Southwestern pub. co. [c1925] 432p. 22½cm.
2d ed. [c1928] 448p. 22½cm.

STOCKWELL, Herbert Grant, 1866–
How to read a financial statement; adapted especially to needs of credit men, bankers, and investors. N. Y. Ronald [c1925] 443p. 22cm.

STONE, William M., and others.
Accountants' and auditors' manual, by William M. Stone . . . in collaboration with Jerome Lee Nicholson . . . Charles J. Nasmyth . . . and others . . . Scranton, International textbk. co. 1925. 422+[5]p. 15cm.
Another ed. Phil. McKay, 1925. 422+[5]p. 15cm.

THOMPSON, William Rodney, 1885– , and others.
Accounting for retail and department stores; principles, procedure, and special problems, by William R. Thompson, A. C. Benton, J. H. Haiman, and R. B. Schreffler. Chic. LaSalle extension univ. [c1925] 158p. 28x21½cm.

WALDRON, Frederick A., 1864–
Simplified factory accounting and routing. N. Y. Ronald [c1925] 113p. 18½cm. (Ronograph library, no.35)

WHITE, Joseph Lowell, 1880–
Analysis of railroad operations. N. Y. Simmons-Boardman pub. co. [c1925] 381p. 23cm.
"The purpose of this book is to review the system of accounts and statistics established on the railroads of the United States by the Interstate commerce commission."—Introd.

WOODBRIDGE, Frederick Wells.
Elements of accounting. N. Y. Ronald [c1925] 700p. 22cm.
A special preliminary edition, being the first section of "Elements of accounting," was published for the use of the author's classes in 1924.
—Solutions to problems, Elements of accounting. N. Y. Ronald [c1927] 216p. 21cm.

1926

ALTHOLZ, Nathaniel, and KLEIN, Anthony W.
Modern bookkeeping practice; first-year course. Chic. Lyons & Carnahan [c1926] 366p. 22½cm.
The second-year course was published in 1930.
[2d ed.] [c1932] 442p. 22½cm.

BAILEY, Warren G., and KNOWLES, Daniel Emerson, 1892–
Accounting procedures for public utilities; with special reference to electric light, gas, water, and electric railway utility companies. Chic. A. W. Shaw, 1926. 471p. 21½cm. (Public utility texts)

BENNETT, George Edward, 1889–
Accounting systems; principles and problems of installation. Chic. A. W. Shaw, 1926. 554p. 21½cm.
Another ed. 1928. 554p. 21½cm.

BERRIGAN, Edmund.
Elements of accounting. N. Y. McGraw-Hill, 1926. 300p. 23½cm.

BOWMAN, Charles Ellis, 1886– , and PERCY, Atlee Lane, 1880–
Principles of bookkeeping and business; elementary course . . . N. Y. Amer. bk. co. [c1926] 287p. 22½cm.
Another ed. 1927. 287p. 22½cm.
—Fundamentals of bookkeeping and business. N. Y. Amer. bk. co. [c1933] 316p. 23cm.
"Published in 1926 under title: 'Principles of bookkeeping and business; elementary course.'"
Practice sets prepared to accompany the elementary and advanced courses separately published.
—Principles of bookkeeping and business; advanced course. N. Y. Amer. bk. co. [c1927] 396p. 22½cm.
—Principles of bookkeeping and business; complete course . . . N. Y. Amer. bk. co. [1927] 287+396p. 23cm.

CASTENHOLZ, William Burtis, 1879–
Accounting and statistical control: a series of practical texts. Chic. LaSalle extension univ. c1926. 3 pamphlets, each 20cm.
The titles of the texts follow:
1. Executive uses of accounting; management and the balance sheet. c1926. 100p. 20cm.
2. Management and the income statement; control through budgeting. c1926. 108p. 20cm.
3. Statistics and quotas; control through charts; control through reports. c1926. 122p. 20cm.

CHAMBER OF COMMERCE OF THE UNITED STATES OF AMERICA. Organization service.
Financial control and accounting for a chamber of commerce. Wash. Chamber of commerce [1926] 65p. 24cm.

DJÖRUP, Christian.
Foreign exchange accounting. N. Y. Prentice-Hall, 1926. 406p. 23½cm.

EGGLESTON, De Witt Carl, 1881–
Auditing procedure. N. Y. Wiley, 1926. 528p. 24cm. (Wiley accounting ser.)

ELWELL, Fayette Herbert, 1885– , and TONER, James Vincent.
Bookkeeping and accounting; first course. Bost. Ginn [c1926] 217p. 24cm. (Elwell and Toner ser.)
—Bookkeeping and accounting; elementary course. Bost. Ginn [c1926] 352p. 24cm. (Elwell and Toner ser.)
Contents as in entry above: p.1–211.
—Bookkeeping and accounting; intermediate course. Bost. Ginn [c1926] p.205–463, 24cm. (Elwell and Toner ser.)
—Bookkeeping and accounting; advanced course. Bost. Ginn [c1926] p.335–596, 24cm. (Elwell and Toner ser.)
—Bookkeeping and accounting; corporation and voucher accounting. Bost. Ginn [c1926] p.457–594, 24cm. (Elwell and Toner ser.)
—Bookkeeping and accounting; complete course. Bost. Ginn [c1926] 465p. 24cm. (Elwell and Toner ser.)

HADLEY, Charles R., company, Los Angeles.
Exhibit and book of instructions; Hadley's pathfinder bookkeeping system for insurance agents. Los Angeles, Hadley, c1926. 63 numb. l.+forms, 28x28cm.
Another ed. 1928. 63 numb. l.+forms, 28x28cm.

—Exhibit of pathfinder trust department accounting system. Los Angeles, Hadley, c1926. 53 numb. l.+forms, 28x36cm.
Another ed. 1932 53 numb. l.+forms, 28x36cm.

—Hadley's pathfinder system for a finance company. Los Angeles, Hadley, c1926. 39 numb. l.+forms, 28x36cm.
Another ed. 1928. 39 numb. l.+forms, 28x36cm.

HEDLAND, Edward W.
Newspaper cost accounting. N. Y. National assn. of cost accountants [c1926] 91p. 23cm.

INTERNATIONAL TEXTBOOK COMPANY, Scranton.
Auditing practices. Scranton, International textbk. co. c1926. 191p. 19½cm. (International library of technology. Blue book ser. v.53)

—Corporation accounting and records. Scranton, International textbk. co. c1926. 96p. 19½cm. (International library of technology. Blue book ser. v.57)

—Cost accounting principles and records. Scranton, International textbk. co. c1926. 135p. 19½cm. (International library of technology. Blue book ser. v.50)

INTERNATIONAL TEXTBOOK COMPANY (continued)
—Cost accounting problems. Scranton, International textbk. co. c1926. 111p. 19½cm. (International library of technology. Blue book ser. v.52)

—Cost control and cost systems. Scranton, International textbk. co. c1926. 128p. 19½cm. (International library of technology. Blue book ser. v.51)

JACKSON, Jacob Hugh, 1891– , SANDERS, Thomas Henry, 1885– and SPROUL, Alexander Hugh.
Bookkeeping and business knowledge . . . Bost. Ginn [c1926] 2v. 24cm.
v.1, first-year course; v.2, second-year course.
Another ed. [c1926] 686p. 24cm.
Edition complete in one volume.
Another ed. [c1928] 364p. 24cm.
v.1, first-year course, separately published.
Another ed. [c1931] 2v. 24cm.
Revised edition.

JOB, Leonard Bliss, 1891–
Business management of institutional homes for children. N. Y. Teachers college, Columbia univ. 1926. 205p. 23cm.
Thesis (Ph.D.)—Columbia university, 1926.
Published also as Teachers college, Columbia university, Contributions to education, no.215.

KOHLER, Eric Louis, 1892– , and MORRISON, Paul Leslie, 1899–
Principles of accounting. Chic. A. W. Shaw, 1926. 446p. 21½cm.
Practice set separately published.
2d ed. N. Y. McGraw-Hill, 1931. 507p. 21cm.

MCCARTY, Wesley James, 1869– , and AMIDON, Luey Earle Cleveland, 1885–
Survey course in accounting. N. Y. Prentice-Hall, 1926. 483p. 23½cm.

MCMURRY, Karl Franklin, 1880– , and MCNALL, Preston Essex, 1888–
Farm accounting principles and problems. Chic. A. W. Shaw, 1926. 329p. 21½cm.

MARTINETTI, Frederick A.
Financial statements and their analysis. Tacoma, Smith-Digby co. [c1926] 41p. 15½cm.

MATHER, Charles Ernest, 1866–
Life insurance accounting. N. Y. Ronald [c1926]
118p. 18½cm. (Ronograph library, no.42)

MAY, Irville Augustus.
Motor bus accounting practice. N. Y. Ronald [c1926]
200p. 22cm.

NEWLOVE, George Hillis, 1893–
Consolidated balance sheets. N. Y. Ronald [c1926]
309p. 22cm.

PARKINSON, Charles W., and MERRELL, Oscar J.
Municipal accountancy. [Stillwater, Okla. c1926] 253 l. 29cm.
Autographed from typewritten copy.

POWELSON, John Abrum, 1883–
Introductory accounting. N. Y. Prentice-Hall, 1926.
719p. 23½cm.
Other eds. 1926; 1927; 1928. 719p. 23½cm.

PRIDGEN, Samuel James.
Pridgen's ready reference method of accounting and suggestions in business administration. [Atlanta, c1926] 55p. 19½x26cm.

RACINE, Samuel Frederick, 1882–
Junior auditing. [Seattle, Western institute of accountancy, commerce & finance] c1926. 236p. 23cm.

REITER, Prosper, jr.
Profits, dividends, and the law; profits available for dividends from standpoint of law and best accounting practice. N. Y. Ronald [c1926] 260p. 22cm.

RUBBER MANUFACTURERS ASSOCIATION, INC.
Manual of accounts and budgetary control for the rubber industry. N. Y. Ronald [c1926] 257p. 22cm.

STEVENSON, Russell Alger, 1890– , and TAYLOR, Robert Emmett, 1889–
Questions and problems in accounting. N. Y. Macmillan, 1926. 234p. 22½cm.

THOMPSON, William Rodney, 1885–
Accounting systems; their design and installation. Chic. LaSalle extension univ. 1926. 743p. 21½cm.

THOMPSON (continued)
Another ed. 1927. 743p. 21½cm.
Another ed. 1932. 736p. 21½cm.
—and KEEN, H. F.
Assignments in Accounting systems; their design and installation: a series of ten coordinated assignments . . . c1926. 47p. 23cm.
Reprinted annually.

WASHBURN, Earle Leroy, 1891–
Accounting for universities. N. Y. Ronald [c1926] 126p. 18½cm. (Ronograph library, no.41)

WIEGAND, William B.
Fire insurance accounting. N. Y. Ronald [c1926] 108p. 18½cm. (Ronograph library, no.43)

1927

ACKERMAN, Paul Frederick, 1871–
Automobile accounting. [Shorewood, Wis. North Shore pub. co.] c1927. 59p. 24cm.

BALDWIN, Harry Glen, 1886–
Accounting for value as well as original cost: a discussion of the necessity and desirability of accounting for value as well as original cost; with a suggested procedure for its accomplishment. Atlanta, Amer. appraisal co. [c1927] 111p. 22½cm.

BEACH, Frank Loomis, 1894–
Bank system and accounting. N. Y. Ronald [c1927] 373p. 22cm.

BELDING, Albert G., 1870– , and GREENE, Russell Thomas, 1873–
Rational bookkeeping and accounting. N. Y. Gregg [c1927] 2v. 24cm.
v.1, elementary course; v.2, advanced course.
Practice set separately published for use in connection with the transaction narrative contained in chapter 19 of the advanced course.
Vol.1 reprinted in 1934; v.2, in 1929.
—Rational bookkeeping and accounting [complete course] N. Y. Gregg [c1927] 383p. 24cm.
BELDING, Albert G., and BERTSCHI, Lloyd.
An interpretation of the objectives, method, and subject matter of

Rational bookkeeping and accounting; elementary course. N.Y. Gregg [c1929] 88p. 18cm.

BENTLEY, Harry Clark, 1877–
Massachusetts certified public accountant examination questions; with answers. Bost. Bentley school of accounting & finance, 1927. 826p. 26cm.

BUDD, Thomas Allibone, 1890– , and WRIGHT, Edward Needles, 1897–
The interpretation of accounts. N.Y. Prentice-Hall, 1927. 416p. 23½cm.

CHAMBER OF COMMERCE OF THE UNITED STATES OF AMERICA. Dept. of manufacture.
The evolution of overhead accounting; part 1, Basic principles in the treatment of manufacturing overhead; part 2, Designing the overhead structure. Wash. Chamber of commerce [1927] 30p. 23cm.

COLLINS, Clem Wetzell, 1883– , and others.
C.P.A. review: a manual for colleges and schools and for accountants preparing for the C.P.A. examination, by Clem Wetzell Collins . . . and special collaborators: Frank C. Onstott . . . Alexander J. Lindsay . . . Ralph J. Cummings . . . Theodore J. Witting . . . N.Y. Wiley, 1927. 490p. 23½cm. (Wiley accounting ser.)
"All questions in all examinations set by the American institute of accountants from . . . June, 1917, to and including . . . November, 1925, are presented."—Pref.
—C.P.A. review answers; covering questions and problems presented in book entitled C.P.A. review. N.Y. Wiley, 1928. 955p. 23½cm. (Wiley accounting ser.)
"The answers to the A.I.A. questions are all by H. A. Finney, as published in the Journal of accountancy, except commercial law questions from June, 1917, to May, 1920, both inclusive. The answers to these law questions . . . have been supplied by Ralph J. Cummings . . . with the exceptions of chapter L . . . by Theodore J. Witting."—Pref.

CROW, William Henry, 1878–
Corporation treasurer's and controller's guide: a guide for the treasurer, controller, and auditor of large and small corporations, as well as unincorporated businesses . . . N.Y. Prentice-Hall, 1927. 1657p. 23½cm.

CURRAN, Con. P., printing company, St. Louis.
The Curran system of hospital accounting, simplified; especially

CURRAN (continued)
adapted to the requirements of hospitals of 100 beds and less. St. L. Curran [c1927] 40p. 29½cm.

DAVIS, Sidney S.
Double entry bookkeeping in its simplest and correct form. N. Y. S. S. Davis corp. c1927. 72p. 18cm.

ENGELHARDT, Fred, 1885– , and VON BORGERSRODE, Fred.
Accounting procedure for school systems. N. Y. Teachers college, Columbia univ. 1927. 130p. 23½cm. (School administration ser.)

"In this manual the authors have endeavored to present in a systematic and simplified form the necessary accounting procedure for the adequate control of the funds of a local school system . . ."—Introd.

—and ENGELHARDT, Nickolaus Louis, 1882–
Complete accounting system for public schools. N. Y. Teachers college, Columbia univ. [1927] [234]p. 36x43cm.

This accounting system comprises a loose-leaf system of forms.

ESQUERRÉ, Paul Joseph, 1872–1934.
Accounting. N. Y. Ronald [c1927] 369p. 22cm.

HADLEY, Charles R., company, Los Angeles.
Hadley's pathfinder accounting system for Ford agencies. Los Angeles, Hadley, c1927. 35 numb. l.+forms, 28x36cm.

HIMMELBLAU, David, 1889–
Auditors' certificates. N. Y. Ronald [c1927] 153p. 22cm.

JASON, Simon J.
Elements of bookkeeping and accounting. N. Y. Globe bk. co. [c1927] 178+[16]p. 19½cm.

KOHLER, Eric Louis, 1892–
Accounting for business executives. Chic. A. W. Shaw, 1927. 115p. 21cm. (Manuals of business management, v.9)

MILLET, John I.
Bank audits and examinations. N. Y. Ronald [c1927] 490p. 22cm.

MOREY, Lloyd, 1886–
Introduction to governmental accounting. N. Y. Wiley, 1927.

285p. 23½cm. (Wiley accounting ser.)
Another ed. 1932. 285p. 23½cm. (Wiley accounting ser.)

—Manual of municipal accounting. N. Y. Wiley, 1927. 187p. 23½cm. (Wiley accounting ser.)

MYER, Joseph Charles, 1893–1934.
Standard accounting text . . . Brooklyn, c1927–[29] 19v. 23½cm.
This work consists of nineteen pamphlets totalling 645 pages. Series 1 consists of seven pamphlets on Elementary accounting and Constructive accounting; series 2 consists of seven pamphlets on Partnerships, Working papers, etc.; series 3 consists of five pamphlets on Corporation accounting and finance.

NEWLOVE, George Hillis, 1893–
Cost accounting; preliminary ed. Balt. The author, 1927. 212p. 23cm.
Another ed. Wash. White press, 1928. 328p. 23½cm. Second preliminary edition.

O'BRIEN, Daniel J., and COUCHMAN, Charles Bennington, 1879–
Hotel administration; accounts and control. N. Y. McGraw-Hill, 1927. 379p. 23½cm.

ROBBINS, Carl Burton.
No-par stock; legal, financial, economic, and accounting aspects. N. Y. Ronald [c1927] 228p. 22cm.

SANDERS, Thomas Henry, 1885–
Plant and shop costs. Chic. A. W. Shaw, 1927. 130p. 21½cm. (Shaw plant and shop management library, v.3)

SCHLATTER, Charles F.
Elementary cost accounting. N. Y. Wiley, 1927. 321p. 23½cm. (Wiley accounting ser.)
Forms for use in solution of problems in "Elementary cost accounting," 114 sheets, separately published.

STOCKWELL, Herbert Grant, 1866–
How to read a profit and loss statement; adapted especially to needs of credit men, bankers, and investors. N. Y. Ronald [c1927] 411p. 22cm.
"The present work is a companion volume to the author's previous work, entitled 'How to read a financial statement.'"—Pref.

VOKE, Albert F., and CUTRIGHT, Harold Glenn.
Auditing case—Ansted jewelry company. Ann Arbor, Mich. Edwards bros. c1927. 29 l. 27½x21½cm.
Mimeographed.
"This case has been prepared primarily to emphasize the mechanics of auditing procedure as well as the theory . . ."—Foreword.

YANG, Ju Mei, 1898–
Goodwill and other intangibles; their significance and treatment in accounts. N. Y. Ronald [c1927] 238p. 22cm.
Thesis (Ph. D.)—University of Michigan, 1926.
Published without thesis note.

1928

AMIDON, Luey Earle Cleveland, 1885– , and LANG, Theodore.
Essentials of cost accounting. N. Y. Ronald [c1928] 383p. 22cm.

BANKERS MAGAZINE.
How to analyze a bank's statement . . . N. Y. Bankers pub. co. [c1928] 32p. 23cm.
Reprinted from the Bankers magazine, Bank credit problems department.

BOLAND, Chester R.
Shoe industry accounting. Detroit, Lawlis pub. co. [c1928] 204p. 22½cm.

BRETT, George Monroe, 1875–
Fundamental accounting. [Lancaster, Pa. Lancaster press [c1928] 541p. 24cm. (College of the city of New York ser. in commerce, civics, and technology)

FILFUS, Nathaniel.
Principles and exercises in accounting. N. Y. Globe bk. co. [c1928] 193p. 19½cm.
Another ed. [c1928] 202p. 19½cm.

GREER, Howard Clark, 1894–
How to understand accounting: a book for everyone in business. N. Y. Ronald [c1928] 255p. 22cm.

GREGORY, Homer Ewart, 1886–
Accounting reports in business management; use of financial and

operating statements; together with a system of standards and performance records in maintaining efficient management and control. N. Y. Ronald [c1928] 445p. 22cm.

HADLEY, Charles R., company, Los Angeles.
Hadley's pathfinder accounting manual for small manufacturing concerns. Los Angeles, Hadley, c1928. 75 numb. l.+forms, 28x36cm.
Another ed. 1931. 75 numb. l.+forms, 28x36cm.

HORWATH, Ernest B., and TOTH, Louis.
Hotel accounting; including departmental control, food costing, and auditing. N. Y. Ronald [c1928] 508p. 22cm.

JAYNE, David A., and company, Charleston, W. Va.
Jayne's rightline accounting systems for automobile dealers; manual of instruction. Charleston, W. Va. Jayne [c1928] 44p. 28x22cm.

JOSEPH, Emrys Sibbering, 1880–
Insurance agency accounting and management; principles and application of the Joseph system. Harrisburg, Pa. Unit system co. [c1928] 137p. 23½cm.

KOCH, Elmer J.
The standard book on cost finding for printers. Chic. Dept. of education, United typothetae of America, 1928. 127p. 28½cm. (Typothetae management ser.)
This text-book aims to present standard methods and practices in accordance with the principles of the United typothetae of America. The publication is approved by the Committee on education of the United typothetae of America as its authorized book on cost finding and is offered as a revision of, or to supplement, its Standard cost finding system for printers, first published in 1909. *cf.* Pref. and Foreword.
The various systems of accounts sponsored by the United typothetae of America are indexed in the Supplement under Printing.

LAZENBY, Charles D.
Basic bookkeeping and accounting; a scientific treatment of these important subjects. Portland, Or. Basic bks. co. [c1928] 216p. 27½cm.
Another ed. Lincoln, Neb. Univ. pub. co. 1932. Various pagings.
"The arrangement has changed materially though the content is about the same."—Author's letter.

LUND, Reuel Ithiel, 1896–
Bookkeeping and business methods; two-year course. Battle Creek, Mich. Ellis pub. co. [c1928] 297p. 23cm.
Laboratory practice sets separately published.
Another ed. [c1928] 201p. 17cm.

MORAN, T. J.
Accounting in olive green: a handbook on the all-in-one simplified system. [Pittsburgh, Moran, c1928] 31p.+forms, 26x32cm.

NATIONAL RETAIL DRY GOODS ASSOCIATION. Controllers' congress.
Expense manual. N. Y. National retail dry goods assn. 1928. 232p. 22½x28cm.
The Expense manual index was added in 1929, and the Expense distribution manual section was added in 1932.

PROCHAZKA, George Anthony, 1889–
Accounting and cost finding for the chemical industries. N. Y. McGraw-Hill, 1928. 242p. 23½cm. (Chemical engineering ser.)

REITELL, Charles Ervin, 1887– , BULLIS, Harry A., TUTTLE, John Raymond, 1890– , and HOWARD, Thomas W.
The presentation of costs for executives; Scovell prize competition. N. Y. National assn. of cost accountants [c1928] 285p. 23cm.
This book contains the four prize winning essays of the competition conducted under the supervision of the National association of cost accountants. *cf.* Foreword.

ROREM, Clarence Rufus, 1894–
Accounting method. Chic. Univ. of Chic. press [1928] 596p. 23½cm. (Materials for the study of business)
"Laboratory exercises": p.[537]–587.
2d ed. [c1930] 644p. 23½cm. (Materials for the study of business)
"Alternative laboratory exercises," by Willard J. Graham (p.589–636) also published separately.

ROWE, Harry Marc, 1860–1926.
Rowe's new cost accounting; rev. by J. W. Alexander and A. E. Lenhart. Balt. Rowe [c1928] 88p. 23cm.
(Alexander, John W., and Lenhart, Arthur E.)
Practice set consisting of a budget, blank books, and outgoing papers separately published.
"New cost accounting" is based upon "Cost accountancy for manufacturing" which was budget 128 accompanying the work "Bookkeeping and accountancy . . ." first published in 1910.

SEIDEMANN, Henry Peter, 1883–
Manual of accounting, reporting, and business procedure for the territorial government of Hawaii. Balt. Johns Hopkins press, 1928. 570p. 22½cm. (Institute for government research. Studies in administration)
This work is now being distributed by Brookings institution, Washington, D. C.

STREIGHTOFF, Frank Hatch, 1886–
Elementary accounting. N. Y. Harper, 1928. 501+[1]p. 24cm.
The author's "Advanced accounting" published in 1932.

WALL, Alexander, 1879– , and DUNING, Raymond William, 1897–
Ratio analysis of financial statements: an explanation of a method of analysing financial statements by the use of ratios. N. Y. Harper, 1928. 353p. 24cm.

WILDMAN, John Raymond, 1878– , and POWELL, Weldon, 1903–
Capital stock without par value. Chic. A. W. Shaw, 1928. 553p. 21½cm.

WOOLLEY, Ernest Stanley, 1886–
Physicians' systems: a short course of business instructions for the doctor and his assistant, divided into three main sections; namely, accounting, collections, income taxes. Kansas City, Mo. Physicians pub. co. 1928. 133p. 20cm.

1929

BROWNELL, Leon Edward, 1894–
Accounting and finance. N. Y. Wiley, 1929. 244p. 23½cm. (Wiley accounting ser.)

CANNING, John Bennett.
The economics of accountancy: a critical analysis of accounting theory. N. Y. Ronald [c1929] 367p. 22cm.
Thesis (Ph.D.)—University of Chicago, 1929.
Published without thesis note.

CASTENHOLZ, William Burtis, 1879–
Bookkeeping practice: an easy introduction to Higher accountancy; written in a unique informal style . . . Chic. LaSalle extension univ. c1929. 100p. 23cm.
Another ed. c1933. 100p. 23cm.

CHAMBERLIN, Newell Kirby.
Power plant costs. [Chic.] National assn. of power engineers [c1929] 95p. 23cm.

COMMERCIAL RESEARCH BUREAU, Chicago.
Commercial research bureau accountancy reports and reference manuals . . . Chic. Commercial research bur. [c1929] 6v. 21cm.
These bound volumes total 667 pages.
Contents.—v.1. The basic accounting; operations and records. —v.2. The balance sheet and interpretation of accounts.—v.3. Partnership and corporation accounting—reserves.—v.4. Depreciation, costs, and consolidated balance sheets.—v.5. Preparation of statements for financing and credit.—v.6. Specialized accounting systems and budgetary control [and] Index.

CONNER, A. H., and GORDON, Robert W.
Merchandise control. Los Angeles, Hadley, c1929. 42p. 28x22cm.
"The purpose of this article is to show by a series of examples how detailed facts regarding merchandising activities may be reflected in properly prepared reports capable of being analyzed and interpreted."—Pref.

COOK, Jonathan Blanchard.
Ice accounting: a manual on uniform accounting for the ice industry—manufactured and natural ice production and distribution with particular reference to the costs—standardization and budgeting of operations—designed for both large and small companies including those combined with allied businesses. Chic. Nickerson & Collins [c1929] 230p. 24cm.

ECKARDT, Hugo William, 1900–
Accounting in the lumber industry. N. Y. Harper, 1929. 291p. 24cm.

EGGLESTON, De Witt Carl, 1881–
Auditors' reports and working papers. N. Y. Wiley, 1929. 305p. 23½cm. (Wiley accounting ser.)

FILFUS, Nathaniel.
Bookkeeping exercises [second-year course] N. Y. Globe bk. co. [c1929] 172+[12]p. 19cm.
The first-year course was written by Rose Gerstein Smolin and published in 1929.

FOLTS, Franklin Erton, and STILLMAN, Arthur B.
Interpretative accounting. N. Y. Longmans, Green, 1929.

432p. 24cm. (Longmans' economics ser.)
Another ed. 1930. 432p. 24cm. (Longmans' economics ser.)

GIFFORD, Luther Erwin, and FAIRWEATHER, Thomas.
Farm accounting course . . . Des Moines, Univ. of commerce [1929] [39]l. 28cm.

GRAHAM, Willard J., 1897–
Cost accounting and office equipment: a comprehensive treatise on process cost accounting, specific order cost accounting, how costs are collected and allocated, accounting and bookkeeping machines, correspondence, filing and mailing equipment. Chic. Amer. technical soc. 1929. 272p. 21½cm.
This work was reprinted in 1929, 1932, and 1934 as part of v.11 of the encyclopedia "Practical business administration" copyrighted by the American technical society.

HADLEY, Charles R., company, Los Angeles.
Manual of pathfinder accounting system for municipalities . . . Los Angeles, Hadley, c1929. 96 numb. l.+forms, 28½x38cm.

HAYES, Monard Vinson, 1896–
Accounting for executive control. N. Y. Harper, 1929. 495p. 24cm.
Thesis (Ph.D.)—Columbia university, 1929.
Published also without thesis note.

HERRICK, Anson.
An outline of brokerage accounting; principles and practices. [San Fran. San Francisco stock exchange, Printing dept. c1929] 94p. 23½cm.

HILL, Frank Hylan, 1902–
Computing cotton fabric costs. N. Y. Pub. for the Textile world by McGraw-Hill, 1929. 122p. 23½cm.

HORNBERGER, Donald Jay, 1897–
Studies in no par stock. Delaware, Ohio, Ohio Wesleyan univ. Bur. of business service, 1929–30. 3 pamphlets, each 23cm.
Titles of the texts follow:
1. No par stock and the public utilities. 1929. 11p. 23cm.
2. A study of the methods of accounting for no par stocks in the public utilities. 1929. 25p. 23cm.
3. A study of the methods of accounting for no par stock in the industrials. 1930. 20p. 23cm.

HOWARD, Stanley Edwin, 1888–
The A B C of accounting. Princeton, N. J. Princeton univ. press, 1929. 302p. 23½cm.

INSTITUTE OF AMERICAN MEAT PACKERS, Chicago.
Packinghouse accounting, prepared by the Committee on accounting of the Institute of American meat packers; rev. and ed. by Howard C. Greer. Chic. Univ. of Chic. press [1929] 404p. 21½cm.

JACKSON, Jacob Hugh, 1891–
Auditing problems: a comprehensive study in principles and procedure. N. Y. Ronald [c1929] 534p. 22cm.

KNIGHT, Robert T.
Cash journal system. Seattle, Western institute of accountancy, commerce & finance, 1929. 230p. 23cm. (Accounting students' ser.)

LASALLE EXTENSION UNIVERSITY, Chicago.
Railway accounting: a series of practical texts. Chic. LaSalle extension univ. c1929–31. 33 pamphlets, each 22x27cm.
Titles of the texts follow:
1. The railroad industry. c1929. 39p. 22x27cm.
2. Scope and purpose of railway accounting. c1929. 26p. 22x27cm.
3. Government regulation of railroads. c1929. 27p. 22x27cm.
4. Government regulation of carriers' accounts. c1929. 36p. 22x27cm.
5. Railway organization. c1929. 48p. 22x27cm.
6. Status of the railroad accounting department. c1929. 23p. 22x27cm.
7. Development of railway accounting. c1929. 30p. 22x27cm.
8. Elementary principles of railway accounting. c1929. 39p. 22x27cm.
9. Interstate commerce commission classification of accounts c1929. 15p. 22x27cm.
10. General railway balance sheet; part 1. c1929. 34p. 22x27cm.
11. General railway balance sheet; part 2. c1930. 34p. 22x27cm.
12. Railway income statement. c1930. 27p. 22x27cm.
13. Interpretation of the I.C.C. classification of income accounts. c1930. 17p. 22x27cm.
14. Profit and loss account. c1930. 22p. 22x27cm.
15. Classification of investment in road and equipment accounts. c1930. 22p. 22x27cm.

16. Interpretation of the classification of road and equipment accounts. c1930. 22p. 22x27cm.
17. Railway operating revenues. c1930. 25p. 22x27cm.
18. Interpretation of the classification of operating revenue accounts. c1930. 18p. 22x27cm.
19. Classification of operating expense accounts. c1930. 31p. 22x27cm.
20. Interpretation of the operating expense classification. c1930. 42p. 22x27cm.
21. Railroad cost accounting. c1930. 38p. 22x27cm.
22. Analysis and interpretation of a railroad income account; part 1. c1930. 28p. 22x27cm.
23. Analysis and interpretation of a railroad income account; part 2. c1930. 18p. 22x27cm.
24. Use and interpretation of the railroad balance sheet. c1930. 18p. 22x27cm.
25. Railway accounting procedure. c1930. 25p. 22x27cm.
26. Machine accounting in the railroad industry. c1930. 106p. 22x27cm.
27. Accounting for freight revenue; part 1. c1930. 49p. 22x27cm.
28. Accounting for miscellaneous freight revenue; part 1. c1930. 28p. 22x27cm.
29. Accounting for miscellaneous freight revenue. c1930. 33p. 22x27cm.
30. Auditing local and interline freight revenue. c1930. 31p. 22x27cm.
31. Accounting for passenger revenue. c1931. 35p. 22x27cm.
32. Railway disbursement accounting. c1931. 25p. 22x27cm.
33. Valuation accounting. c1931. 41p. 22x27cm.

McKINSEY, James Oscar, 1889–
Accounting principles. Cin. South-western pub. co. [c1929] 640p. 22cm.
Practice sets and two work books separately published.
Another ed. 1931. 736p. 22cm.
Supplementary problems and practice set added as an appendix.

MAZE, Coleman Lloyd, and GLOVER, John George.
How to analyze costs. N. Y. Ronald [c1929] 389p. 22cm.

MONTGOMERY, Robert Hiester, 1872– , and GRAHAM, Willard J., 1897–
Auditing: a comprehensive treatise on duties of auditor, method of audit, special classes of audits, depreciation, reserves, reserve funds, revenue receipts and expenses, investigations, audit reports and cer-

MONTGOMERY (continued)
tificates; rev. by Willard J. Graham. Chic. Amer. technical soc. 1929. 221+8p. 21½cm.

This work is based on a work on auditing prepared by Montgomery as part of a course for American school of correspondence students and reprinted in 1927 as part of v.11 of the encyclopedia "Practical business administration." The revision by Graham was reprinted in 1929, 1932, and 1934 as v.11 of the encyclopedia "Practical business administration."

PHENEY, Edward Thomas, 1895–
College fraternity finances. Detroit, Pheney [c1929] 67p. 23½cm.

ROSENKAMPFF, Arthur Henry, 1884– , and WALLACE, William Carroll.
Bookkeeping principles and practice; advanced course. N. Y. Prentice-Hall, 1929. 491p. 23½cm.

This text continues the presentation of the principles and practices of bookkeeping begun in the introductory course published in 1923.

SANDERS, Thomas Henry, 1885–
Industrial accounting; control of industry through costs. N. Y. McGraw-Hill, 1929. 371p. 21½cm.
—Cost accounting for control; 2d ed. completely rev. N. Y. McGraw-Hill, 1934. 517p. 23½cm.

Published in 1929 under title: "Industrial accounting."

SAWYER, Albert E.
Problems of hospital management; with special reference to the University of Michigan hospital. Ann Arbor [Mich.] Univ. of Mich. School of business administration, Bur. of business research, 1929. 83p. 23cm. (Michigan. University. School of business administration. Bureau of business research. Michigan business studies, v.2, no.2)

SAYPOL, Julian H., 1896–
Principles of modern bookkeeping. Balt. Rowe [c1929] 249p. 23cm.

SCHMIDT, Leo Anton.
Mechanics of accounting: a first course textbook by the problem method. N. Y. Prentice-Hall, 1929. 230p. 23½cm.

SCHNACKEL, Harry Gregory, 1894– , and LANG, Henry Carleton, 1898–

Accounting by machine methods; the design and operation of modern systems. N. Y. Ronald [c1929] 563p. 22cm.

SCHREFFLER, Robert Bruce, 1879–
The retail inventory; how to install it; how to operate it . . . Chic. [c1929] 40p. 22½x28½cm.

SHERWOOD, John F., 1890–
Constructive accounting; associate editors, H[arry] I. Good . . . and D[onald] J[ay] Hornberger . . . Cin. South-western pub. co. [c1929] 252p. 22½cm. (His Accountancy, unit 2)
Work book for "Constructive accounting" separately published.
Another ed. 1931. 278p. 22½cm.

—Fundamentals of accounting; associate editors, H[arry] I. Good . . . and D[onald] J[ay] Hornberger . . . Cin. South-western pub. co. [c1929] 221p. 22½cm. (His Accountancy, unit 1)
Work book separately published.

SMOLIN, Rose Gerstein, 1893–
Bookkeeping exercises . . . [first-year course] N. Y. Globe bk. co. [c1929] 131p. 18½cm.
The second-year course was written by Nathaniel Filfus and published in 1929.

STRAIN, Myron M.
Industrial balance sheets: a study in business analysis. N. Y. Harper, 1929. 182p. 24cm.

WALKER, Ross Graham, and COFFMAN, Paul Brown.
Problems in accounting principles; with advice and editorial assistance from Paul Brown Coffman . . . Chic. A. W. Shaw, 1929. 620p. 24cm.

1930

ALEXANDER, John W., and LENHART, Arthur E.
Introductory accounting. Balt. Rowe [c1930] 52p. 22½cm.
Book of working papers separately published.

ALTHOLZ, Nathaniel.
Modern bookkeeping practice; second-year course. Chic. Lyons & Carnahan [c1930] 439p. 22½cm.
The first-year course published in 1926.
Another ed. 1930. 467p. 22½cm.

BANGS, John Robert, jr.
Industrial accounting for executives. N. Y. McGraw-Hill, 1930. 449p. 23½cm. (McGraw-Hill industrial management ser.)

BAUGHMAN, Charles E.
Farm accounting and agricultural economics. Austin, Tex. c1930. 182p. 19cm.

BENNETT, George Edward, 1889–
Fraud; its control through accounts; published under the auspices of American institute of accountants. N. Y. Century co. 1930. 135p. 24cm.

CASTENHOLZ, William Burtis, 1879–
The control of distribution costs and sales. N. Y. Harper, 1930. 194p. 24cm.

CHURCH, Alexander Hamilton, 1866–
Overhead expense in relation to costs, sales, and profits. N. Y. McGraw-Hill, 1930. 418p. 23½cm.

EGGLESTON, De Witt Carl, 1881–
Modern accounting theory and practice. N. Y. Wiley, 1930. 2v. 24cm. (Wiley accounting ser.)

—Wall street procedure; with special reference to brokers' accounts; with 88 charts. N. Y. Greenberg [c1930] 301p. 23½cm.

GEIER, George Jacob, and MAUTNER, Oscar.
Practical corporation accounting. N. Y. Burrell-Snow, 1930. 824p. 23½cm.

GOGGIN, Walter John, 1882– , and TONER, James Vincent.
Accounting principles and procedure. Bost. Houghton Mifflin [c1930] 476p. 21cm.
"Under the editorship of Edgar S. Furniss."
—Laboratory manual to accompany Accounting principles and procedure; part 1. Bost. Houghton Mifflin [c1930] 272p. 28cm.
—Laboratory manual to accompany Accounting principles and procedure; part 2. Bost. Houghton Mifflin [c1930] 258p. 28cm.

HANSON, Arthur Warren, 1890– , and COFFMAN, Paul Brown.
Problems in auditing. N. Y. McGraw-Hill, 1930. 754p. 24cm.

HARRISON, George Charter, 1881–
Standard costs; installation, operation, and use. N. Y. Ronald [c1930] 308p. 22cm.

HULL, Robert Sedgwick, 1884–
Casualty insurance accounting; published under the auspices of the Casualty actuarial society. N. Y. Ronald [c1930] 325p. 22cm.

HUSBAND, George R., and THOMAS, Olin Eugene, 1900–
Elementary accounting: manual of instructions for accounting laboratory. Ann Arbor, Mich. G. Wahr [c1930] 26p. 25½cm.

ILLINOIS. UNIVERSITY. College of commerce and business administration. Bureau of business research.
Balance sheet structure of automobile manufacturing companies. Urbana, Ill. Univ. of Illinois, 1930. 65p. 23cm. (Bulletin no.29)

KEMMERER, Walter William, 1903–
School accounting by machine methods . . . [Houston, Tex. Printed by Auxiliary directory co.] 1930. 179p. 24cm.
Thesis (Ph.D.)—Columbia university, 1930.
Published also without thesis note.

KLOOSTER, Bert Louis.
Patent accountings; a phase of cost accounting; rules and principles for determining profits and deductions, advantage derived, damages, and reasonable royalty, as evolved by the courts in patent infringement accountings . . . with a foreword by David Himmelblau. N. Y. Prentice-Hall, 1930. 795p. 23½cm.

KNIGHT, Robert T.
Bookkeeping. Seattle, Western institute of accountancy, commerce & finance, 1930. 226p. 23cm.

LAMBERTON, Robert Alexander, 1896–
Fundamental principles of accounting. [New Brunswick, N. J. Thatcher Anderson co. c1930] 2v. 22½cm.
Preliminary mimeographed edition issued in 1930 by Edwards brothers, Ann Arbor, Mich.
Another ed. Ann Arbor, Mich. Edwards bros. 1934. 205p. 28cm.
The title of this edition is "Fundamentals of accounting."

LEE, E. B., compiler.
Bookkeeping (second year) tests and forms. N. Y. Globe bk. co. [c1930] 60p. 19½cm.
Includes complete recent examination papers (offered by the Board of regents of the state of New York) as well as approved bookkeeping forms. Later editions which include 1931, 1932 and 1933 examinations have been published. The examinations have also been reprinted separately.

METROPOLITAN LIFE INSURANCE COMPANY, New York. Policyholders service bureau.
Financial statements in annual reports to stockholders of industrial and mercantile companies. N. Y. Metropolitan life insurance co. 1930. 72p. 24cm.

—Methods of determining distribution costs. N. Y. Metropolitan life insurance co. 1930. 40 l. 28cm.
Mimeographed.
Another ed. 1933. 40 l. 28cm.
Mimeographed.

MILLER, FRANKLIN & company, New York.
How to audit: a manual of procedure. N. Y. Harper, 1930. 233p. 24cm.

MOREY, Lloyd, 1886–
University and college accounting. N. Y. Wiley, 1930. 323p. 23½cm. (Wiley accounting ser.)

NATIONAL COMMITTEE ON STANDARD REPORTS FOR INSTITUTIONS OF HIGHER EDUCATION.
Bulletins. Urbana, Ill. 1930–33. 8 nos. 23cm.
These bulletins were prepared at the suggestion of the United States Office of education and were financed by the General education board. Bulletins 1 to 7 are now (1934) out of print. The University of Chicago press will publish in 1935 the final revised report of the committee under the title: "Financial reports for colleges and universities." Though the bulletins do not all deal with accounting data primarily, the title of each is listed as follows:

1. A study of financial reports of colleges and universities in the United States. 1930. 48p. 23cm.
2. Suggested forms for financial reports of colleges and universities. 1931. 88p. 23cm.
3. A study of methods used in unit-cost studies in higher education. 1932. 34p. 23cm.
4. Recommended classification of expenditures by object. 1932. 9p. 23cm.
5. Suggested forms for internal financial reports of colleges and universities. 1932. 47p. 23cm.
6. Suggested forms for enrolment reports of colleges and universities. 1932. 29+[1]p. 23cm.
7. Suggested forms for financial reports of auxiliary activities and organized activities relating to instructional departments and supplementary suggestions concerning general financial report forms of colleges and universities. 1933. 63p. 23cm.

8. Suggested methods and forms for use in unit-cost studies in colleges and universities. 1933. 26 l.+forms, 28x28cm. This bulletin issued only in mimeographed form, is not a final report.

PRICKETT, Alva Le Roy, 1890– , and MIKESELL, Rufus Merrill.
Introduction to accounting. N. Y. Macmillan, 1930.
374p. 20½cm.

REITELL, Charles Ervin, 1887– , and VAN SICKLE, Clarence, 1892–
Cost finding for engineers. N. Y. McGraw-Hill, 1930.
518p. 23½cm.
"The material embodied in this book, in the sequence in which it is here presented, has been offered for two years at the University of Pittsburgh in cost-finding classes for engineers."—Pref.

ROBINSON, Nathaniel.
Bookkeeping. N. Y. Oxford bk. co. 1930. 111+[38]p. 19cm. (Oxford review ser.)
"Recent examination papers . . . set by the University of the state of New York": p.[13]–[38] at end.
Another ed. 1934. 111+[38]p. 19cm. (Oxford review ser.)
This reprint is called: "Bookkeeping review book."

SAXE, Emanuel, and LEVY, Walter Arthur, 1899–
Estate accounting and taxation. N. Y. Burrell-Snow, 1930.
267p. 23½cm.

SHERWOOD, John F., 1890– , and HORNBERGER, Donald Jay, 1897–
Fundamentals of auditing. Cin. South-western pub. co. [c1930]
341p. 22½cm. (His Accountancy, unit 6)
Work book for "Fundamentals of auditing" separately published.
2d ed. 1933. 363p. 22cm.
Work book for "Fundamentals of auditing" separately published.

STONE, Clarence L.
Consolidations. Seattle, Western institute of accountancy, commerce & finance, 1930. 165p. 23cm.

TAGGART, Herbert Francis, 1898–
Subdivision accounts. Ann Arbor [Mich.] Univ. of Mich. School of business administration, Bur. of business research, 1930.
89p. 22½cm. (Michigan. University. School of business admin-

TAGGART (continued)
istration. Bureau of business research. Michigan business studies, v.2, no.7)
Thesis (Ph.D.)—University of Michigan, 1928.
Published without thesis note.

TAYLOR, Jacob Bacchus, 1898– , and MILLER, Hermann Clinton, 1895–
C.P.A. problems and questions in theory and auditing. N. Y. McGraw-Hill, 1930. 603p. 24cm. (McGraw-Hill accounting ser.)
—Solutions to C.P.A. problems. N. Y. McGraw-Hill, 1931. 486p. 23½cm. (McGraw-Hill accounting ser.)
"A companion book to and the outgrowth of 'C.P.A. problems and questions in theory and auditing.'"—Pref.

TAYLOR, Robert Emmett, 1889– , and OWENS, Richard Norman, 1894–
Elements of accounting. N.Y. Macmillan, 1930. 518p. 20½cm.

THORNTON, Frank Weldon, 1863–
Stock brokerage and investment house accounting; with notes on auditing procedure. N. Y. Harper, 1930. 188p. 24cm.

WALL, Alexander, 1879– , and DUNING, Raymond William, 1897–
Analyzing financial statements. N. Y. Amer. institute of banking [c1930] 368p. 21cm.

WINTER, Sidney Graham, 1896–
C. P. A. review; questions and problems in auditing and in accounting theory and practice. N. Y. Prentice-Hall, 1930. 556p. 23½cm.
—C. P. A. review; answers to questions and solutions to problems. N. Y. Prentice-Hall, 1930. 763p. 23½cm.

WOODBRIDGE, Frederick Wells.
A system of accounting procedure for livestock ranches. Austin, Tex. [c1930] 193p. 22cm. (Texas. University. Bureau of business research. Research monograph no.5)
At head of title: The University of Texas bulletin no. 3040: October 22, 1930.

1931

AMERICAN INSTITUTE OF ACCOUNTANTS. Special committee on terminology.
Accounting terminology; preliminary report of a Special committee

on terminology; pub. under the auspices of American institute of accountants. N. Y. Century co. [c1931] 126p. 24cm.
Walter Mucklow, chairman; A. P. Richardson, editor.

BOLON, Dallas Sinclaire, 1894– , and ECKELBERRY, George Wendell, 1892–
Introduction to accounting. N. Y. Wiley, 1931. 572p. 23½cm. (Wiley accounting ser.)
Preliminary edition of 218 pages with Eckelberry's name appearing first on the title-page published in 1930.
Accounting laboratory materials separately published in two parts.

CASTENHOLZ, William Burtis, 1879–
A solution to the appreciation problem; with a supplementary article entitled: This thing called depreciation. Chic. LaSalle extension univ. 1931. 95p. 20½cm.

DILS, Frank Lee.
Farm accounting. Covington, Ky. Agricultural service corp. of America, inc. [1931] 100p. 29cm.

DUNCAN, John Christie, 1881–
Principles of analytical accounting. Cin. Printed for the author by the Ruter press [c1931] 534p. 23½cm.

EGGLESTON, De Witt Carl, 1881–
Department store accounting; with 180 charts. N. Y. Greenberg [c1931] 422p. 23½cm.

GREER, Howard Clark, 1894– , and WILLCOX, Russell Stuart, 1898–
Problems in cost accounting. N. Y. McGraw-Hill, 1931. 379p. 23½cm. (McGraw-Hill accounting ser.)

HADLEY, Charles R., company, Los Angeles.
Hadley's pathfinder accounting system for radio dealers. Los Angeles, Hadley, c1931. 63 numb. l.+forms, 11x14cm.

INTERNATIONAL TEXTBOOK COMPANY, Scranton.
Branches, consolidations, municipal accounts. Scranton, International textbk. co. c1931. 136p. 19½cm. (International library of technology. Blue book ser. v.233B)

—C. P. A. questions and coaching. Scranton, International textbk. co. c1931–32. 187p. 19½cm. (International library of technology. Blue book ser. v.69)

MEREDITH, Spencer B.
What the figures mean. Bost. Financial pub. co. [c1931] 77p. 19½cm.

METROPOLITAN LIFE INSURANCE COMPANY, New York. Policyholders service bureau.
Cost accounting for advertising agencies. N. Y. Metropolitan life insurance co. 1931. 20 l.+[7] l. 28cm.
Mimeographed.
Another ed. 1932. 20 l.+[7] l. 28cm.
Mimeographed.

MYERS, Herbert J., KEATING, William L., and METSCH, J. C.
How to set standards; Jordan prize competition. N. Y. National assn. of cost accountants [c1931] 98p. 22½cm.
Contains the three prize winning essays of a competition open to members of the National association of cost accountants. *cf.* Foreword.

NOBLE, L. Scott.
Student body finances and accounting. Cin. South-western pub. co. [c1931] 256p. 22cm.

O'HARA, Allen.
Accounting to increase profits . . . Holyoke, Mass. National blank bk. co. c1931. 130p. 29x37½cm.
Loose-leaf sheets in binder.
"This modern unit accounting system, applicable to any type of business, makes it possible for executives to know monthly the vital facts about the current history of the business."

PACE, Homer St. Clair, 1879– , and BRYAN, Charles Teitge, 1890–
Comprehensive propositions in accounting. N. Y. Pace institute publishers, inc. 1931. 398p. 23½cm.

PEARSON, M. L.
Progressive bookkeeping and accounting. Cin. South-western pub. co. [c1931] 325p. 22cm.

SANFORD, Emmett Reid.
Applied accounting principles. N. Y. Crowell [c1931] 538p. 23½cm.

SUNLEY, William Terry, and PINKERTON, Paul Whittier, 1887–
Corporation accounting. N. Y. Ronald [c1931] 570p. 22cm.

1932

AMERICAN INSTITUTE OF ACCOUNTANTS. Board of examiners.
Examination questions prepared by the Board of examiners of the American institute of accountants for the examinations conducted from May, 1927, to November, 1931, inclusive. N. Y. Pub. for the Amer. institute of accountants by Amer. institute pub. co. [c1932] 281p. 18½cm.
(For "Examination questions" prepared previous to Nov. 1927, see 1921, American institute of accountants)

CAMMAN, Eric A., 1891–
Basic standard costs; control accounting for manufacturing industries. N. Y. Amer. institute pub. co. 1932. 232p. 24½cm.
Appendix, containing tables (in part folded) folded diagrams and folded forms, in pocket.

DELEVANTI, A. C.
Systematizing an attorney's office. Chic. Callaghan, 1932. 66p. 27cm.

DICKERSON, William E., and JONES, J. Weldon.
Ohio C. P. A. problems: an analytical study of and solution to the problems given by the Ohio state board of accountancy, 1928–1931. Columbus, Ohio [Ohio state univ. press] c1932. [252]p. 29cm.
—Ohio C. P. A. problems and solutions, 1932 supplement. 1933. 72p. 29cm.
—Ohio C. P. A. problems and solutions, 1933 supplement. 1934. 67p. 29cm.

DODGE, Chester Joseph.
Estate administration and accounting. Brooklyn, Standard text press [c1932] 453p. 23½cm.
2d ed. [c1933] 450p. 24cm.

ELWELL, Fayette Herbert, 1885–
Bookkeeping for today; first course. Bost. Ginn [c1932] 277p. 24cm.
This work and those which immediately follow are based upon the volumes written by Elwell and Toner in 1926. Elwell has entirely rewritten this series of volumes. They are essentially new works.
—Bookkeeping for today; elementary course. Bost. Ginn [c1932] 436p. 24cm.
—Bookkeeping for today; advanced course. Bost. Ginn [c1932] p.415–770, 24cm.

ELWELL (continued)
—Bookkeeping for today; combined course. Bost. Ginn [c1932] 598p. 24cm.
—Bookkeeping for today; corporation and voucher accounting. Bost. Ginn [c1932] p.599–768, 24cm.

FINNEY, Harry Anson, 1886–
Introduction to principles of accounting. N. Y. Prentice-Hall, 1932. 649p. 23½cm.

—BAUMANN, Harry Paul, 1892– , and GORDON, Spencer, 1887–
Unofficial answers to the examination questions of the American institute of accountants, May, 1927, to November, 1931. N. Y. Amer. institute pub. co. [c1932] 423p. 24½cm.
Editor's note signed: A. P. Richardson, editor.

GEIER, George Jacob, and MAUTNER, Oscar.
Systems installation in accounting. N. Y. Burrell-Snow, 1932. 500p. 23½cm.
Sets of problems in accounting systems and methods of installation separately published.

GRAHAM, Willard J., 1897– , and KATZ, Wilber Griffith.
Accounting in law practice. Chic. Callaghan, 1932. 444p. 26cm.
This work is primarily intended to furnish law students and lawyers with a thorough treatise on elementary and advanced accounting principles and practice. It is equally valuable as a general treatise for students of accounting.
—Problems and exercises for use with Graham and Katz' "Accounting in law practice." Chic. Callaghan, 1932. 81p. 23½cm.

GRAHAME, J. W. F., and MYERS, Preston E.
"Unaform" accounting schedules. Belleville, N. J. Yerg, inc. c1932. [82]p. 36½x23cm.
A treatise on auditing procedure which includes form sheets, set of schedules with captions inserted, and outline of audit procedure relative to each schedule printed on reverse side.

HADLEY, Charles R., company, Los Angeles.
Hadley's pathfinder accounting system for attorneys-at-law. Los Angeles, Hadley, c1932. 51 numb. l.+forms, 28x34cm.

—Hadley's pathfinder accounting system for service stations and garages. Los Angeles, Hadley, c1932. 89 numb. l.+forms, 28x28cm.

Another ed. c1934. 89 numb. l.+forms, 28x28cm.
The title of this edition was changed to "garages and service stations."

LIEBERMAN, Bernard.
Accounting system for retail stores. N. Y. Accounting systems & forms co. c1932. 26p. 18cm.
Set of forms separately published.

METROPOLITAN LIFE INSURANCE COMPANY, New York. Policyholders service bureau.
Annual reports to stockholders of chain stores. N. Y. Metropolitan life insurance co. 1932. 38 l. 28cm.

MORRIS, Anthony William, and KINMAN, James Irvin, 1887–
Accountancy and business procedure; series one. Spokane, Kinman-Morris [c1932] 466+[12]p. 23½cm.

PATON, William Andrew, 1889– , editor.
Accountants' handbook; 2d ed. N. Y. Ronald, 1932.
1873p. 19cm.
"This second edition . . . supersedes the first edition issued in 1923 under the able editorship of Dr. Earl A. Saliers . . . the present book, although built upon the foundation of the earlier work, is in both content and arrangement an entirely new publication."—Publisher's pref.
Another ed. 1933. 1873p. 19cm.
9th printing.
Another ed. 1934. 1742p. 19cm.
Revised printing.

SHERWOOD, John F., 1890–
C. P. A. problems. Cin. South-western pub. co. [c1932]
108p. 22cm.
Problems selected from examinations of the American institute of accountants and state examinations given applicants for the certified public accountant certificate.
Model solutions for C. P. A. problems (loose-leaf) separately published.

STREIGHTOFF, Frank Hatch, 1886–
Advanced accounting. N. Y. Harper, 1932. 656p. 24cm.
The author's "Elementary accounting" published in 1928.

STUDEBAKER, Mark E.
Bookkeeping and accounting for rural schools. Cin. South-western pub. co. [c1932] 380p. 22½cm.

THORNTON, Frank Weldon, 1863–
Duties of the senior accountant. N.Y. Pub. for the Amer. institute of accountants by the Amer. institute pub. co. [c1932] 91p. 18cm.
Editor's note signed: A. P. Richardson.

VAN BENTHUYSEN, Alvin Seaward, 1884–
Newspaper organization and accounting. N.Y. Prentice-Hall, 1932. 544p. 27½cm.

1933

AZIERE, Charles, father, 1905–
Accounting for Catholic institutions of higher education. Atchison, Kan. National Benedictine educational assn. [c1933] p.29–57, 22½cm. (National Benedictine educational association. Bulletin, v.16, no.2)

BURTON, Norman Lee, 1890–
Analytical accounting. Ann Arbor, Mich. Edwards bros. c1933. 82 numb. l. 28½cm.

CHASE, Harvey Stuart, 1861–
A plan for a standard form of municipal reports to be published annually by towns in the commonwealth, prepared by Harvey S. Chase, C.P.A., for a special committee of the National economy league, Massachusetts state branch, inc., for presentation to the Recess commission on public expenditures of the General court of Massachusetts, October, 1933. [Salem, Mass. Printed by Newcomb & Gauss co. 1933] 31p. 23½cm.

CHATTERS, Carl H.
Accounting manual for small cities (under 25,000 population) Chic. Municipal finance officers' assn. of the United States & Canada, 1933. 79p. 25½cm. (Municipal finance officers' association of the United States and Canada. Publication no.1)

CIPRIANI, Alfred B.
Duties of the junior accountant. N.Y. Amer. institute pub. co. [c1933] 170p. 18cm.
Lettered on cover: Revised and enlarged edition.
Based to some extent on an earlier work under the same title by W. B. Reynolds and F. W. Thornton. *cf.* Editor's note. (See 1918, Reynolds, W. B. and Thornton, F. W.)

GOETTSCHE, H. C. & co., Chicago.
Standard brewery systems. Chic. H. C. Goettsche & co. c1933. Various pagings, 29½cm.

—Brewery accounting; complete system and forms. Crawfordsville, Ind. R. R. Donnelley, 1934. 279p. 22cm.
Harty C. Goettsche is named as author of this second edition.

GRANGE, William James, STAUB, Walter Adolph, 1881– , and BLACKFORD, Eugene G.
Wills, executors, and trustees: a practical work on the law, accounting, and taxation of estates and trusts—including the bank and trust company as a fiduciary. N. Y. Ronald [c1933]
844p. 22cm.

HELMSTADTER, Carl W.
Elementary college accounting. Minneapolis, Burgess pub. co. c1933. 121 numb. l. 27½cm.
Mimeographed.
Ruled leaves for "Journal" inserted.

HOGAN, Thomas J., and FINNEN, Malachi A., 1889–
Outline of audit procedure. Brooklyn, Standard text press [c1933] 142p. 23½cm.
The classification of accounting services of the New Jersey state society is given in this volume. *cf.* p.10.

JONES, Ralph C.
Allocation accounting for the taxable income of industrial enterprises. Geneva, League of Nations, 1933. 78p. 26cm. (Taxation of foreign and national enterprises, v.5)
This work was written by Ralph C. Jones, C. P. A., Associate professor of accounting, Yale university, and is distributed in this country by the World peace foundation, Boston.
A preliminary report was published by Yale university in 1932.

LAFFERTY, William A.
The auditing of municipal accounts in New York state. Albany, New York state conference of mayors and other municipal officials, Bureau of training and research, 1933. 83p. 23cm. (Publication no.28)

LANGER, Charles Heinrichs, 1876–
Accounting principles and procedure . . . Chic. Walton pub. co. [c1933] [301]p. 28½cm. (Walton accounting ser.)

McGINLEY, Lee.
Public accounting procedure: a working manual on audits, systems, and income taxes. N. Y. Gregg [c1933] 169p. 21cm.

METROPOLITAN LIFE INSURANCE COMPANY, New York. Policyholders service bureau.
Annual reports to stockholders of banking institutions. N. Y. Metropolitan life insurance co. 1933. 43 l. 28cm.
Another ed. 1934. 43 l. 28cm.

MYER, Joseph Charles, 1893–1934.
New York C. P. A. theory questions with answers. Brooklyn, Standard text press [c1933] 512p. 23½cm.
"Includes all of the questions that have been asked on the theory part of each New York C. P. A. examination from November, 1915, through April, 1933."—Pref.

NEW YORK CONFERENCE ON HOSPITAL ACCOUNTING.
Accounting and business procedure for hospitals; prepared by New York conference on hospital accounting, Herbert R. Sands, consulting accountant. N. Y. United hospital fund of New York [c1933] 195p. 26cm.

REITELL, Charles Ervin, 1887–
Cost accounting principles and methods. Scranton, International textbk. co. 1933. 441p. 24cm.
"Questions, discussion cases, and problems" separately published in 1934.

SHERWOOD, John F., 1890–
Modern accounting principles and procedure. [Cin. South-western pub. co. c1933] 358p. 29cm.

SMITH, Charles Aubrey, 1901–
Internal audit control. Austin, Tex. Univ. co-operative soc. 1933. 205p. 23½cm.
Thesis (Ph.D.)—Columbia university, 1933.

TANZ, Louis.
Bookkeeping workbook (second year) N. Y. Globe bk. co. [c1933] 60p. 28cm.

TAYLOR, Jacob Bacchus, 1898– , and MILLER, Hermann Clinton, 1895–
Intermediate accounting. N. Y. McGraw-Hill, 1933–[34] 2v. 23½cm. (McGraw-Hill accounting ser.)
v.1, 1933; v.2, 1934.

THORNTON, Frank Weldon, 1863–
Financial examinations. N. Y. Amer. institute pub. co. [c1933] 282p. 18cm.

Editor's note signed: A. P. Richardson.
A revision of "Approved methods for the preparation of balance sheet statements" with the title "Verification of financial statements" was completed by a committee of the American institute of accountants in 1929 and published by the Federal reserve board. It is submitted as an appendix to this book which is written as an amplification of the procedure contained therein. *cf.* Pref.

WISCONSIN. PUBLIC SERVICE COMMISSION.
Depreciation; a review of legal and accounting problems . . . Madison, Wis. Public service commission of Wisconsin [c1933] 196p. 22½cm.

YOUNG, Benjamin E.
Bank cost control; with a foreword by R. H. Brunkhorst . . . N. Y. Rand, McNally [c1933] 299p. 22½cm.

1934

ALFORD, Leon Pratt, 1877– , editor.
Cost and production handbook. N. Y. Ronald, 1934. 1544p. 19cm.

ATKINSON, Sterling Krick, 1904–
A model cost control plan for delivery organizations of department stores doing an annual business of from two to ten million dollars . . . Phil. 1934. 124p. 23cm.
Thesis (Ph.D.)—Columbia university, 1934.

BELLOWS, Frederick M.
How to read a financial statement. N. Y. System & business management [c1934] 33p. 23x11cm.

DANIELS, Mortimer B.
Corporation financial statements. Ann Arbor, Mich. Univ. of Mich. School of business administration, Bur. of business research, 1934. 131p. 23cm. (Michigan. University. School of business administration. Bureau of business research. Michigan business studies, v.6, no.1)

FOWLKES, John Guy, 1898–
Principles and practices of financial accounting for schools. Milw. E. M. Hale, 1934. 238p. 23½cm.

GRAHAM, Willard J., 1897–
Public utility valuation; reproduction cost as a basis for deprecia-

GRAHAM (continued)
tion and rate-base determination. Chic. [Univ. of Chic. press] 1934. 95p. 23cm. (Studies in business administration, v.4, no.3)
Thesis (Ph.D.)—University of Chicago, 1934.
Published also without thesis note.

HADLEY, Charles R., company, Los Angeles.
Hadley's accounting manual for Federal savings and loan associations. Los Angeles, Hadley, c1934.
77 numb. l.+forms, 28x35cm.

HARRIS, Walter O.
A municipal general ledger and principal supporting records (based on accounting systems in Flint and Grand Rapids, Michigan) Chic. Municipal finance officers' assn. of the United States and Canada, 1934. 44p. 27½cm.

HOSMER, Windsor Arnold, SANDERS, Thomas Henry, 1885– , and HANSON, Arthur Warren, 1890–
Problems in accounting. N. Y. McGraw-Hill, 1934.
463p. 23½cm.

HUMPHREYS, HUGH G.
The accounts of an oil company. N. Y. Amer. institute pub. co. 1934. 136p. 24cm.

JAFFE, John, 1895–
Labor cost records; their forms and preparation. Lancaster, Pa. 1934. 141p. 23½cm.
Thesis (Ph.D.)—Columbia university, 1934.

KIRK, John George, 1881– , STREET, James Layman, 1879– , and ODELL, William Rockhold, 1906–
Bookkeeping for immediate use; script illus. by Edward C. Mills. Phil. Winston, 1934. 393p. 22cm.
Two workbooks separately published.

LINDSAY, Maurice M.
Corporate organization and accounts [preliminary ed.] Bost. Bentley school of accounting & finance [c1934] 164p. 29cm.

LYANS, Cecil Kenyon, and BRISCO, Norris Arthur, 1875–
Retail accounting. N. Y. Prentice-Hall, 1934. 590p. 23½cm. (Retailing ser.)

MANNIX, Raymond Leo.
Accounting for corporations. Bost. [Printed by Insurance press] 1934. 344p. 24cm.

METROPOLITAN LIFE INSURANCE COMPANY, New York. Policyholders service bureau.
Accounting policies in inter-company sales and transfers. N. Y. Metropolitan life insurance co. 1934. 26 l. 28cm.

—Inventory control methods. N. Y. Metropolitan life insurance co. 1934. 30 l. 28cm.

MOORE, Franklin Frazee, and GILL, John Goodner, editors.
Municipal accounting and auditing. Trenton, N. J. Rider college, c1934. 321p. 23½cm.
"The most important laws and requirements governing municipal accounting in the state of New Jersey."—Pref.
"Requirements of an audit [published in 1931 by Walter R. Darby] :" p. 237–314.

NATIONAL COMMITTEE ON MUNICIPAL ACCOUNTING, Chicago.
Tentative outline of a suggested method of procedure for a detailed municipal audit . . . Chic. National committee on municipal accounting [c1934] 25+[1]p. 23cm. (Bulletin no.2)
Bulletin no.1, "Tentative outline: principles of municipal accounting," is a pamphlet of four pages published in January, 1934.

SCHMIDT, Leo Anton.
Bookkeeping-accounting; comprising hundreds of test questions and accounting problems of the latest style in use in city, county, state, and federal civil service examinations for bookkeepers and accountants. Milw. Pergande pub. co. c1934. 96p. 23½cm.

SEIDMAN, Henry L.
New York C. P. A. problems and solutions, 1924–1933. N. Y. C. P. A. examinations review [c1934] 2v. 29½cm.
v.1, 1924–1928; v.2, 1929–1933.
Loose-leaf mimeographed sheets in two binders.

WADE, Harry Henchell.
Fundamentals of accounting: a text designed primarily for a survey course. N. Y. Wiley, 1934. 281p. 23½cm. (Wiley accounting ser.)
"The material in this book has been developed during seven years of teaching, and it has been used in mimeographed form for the

WADE (continued)
last two years in the instruction of engineering students in the University of Iowa."—Pref.

—Laboratory material for Fundamentals of accounting. N. Y. Wiley, 1934. 121p. 28cm.

WIGHTMAN, Earl Charles, 1889–
Life insurance accounts. [Fort Wayne, Ind.] Life office management assn. 1934. 281p. 21cm. (Life office management association. Institute ser.)

WILLCOX, Russell Stuart, 1898–
Cost accounting. Chic. Business publications co. 1934. 328+[1]p. $23\frac{1}{2}$cm.

PART TWO

PART TWO

Classification of works listed in Part One

INTRODUCTION

FOR practical reference purposes the works on accounting listed in Part One are divided into the seven classes designated hereunder. Twentieth century editions of 19th century titles are also classified.

1. Works on bookkeeping intended primarily for use in high schools and private business schools
2. Works on elementary and advanced accounting intended primarily for students of college grade or for general reference purposes
3. Works dealing with the preparation and interpretation of financial statements
4. Cost accounting and system building:
   (a) Works dealing chiefly or wholly with general principles and practice
   (b) Treatises applicable to specific businesses and professions
5. Auditing:
   (a) Works dealing chiefly or wholly with general principles and procedure
   (b) Treatises applicable to specific businesses and professions
6. C. P. A. examination questions and answers
7. Encyclopedias, handbooks, etc.

The works in each class are listed chronologically. Each first edition is recorded under the date of its publication with a reference to the date of the latest edition, if any. The latest "edition" of each title, regardless of whether it is a reprint or a revised edition, is recorded under the date of its publication with a reference to the date of the first edition. This method of arrangement serves a double purpose by showing the development in each field of accounting, and by providing a ready reference to the first and latest works in each field.

The Author Index makes it possible to ascertain the pages where each author's work is classified.

The Subject Index lists the pages where accounting material for specific businesses and professions can be found in this part and also in the Supplement.

Only as much of the title is recorded in Part Two as is necessary to identify it. For full bibliographical information concerning each title, see Part One.

Part Two

CLASS I

Works on bookkeeping intended primarily for use in high schools and private business schools

1901

FIELD, Millard Lincoln.
Outlines in bookkeeping. 64p.

INGERSON, Carlos Ira.
A normal method in double entry bookkeeping. 88p.

MULLER, S. F.
A graded system of book-keeping. 155p.

ROBERTSON, Powhatan Wyndham.
Robertson's bookkeeping and science of accounts; 4th ed. rev. and enl. 183p.
First edition, 1894.

TANNER, Henry T.
Practical business instructor. 151p.
Latest edition, 1907.

WRIGHT, Prince Albert.
Wright's bookkeeping simplified; Wall street ed. 368p.
First edition, 1881.

1902

ATKINSON, Edmund Clement.
Modern methods in bookkeeping; 2d ed. 160p.
First edition, 1894.

CURTISS, Charles Carroll.
The American standard bookkeeping. 192p.

GILBERT, Adelbert Lorenzo.
Modern business bookkeeping. 215p.
Latest edition, 1912.

1902 (continued)

GROVER, Preston Henry.
Corporation book-keeping in a nut-shell. 52p.
First edition, 1897.

MCKINNEY, W. J.
The ideal self-instructor in double entry book-keeping. 110p.

MARSHALL, Carl Coran.
Marshall's corporation and voucher accounting. 68p.
Latest edition, 1907.

MOORE, John Henry, and MINER, George Washington.
Accounting and business practice. 400p.

READ, Frederick H.
Bookkeeping, business arithmetic, and correspondence. 262p.

SNYDER, Carrie, and THURSTON, Ernest Lawton.
The universal system of practical bookkeeping. 192p.
Latest edition, 1915.

1903

BAKER, James William.
Reference book: 20th century bookkeeping and office practice. 116p.
Latest edition, 1929.

FOELLER, Joseph Paul.
A short and practical illustration of double entry book-keeping. 35p.

GOODWIN, Phillip C.
Bookkeeping self-taught. 127p.

HIRSCH, Adolph.
The science of commercial bookkeeping. 139p.
Latest edition, 1910.

MARSHALL, Carl Coran.
Marshall's double entry drills. 60p.
Latest edition, 1920.

UNTERBRINK, John Roman.
The bookkeeping owl; or, Practical bookkeeping explained. 102p.

WHINYATES, John W.
Bookkeeping with or without a master. 73p.
First edition, 1898.

1904

BRYANT, Henry Willis.
Bryant's practical book-keeping. 116p.
Latest edition, 1920.

DRAUGHON, James William.
Draughon's practical accountant and commercial law. 178p.

DUFF, Charles Peter, DUFF, William Henry, and DUFF, Robert Peel.
Duff's common school book-keeping. 192p.
First edition, 1877.

HOOKLAND, Seibert S., and HAYWARD, William Richart.
Inductive bookkeeping and business practice. 147p.

MEREDITH, Reuben Leslie.
Practical exercises in higher accounting. 59p.

MILLER, O. L.
Miller's system of bookkeeping and business. 181p.

MOORE, John C.
Moore's modern methods; containing . . . valuable information on the science of bookkeeping and loose leaf accounting. 80p.

SANDY, William Charles.
The American accountant; part 1, rev. 118p.
First edition, 1894.

STRAYER, S. Irving.
Modern bookkeeping. 164p.

THORNE, William Winter.
Thorne's twentieth century book-keeping and business practice. 384p.
Latest edition, 1910.

1905

BOGLE, Artemas Melvin.
Comprehensive bookkeeping. 142p.
Latest edition, 1919.

BUCHANAN, William.
The journal dictionary and bookkeepers' proof book. 534p.

BYRNE, Henry Edward.
Byrne practical bookkeeping. 90p.

CLEARY, P. Roger.
Study and practice of business bookkeeping and accounting. 216p.

DARBY, Willis W., and RAGLAND, Alphonso.
Darby & Ragland's practical bookkeeping. 203p.

EATON, Abijah H., STALEY, H. N., and DIXON, J. W.
Corporation bookkeeping. 72p.

INTERNATIONAL TEXTBOOK COMPANY, Scranton.
Single-entry bookkeeping; double-entry bookkeeping; opening, closing, and changing books [etc.] Various pagings.

LYONS, James A.
Wholesale accounting. 37p.
Latest edition, 1920.

—and WHIGAM, Wallace Hugh.
Modern accountant. 130p.
Latest edition, 1911.

MAYNE, Dexter Dwight, editor.
Office methods and practical bookkeeping. 147p.
First edition, 1900.

SMITH, John Coley, and JENKINS, Friend W.
The national accountant. 320p.
First edition, 1865.

SNYDER, William Thomas.
A brief exposition of the fundamental principles of bookkeeping. 51p.

1906

DELAY, David W.
DeLay's manual of bookkeeping. 98p.

GOODYEAR, Lloyd Earnest.
Goodyear's bank accounting; tablet method. 68p.

KING, Thomas.
Expert King's double entry bookkeeping manual. 113p.

LYTE, Eliphalet Oram.
Practical book-keeping. 224p.
First edition, 1880.

MONTGOMERY, James Louis.
Modern book-keeping and business practice. 381p.
First edition, 1897.

PRINCE, William Layphayette.
New practical bookkeeping and short system of double entry. 110p.

THORNE, William Winter.
The abolition of the trial balance; together with twelve studies in book-keeping and accounting. 168p.

1907

CLEARY, P. Roger.
Student's guide to the Cleary system of business, bookkeeping, accounting, and auditing. 2v.
v.1, 108p., 1907. v.2, 62p., 1908.
Latest edition, 1909.

CROXTON, Oscar Charles.
Short cuts to practical bookkeeping. 44p.

DEYO, Willet Abram.
A manual for actual business practise in high schools. 43p.

ELLIS, Carlos Bent.
Practical bookkeeping. 252p.
Latest edition, 1908.

1907 (continued)

GOODYEAR, Samuel Horatio.
The theory of accounts. 206p.
First edition, 1890.

—and GOODYEAR, Lloyd Earnest.
Goodyear's higher accounting. 112p.
Latest edition, 1909.

—Wholesale accounting. 26p.

—and MARSHALL, Carl Coran.
Modern inductive bookkeeping. 159p.

McKINNEY, Winfield S.
Mercantile accounting. 59p.

MARSHALL, Carl Coran.
Marshall's corporation and voucher accounting. 68p.
First edition, 1902.

MURRAY, George Stanley.
Elements of accounts. 92p.

SMITH, Ephraim Waldo, and SMITH, Wilbur Rush.
The text-book on book-keeping; 22d ed. 302p.
First edition, 1885.

TANNER, Henry T.
Practical business instructor. 151p.
First edition, 1901.

VAN CLEVE, Charles McKinstry.
Theory of double-entry bookkeeping. 60p.

WEBER, Fred Charles.
Introductory bookkeeping. 66p.
Latest edition, 1920.

1908

BYRNE, Henry Edward.
Byrne bookkeeping for business colleges, high schools, and self instructions. 110p.
Latest edition, 1923.

CORNEIL, George Russel.
A text-book in bookkeeping. 79p.

ELLIS, Carlos Bent.
Practical bookkeeping. 252p.
First edition, 1907.

LYONS, James A.
Modern corporation accounting (voucher system) 80p.

—The new complete accountant. 222p.

NELSON, Richard James.
Nelson's new book-keeping. 330p.

1909

ALLEN, George.
The science of accounts made clear and simple. 136p.

BEVERSDORF, Allen A.
The self-instructing book-keeper. 112p.

BISHOP, William George.
A short course in business training. 85p.
Latest edition, 1914.

CLEARY, P. Roger.
Student's guide to the Cleary system of business, bookkeeping, accounting, and auditing. 2v.
v.1, 121p. v.2, 76p.
First edition, 1907.

ELLIS PUBLISHING COMPANY, Battle Creek, Mich.
Bookkeeping outlines. 56p.

GOODYEAR, Samuel Horatio.
Goodyear's advanced accounting. 114p.

1909 (continued)

GOODYEAR, Samuel Horatio, and GOODYEAR, Lloyd Earnest.
Goodyear's higher accounting; 2d ed. 132p.
First edition, 1907.

LYONS, James A., and READ, Walter L.
Bookkeeping from vouchers: a course in bookkeeping for beginners. 189p.
Latest edition, 1913.

MUSSELMAN, De Lafayette.
Musselman's bookkeeping. 73p.
Latest edition, 1911.

PACKARD, Silas Sadler, and BRYANT, Henry Beadman.
The new Bryant & Stratton high-school book-keeping. 166p.
First edition, 1860.

SPENCER, Enos.
Art of modern bookkeeping and accounting; 3d ed. 446p.
First edition, 1899.

STEPHENS, John Rittenhouse.
Principles of accounting. 91p.

WEBER, Fred Charles.
Corporation bookkeeping. 41p.

WIGHTMAN, William W., compiler.
Student's guide to the principles of bookkeeping. 116p.

1910

BARDEEN, Charles William.
Question book of book-keeping. 27p.
First edition, 1888.

BENTON, Charles William.
Practical bookkeeping. 222p.
First edition, 1896.

DEWHIRST, John Mark.
Elements of bookkeeping. 63p.

EATON, Abijah H.
The Eaton & Burnett bookkeeping; 6th ed. 264p.
First edition, 1881.

GOODYEAR, Lloyd Earnest.
Progressive business accounting. 155p.
Latest edition, 1912.

GRIFFITH, James Bray.
Corporation accounts and voucher system. 132p.
Latest edition, 1919.

—Practical bookkeeping. 288p.
Latest edition, 1919.

HEITMANN, Henry.
A course in the theory and practice of higher acounting. 240p.

HIRSCH, Adolph.
The science of commercial bookkeeping. 139p.
First edition, 1903.

ROWE, Harry Marc.
Bookkeeping and accountancy. 263p.
Latest edition, 1927.

THORNE, William Winter.
The international accountant's manual; or, Twentieth century bookkeeping and business practice. 384p.
No author is named on the title-page, but it is a reprint of Thorne's work published in 1904.

WHIGAM, Wallace Hugh, and FREDERICK, Oliver Detwiler.
Bookkeeping and business practice. 142p.

WITTER, Charles Asa.
Witter's business and accounts; 6th ed. 112p.
First edition, 1886.

1911

CAMPBELL, Thomas Findley.
Campbell's actual accounting. 135p.
Latest edition, 1912.

1911 (continued)

FREEMAN, Charles Edmund.
Adjustments through elimination. 49p.

LOCKYEAR, Melvin H.
An introductory course: Lockyear's bookkeeping. 105p.
Latest edition, 1931.

LYONS, James A., and READ, Walter L.
Modern accountant; rev. 168p.
First edition, 1905.

MUSSELMAN, De Lafayette.
Musselman's bookkeeping. 143p.
First edition, 1909.

1912

BENNETT, Robert Joseph.
Bookkeeping and accounting exercises. 2v.
v.1, 96p. v.2, 112p.

BLISS, Fred H.
Bliss system of bookkeeping and office practice. 154p.
Latest edition, 1920.

BROTHERS OF THE CHRISTIAN SCHOOLS.
First steps in bookkeeping. 68p.

CAMPBELL, Thomas Findley.
Campbell's actual accounting. 267p.
First edition, 1911.

ELLIS PUBLISHING COMPANY, Battle Creek, Mich.
Business directions used in connection with Ellis industrial bookkeeping. 75p.
Latest edition, 1920.

GILBERT, Adelbert Lorenzo.
Modern business bookkeeping. 216p.
First edition, 1902.

GOODYEAR, Lloyd Earnest.
Progressive business accounting. 154p.
First edition, 1910.

LYONS, James A.
The Lyons accounting; series A.

—The Lyons accounting; series B.

MEREDITH, Arthur John.
Meservey's new bookkeeping. 276p.

MINER, George Washington.
Bookkeeping; complete course. 334p.
Various parts of this work, including the introductory course, intermediate course, and advanced course, published separately. Latest edition, 1916.

VAUGHAN, L. Brent.
Complete course in bookkeeping, double and single entry. 91p.

1913

BEXELL, John Andrew, and NICHOLS, Frederick George.
Principles of bookkeeping and farm accounts. 184p.
Latest edition, 1927.

BROWN, Michael J.
"Tally"; or, Every debit has its credit. 40p.

GOODWIN, Joseph Henry.
Goodwin's improved book-keeping and business manual; 28th ed. 301p.
First edition, 1881.

GOODYEAR, Lloyd Earnest.
Principles of accountancy. 189p.
Latest edition, 1924.

HALL, Marshall Parker.
The art of accounts; 2d ed. 86p.
First edition, 1898.

LYONS, James A., and READ, Walter L.
Lyons' bookkeeping: a course for beginners. 236p.
First edition, 1909.

1913 (continued)

MacFarland, George Arthur, and Rossheim, Irving David.
A first year in bookkeeping and accounting. 227p.

Miner, George Washington.
Bookkeeping: banking. 104p.

Powers, Orville Marcellus.
Theory of bookkeeping. 125p.

Sweet, James Sylvester.
Business practice bookkeeping. 192p.

Van Cleve, Charles McKinstry.
Principles of double-entry bookkeeping. 210p.

1914

Bishop, William George.
A short course in business training. 149p.
First edition, 1909.

Detroit school of accounts and commerce.
Book-keeping in six lessons. 94p.

Dudley, George Osgood.
Corporation accounting. 86p.

Mankato commercial college, Mankato, Minn.
Student's guide to accompany the Brandrup & Nettleton system of teaching bookkeeping and business practice. 255p.

Mann, Jasper Dalton.
Mann's agricultural bookkeeping instructor. 55p.

Peck, Roscoe H., and Read, Harlan Eugene.
Peck and Read's bookkeeping. 2v.
v.1, 140p. v.2, 76p.

Sheaffer, William Adam.
Metropolitan system of bookkeeping. 2v.
v.1, 210p. v.2, 185p.
Latest edition, 1922.

1915

ARMSTRONG, Augustus.
Double entry bookkeeping. 64p.

BELDING, Albert G.
Accounts and accounting practice. 224p.
Latest edition, 1918.

BRADLEY, Carolyn H.
Suggestive exercises in bookkeeping for grammar schools. 30p.

MARSHALL, Carl Coran.
Bookkeeping and business training. 115p.
First edition, 1900.

MELCHIOR, Roger Logan.
Hints on bookkeeping. 60p.

SNYDER, Carrie, and THURSTON, Ernest Lawton.
The universal system of practical bookkeeping. 192p.
First edition, 1902.

SOBEL, Joseph.
Practical accounting. 7 pamphlets.
These pamphlets total 124 pages.

1916

BRYANT, John Collins.
The new standard practical and progressive book-keeping (counting-house ed.) 223p.
—The new standard practical and progressive book-keeping (commercial ed.) 155p.
First edition, 1869.

HAWORTH, Smith Gordon, and ASHBY, William Silas.
Cotton seed oil mill bookkeeping. 55p.

HOFFMAN, George Lawrence.
Simplified bookkeeping. 60p.

1916 (continued)

MINER, George Washington.
Bookkeeping; complete course. 334p.
Various parts of this work, including the introductory course, intermediate course, and advanced course, published separately.
First edition, 1912.

RATIONAL BUSINESS SYSTEM, Cedar Rapids, Ia.
The rational business system. 95p.

WALKER, James Cree.
Retail accounting and store management. 91p.

1917

BOGLE, Artemas Melvin.
Everyday bookkeeping. 126p.
Latest edition, 1918.

BOOKMAN, Clarence Monroe, and BLUE, Franz Sigel.
First steps in bookkeeping. 86p.

EATON, Abijah H.
The Eaton and Burnett revised and improved bookkeeping, corporation, voucher, and cost accounting. 261p.
Latest edition, 1918.

HATTON, Linius Monroe, and PROWINSKY, Joseph Albert.
The H. and P. practical bookkeeping. 48p.
Latest edition, 1920.

HAYES, Pryor Lee.
The bookkeeping teacher: a treatise on the science of double entry bookkeeping. 126p.

KLEIN, Joseph Jerome.
Bookkeeping and accounting; complete course. 453p.
This work was also published in two separate parts: part 1, introductory course; part 2, advanced course.
Latest edition, 1929.

MORTON, Davis Walter.
Banking and bank accounting. 112p.
Latest edition, 1933.

ROWE, Harry Marc.
Junior arithmetic-bookkeeping. 2v.
v.1, 131p., 1917. v.2, 88p., 1918.

WINSPEAR, Clara Schmudde.
Winspear's 1917 bookkeeping manual. 40p.

WOLFF, Mark.
Bookkeeper and accountant civil service examination instruction. 108p.
Latest edition, 1918.

1918

ALCORN, Edgar Greenville.
The Alcorn system of modern bank book-keeping. 3v.
v.1, 132p. v.2, 92p. v.3, 48p.

BELDING, Albert G.
Accounts and accounting practice. 224p.
First edition, 1915.

BOGLE, Artemas Melvin.
Everyday bookkeeping. 126p.
First edition, 1917.

EATON, Abijah H.
The Eaton and Burnett revised and improved bookkeeping, corporation, voucher, and cost accounting. 261p.
First edition, 1917.

McCORMACK, Charles Thomas.
The bookkeeper's ready reference manual. 80p.

MINER, George Washington, and ELWELL, Fayette Herbert.
Principles of bookkeeping.
The first course, introductory course, intermediate course, advanced course, and combined course published separately.

NICHOLS, Frederick George.
Elementary bookkeeping. 115p.
Latest edition, 1922.

1918 (continued)

PRICE, Isaac.
Questions in advanced bookkeeping for drill, test, and review. 187p.

—Questions in elementary bookkeeping for drill, test, and review. 185p.

STRAYER, S. Irving, and WRIGHT, H. Winfield.
Modern bookkeeping, accounting, and business practice. 258p.

WOLFF, Mark.
Bookkeeper and accountant civil service examination instruction. 108p.
First edition, 1917.

1919

ADAMS, William James.
Up-to-date regents questions in bookkeeping. 49p.
Another ed. 1919. 57p.

BARTHOLOMEW, Wallace Edgar.
Bookkeeping exercises. 2v.
v.1, 105p. v.2, 118p.
Latest edition, v.1, 1932; v.2, 1923.

BENDER, George De Witt.
Accounting and business secrets. 64p.

BOGLE, Artemas Melvin.
Comprehensive bookkeeping. 142p.
First edition, 1905.

DRAUGHON, John Franklin.
Draughon's progressive bookkeeping and business manual. 2v.
v.1, 216p. v.2, 376p.
First edition, 1895.

ELLIS PUBLISHING COMPANY, Battle Creek, Mich.
Guide to accompany the Ellis tablet method of teaching book-keeping. 2v.
v.1, 93p. v.2, 122p.
First edition, 1892.

GRIFFITH, James Bray.
Corporation accounts and voucher system. 132p.
First edition, 1910.

—Practical bookkeeping. 264p.
First edition, 1910.

LEMOWITZ, Nathan H.
Bookkeeping made easy. 193p.

LITTLETON, Ananias Charles.
An introduction to elementary accounting. 64p.
Latest edition, 1920.

RITTENHOUSE, Charles Forest.
New modern illustrative bookkeeping; advanced course. 172p.
—New modern illustrative bookkeeping; complete course. 326p.
The two volumes listed above are based upon the advanced course and the complete course of "Modern illustrative bookkeeping . . ." by Neal and Cragin, copyrighted in 1901 (listed in Volume I under 1900).

VINCENT, John P.
Cost accountancy and profit figuring. 68p.

1920

BLISS, Fred H.
Bliss system of bookkeeping and office practice. 188p.
First edition, 1912.

BRIERLEY, John Thomas.
Book-keeping at a glance. 135p.
First edition, 1893.

BRYANT, Henry Willis.
Bryant's practical book-keeping. 110p.
First edition, 1904.

1920 (continued)

ELLIS PUBLISHING COMPANY, Battle Creek, Mich.
Business directions used in connection with Ellis industrial bookkeeping. 75p.
First edition, 1912.

HATTON, Linius Monroe, and PROWINSKY, Joseph Albert.
The H. and P. practical bookkeeping; 3d ed. 52p.
First edition, 1917.

HOOVER, Simon Robert.
Bookkeeping and accounting practice. 301p.
Latest edition, 1927.

KIRK, John George, and STREET, James Layman.
Bookkeeping for modern business. 236p.

LITTLETON, Ananias Charles.
An introduction to elementary accounting. 64p.
First edition, 1919.

LYNAUGH, Matthew Edmund, and THOMPSON, Clyde Ordell.
Practice exercises in bookkeeping. 144p.

LYONS, James A., and SMITH, Oliver Saxton.
Lyons' bookkeeping and accounting. 240p.
Latest edition, 1922.

—Wholesale accounting; rev. ed. 51p.+forms.
First edition, 1905.

McKINSEY, James Oscar.
Bookkeeping and accounting [series A] 2v.
v.1, 504p. v.2, 569p.
Latest edition, 1931.
—Bookkeeping and accounting [series B] 3v.
v.1, 335p. v.2, 391p. v.3, 361p.
Latest edition, 1931.

MARSHALL, Carl Coran.
Marshall's double entry drills; 9th ed. 60p.
First edition, 1903.

VAN DE WALKER, Frank C., and ROWE, Harry Marc.
Logging and lumber manufacturing set. 68p.

WEBER, Fred Charles.
Bookkeeping and accountancy revised ; 6th ed. 275p.
First edition, 1907.

1921

ALGER, Francis Russell.
Actual business bookkeeping and accounting. 78p.
Latest edition, 1930.

BEACH, Frank Loomis.
Twenty twenty-minute lessons in bookkeeping. 124p.

BOURNE, Clifford Norman.
A special course in accounting and commercial law. 125p.

DUDLEY, A. W.
Modern commercial bookkeeping. 200p.

GARBER, Osborne.
20th century bank accounting. 79p.
Latest edition, 1922.

KIRK, John George, and STREET, James Layman.
Bookkeeping for modern business ; advanced course. 118p.

KOOPMAN, Sietse Bernard, and KESTER, Roy Bernard.
Fundamentals of accounting. 2v.
v.1, 404p., 1921. v.2, 525p., 1923.
Latest edition, v.1, 1930.

LOOMIS, Henry Thomas, BRYANT, James H., and STEVENS, Charles E.
Progressive practical bookkeeping. 96p.
First edition, 1894.

MUSICK, William L.
Practical bookkeeping and accounting. 248p.

SALIERS, Earl Adolphus.
Principles of accounting. 72p.
Latest edition, 1930.

1921 (continued)

SMITH, W. J.
Modern commercial banking. 47p.

WILLIAMS, Louis Lafayette, and ROGERS, Fernando E.
New complete bookkeeping. 288p.
First edition, 1882.

1922

BORSODI, Ralph.
The new accounting. 127p.

GARBER, Osborne.
20th century bank accounting. 79p.
First edition, 1921.

HAYWARD, William Richart, and PRICE, Isaac.
Progressive problems in bookkeeping and accountancy. 149p.

KILBURN, Florence M.
Bookkeeping exercises. 32p.
Latest edition, 1923.

LYONS, James A., and SMITH, Oliver Saxton.
Lyons' bookkeeping and accounting. 240p.
First edition, 1920.

NICHOLS, Frederick George.
Elementary bookkeeping. 156p.
First edition, 1918.

ROWE, Harry Marc, 1860–1926, and ROWE, Harry Marc, 1887–
Accountancy and business management. 132p.
Complete edition in which Part 1 entered above is incorporated, published in 1923.
Latest edition, 1925.

SHEAFFER, William Adam.
Metropolitan system of bookkeeping. 226p.
Parts 1 and 2 reprinted in one volume.
First edition, 1914.

SHEPHERD, Jessie M.
Practical accounting problems. 94p.

1923

BARTHOLOMEW, Wallace Edgar.
Bookkeeping exercises. v.2, 118p.
First edition, 1919.

BYRNE, Henry Edward.
Byrne bookkeeping for business colleges, high schools, and self instructions; 4th ed. 163p.
First edition, 1908.

CAREY, Thomas Joseph.
Vest pocket bookkeeper. 160p.

COWLES, Clarence E.
Elements of bookkeeping. 2v.
v.1, 221p., 1923. v.2, 295p., 1925.
Latest edition, 1926.

ELLIS, Carlos Bent.
Elementary bookkeeping. 142p.

FILFUS, Nathaniel, and ROBINSON, Nathaniel.
Graded exercises in bookkeeping and accounting. 3v.
v.1, 136p., 1923. v.2, 153p., 1923. v.3, 216p., 1924.

FRITCH, Edouard Henri.
Simplified bookkeeping. 219p.

GOODYEAR, Samuel Horatio.
New inductive accounting. 142p.

HADLEY, Charles R., company, Los Angeles.
Exhibit and book of instructions of Hadley's pathfinder "straight line" bookkeeping system. 31p.+forms.
Latest edition, 1928.

KILBURN, Florence M.
Bookkeeping exercises. 47p.
First edition, 1922.

LEIDNER, Walter E., and RITTENHOUSE, Charles Forest.
Essential exercises in bookkeeping. 171p.

1923 (continued)

NUESE, Marie A.
Elementary bookkeeping. 116p.

ROSENKAMPFF, Arthur Henry, and WALLACE, William Carroll.
Bookkeeping principles and practice; introductory course. 232p.
Latest edition, 1932.

SHEAFFER, William Adam, and MCINTOSH, Robert James.
Common sense course in accounting. 740p.

1924

BERG, John.
Elementary accounting problems and solutions. 43p.

COWAN, Harold E., and LOKER, Harold W.
Exercises in bookkeeping and business problems. 3v.
v.1, 196p., 1924. v.2, 156p., 1925. v.3, 157p., 1925.

FINNEY, Harry Anson.
Accounting principles and bookkeeping methods. 2v.
v.1, 329p. v.2, 248p.

FISHER, Everard Ellsworth.
Condensed practical bookkeeping and accounting. 34p.

GOODYEAR, Lloyd Earnest.
Principles, rules, and definitions for bookkeeping; 8th ed. rev. 238p.
First edition, 1913.

READ, Harlan Eugene, and HARVEY, Charles J.
Bookkeeping and accounting. 207p.

WILLIAMS, Louis Lafayette, and ROGERS, Fernando E.
First lessons in bookkeeping. 100p.
First edition, 1889 (listed in 1882)

1925

FILFUS, Nathaniel, and ROBINSON, Nathaniel.
Bookkeeping and accounting; elementary course. 130p.
Latest edition, 1928.

KINMAN, James Irvin, and MORRIS, Anthony William.
Kinman's bookkeeping and accounting. 156p.
Latest edition, 1930.

PEEL, Arthur J.
Simplified school accounting. 118p.

ROWE, Harry Marc, 1860–1926, and ROWE, Harry Marc, 1887–
Accountancy and business management. 270p.
Complete edition.
First edition, part 1, 1922.

1926

ALTHOLZ, Nathaniel, and KLEIN, Anthony W.
Modern bookkeeping practice; first-year course. 366p.
Latest edition, 1932.

BOWMAN, Charles Ellis, and PERCY, Atlee Lane.
Principles of bookkeeping and business; elementary course. 287p.
Advanced and complete courses published separately in 1927.
Latest edition, elementary course, 1933.

COWLES, Clarence E.
Elements of bookkeeping. 2v.
v.1, 236p. v.2, 305p.
First edition, 1923.

ELWELL, Fayette Herbert, and TONER, James Vincent.
Bookkeeping and accounting.
The first course, elementary course, intermediate course, advanced course, and complete course published separately in 1926.

JACKSON, Jacob Hugh, SANDERS, Thomas Henry, and SPROUL, Alexander Hugh.
Bookkeeping and business knowledge. 2v.
v.1, 332p. v.2, 355p.
Latest edition, 1931.

1926 (continued)

PRIDGEN, Samuel James.
Pridgen's ready reference method of accounting and suggestions in business administration. 55p.

1927

BELDING, Albert G., and GREENE, Russell Thomas.
Rational bookkeeping and accounting. 2v.
v.1, elementary course, 253p. v.2, advanced course, 267p.
Complete course published separately in 1927.
Latest edition, v.1, 1929; v.2, 1934.

BEXELL, John Andrew, and NICHOLS, Frederick George.
Principles of bookkeeping and farm accounts. 180p.
First edition, 1913.

DAVIS, Sidney S.
Double entry bookkeeping. 72p.

HOOVER, Simon Robert.
Bookkeeping and accounting practice. 309p.
First edition, 1920.

JASON, Simon J.
Elements of bookkeeping and accounting. 194p.

ROWE, Harry Marc.
Bookkeeping and accountancy. 264p.
First edition, 1910.

1928

FILFUS, Nathaniel.
Principles and exercises in accounting. 193p.
Another ed. [c1928] 202p.

—and ROBINSON, Nathaniel.
Fundamentals of bookkeeping and accounting. 2v.
v.1, 230p. v.2, 228p.
First edition, v.1, elementary course, 1925.

HADLEY, Charles R., company, Los Angeles.
Exhibit and book of instructions of Hadley's pathfinder "straight line" bookkeeping system. 31p.+forms.
First edition, 1923.

LAZENBY, Charles D.
Basic bookkeeping and accounting. 216p.
Latest edition, 1932.

LUND, Reuel Ithiel.
Bookkeeping and business methods. 297p.

ROWE, Harry Marc.
Rowe's new cost accounting; rev. by J. W. Alexander and A. E. Lenhart. 88p.

1929

BAKER, James William.
20th century accounting; college ed.; ed. by John F. Sherwood. 364p.
First edition, 1903.

BELDING, Albert G., and GREENE, Russell Thomas.
Rational bookkeeping and accounting. v.1, 253p.
First edition, 1927.

FILFUS, Nathaniel.
Bookkeeping exercises [second-year course] 184p.

KLEIN, Joseph Jerome.
Bookkeeping and accounting; complete course. 453p.
First edition, 1917.

ROSENKAMPFF, Arthur Henry, and WALLACE, William Carroll.
Bookkeeping principles and practice; advanced course. 491p.

SAYPOL, Julian H.
Principles of modern bookkeeping. 249p.

SMOLIN, Rose Gerstein.
Bookkeeping exercises [first-year course] 131p.

1930

ALEXANDER, John W., and LENHART, Arthur E.
Introductory accounting. 52p.

ALGER, Francis Russell.
Bliss-Alger bookkeeping and accounting theory and practice. 217p.
First edition, 1921.

ALTHOLZ, Nathaniel.
Modern bookkeeping practice; second-year course. 439p.
Another ed. 1930. 467p.

KINMAN, James Irvin, and MORRIS, Anthony William.
Kinman's bookkeeping and accounting. 180p.
First edition, 1925.

KOOPMAN, Sietse Bernard, and KESTER, Roy Bernard.
Fundamentals of bookkeeping and accounting. v.1, 404p.
First edition, 1921.

LEE, E. B., compiler.
Bookkeeping (second year) tests and forms. 60p.

ROBINSON, Nathaniel.
Bookkeeping. 149p.
Latest edition, 1934.

SALIERS, Earl Adolphus.
Principles of accounting. 76p.
First edition, 1921.

TAYLOR, Robert Emmett, and OWENS, Richard Norman.
Elements of accounting. 518p.

WILLIAMS, Louis Lafayette, and ROGERS, Fernando E.
New introductive bookkeeping. 131p.
First edition, 1890 (listed in 1882)

1931

JACKSON, Jacob Hugh, SANDERS, Thomas Henry, and SPROUL, Alexander Hugh.

Bookkeeping and business knowledge. 2v.
v.1, 398p. v.2, 416p.
First edition, 1926.

LOCKYEAR, Melvin H.
An introductory course: Lockyear's bookkeeping. 105p.
First edition, 1911.

MCKINSEY, James Oscar.
Bookkeeping and accounting [series A]
v.1, 541p., 1931. v.2, 547p., 1933.
First edition, 1920.
—Bookkeeping and accounting [series B]
v.1, 392p., 1931. v.2, 442p., 1932.
First edition, 1920.

NOBLE, L. Scott.
Student body finances and accounting. 256p.

PEARSON, M. L.
Progressive bookkeeping and accounting. 325p.

ROGERS, Ralph Ernest.
New modern illustrative bookkeeping; elementary course. 152p.
Based upon "Modern illustrative bookkeeping . . . introductory course," by Neal and Cragin.
First edition, 1900.

1932

ALTHOLZ, Nathaniel, and KLEIN, Anthony W.
Modern bookkeeping practice; first-year course; 2d ed. 442p.
First edition, 1926.

BARTHOLOMEW, Wallace Edgar.
Bookkeeping exercises. v.1, 105p.
First edition, 1919.

ELWELL, Fayette Herbert.
Bookkeeping for today.
The first, elementary, advanced, and combined courses published separately in 1932.

LAZENBY, Charles D.
Basic bookkeeping and accounting. Various pagings.
First edition, 1928.

1932 (continued)

MORRIS, Anthony William, and KINMAN, James Irvin.
Accountancy and business procedure. 478p.

ROSENKAMPFF, Arthur Henry, and WALLACE, William Carroll.
Bookkeeping principles and practice; introductory course. 426p.
First edition, 1923.

SOULÉ, George.
Soulé's new science and practice of accounts; 12th ed. 567p.
First edition, 1881.

STUDEBAKER, Mark E.
Bookkeeping and accounting for rural schools. 380p.

1933

BOWMAN, Charles Ellis, and PERCY, Atlee Lane.
Fundamentals of bookkeeping and business [elementary course] 316p.
First edition, 1926.

MORTON, Davis Walter, and COX, John Henry.
Banking and bank accounting. 112p.
First edition, 1917.

TANZ, Louis.
Bookkeeping workbook (second year) 60p.

1934

BELDING, Albert G., and GREENE, Russell Thomas.
Rational bookkeeping and accounting. v.2, 267p.
First edition, 1927.

KIRK, John George, STREET, James Layman, and ODELL, William Rockhold.
Bookkeeping for immediate use. 393p.

ROBINSON, Nathaniel.
Bookkeeping review book. 149p.
First edition, 1930.

Part Two

CLASS 2

Works on elementary and advanced accounting intended primarily for students of college grade or for general reference purposes

1905

HYANS, Edward Malcolm.
Theory of accounts. 144p.
Latest edition, 1918.

WOLFF, Arthur.
Practical accounting. 66p.
Latest edition, 1918.

1907

RAHILL, John Joseph.
Corporation accounting and corporation law. 452p.
First edition, 1899.

1908

BENTLEY, Harry Clark.
Corporate finance and accounting. 525p.
Latest edition, 1911.

COLE, William Morse.
Accounts; their construction and interpretation. 346p.
Latest edition, 1915.

SPRAGUE, Charles Ezra.
The philosophy of accounts. 161p.
Latest edition, 1923.

1909

GARRISON, Elisha Ely.
Accounting every business man should know. 188p.
Latest edition, 1925.

HATFIELD, Henry Rand.
Modern accounting; its principles and some of its problems. 367p.
Latest edition, 1930.

1910

COLE, William Morse.
Accounting and auditing. 479p.
Latest edition, 1921.

RUSSELL, Thomas Herbert, and JACKMAN, William James.
Bookkeeping, accounting, and auditing. 415p.
Latest edition, 1916.

WILLIS, Henry Parker, and others.
Accounting theory and practice. 545p.

1911

BENTLEY, Harry Clark.
Corporate finance and accounting. 525p.
First edition, 1908.

—The science of accounts. 393p.
Latest edition, 1913.

1913

BENTLEY, Harry Clark.
The science of accounts. 393p.
First edition, 1911.

KLEIN, Joseph Jerome.
Elements of accounting theory and practice. 422p.
Latest edition, 1927.

RACINE, Samuel Frederick.
Accounting principles. 280p.
Latest edition, 1917.

1914

DICKINSON, Arthur Lowes.
Accounting practice and procedure. 315p.
Latest edition, 1922.

ESQUERRÉ, Paul Joseph.
The applied theory of accounts. 519p.
Latest edition, 1926.

MCINTOSH, Robert James.
Reference book of accounts for manufacturing and mercantile companies. 300p.
Latest edition, 1923.

RACINE, Samuel Frederick.
Graded corporation problems. 54p.

—Guide to the study of accounting. 76p.
Latest edition, 1916.

WILDMAN, John Raymond.
Elementary accounting problems. 218p.
Latest edition, 1918.

1915

COLE, William Morse.
Accounts; their construction and interpretation; rev. and enl. ed. 446p.
First edition, 1908.

—Problems in the principles of accounting. 102p.
Latest edition, 1927.

INTERNATIONAL TEXTBOOK COMPANY, Scranton.
Corporation organization and accounting [etc.] Various pagings.

SALIERS, Earl Adolphus.
Depreciation in theory and practice. 27p.
Latest edition, 1932.

—Principles of depreciation. 200p.
Latest edition, 1923.

1916

BENNETT, Robert Joseph.
Corporation accounting. 563p.
Latest edition, 1922.

CONSOLIDATED GAS COMPANY OF NEW YORK.
In re theoretical depreciation. 155p.

GILMAN, Stephen.
Principles of accounting. 415p.
Latest edition, 1920.

HUNTER, Joel.
Thinking in figures; commerce, finance and accounts, business systems, and short cuts. 234p.

PATON, William Andrew, and STEVENSON, Russell Alger.
Principles of accounting. 222p.
Latest edition, 1928.

RACINE, Samuel Frederick.
Guide to the study of accounting. 91p.
First edition, 1914.

—Practical problems graded; series "A." 116p.
Latest edition, 1926.

RUSSELL, Thomas Herbert, and JACKMAN, William James.
Bookkeeping, accounting, and auditing. 415p.
First edition, 1910.

1917

ANDERSEN, Arthur, HIMMELBLAU, David, and KOHLER, Eric Louis.
Complete accounting course. 3v.
v.1, 282p., 1917. v.2, 435p., 1919. v.3, various pagings, 1921.

KESTER, Roy Bernard.
Accounting theory and practice. 3v.
v.1, "Principles of accounting," 607p., 1917.
v.2, "Advanced accounting," 796p., 1918.
v.3, "Accounting applications to various forms of industry," 1921 (classified with Specialized costs and systems)
Latest edition, v.1, 1930; v.2, 1933.

RACINE, Samuel Frederick.
Accounting principles. 320p.
First edition, 1913.

RITTENHOUSE, Charles Forest, and CLAPP, Philip Francis.
Advanced accounting problems. 96p.

—Exercises in accounting. 117p.
Latest edition, 1920.

—Notes on accounting theory and practice. 85p.

1918

HYANS, Edward Malcolm.
Theory of accounts. 208p.
First edition, 1905.

RACINE, Samuel Frederick.
Syllabus of bookkeeping. 26p.
Latest edition, 1920.

RITTENHOUSE, Charles Forest, and CLAPP, Philip Francis.
Accounting theory and practice. 2v.
v.1, 165p. v.2, 186p.
Latest edition, v.1, 1933; v.2, 1929.

WILDMAN, John Raymond.
Elementary accounting problems. 218p.
First edition, 1914.

WOLFF, Arthur.
Practical accounting. 167p.
First edition, 1905.

1920

BENNETT, George Edward.
Accounting principles and practice. 2v.
v.1, 430p., 1920. v.2, 461p., 1921.
Latest edition, 1923.

COX, Henry Clay.
Advanced and analytical accounting. 459p. (Business accounting; ed. by Harold Dudley Greeley, v.4)

1920 (continued)

CUNNINGHAM, Earle H.
Bookkeeping and elementary accounting. 409p.

GILMAN, Stephen.
Principles of accounting. 415p.
First edition, 1916.

GREELEY, Harold Dudley.
Theory of accounts. 442p. (Business accounting, v.1)

HODGE, Albert Claire, and MCKINSEY, James Oscar.
Principles of accounting. 389p.
Latest edition, 1927.

RACINE, Samuel Frederick.
Practical problems graded; series "C." 96p.
Latest edition, 1926.

—Syllabus of bookkeeping. 86p.
First edition, 1918.

RITTENHOUSE, Charles Forest, and CLAPP, Philip Francis.
Exercises in accounting. 114p.
First edition, 1917.

RITTENHOUSE, Charles Forest, and GREELEY, Harold Dudley.
Illustrative accounting problems. 413p. (Business accounting; ed. by Harold Dudley Greeley, v.5)

SALIERS, Earl Adolphus.
Accounts in theory and practice. 301p.

THOMPSON, Alfred J.
Supplementary exercises for schools of accountancy and business administration. 68p.

1921

BELL, Spurgeon.
Accounting principles. 482p.

COLE, William Morse.
Bookkeeping, accounting, and auditing. 479p.
First edition, 1910.

COLE, William Morse, and GEDDES, Anne Elizabeth.
The fundamentals of accounting. 434p.

ESQUERRÉ, Paul Joseph.
Practical accounting problems. 2v.
v.1, 353p., 1921. v.2, 356p., 1922.

NEWLOVE, George Hillis, and PRATT, Lester Amos.
Industrial accounting; with C. P. A. questions and problems. 266p.

RACINE, Samuel Frederick.
Practical problems graded; series "B." 93p.

1922

BELL, Spurgeon.
Theory and practice of accounting. 2v.
v.1, 302p. v.2, 544p.
Latest edition, 1934.

BENNETT, George Edward.
Advanced accounting. 661p.

BENNETT, Robert Joseph.
Corporation accounting. 563p.
First edition, 1916.

BOSTON. CHAMBER OF COMMERCE. Bureau of commercial and industrial affairs.
Classification and definitions of ledger accounts. 34p.

CONYNGTON, Thomas, BENNETT, Robert Joseph, and PINKERTON, Paul Whittier.
Corporation procedure; law, finance, accounting. 1689p.
Latest edition, 1927.

DICKINSON, Arthur Lowes.
Accounting practice and procedure. 309p.
First edition, 1914.

FINNEY, Harry Anson.
Consolidated statements for holding company and subsidiaries. 229p.
Latest edition, 1924.

1922 (continued)

KOEHLER, Theodore, and KOEHLER, Theodora.
The accounting mentor of theory and practice. 2v.
v.1, 421p. v.2, various pagings.

LYBRAND, William M., MACPHERSON, Frank Herbert, and DICKINSON, Arthur Lowes.
Accounting for modern corporations. 91p.

PATON, William Andrew.
Accounting theory. 508p.

RACINE, Samuel Frederick.
Practical problems graded; series "D." 89p.

RITTENHOUSE, Charles Forest, and PERCY, Atlee Lane.
Accounting problems; intermediate. 429p.
Latest edition, 1931.

THEISS, Edwin Leodgar.
Elements of accounting practice. 30 pamphlets.
These pamphlets total 560 pages.
Latest editions, 1927–1932, not listed separately.

WALKER, Ross Graham.
A classified selection of problems in accounting. 181p.

WILDMAN, John Raymond.
Principles of accounting. 310p.

1923

BENNETT, George Edward.
Accounting principles and practice. 2v.
v.1, 430p. v.2, 461p.
First edition, 1920.

EGGLESTON, De Witt Carl.
Principles of accounting practice. 15 pamphlets.
These pamphlets total 414 pages.
Latest editions, 1929–1934, not listed separately.

FINNEY, Harry Anson.
Principles of accounting. 2v.
v.1, 622p. v.2, 536p.
Latest edition, 1934.

INTERNATIONAL TEXTBOOK COMPANY, Scranton.
Theory of accounts. 118p.

KREBS, William Samuel.
Outlines of accounting. 2v.
v.1, 594p., 1923. v.2, 1049p., 1927.

—Valuation accounts. 45p.

McINTOSH, Robert James.
Reference book of accounts for manufacturing and mercantile companies; 2d ed. 300p.
First edition, 1914.

PUTNAM, Alonzo.
Putnam's practical principles of accounting. 102p.

RACINE, Samuel Frederick.
Elementary accounting. 277p.
Latest edition, 1929.

ROSS, Francis Ellsworth.
Elementary accounting; practice set; part 1. 30p.
Part 2 published in 1924.

SALIERS, Earl Adolphus, editor.
Accountants' handbook. 1675p.
For second edition, see 1932, Paton, William Andrew.

—Depreciation; principles and applications. 590p.
First edition, 1915.

SPRAGUE, Charles Ezra.
The philosophy of accounts. 183p.
First edition, 1908.

1924

ALTMAN, George T.
Cash records. 117p.

1924 (continued)

BLISS, James Harris.
Management through accounts. 851p.

FINNEY, Harry Anson.
Consolidated statements for holding company and subsidiaries. 229p.
First edition, 1922.

HIMMELBLAU, David.
Fundamentals of accounting. 212p. (Complete accounting course, v.1)
Latest edition, 1933.

—Principles of accounting. 211p. (Complete accounting course, v.2)
Latest edition, 1934.

INTERNATIONAL TEXTBOOK COMPANY, Scranton.
Insolvent and decedents' estates; accounting methods of banks; consignment, joint trading and branch office accounting [etc.] Various pagings.

KESTER, Roy Bernard.
Depreciation. 105p.

KILDUFF, Frederic W.
Auditing and accounting handbook. 813p.

McKINSEY, James Oscar.
Managerial accounting. 655p.
Latest edition, 1925.

PATON, William Andrew.
Accounting. 894p.
Latest edition, 1926.

PINKERTON, Paul Whittier.
Accounting for surplus. 120p.

RITTENHOUSE, Charles Forest, and PERCY, Atlee Lane.
Accounting problems; advanced. 402p.

—Accounting problems; elementary. 266p.

SCOVILL, Hiram Thompson, and BAILY, Henry Heaton.
Elementary accounting. 2v.
v.1, 435p., 1924. v.2, 457p., 1926.
Vol.2, by Scovill and Baily, entitled "Accounting procedure."

SWEENEY, Henry Whitcomb.
Bookkeeping and introductory accounting. 545p.

1925

BENNETT, George Edward.
Basic accounting. 777p.
Latest edition, 1928.

BLANK, Rudolph.
Bookkeeping and elementary accounting. 212p.

GARRISON, Elisha Ely.
Principles of business accounting. 272p.
First edition, 1909.

JONES, Edwin E., and others.
American business accounting. 3v.
v.1, 423p. v.2, 446p. v.3, 463p.

McCARTY, Wesley James.
Accounting elements. 375p.

McKINSEY, James Oscar.
Managerial accounting. 655p.
First edition, 1924.

SALIERS, Earl Adolphus.
Intermediate accounting. 256p. (Complete accounting course; ed. by David Himmelblau, v.3)
For revised edition, see 1932, Altschuler, Harry.
(See part I, 1924, Himmelblau, David, for the "Complete accounting course")

SCOTT, D R
Theory of accounts. 284p.

SHERWOOD, John F.
Accountancy; the theory and practice of accounting. 432p.
Latest edition, 1928.

STONE, William M., and others.
Accountants' and auditors' manual. 427p.

WOODBRIDGE, Frederick Wells.
Elements of accounting. 700p.

1926

BERRIGAN, Edmund.
Elements of accounting. 300p.

ESQUERRÉ, Paul Joseph.
The applied theory of accounts. 575p.
First edition, 1914.

INTERNATIONAL TEXTBOOK COMPANY, Scranton.
Corporation accounting and records. 96p.

KOHLER, Eric Louis, and MORRISON, Paul Leslie.
Principles of accounting. 446p.
Latest edition, 1931.

McCARTY, Wesley James, and AMIDON, Luey Earle Cleveland.
Survey course in accounting. 483p.

NEWLOVE, George Hillis.
Consolidated balance sheets. 309p.

PATON, William Andrew.
Accounting. 894p.
First edition, 1924.

POWELSON, John Abrum.
Introductory accounting. 719p.
Latest edition, 1928.

RACINE, Samuel Frederick.
Practical problems graded; series "A." 162p.
First edition, 1916.

—Practical problems graded; series "C." 143p.
First edition, 1920.

REITER, Prosper, jr.
Profits, dividends, and the law. 260p.

STEVENSON, Russell Alger, and TAYLOR, Robert Emmett.
Questions and problems in accounting. 234p.

1927

BALDWIN, Harry Glen.
Accounting for value as well as original cost. 111p.

BUDD, Thomas Allibone, and WRIGHT, Edward Needles.
The interpretation of accounts. 416p.

COLE, William Morse.
Problems in the principles of accounting. 102p.
First edition, 1915.

CONYNGTON, Thomas, and BENNETT, Robert Joseph.
Corporation procedure; rev. by Hugh R. Conyngton. 1479p.
First edition, 1922.

CROW, William Henry.
Corporation treasurer's and controller's guide. 1657p.

ESQUERRÉ, Paul Joseph.
Accounting. 369p.

HODGE, Albert Claire, and McKINSEY, James Oscar.
Principles of accounting. 394p.
First edition, 1920.

KLEIN, Joseph Jerome.
Elements of accounting theory and practice. 422p.
First edition, 1913.

KOHLER, Eric Louis.
Accounting for business executives. 115p.

MYER, Joseph Charles.
Standard accounting text. 19 pamphlets.
These pamphlets total 645 pages.

RICHARDSON, Franklin Whittemore.
The check list method of auditing & bookkeeping. 100p.
First edition, 1922.

ROBBINS, Carl Burton.
No-par stock; legal, financial, economic, and accounting aspects. 228p.

1927 (continued)

TINEN, John V.
Advanced accounting. 273p. (Complete accounting course; ed. by David Himmelblau, v.5)
(See part I, 1924, Himmelblau, David, for the "Complete accounting course")

YANG, Ju Mei.
Goodwill and other intangibles. 238p.

1928

BENNETT, George Edward.
Basic accounting. 777p.
First edition, 1925.

BRETT, George Monroe.
Fundamental accounting. 541p.

GREER, Howard Clark.
How to understand accounting. 255p.

PATON, William Andrew, and STEVENSON, Russell Alger.
Principles of accounting. 685p.
First edition, 1916.

POWELSON, John Abrum.
Introductory accounting. 719p.
First edition, 1926.

ROREM, Clarence Rufus.
Accounting method. 596p.
Latest edition, 1930.

SHERWOOD, John F.
Accountancy; the theory and practice of accounting; 2d ed. 448p.
First edition, 1925.

STREIGHTOFF, Frank Hatch.
Elementary accounting. 502p.

WILDMAN, John Raymond, and POWELL, Weldon.
Capital stock without par value. 553p.

1929

BROWNELL, Leon Edward.
Accounting and finance. 244p.

CANNING, John Bennett.
The economics of accountancy. 367p.

CASTENHOLZ, William Burtis.
Bookkeeping practice. 100p.
Latest edition, 1933.

COMMERCIAL RESEARCH BUREAU, Chicago.
Commercial research bureau accountancy reports and reference manuals. 6v.
These bound volumes total 667 pages.

FOLTS, Franklin Erton, and STILLMAN, Arthur B.
Interpretive accounting. 432p.
Latest edition, 1930.

HAYES, Monard Vinson.
Accounting for executive control. 495p.

HORNBERGER, Donald Jay.
Studies in no par stock. 3 pamphlets.
These pamphlets total 56 pages.

HOWARD, Stanley Edwin.
The A B C of accounting. 302p.

KNIGHT, Robert T.
Cash journal system. 230p.

McKINSEY, James Oscar.
Accounting principles. 640p.
Latest edition, 1931.

RACINE, Samuel Frederick.
Introduction to accounting. 288p.
First edition, 1923.

RITTENHOUSE, Charles Forest, and CLAPP, Philip Francis.
Accounting theory and practice. v.1, 165p.
First edition, 1918.

1929 (continued)

SCHMIDT, Leo Anton.
Mechanics of accounting. 230p.

SHERWOOD, John F.
Fundamentals of accounting. 221p.

WALKER, Ross Graham, and COFFMAN, Paul Brown.
Problems in accounting principles. 620p.

1930

EGGLESTON, De Witt Carl.
Modern accounting theory and practice. 2v.
v.1, 431p. v.2, 579p.

FOLTS, Franklin Erton, and STILLMAN, Arthur B.
Interpretive accounting. 432p.
First edition, 1929.

GEIER, George Jacob, and MAUTNER, Oscar.
Practical corporation accounting. 824p.

GOGGIN, Walter John, and TONER, James Vincent.
Accounting principles and procedure. 476p.

HATFIELD, Henry Rand.
Accounting; its principles and problems. 548p.
First edition, 1909.

HUSBAND, George R., and THOMAS, Olin Eugene.
Elementary accounting. 26p.

KESTER, Roy Bernard.
Accounting theory and practice. v.1, 835p.
First edition, 1917.

KNIGHT, Robert T.
Bookkeeping. 226p.

LAMBERTON, Robert Alexander.
Fundamental principles of accounting. 2v.
v.1, 95p. v.2, 165p.
Latest edition, 1934.

PRICKETT, Alva Le Roy, and MIKESELL, Rufus Merrill.
Introduction to accounting. 374p.

ROREM, Clarence Rufus.
Accounting method; 2d ed. 644p.
First edition, 1928.

STONE, Clarence L.
Consolidations. 165p.

TAGGART, Herbert Francis.
Subdivision accounts. 89p.

1931

BOLON, Dallas Sinclaire, and ECKELBERRY, George Wendell.
Introduction to accounting. 572p.

CASTENHOLZ, William Burtis.
A solution to the appreciation problem. 95p.

DUNCAN, John Christie.
Principles of analytical accounting. 534p.

INTERNATIONAL TEXTBOOK COMPANY, Scranton.
Branches, consolidations, municipal accounts. 136p.

KOHLER, Eric Louis, and MORRISON, Paul Leslie.
Principles of accounting; 2d ed. 507p.
First edition, 1926.

McKINSEY, James Oscar.
Accounting principles. 736p.
First edition, 1929.

PACE, Homer St. Clair, and BRYAN, Charles Teitge.
Comprehensive propositions in accounting. 398p.

RITTENHOUSE, Charles Forest, and PERCY, Atlee Lane.
Accounting problems; intermediate. 460p.
First edition, 1922.

SANFORD, Emmett Reid.
Applied accounting principles. 538p.

1931 (continued)

SUNLEY, William Terry, and PINKERTON, Paul Whittier.
Corporation accounting. 570p.

1932

ALTSCHULER, Harry.
Intermediate accounting. 335p. (Complete accounting course; ed. by David Himmelblau, v.3)
For first edition, see 1925, Saliers, Earl Adolphus.

FINNEY, Harry Anson.
Introduction to principles of accounting. 649p.

GRAHAM, Willard J., and KATZ, Wilber Griffith.
Accounting in law practice. 444p.

PATON, William Andrew, editor.
Accountants' handbook; 2d ed. 1873p.
For first edition, see 1923, Saliers, Earl Adolphus.
For latest edition of Paton's Accountants' handbook, see 1934, Paton, William Andrew.

SALIERS, Earl Adolphus.
Depreciation in theory and practice. 28p.
First edition, 1915.

STREIGHTOFF, Frank Hatch.
Advanced accounting. 656p.

1933

BURTON, Norman Lee.
Analytical accounting. 82p.

CASTENHOLZ, William Burtis.
Bookkeeping practice. 100p.
First edition, 1929.

HELMSTADTER, Carl W.
Elementary college accounting. 121p.

HIMMELBLAU, David.
Fundamentals of accounting. 236p. (Complete accounting course, v.1)
First edition, 1924.

KESTER, Roy Bernard.
Accounting theory and practice. v.2, 846p.
First edition, 1918 (listed with v.1 under 1917)

LANGER, Charles Heinrichs.
Accounting principles and procedure. 301p.

RITTENHOUSE, Charles Forest, and CLAPP, Philip Francis.
Accounting theory and practice. v.2, 186p.
First edition, 1918.

SHERWOOD, John F.
Modern accounting principles and procedure. 358p.

TAYLOR, Jacob Bacchus, and MILLER, Hermann Clinton.
Intermediate accounting. 2v.
v.1, 409p., 1933. v.2, 476p., 1934.

1934

BELL, Spurgeon.
Theory and practice of accounting. 2v.
v.1, 302p. v.2, 550p.
The work was published as v.5 and v.6 of the encyclopedia "Practical business administration," in 1934.
First edition, 1922.

FINNEY, Harry Anson.
Principles of accounting. 2v.
v.1, 765p. v.2, 825p.
First edition, 1923.

HIMMELBLAU, David.
Principles of accounting. 274p. (Complete accounting course, v.2)
First edition, 1924.

HOSMER, Windsor Arnold, SANDERS, Thomas Henry, and HANSON, Arthur Warren.
Problems in accounting. 463p.

LAMBERTON, Robert Alexander.
Fundamentals of accounting. 205p.
First edition, 1930.

1934 (continued)

LINDSAY, Maurice M.
Corporate organization and accounts. 164p.

MANNIX, Raymond Leo.
Accounting for corporations. 344p.

METROPOLITAN LIFE INSURANCE COMPANY, New York. Policyholders service bureau.
Accounting policies in inter-company sales and transfers. 26p.

PATON, William Andrew, editor.
Accountants' handbook; 2d ed. rev. printing. 1742p.
For first printing of Paton's Accountants' handbook; 2d ed., see 1932, Paton, William Andrew.

SCHMIDT, Leo Anton.
Bookkeeping-accounting. 96p.

WADE, Harry Henchell.
Fundamentals of accounting. 281p.

Part Two

CLASS 3

Works dealing with the preparation and interpretation of financial statements

1901

WOODLOCK, Thomas Francis.
The anatomy of a railroad report and ton-mile cost. 121p.
First edition, 1895.

1912

MOODY, John.
How to analyze railroad reports. 224p.
Latest edition, 1919.

STOCKWELL, Herbert Grant.
Net worth and the balance sheet. 206p.

1913

BARNETT, Samuel.
The statements of a life insurance company. 57p.

1917

U. S. FEDERAL RESERVE BOARD.
Uniform accounting. 25p.
Reprinted in 1918 under title: "Approved methods for the preparation of balance sheet statements."
Latest edition, 1929.

1918

WILSON, Richard Patrick, and CARPENTER, Harry James.
Analysis of financial statements. 38p.
Latest edition, 1931.

1919

MOODY, John.
How to analyze railroad reports. 218p.
First edition, 1912.

1922

BOSTON. CHAMBER OF COMMERCE. Bureau of commercial and industrial affairs.
Balance sheets and profit and loss statements analyzed and defined. 36p.
Latest edition, 1923.

ROBERT MORRIS ASSOCIATES.
The financial audit as viewed by bankers; statement analysis; suggested methods for a credit index. 56p.

WOODS, Clinton Edgar.
Analytical balance sheets for industrials. 32p.

1923

BLISS, James Harris.
Financial and operating ratios in management. 396p.

BOSTON. CHAMBER OF COMMERCE. Bureau of commercial and industrial affairs.
Balance sheets and profit and loss statements analyzed and defined. 36p.
First edition, 1922.

—Financial reports for industrial executives. 42p.

INTERNATIONAL TEXTBOOK COMPANY, Scranton.
Reserves and the balance sheet. 81p.

SAKOLSKI, Aaron Morton.
The analysis of financial statements. 48p.

1924

BLISS, James Harris.
Management through accounts. 851p.

COUCHMAN, Charles Bennington.
The balance-sheet; its preparation, content, and interpretation. 288p.

1925

GILMAN, Stephen.
Analyzing financial statements. 222p.
Latest edition, 1934.

GUTHMANN, Harry George.
The analysis of financial statements. 454p.
Latest edition, 1930.

STOCKWELL, Herbert Grant.
How to read a financial statement. 443p.

1926

CASTENHOLZ, William Burtis.
Accounting and statistical control. 3 pamphlets.
These pamphlets total 330 pages.

MARTINETTI, Frederick A.
Financial statements and their analysis. 41p.

1927

STOCKWELL, Herbert Grant.
How to read a profit and loss statement. 411p.

1928

BANKERS MAGAZINE.
How to analyze a bank's statement. 32p.

GREGORY, Homer Ewart.
Accounting reports in business management. 445p.

WALL, Alexander, and DUNING, Raymond William.
Ratio analysis of financial statements. 353p.

1929

STRAIN, Myron M.
Industrial balance sheets. 182p.

U. S. FEDERAL RESERVE BOARD.
Verification of financial statements (rev.) 26p.
First edition, 1917.

1930

GUTHMANN, Harry George.
The analysis of financial statements. 454p.
First edition, 1925.

ILLINOIS. UNIVERSITY. College of commerce and business administration. Bureau of business research.
Balance sheet structure of automobile manufacturing companies. 65p.

METROPOLITAN LIFE INSURANCE COMPANY, New York. Policyholders service bureau.
Financial statements in annual reports to stockholders of industrial and mercantile companies. 72p.

WALL, Alexander, and DUNING, Raymond William.
Analyzing financial statements. 368p.

1931

MEREDITH, Spencer B.
What the figures mean. 77p.

WILSON, Richard Patrick, and CARPENTER, Harry James.
Analysis of financial statements. 38p.
First edition, 1918.

1932

METROPOLITAN LIFE INSURANCE COMPANY, New York. Policyholders service bureau.
Annual reports to stockholders of chain stores. 38p.

1933

METROPOLITAN LIFE INSURANCE COMPANY, New York. Policyholders service bureau.
Annual reports to stockholders of banking institutions. 43p.
Latest edition, 1934.

1934

BELLOWS, Frederick M.
How to read a financial statement. 33p.

DANIELS, Mortimer B.
Corporation financial statements. 131p.

GILMAN, Stephen.
Analyzing financial statements. 475p.
First edition, 1925.

METROPOLITAN LIFE INSURANCE COMPANY, New York. Policyholders service bureau.
Annual reports to stockholders of banking institutions. 43p.
First edition, 1933.

Part Two

CLASS 4a

Works dealing chiefly or wholly with general principles and practice of cost accounting and system building

1902

SWEETLAND, Charles Augustus.
The science of loose-leaf bookkeeping and accounting. 238p.
Latest edition, 1905.

WATTS, Charles J.
The cost of production. 64p.

1904

HALL, Harry Lovinas Cephas.
Manufacturing cost. 191p.
Latest edition, 1907.

1905

BEAN, Burt Clifford, editor.
The cost of production: the principles of the science of costs. 198p.
Latest edition, 1916.

BOOK-KEEPER PUBLISHING COMPANY, LTD., Detroit.
Improved balance system of cost accounting. 48p.

MULHALL, John Francis Joseph.
Quasi-public corporation accounting and management. 201p.

SWEETLAND, Charles Augustus.
The science of loose-leaf bookkeeping and accounting. 239p.
First edition, 1902.

1906

COOK, Charles Bannister.
Factory management. 215p.

1907

BOOTH, W. Vernon, and others.
Accounting and office methods. 181p.

HALL, Harry Lovinas Cephas.
Manufacturing cost. 191p.
First edition, 1904.

METCALFE, Henry.
The cost of manufactures and the administration of workshops. 366p.
First edition, 1885.

RISQUE, Ferdinand William.
Loose-leaf books and systems for general business. 174p.

1908

CHURCH, Alexander Hamilton.
The proper distribution of expense burden. 116p.
Latest edition, 1921.

WOODS, Clinton Edgar.
Practical cost accounting for accountant students. 2v.
v.1, 119p. v.2, 139p.
Latest edition, 1918.

—Woods' reports on industrial organization, systematization, and accounting. 12 reports.
The reports, published separately, total 344 pages.
Charts and forms added to each report.
Latest edition, 1914.

1909

NICHOLSON, Jerome Lee.
Nicholson on factory organization and costs. 410p.
Latest edition, 1911.

1909 (continued)

UNCKLESS, Leslie.
How to find manufacturing costs and selling costs. 90p.

1910

CHASE, William Arthur, and others.
Auditing and cost accounting. 517p.

CHURCH, Alexander Hamilton.
Production factors in cost accounting and works management. 187p.
Latest edition, 1919.

GOODWIN, Frank Elbert.
Cost accounting pathfinder. 128p.
7th ed. 1910. 267p.

HATHAWAY, Charles E., and GRIFFITH, James Bray.
Factory accounts. 207p.
Latest edition, 1913.

1911

BUNNELL, Sterling Haight.
Cost-keeping for manufacturing plants. 232p.

DENHAM, Robert Scudder.
The science of cost-finding applied to factories making products to special or shop orders. 104p.
Latest edition, 1914.

EVANS, Holden A.
Cost keeping and scientific management. 252p.

NICHOLSON, Jerome Lee.
Nicholson on factory organization and costs. 410p.
First edition, 1909.

WEBNER, Frank Erastus.
Factory costs: a work of reference for cost accountants and factory managers. 611p.

WILDMAN, John Raymond.
Cost accounting. 106p.
Latest edition, 1916.

1912

ARNOLD, Horace Lucian, compiler.
The complete cost-keeper. 408p.
First edition, 1900.

1913

BRIERLEY, John Thomas.
Manufacturing cost accounts. 42p.

FRANKLIN, Benjamin Alvey.
Cost reports for executives as a means of plant control. 149p.

HATHAWAY, Charles E., and GRIFFITH, James Bray.
Factory accounts. 207p.
First edition, 1910.

MOXEY, Edward Preston.
Principles of factory cost keeping. 102p.
Latest edition, 1920.

NICHOLSON, Jerome Lee.
Cost accounting theory and practice. 341p.
Latest edition, 1917.

1914

DENHAM, Robert Scudder.
The science of cost-finding applied to factories making products to special or shop orders. 104p.
First edition, 1911.

SHAW, A. W., company, Chicago.
Accounting and office methods. 200p.
Latest edition, 1917.

—Costs and statistics. 200p.
Latest edition, 1920.

TIMKEN, Frank Herrmann.
General factory accounting. 171p.

1914 (continued)

WOODS, Clinton Edgar.
Woods' reports on industrial organization, systematization, and accounting. 12 reports.
The reports, published separately, total 344 pages.
Charts and forms added to each report.
First edition, 1908.

1915

BAILLET, Henry F.
Overhead expense and percentage methods. 128p.

BAUGH, Frederick Henry.
Principles and practice of cost accounting. 194p.

INTERNATIONAL TEXTBOOK COMPANY, Scranton.
Cost accounting [etc.] Various pagings.

SHAW, A. W., company, Chicago.
Operation and costs. 216p.

1916

BEAN, Burt Clifford, editor.
The cost of production: the principles of the science of costs. 196p.
First edition, 1905.

PARKHURST, Frederic Augustus.
The predetermination of true costs and relatively true selling prices. 96p.

SCOVELL, Clinton Homer.
Cost accounting and burden application. 328p.
Latest edition, 1920.

THOMPSON, Clarence Bertrand.
How to find factory costs. 191p.
Latest edition, 1925.

U. S. FEDERAL TRADE COMMISSION.
Fundamentals of a cost system for manufacturers. 31p.
Latest edition, 1922.

WILDMAN, John Raymond.
Principles of cost accounting. 96p.
First edition, 1911.

1917

CHURCH, Alexander Hamilton.
Manufacturing costs and accounts. 452p.
Latest edition, 1929.

FICKER, Nicholas Thiel.
Industrial cost-finding. 511p.
Latest edition, 1922.

—Shop expense analysis and control. 236p.

NICHOLSON, Jerome Lee.
Cost accounting theory and practice. 341p.
First edition, 1913.

SHAW, A. W., company, Chicago.
Accounting and office methods. 200p.
First edition, 1914.

WEBNER, Frank Erastus.
Factory accounting. 345p.
Latest edition, 1918.

WOODS, Clinton Edgar.
Unified accounting methods for industrials. 484p.
Latest edition, 1919.

1918

BASSET, William Rupert.
Accounting as an aid to business profits. 316p.
Latest edition, 1926.

CLEARY, P. Roger.
How to figure profit. 265p.

DENHAM, Robert Scudder.
Fundamentals of cost and profit calculation. 120p.
Latest edition, 1919.

1918 (continued)

EGGLESTON, De Witt Carl.
Problems in cost accounting. 349p.

KENT, William.
Bookkeeping and cost accounting for factories. 261p.

WEBNER, Frank Erastus.
Factory accounting. 345p.
First edition, 1917.

WOODS, Clinton Edgar.
Practical cost accounting for accountant students. 2v.
v.1, 119p. v.2, 139p.
First edition, 1908.

1919

CHURCH, Alexander Hamilton.
Production factors in cost accounting and works management. 187p.
First edition, 1910.

DENHAM, Robert Scudder.
The A-B-C of cost engineering. 105p.
Latest edition, 1922.

—Fundamentals of cost and profit calculation. 126p.
First edition, 1918.

NICHOLSON, Jerome Lee, and ROHRBACH, John Francis Deems.
Cost accounting. 576p.
Latest edition, 1923.

WOODS, Clinton Edgar.
Unified accounting methods for industrials. 484p.
First edition, 1917.

1920

BENNETT, George Edward.
Constructive accounting. 501p. (Business accounting; ed. by Harold Dudley Greeley, v.2)

BERNDT, Irving A.
Costs; their compilation and use in management. 235p.

EGGLESTON, De Witt Carl.
Cost and accounting. 444p. (Business accounting; ed. by Harold Dudley Greeley, v.3)

JORDAN, John Packard, and HARRIS, Gould Leach.
Cost accounting principles and practice. 529p.
Latest edition, 1925.

MOXEY, Edward Preston.
Principles of factory cost keeping. 102p.
First edition, 1913.

SCOVELL, Clinton Homer.
Cost accounting and burden application. 328p.
First edition, 1916.

SHAW, A. W., company, Chicago.
Costs and statistics. 216p.
First edition, 1914.

1921

ARMSTRONG, George Simpson.
Essentials of industrial costing. 297p.

CHURCH, Alexander Hamilton.
The proper distribution of expense burden. 144p.
First edition, 1908.

EGGLESTON, De Witt Carl, and ROBINSON, Frederick Bertrand.
Business costs. 587p.

GOGGIN, Walter John.
Cost accounting. 86p.
Latest edition, 1930.

HARRISON, George Charter.
Cost accounting to aid production. 234p.
Latest edition, 1924.

RACINE, Samuel Frederick.
Cost accounts. 183p.

1922

CASTENHOLZ, William Burtis.
Cost accounting procedure. 333p.
Latest edition, 1932.

DENHAM, Robert Scudder.
The A-B-C of cost engineering. 109p.
First edition, 1919.

FICKER, Nicholas Thiel.
Industrial cost-finding. 511p.
First edition, 1917.

HIBBS, Weston J.
Cost system of the U. G. I. [United gas improvement] contracting co. 63p.

NEWLOVE, George Hillis.
Cost accounts. 166p.
Latest edition, 1923.

RISQUE, Ferdinand William.
Risque's bookkeeping and business management. 189p.

U. S. FEDERAL TRADE COMMISSION.
Fundamentals of a cost system for manufacturers. 31p.
First edition, 1916.

WILLARD, Raymond Delmar.
System building and constructive accounting. 307p.
Latest edition, 1924.

1923

ATKINS, Paul Moody.
Industrial cost accounting for executives. 322p.
Latest edition, 1924.

BORTON, E. J.
Cost accounting principles and methods. 243p.

KEMP, William S.
Departmental and standard costs. 85p.

NEWLOVE, George Hillis.
Cost accounts; 3d ed. 183p.
First edition, 1922.

NICHOLSON, Jerome Lee, and ROHRBACH, John Francis Deems.
Cost accounting. 576p.
First edition, 1919.

SANDERS, Thomas Henry.
Problems in industrial accounting. 643p.
Latest edition, 1930.

1924

ATKINS, Paul Moody.
Textbook of industrial cost accounting. 396p.
First edition, 1923.

BLISS, James Harris.
Management through accounts. 851p.

DOHR, James Lewis.
Cost accounting theory and practice. 631p.

HARRISON, George Charter.
Cost accounting to aid production; 2d ed. 234p.
First edition, 1921.

KONOPAK, Lothar Theodore.
Cost accounting fundamentals from the standpoint of management. 235p.

MANNING, Anthony B.
Elements of cost accounting. 166p.

SCOVELL, Clinton Homer.
Interest as a cost. 254p.

WEBNER, Frank Erastus.
Factory overhead. 456p.

WILLARD, Raymond Delmar.
System building and constructive accounting; 2d ed. 361p.
First edition, 1922.

1924 (continued)

WRIGHT, H. Winfield.
Cost accounting theory and practice. 68p.

1925

CHAMBER OF COMMERCE OF THE UNITED STATES OF AMERICA. Dept. of manufacture.
Cost accounting through the use of standards. 27p.
Latest edition, 1933.

JORDAN, John Packard, and HARRIS, Gould Leach.
Cost accounting principles and practice; 2d ed. rev. 562p.
First edition, 1920.

LAWRENCE, William Beaty.
Cost accounting. 528p.
Latest edition, 1930.

NEWLOVE, George Hillis, and PRATT, Lester Amos.
Specialized accounting. 475p.

THOMPSON, Clarence Bertrand.
A report: factory costs as an aid to greater profits. 208p.
First edition, 1916.

WALDRON, Frederick A.
Simplified factory accounting and routing. 113p.

1926

BASSET, William Rupert.
Accounting as an aid to business profits; 3d rev. ed. 315p.
First edition, 1918.

INTERNATIONAL TEXTBOOK COMPANY, Scranton.
Cost accounting principles and records. 135p.

—Cost accounting problems. 111p.

—Cost control and cost systems. 128p.

THOMPSON, William Rodney.
Accounting systems; their design and installation. 743p.
Latest edition, 1932.

1927

CHAMBER OF COMMERCE OF THE UNITED STATES OF AMERICA. Dept. of manufacture.
The evolution of overhead accounting. 30p.

NEWLOVE, George Hillis.
Cost accounting. 212p.
Latest edition, 1928.

SANDERS, Thomas Henry.
Plant and shop costs. 130p.

SCHLATTER, Charles F.
Elementary cost accounting. 321p.

1928

AMIDON, Lucy Earle Cleveland, and LANG, Theodore.
Essentials of cost accounting. 383p.

HADLEY, Charles R., company, Los Angeles.
Hadley's pathfinder accounting manual for small manufacturing concerns. 75p.
Latest edition, 1931.

MORAN, T. J.
Accounting in olive green. 31p.

NEWLOVE, George Hillis.
Cost accounting. 328p.
First edition, 1927.

REITELL, Charles Ervin, BULLIS, Harry A., TUTTLE, John Raymond, and HOWARD, Thomas W.
The presentation of costs for executives; Scovell prize competition. 285p.

1929

CHURCH, Alexander Hamilton.
Manufacturing costs and accounts; 2d ed. rev. and enl. 516p.
First edition, 1917.

1929 (continued)

GRAHAM, Willard J.
Cost accounting and office equipment. 272p.

MAZE, Coleman Lloyd, and GLOVER, John George.
How to analyze costs. 389p.

SANDERS, Thomas Henry.
Industrial accounting; control of industry through costs. 371p.
Latest edition, 1934.

SCHNACKEL, Harry Gregory, and LANG, Henry Carleton.
Accounting by machine methods. 563p.

SHERWOOD, John F.
Constructive accounting. 252p.
Latest edition, 1931.

1930

BANGS, John Robert, jr.
Industrial accounting for executives. 449p.

CASTENHOLZ, William Burtis.
The control of distribution costs and sales. 194p.

CHURCH, Alexander Hamilton.
Overhead expense in relation to costs, sales, and profits. 418p.

GOGGIN, Walter John.
Cost accounting. 88p.
First edition, 1921.

HARRISON, George Charter.
Standard costs; installation, operation, and use. 308p.

LAWRENCE, William Beaty.
Cost accounting. 548p.
First edition, 1925.

METROPOLITAN LIFE INSURANCE COMPANY, New York. Policyholders service bureau.
Methods of determining distribution costs. 40p.
Latest edition, 1933.

REITELL, Charles Ervin, and VAN SICKLE, Clarence.
Cost finding for engineers. 518p.

SANDERS, Thomas Henry, and COFFMAN, Paul Brown.
Problems in industrial accounting; 2d ed. completely rev. 816p.
First edition, 1923.

1931

GREER, Howard Clark, and WILLCOX, Russell Stuart.
Problems in cost accounting. 379p.

HADLEY, Charles R., company, Los Angeles.
Hadley's pathfinder accounting manual for small manufacturing concerns. 75p.
First edition, 1928.

MYERS, Herbert J., KEATING, William L., and METSCH, J. C.
How to set standards; Jordan prize competition. 98p.

O'HARA, Allen.
Accounting to increase profits. 130p.

SHERWOOD, John F.
Constructive accounting. 278p.
First edition, 1929.

1932

CAMMAN, Eric A.
Basic standard costs; control accounting for manufacturing industries. 232p.

CASTENHOLZ, William Burtis.
Cost accounting procedure. 359p.
First edition, 1922.

GEIER, George Jacob, and MAUTNER, Oscar.
Systems installation in accounting. 500p.

GILLESPIE, Cecil Merle.
Introductory cost accounting. 253p. (Complete accounting course; ed. by David Himmelblau, v.4)
(See part I, 1924, Himmelblau, David, for the "Complete accounting course")

1932 (continued)

THOMPSON, William Rodney.
Accounting systems; their design and installation. 736p.
First edition, 1926.

1933

CHAMBER OF COMMERCE OF THE UNITED STATES OF AMERICA. Dept. of manufacture.
Cost accounting through the use of standards. 52p.
First edition, 1925.

METROPOLITAN LIFE INSURANCE COMPANY, New York. Policyholders service bureau.
Methods of determining distribution costs. 40p.
First edition, 1930.

REITELL, Charles Ervin.
Cost accounting principles and methods. 441p.

1934

ALFORD, Leon Pratt, editor.
Cost and production handbook. 1544p.

JAFFE, John.
Labor cost records; their forms and preparation. 141p.

SANDERS, Thomas Henry.
Cost accounting for control; 2d ed. completely rev. 517p.
First edition, 1929.

WILLCOX, Russell Stuart.
Cost accounting. 329p.

Part Two

CLASS 4b

Treatises on cost accounting and system building applicable to the following businesses and professions

(The *see* and *see also* references in the Subject Index at the back of the book should be used to direct the reader to works on related or subordinate subjects classified in this list and also to those classified in the Supplement)

Advertising agencies
Agriculture
Automobiles
Bakeries
Banks
Breweries
Bricks
Building and loan associations
Building trades
Chain stores
Charitable and penal institutions
Chemicals
Clergy
Coal trade
Coffee
Construction
Cooperative stores and societies
Cotton mills
Electric construction
Electric light and power companies
Electric railways
Finance companies
Foreign exchange and foreign branch accounting
Foundries
Furniture
Garages and service stations
Gas companies
Government accounting (National, state, and municipal)
Hospitals
Hotels
Ice
Insurance
Knit goods
Laundries
Lawyers
Live stock
Lumber
Machine shops
Meat packers
Milk
Mining
Mining, Coal
Mining, Metal
Motion pictures
Motor bus transportation
Newspapers
Oil
Paints and varnishes
Patent accounting
Personal and household accounting
Physicians
Plumbing and heating
Printing
Probate accounting
Public accountants
Public utilities
Radio dealers
Railroads
Ranches
Real estate
Retail stores
Rubber goods

Sawmills
Schools, Public
Sheet metal work
Shoes
Silk
Societies, associations, etc.
Stock brokerage
Sugar
Tanneries
Telephone companies
Textiles
Universities and colleges
Water works
Woodworking
Woolens and worsteds

ADVERTISING AGENCIES

1921

WOOLHOUSE, T. L.
Accounting for an advertising agency. (In Kester, Roy Bernard. Accounting theory and practice. v.3, p.465–487)

1931

METROPOLITAN LIFE INSURANCE COMPANY, New York. Policyholders service bureau.
Cost accounting for advertising agencies. 27p.
Latest edition, 1932.

1932

METROPOLITAN LIFE INSURANCE COMPANY, New York. Policyholders service bureau.
Cost accounting for advertising agencies. 27p.
First edition, 1931.

AGRICULTURE

1903

ROBERTS, Isaac Phillips.
The farmer's business handbook. 300p.
Latest edition, 1913.

1905

STEINER, Harry Lee.
How to keep farm accounts. 150p.
Latest edition, 1909.

1906

VYE, John Alexander.
Farm accounts. 141p.
Latest edition, 1910.

1908

LAMB, Henry Grant.
Farm book-keeping. 69p.

1909

BEXELL, John Andrew.
The business side of farming. 71p
Latest edition, 1911.

STEINER, Harry Lee.
How to keep farm accounts; 3d ed. 154p.
First edition, 1905.

1910

VYE, John Alexander.
Farm accounts; 2d ed. 141p.
First edition, 1906.

1911

BEXELL, John Andrew.
The business side of farming; 2d ed. 53p.
First edition, 1909.

—Farm accounting and business methods. 161p.

AGRICULTURE, 1911 (continued)

GOODYEAR, Lloyd Earnest.
Farm accounting. 36p.

1913

ROBERTS, Isaac Phillips.
The farmer's business handbook; 6th ed. 300p.
First edition, 1903.

SMITH, Chester William, and THOMAS, S. M.
Farm accounts. 82p.

1915

BONNER, Joseph Claybaugh.
Farm cost system. 58p.

OTIS, Daniel Henry.
Farm accounts simplified. 42p.
Latest edition, 1918.

1918

OTIS, Daniel Henry.
Farm accounts simplified; 6th ed. 40p.
First edition, 1915.

SCOVILL, Hiram Thompson.
Farm accounting. 429p.
Latest edition, 1921.

1919

BEXELL, John Andrew, and SCUDDER, H. D.
The standard farm accounts and records. 72p.

1920

ATKESON, Thomas Clark.
Bookkeeping for farmers. 40p.
First edition, 1892.

1921

SCOVILL, Hiram Thompson.
Farm accounting. 429p.
First edition, 1918.

1922

GILES, John Henry.
Farm-ranch bookkeeping. 45p.

WILLARD, Rex Ethan.
Simple farm accounts. 106p.
Latest edition, 1930.

1924

CURRIER, Edwin Lovejoy, LENNES, Nels Johann, and MERRILL, Archibald Shepard.
Farm accounting. 287p.

1926

McMURRY, Karl Franklin, and McNALL, Preston Essex.
Farm accounting. 329p.

1929

GIFFORD, Luther Erwin, and FAIRWEATHER, Thomas.
Farm accounting course. 39p.

1930

BAUGHMAN, Charles E.
Farm accounting and agricultural economics. 182p.

WILLARD, Rex Ethan.
Simple farm accounts; 4th ed. 102p.
First edition, 1922.

1931

DILS, Frank Lee.
Farm accounting. 100p.

AUTOMOBILES

1923

HADLEY, Charles R., company, Los Angeles.
Exhibit and book of instructions of Hadley's pathfinder bookkeeping system for automobile dealers. 67p.+forms.

1927

ACKERMAN, Paul Frederick.
Automobile accounting. 59p.
Dealer accounting system.

HADLEY, Charles R., company, Los Angeles.
Hadley's pathfinder accounting system for Ford agencies. 35p.+forms.

1928

JAYNE, David A., and company, Charleston, W. Va.
Jayne's rightline accounting systems for automobile dealers. 44p.

BAKERIES

1917

WIHLFAHRT, Julius Emil.
Treatise on increasing bakery efficiency. 38p.
Latest edition, 1927.

1927

WIHLFAHRT, Julius Emil.
Treatise on increasing bakery efficiency. 45p.
First edition, 1917.

BANKS

1902

BARRETT, Albert Reed.
Modern banking methods and practical bank bookkeeping. 325p.
Latest edition, 1907.

1904

FROST, Edward Allin, and TALBERT, Joseph T.
System of accounts for receivers of national banks. 63p.

1907

BARRETT, Albert Reed.
Modern banking methods and practical bank bookkeeping; 5th ed. 325p.
First edition, 1902.

1910

SWEETLAND, Charles Augustus.
Bank bookkeeping. 140p.
Latest edition, 1914.

1913

BORDWELL, George Otis.
Modern banking methods. 123p.

MOXEY, Edward Preston, GREELEY, Harold Dudley, JEFFERSON, Howard McNayr, and GRUNDMAN, Otto A.
Bank accounting. (In their Practical accounting methods. p.123–134)

1914

SWEETLAND, Charles Augustus.
Bank bookkeeping. 140p.
First edition, 1910.

BANKS (continued)

1918

JEFFERSON, Howard McNayr.
Accrued interest receivable and payable. 93p.

SHAW, A. W., company, Chicago.
Accounting and costs; finding bank costs. 229p.

1920

FOOTE, Lewis A.
The Adap-table system; a practical and economic solution of the accrual accounting problems. 2v.
v.1, 85p. v.2, 41 l.

1921

KESTER, Roy Bernard.
Savings bank accounting. (In his Accounting theory and practice. v.3, p.101–136)

1922

INTERNATIONAL TEXTBOOK COMPANY, Scranton.
Bank accounting; financial calculations. 158p.

SCHULZ, Arthur Karl.
Bank bookkeeping. 189p.

1924

GORDON, William Duncan, and LOCKWOOD, Jeremiah.
Banks. (In their Modern accounting systems. p.131–191)
Latest edition, 1933.

1927

BEACH, Frank Loomis.
Bank system and accounting. 373p.

1933

GORDON, William Duncan, and LOCKWOOD, Jeremiah.
Banks. (In their Modern accounting systems; 2d ed. p.123-184)
First edition, 1924.

YOUNG, Benjamin E.
Bank cost control. 299p.

BREWERIES

1913

MOXEY, Edward Preston, GREELEY, Harold Dudley, JEFFERSON, Howard McNayr, and GRUNDMAN, Otto A.
Brewery accounting. (In their Practical accounting methods. p.135-163)

THORNTON, Frank Weldon.
Brewery accounts. 102p.

1933

GOETTSCHE, H. C. & co., Chicago.
Standard brewery systems. Various pagings.
Latest edition, 1934.

1934

GOETTSCHE, Harty C.
Brewery accounting. 279p.
Harty C. Goettsche is named as sole author of the second edition.
First edition, 1933.

BRICKS

1923

GREENWOOD, G. W.
Accounting simplified. 48p.

BUILDING AND LOAN ASSOCIATIONS

1913

MOXEY, Edward Preston, GREELEY, Harold Dudley, JEFFERSON, Howard McNayr, and GRUNDMAN, Otto A.
[Building and loan association accounting] (In their Practical accounting methods. p.7–57)

1923

YEO & LUKENS co., Philadelphia.
Building and loan association accounting. 54p.

1924

BENNETT, Robert Joseph.
Accounting for building and loan associations. 45p.

GORDON, William Duncan, and LOCKWOOD, Jeremiah.
Building and loan associations. (In their Modern accounting systems. p.7–50)
Latest edition, 1933.

1925

HADLEY, Charles R., company, Los Angeles.
Hadley's pathfinder system for building and loan associations. Various pagings.

1933

GORDON, William Duncan, and LOCKWOOD, Jeremiah.
Building and loan associations. (In their Modern accounting systems; 2d ed. p.7–55)
First edition, 1924.

1934

HADLEY, Charles R., company, Los Angeles.
Hadley's accounting manual for Federal savings and loan associations. 77p.+forms.

BUILDING TRADES

1922

HAFNER, George W.
The dealers' handy cost book; containing the Building supply news' adaptable uniform cost accounting system for every building supply, lumber, and coal retail merchant. 158p.

1923

HADLEY, Charles R., company, Los Angeles.
Exhibit and book of instructions of Hadley's pathfinder building trades bookkeeping system for plumbers, electrical contractors and dealers, tinners, roofers [etc.] 58p.+forms.
Latest edition, 1931.

1931

HADLEY, Charles R., company, Los Angeles.
Exhibit and book of instructions of Hadley's pathfinder building trades bookkeeping system for plumbers, electrical contractors and dealers, tinners, roofers [etc.] 84p.+forms.
First edition, 1923.

CHAIN STORES

1924

GREER, Howard Clark.
Chain store accounting. 312p.

CHARITABLE AND PENAL INSTITUTIONS

1913

COLE, William Morse.
Cost accounting for institutions. 248p.
Latest edition, 1920.

CHARITABLE AND PENAL INSTITUTIONS (continued)

1918

RITTENHOUSE, Charles Forest.
Elements of accounts for individuals, professional men, and institutions. 264p.

1920

COLE, William Morse.
Cost accounting for institutions. 248p.
First edition, 1913.

1926

JOB, Leonard Bliss.
Business management of institutional homes for children. 205p.

CHEMICALS

1928

PROCHAZKA, George Anthony.
Accounting and cost finding for the chemical industries. 242p.

CLERGY

1910

KAIB, Daniel Joseph.
Bookkeeping for parish priests. 129p.
Latest edition, 1931.

1923

SCHAAFS, Francis J.
Simplified parish accounting. 26p.

1931

KAIB, Daniel Joseph.
Bookkeeping for parish priests; 3d rev. ed. 154p.
First edition, 1910.

COAL TRADE

1922

HAFNER, George W.
The dealers' handy cost book; containing the Building supply news' adaptable uniform cost accounting system for every building supply, lumber, and coal retail merchant. 158p.

COFFEE

1921

KESTER, Roy Bernard.
Accounting in the coffee trade. (In his Accounting theory and practice. v.3, p.345-395)

CONSTRUCTION

1909

GILLETTE, Halbert Powers, and DANA, Richard Turner.
Cost keeping and management engineering. 346p.
Latest edition, 1922.

1912

JOYCE, Bryan Pope.
The Joyce system of cost keeping. 29p.

CONSTRUCTION (continued)

1914

ALLEN, Leslie Herbert.
Cost accounting on construction work. 46p.
Latest edition, 1915.

1915

ALLEN, Leslie Herbert.
Cost accounting on construction work; 2d ed. 46p.
First edition, 1914.

1916

WALKER, Frank Rabold.
Practical cost keeping for contractors. 273p.
Latest edition, 1918.

1917

ROSS, George Edward.
Cost keeping and construction accounting. 59p.
Latest edition, 1919.

1918

WALKER, Frank Rabold.
Practical cost keeping for contractors. 275p.
First edition, 1916.

1919

ROSS, George Edward.
Cost keeping and construction accounting. 171p.
First edition, 1917.

1921

BYRNES, Thomas W., and BAKER, K. Lanneau.
Contractors' accounts. (In Kester, Roy Bernard. Accounting theory and practice. v.3, p.316–344)

CONNOR, W. N.
Construction costs. 41p.

1922

GILLETTE, Halbert Powers, and DANA, Richard Turner.
Construction cost keeping and management. 572p.
First edition, 1909.

GRANT, Harris Denison.
Practical accounting for general contractors. 254p.
Latest edition, 1925.

HADLEY, Charles R., company, Los Angeles.
Exhibit and book of instructions of Hadley's pathfinder bookkeeping system for contractors and builders. 36p.+forms.
Latest edition, 1931.

1924

AFFELDER, William Maurice.
Contractors' accounting practice. 386p.

DINGMAN, Charles Francis.
Accounting and business methods for contractors. 175p.

WALKER, Frank Rabold.
Practical accounting and cost keeping for contractors. 169p.
Latest edition, 1926.

1925

BLOCK, Milton D., and ALLEN, Leslie Herbert.
Accounting for construction companies. 75p.

GRANT, Harris Denison.
Practical accounting for general contractors. 329p.
First edition, 1922.

1926

WALKER, Frank Rabold.
Practical accounting and cost keeping for contractors. 169p.
First edition, 1924.

CONSTRUCTION (continued)

1931

HADLEY, Charles R., company, Los Angeles.
Exhibit and book of instructions of Hadley's pathfinder bookkeeping system for contractors and builders. 36p.+forms.
First edition, 1922.

COOPERATIVE STORES AND SOCIETIES

1917

DWORAK, E. A., compiler.
The Corey & McKenzie complete accounting system and record for national farm loan associations. 49p.

COTTON MILLS

1908

DAY, Clarence Munro.
Cost accounting [cotton mill costs] (In his Accounting practice. p.89–169)
Latest edition, 1924.

1915

NICHOLS, Henry Wyman.
A method of determining costs in a cotton mill. 115p.

1924

DAY, Clarence Munro.
Cost accounting [cotton mill costs] (In his Accounting practice. p.89–169)
First edition, 1908.

1929

HILL, Frank Hylan.
Computing cotton fabric costs. 122p.

ELECTRIC CONSTRUCTION

1916

MOXEY, Louis White.
The electrical contractor. 86p.

1923

HADLEY, Charles R., company, Los Angeles.
Exhibit and book of instructions of Hadley's pathfinder building trades bookkeeping system for plumbers, electrical contractors and dealers, tinners, roofers [etc.] 58p.+forms.
Latest edition, 1931.

1931

HADLEY, Charles R., company, Los Angeles.
Exhibit and book of instructions of Hadley's pathfinder building trades bookkeeping system for plumbers, electrical contractors and dealers, tinners, roofers [etc.] 84p.+forms.
First edition, 1923.

ELECTRIC LIGHT AND POWER COMPANIES

1914

EDWARDS, Henry Moore.
Electric light accounts and their significance. 172p.

ELECTRIC LIGHT AND POWER COMPANIES (continued)

1929

CHAMBERLIN, Newell Kirby.
Power plant costs. 95p.

ELECTRIC RAILWAYS

1906

BROCKWAY, Walter Belding.
Electric railway accounting. 84p.

FORSE, William Harry.
Electric railway auditing and accounting. 157p.

1913

MOXEY, Edward Preston, GREELEY, Harold Dudley, JEFFERSON, Howard McNayr, and GRUNDMAN, Otto A.
Street railroad accounting. (In their Practical accounting methods. p.331–350)

1917

MAY, Irville Augustus.
Street railway accounting. 454p.

FINANCE COMPANIES

1926

HADLEY, Charles R., company, Los Angeles.
Hadley's pathfinder system for a finance company. 39p.+forms.
Latest edition, 1928.

1928

HADLEY, Charles R., company, Los Angeles.
Hadley's pathfinder system for a finance company. 39p.+forms.
First edition, 1926.

FOREIGN EXCHANGE AND FOREIGN BRANCH ACCOUNTING

1921

SCHOLZ, Frederick W.
Foreign exchange accounting. (In Kester, Roy Bernard. Accounting theory and practice. v.3, p.49–100)

1925

BERGER, J. A.
Foreign branch accounting. 43p.
Latest edition, 1931.

1926

DJÖRUP, Christian.
Foreign exchange accounting. 406p.

1931

BERGER, J. A.
Foreign branch accounting. 43p.
First edition, 1925.

1933

JONES, Ralph C.
Allocation accounting for the taxable income of industrial enterprises. 78p.

FOUNDRIES

1910

LOUGHRY, James Cooper.
How to install a foundry cost system. 41p.

FOUNDRIES (continued)

1919

BELT, Robert E.
Foundry cost accounting. 271p.
Latest edition, 1926.

1921

MILLER, Nina M.
Accounting for malleable iron industry. (In Kester, Roy Bernard. Accounting theory and practice. v.3, p.275–315)

1923

EVERITT, Frank, and HEYWOOD, Johnson.
Cost control for foundries; ed. by William R. Basset. 226p.

1926

BELT, Robert E.
Foundry cost accounting; 2d ed. rev. and enl. 267p.
First edition, 1919.

BENNETT, George Edward.
Foundries. (In his Accounting systems. p.381–410)

FURNITURE

1915

TIMKEN, Frank Herrmann.
Accounting in the furniture and woodworking industries. 118p.

1924

POTTER, Homer D.
Cost finding principles for furniture factories. 140p.

GARAGES AND SERVICE STATIONS

1915

HOLLISTER, Horace Edward.
Practical garage accounting. 57p.
Latest edition, 1916.

1916

HOLLISTER, Horace Edward.
Practical garage accounting; 2d ed. 173p.
First edition, 1915.

1926

BENNETT, George Edward.
Garages. (In his Accounting systems. p.357–380)

1932

HADLEY, Charles R., company, Los Angeles.
Hadley's pathfinder accounting system for service stations and garages. 89p.+forms.
Latest edition, 1934.

1934

HADLEY, Charles R., company, Los Angeles.
Hadley's pathfinder accounting system for garages and service stations. 89p.+forms.
First edition, 1932.

GAS COMPANIES

1913

MOXEY, Edward Preston, GREELEY, Harold Dudley, JEFFERSON, Howard McNayr, and GRUNDMAN, Otto A.
Gas accounting. (In their Practical accounting methods. p.202–242)

GAS COMPANIES (continued)

1924

GORDON, William Duncan, and LOCKWOOD, Jeremiah.
Gas companies. (In their Modern accounting systems. p.287–327)
Latest edition, 1933.

1933

GORDON, William Duncan, and LOCKWOOD, Jeremiah.
Gas companies. (In their Modern accounting systems; 2d ed. p.294–340)
First edition, 1924.

GOVERNMENT ACCOUNTING (NATIONAL, STATE, AND MUNICIPAL)

1901

MACPHERSON, Frank Herbert.
Municipal accounting. 47p.

1909

CLEVELAND, Frederick Albert.
Chapters on municipal administration and accounting. 361p.

1913

BUREAU OF MUNICIPAL RESEARCH, New York. Metz fund.
Handbook of municipal accounting. 318p.

MOXEY, Edward Preston, GREELEY, Harold Dudley, JEFFERSON, Howard McNayr, and GRUNDMAN, Otto A.
Municipal accounting. (In their Practical accounting methods. p.351–373)

1914

EGGLESTON, De Witt Carl.
Municipal accounting. 456p.
Latest edition, 1922.

1915

SULLIVAN, Frank Joseph.
System of accounts for county government. 72p.

1916

BLACHLY, Frederick Frank.
The accounting and reporting methods of the state of New York. 151p.

1921

DOHR, James Lewis.
Municipal accounting. (In Kester, Roy Bernard. Accounting theory and practice. v.3, p.523–585)

OAKEY, Francis.
Principles of government accounting and reporting. 561p.

1922

EGGLESTON, De Witt Carl.
Municipal accounting. 456p.
First edition, 1914.

1923

BEASLEY, Leonard.
An outline of municipal accounts. 48p.

1924

GORDON, William Duncan, and LOCKWOOD, Jeremiah.
Municipalities. (In their Modern accounting systems. p.391–453)
Latest edition, 1933.

GOVERNMENT ACCOUNTING, 1924 (continued)

MacDonald, Ernest F.
Municipal accounting. 59p.

Seidemann, Henry Peter.
Manual of governmental accounting. 229p.
Latest edition, 1926.

1926

Parkinson, Charles W., and Merrell, Oscar J.
Municipal accountancy. 253p.

Seidemann, Henry Peter.
Manual of accounting and reporting for the operating services of the national government. 399p.
First edition, 1924.

1927

Morey, Lloyd.
Introduction to governmental accounting. 285p.
Latest edition, 1932.

—Manual of municipal accounting. 187p.

1928

Seidemann, Henry Peter.
Manual of accounting, reporting, and business procedure for the territorial government of Hawaii. 570p.

1929

Hadley, Charles R., company, Los Angeles.
Manual of pathfinder accounting system for municipalities. 96p.+forms.

1932

Morey, Lloyd.
Introduction to governmental accounting. 285p.
First edition, 1927.

1933

CHASE, Harvey Stuart.
A plan for a standard form of municipal reports to be published annually by towns in the commonwealth. 31p.

CHATTERS, Carl H.
Accounting manual for small cities (under 25,000 population) 79p.

GORDON, William Duncan, and LOCKWOOD, Jeremiah.
Municipalities. (In their Modern accounting systems; 2d ed. p.405-472)
First edition, 1924.

1934

HARRIS, Walter O.
A municipal general ledger and principal supporting records. 44p.

MOORE, Franklin Frazee, and GILL, John Goodner, editors.
Municipal accounting and auditing. 321p.

HOSPITALS

1906

THOMPSON-BROWN COMPANY, Boston.
The forms of hospital financial reports.
Latest edition, 1918.

1918

THOMPSON-BROWN COMPANY, Boston.
Hospital accounting and statistics; 4th ed. 119p.
William V. Thorne is named as compiler of the fourth edition.
First edition, 1906.

HOSPITALS (continued)

1924

CURTIS, Gay Waite.
Improved methods in hospital management. 176p.

1925

HADLEY, Charles R., company, Los Angeles.
Exhibit and book of instructions; Hadley's pathfinder bookkeeping system for hotels [applicable also to hospitals and clubs] 82p.+forms.
Latest edition, 1928.

1927

CURRAN, Con. P., printing company, St. Louis.
The Curran system of hospital accounting, simplified. 40p.

1928

HADLEY, Charles R., company, Los Angeles.
Exhibit and book of instructions; Hadley's pathfinder bookkeeping system for hotels [applicable also to hospitals and clubs] 82p.+forms.
First edition, 1925.

1929

SAWYER, Albert E.
Problems of hospital management. 83p.

1933

NEW YORK CONFERENCE ON HOSPITAL ACCOUNTING.
Accounting and business procedure for hospitals. 195p.
(Herbert R. Sands, consulting accountant)

HOTELS

1907

CLARENBACH, Ernst, and WILLY, John.
Clarenbach system of hotel accounting. 46p.
Latest edition, 1930.

1921

KESTER, Roy Bernard.
Hotel accounting. (In his Accounting theory and practice. v.3, p.488–522)

1925

HADLEY, Charles R., company, Los Angeles.
Exhibit and book of instructions; Hadley's pathfinder bookkeeping system for hotels [applicable also to hospitals and clubs] 82p.+forms.
Latest edition, 1928.

1926

BENNETT, George Edward.
Summer hotels. (In his Accounting systems. p.329–356)

1927

O'BRIEN, Daniel J., and COUCHMAN, Charles Bennington.
Hotel administration; accounts and control. 379p.

1928

HADLEY, Charles R., company, Los Angeles.
Exhibit and book of instructions; Hadley's pathfinder bookkeeping system for hotels [applicable also to hospitals and clubs] 82p.+forms.
First edition, 1925.

HORWATH, Ernest B., and TOTH, Louis.
Hotel accounting. 508p.

HOTELS (continued)

1930

CLARENBACH, Ernst.
Clarenbach's hotel accounting. 66p.
First edition, 1907.

ICE

1911

BLUIM, J. M.
The accounting system of an ice company. 104p.

1912

CAROLINA PUBLIC SERVICE COMPANY, Columbia, S. C.
Classification of accounts. 46p.

1929

COOK, Jonathan Blanchard.
Ice accounting. 230p.

INSURANCE

1909

BARNETT, Samuel.
Life insurance accounting. 112p.

1910

SWEETLAND, Charles Augustus.
Insurance accounts. (In his Insurance and real estate accounts. pt.1, p.1–154)

1911

SEITZ, Jacob Charles.
A system and accounting for a life insurance company. 112p.
Latest edition, 1931.

1913

MOXEY, Edward Preston, GREELEY, Harold Dudley, JEFFERSON, Howard McNayr, and GRUNDMAN, Otto A.
Fire insurance accounting. (In their Practical accounting methods. p.97–107)

—[Life insurance company accounting] (In their Practical accounting methods. p.58–96)

1920

PARSONS, Theodore C.
Parsons' [insurance] accounting system. 26p.

1922

AMERICAN SYSTEM COMPANY, Roanoke, Va.
American agency accounting system. 28p.
Latest edition, 1924.

1923

WIEGAND, William B.
Accounting for fire insurance companies. 95p.

1924

AMERICAN SYSTEM COMPANY, Roanoke, Va.
American agency accounting system. 31p.
First edition, 1922.

GORDON, William Duncan, and LOCKWOOD, Jeremiah.
Insurance companies. (In their Modern accounting systems. p.51–129)
Latest edition, 1933.

INSURANCE (continued)

1925

GLOVER, James Waterman, and WIGHTMAN, Earl Charles.
Life insurance accounting. 178p.

1926

HADLEY, Charles R., company, Los Angeles.
Exhibit and book of instructions; Hadley's pathfinder bookkeeping system for insurance agents. 63p.+forms.
Latest edition, 1928.

MATHER, Charles Ernest.
Life insurance accounting. 118p.

WIEGAND, William B.
Fire insurance accounting. 108p.

1928

HADLEY, Charles R., company, Los Angeles.
Exhibit and book of instructions; Hadley's pathfinder bookkeeping system for insurance agents. 63p.+forms.
First edition, 1926.

JOSEPH, Emrys Sibbering.
Insurance agency accounting and management. 137p.

1930

HULL, Robert Sedgwick.
Casualty insurance accounting. 325p.

1931

SEITZ, Jacob Charles.
A system and accounting for a life insurance company; 2d ed. rev. and enl. 190p.
First edition, 1911.

1933

GORDON, William Duncan, and LOCKWOOD, Jeremiah.
Insurance company accounting. (In their Modern accounting systems; 2d ed. p.57–122)
First edition, 1924.

1934

WIGHTMAN, Earl Charles.
Life insurance accounts. 281p.

KNIT GOODS

1923

GORDON, Stephen Robbins.
Cost finding in knitting mills. 204p.

1924

LUTZ, Werner, and GORDON, Stephen Robbins.
Cost accounting manual for the knitted outerwear industry. 145p.

MILLER, FRANKLIN & company, New York (formerly Miller, Franklin, Basset & co.)
Cost control for knit underwear factories. 259p.

1926

BENNETT, George Edward.
Knit goods. (In his Accounting systems. p.434–455)

LAUNDRIES

1925

HADLEY, Charles R., company, Los Angeles.
Exhibit and book of instructions of Hadley's pathfinder bookkeeping system for laundries. 47p.+forms.
Latest edition, 1929.

LAUNDRIES (continued)

1929

HADLEY, Charles R., company, Los Angeles.
Exhibit and book of instructions of Hadley's pathfinder bookkeeping system for laundries. 47p.+forms.
First edition, 1925.

LAWYERS

1932

DELEVANTI, A. C.
Systematizing an attorney's office. 66p.

GRAHAM, Willard J., and KATZ, Wilber Griffith.
Accounting in law practice. 444p.

HADLEY, Charles R., company, Los Angeles.
Hadley's pathfinder accounting system for attorneys-at-law. 51p.+forms.

LIVE STOCK

1930

WOODBRIDGE, Frederick Wells.
A system of accounting procedure for livestock ranches. 193p.

LUMBER

1914

JONES, Arthur Francis.
Lumber manufacturing accounts. 112p.
Latest edition, 1919.

1919

JONES, Arthur Francis.
Lumber manufacturing accounts. 112p.
First edition, 1914.

1922

HAFNER, George W.
The dealers' handy cost book; containing the Building supply news' adaptable uniform cost accounting system for every building supply, lumber, and coal retail merchant. 158p.

1923

HAFNER, George W.
An accounting system for retailers. 49p.

1929

ECKARDT, Hugo William.
Accounting in the lumber industry. 291p.

MACHINE SHOPS

1903

ARNOLD, Horace Lucian, compiler.
The factory manager and accountant. 431p.
This work includes cost systems for boilers, link-belts, machines, metal working machine-tools, printing presses, and taps, dies, and reamers.
Latest edition, 1905.

1905

ARNOLD, Horace Lucian, compiler.
The factory manager and accountant. 431p.
First edition, 1903.

MACHINE SHOPS (continued)

1922

BASSET, William Rupert, and HEYWOOD, Johnson.
Production engineering and cost keeping for machine shops. 311p.

1926

BENNETT, George Edward.
Machine-shop. (In his Accounting systems. p.411–433)

MEAT PACKERS

1929

INSTITUTE OF AMERICAN MEAT PACKERS, Chicago.
Packinghouse accounting. 404p.

MILK

1916

LARSON, Carl William.
Milk production cost accounts. 61p.

1926

BENNETT, George Edward.
Cooperative milk manufacturing. (In his Accounting systems. p.464–545)

MINING

1908

DAVIS, Walter.
Simple mine accounting. 63p.
Latest edition, 1909.

1909

DAVIS, Walter.
Simple mine accounting; 2d ed. 78p.
First edition, 1908.

1920

MCGARRAUGH, Robert.
Mine bookkeeping. 118p.

MINING, COAL

1912

CHARLTON, William Hurst.
[Coal mining] (In his American mine accounting. p.203–274)
Latest edition, 1913.

1913

CHARLTON, William Hurst.
[Coal mining] (In his American mine accounting. p.203–274)
First edition, 1912.

ROBY, James J.
A treatise on cost accounting as applied to coal mining. 16p.
Latest edition, 1914.

1914

ROBY, James J.
Cost accounting as applied to coal mining. 32p.
First edition, 1913.

1921

THOMPSON, William J.
Bituminous coal mine accounting. (In Kester, Roy Bernard. Accounting theory and practice. v.3, p.137–201)

MINING, COAL (continued)

1922

REED, William Blose.
Bituminous coal mine accounting. 221p.

SHURICK, Adam Thomas.
Coal mining costs. 515p.

MINING, METAL

1912

CHARLTON, William Hurst.
[Metal mining] (In his American mine accounting)
Contents: Copper mining, p.58–202; Gold mining, p.275–316; Iron mining, p.1–57.
Latest edition, 1913.

1913

CHARLTON, William Hurst.
[Metal mining] (In his American mine accounting)
Contents: Copper mining, p.58–202; Gold mining, p.275–316; Iron mining, p.1–57.
First edition, 1912.

1914

JONES, E. Horton.
Unit construction costs from the new smelter of the Arizona copper co. ltd. 153p.

1921

McGRATH, Thomas Orrin.
Mine accounting and cost principles. 257p.

THOMAS, Reginald.
Precious metal mine accounting. (In Kester, Roy Bernard. Accounting theory and practice. v.3, p.202–225)

MOTION PICTURES

1916

THORNTON, Frank Weldon.
Memorandum on moving picture accounts. 54p.

1923

MORRIS, William F.
Motion picture theatre accounting. 144p.

MOTOR BUS TRANSPORTATION

1926

MAY, Irville Augustus.
Motor bus accounting practice. 200p.

NEWSPAPERS

1921

WALKER, Edmund.
Newspaper accounting and federal taxation. 27p.

1924

SWINDELL, Walter B.
Newspaper accounting and cost finding. 87p.

1926

HEDLAND, Edward W.
Newspaper cost accounting. 91p.

NEWSPAPERS (continued)

1932

VAN BENTHUYSEN, Alvin Seaward.
Newspaper organization and accounting. 544p.

OIL

1925

MORLAND, David F., and MCKEE, Raymond W.
Accounting for the petroleum industry. 304p.

1934

HUMPHREYS, H. G.
The accounts of an oil company. 136p.

PAINTS AND VARNISHES

1917

STOREY, Eugene Wilfred.
Monthly cost accounting for varnish plants. 51p.

PATENT ACCOUNTING

1930

KLOOSTER, Bert Louis.
Patent accountings; a phase of cost accounting. 795p.

PERSONAL AND HOUSEHOLD ACCOUNTING

1903

HASKINS, Charles Waldo.
How to keep household accounts. 117p.

1912

ROGERS, C. S., and ROGERS, O. L.
Personal bookkeeping. 62p.

1913

WHIGAM, Wallace Hugh, and FREDERICK, Oliver Detwiler.
Household accounting. 47p.

1917

CRANDELL, John Chester, and CRANDELL, Mercy Frye.
A manual of household accounts. 24p.+68 forms.

HARPMAN, Charles Andrew.
Home bookkeeping for the thrifty. 98p.

SHEAFFER, William Adam.
Household accounting and economics. 161p.

1918

RITTENHOUSE, Charles Forest.
Elements of accounts for individuals, professional men, and institutions. 264p.

1923

HADLEY, Charles R., company, Los Angeles.
Exhibit and book of instructions of Hadley's pathfinder personal accounting system, double entry. 26p.+forms.
Latest edition, 1934.

PERSONAL AND HOUSEHOLD ACCOUNTING, 1923 (continued)

TABER, Clarence Wilbur, and WARDALL, Ruth Aimee.
Economics of the family. 224p.

1934

HADLEY, Charles R., company, Los Angeles.
Exhibit and book of instructions of Hadley's pathfinder personal accounting system, double entry. 38p.+forms.
First edition, 1923.

PHYSICIANS

1928

WOOLLEY, Ernest Stanley.
Physicians' systems. 133p.

PLUMBING AND HEATING

1905

RYAN, George Weiser.
Bookkeeping for the plumber. 62p.
Latest edition, 1910.

1910

RYAN, George Weiser.
Bookkeeping for the plumber; 2d ed. 58p.
First edition, 1905.

1911

PRIOR, Frank Samuel.
Office methods for the plumber. 47p.

1914

METAL WORKER, PLUMBER AND STEAM FITTER.
Estimating, cost keeping, and profit making in the plumbing, heating, and sheet metal trades. 380p.

1918

FINK, Wesley Albert.
Bookkeeping and cost-finding for the plumber. 128p.

1923

HADLEY, Charles R., company, Los Angeles.
Exhibit and book of instructions of Hadley's pathfinder building trades bookkeeping system for plumbers, electrical contractors and dealers, tinners, roofers [etc.] 58p.+forms.
Latest edition, 1931.

1931

HADLEY, Charles R., company, Los Angeles.
Exhibit and book of instructions of Hadley's pathfinder building trades bookkeeping system for plumbers, electrical contractors and dealers, tinners, roofers [etc.] 84p.+forms.
First edition, 1923.

PRINTING

1901

BLANCHARD, Isaac H.
Actual costs in printing and how to discover and reckon them. 58p.

DANDO, J. Clifford.
Fundamental principles of ascertaining cost of manufacturing; applied to manufacturing printing. 82p.
3d ed. 1901. 81p.

PRINTING (continued)

1905

STUART, Eden Burroughs.
A money-making system for the employing printer. 99p.

1908

PORTE, Roy Trewin.
The practical cost system for printing offices.
Latest edition, 1925.

1912

JOBSON, Walter Paxton.
An accounting system for printing concerns. 76p.
Latest edition, 1914.

1913

WINCHELL, Samuel Dixon.
The model system of bookkeeping and cost finding; prepared especially for the printing and allied industries. 36p.

1914

DAVIS, Albert Eugene.
How to find costs in printing. 120p.

JOBSON, Walter Paxton.
An accounting system for printing concerns. 106p.
First edition, 1912.

PORTE, Roy Trewin.
How to figure costs in printing offices. 134p.
Latest edition, 1924.

1922

PORTE, Roy Trewin.
John Smith's bookkeeping. 168p.
Latest edition, 1924.

1924

PORTE, Roy Trewin.
How to figure costs in printing offices; rev. ed. 181p.
First edition, 1914.

—John Smith's bookkeeping. 187p.
First edition, 1922.

1925

PORTE, Roy Trewin.
The practical cost system for printing offices; rev. ed. 159p.
First edition, 1908.

1928

KOCH, Elmer J.
The standard book on cost finding for printers. 127p.

PROBATE ACCOUNTING

1902

GOTTSBERGER, Francis.
Accountant's guide for executors, administrators, assignees, receivers, and trustees. 196p.

1910

BAUGH, Frederick Henry, and SCHMEISSER, William Christian.
Theory and practice of estate accounting. 321p.
Latest edition, 1925.

1912

VIERLING, Frederick
Fiduciary accounting. 47p.
Latest edition, 1931.

PROBATE ACCOUNTING (continued)

1913

MOXEY, Edward Preston, GREELEY, Harold Dudley, JEFFERSON, Howard McNayr, and GRUNDMAN, Otto A.
Executor's work and estate bookkeeping. (In their Practical accounting methods. p.374–441)

1915

INTERNATIONAL TEXTBOOK COMPANY, Scranton.
Cost accounting; analysis of accounts; insolvent and decedents' estates. Various pagings.

1921

CONYNGTON, Thomas, KNAPP, Harold C., and PINKERTON, Paul Whittier.
Wills, estates, and trusts. 2v.
v.1, 355p. v.2, 470p.
Latest edition, 1922.

1922

CONYNGTON, Thomas, KNAPP, Harold C., and PINKERTON, Paul Whittier.
Wills, estates, and trusts. 2v.
v.1, 355p. v.2, 470p.
First edition, 1921.

1923

RACINE, Samuel Frederick.
Estate accounts. 191p.

1924

GREELEY, Harold Dudley.
Estate accounting. 110p.
Latest edition, 1930.

1925

BAUGH, Frederick Henry, and SCHMEISSER, William Christian.
Theory and practice of estate accounting. 321p.
First edition, 1910.

1926

HADLEY, Charles R., company, Los Angeles.
Exhibit of pathfinder trust department accounting system. 53p.+forms.
Latest edition, 1932.

1930

GREELEY, Harold Dudley.
Estate accounting. 114p.
First edition, 1924.

SAXE, Emanuel, and LEVY, Walter Arthur.
Estate accounting and taxation. 267p.

1931

VIERLING, Frederick.
Fiduciary accounting. 49p.
First edition, 1912.

1932

DODGE, Chester Joseph.
Estate administration and accounting. 453p.
Latest edition, 1933.

HADLEY, Charles R., company, Los Angeles.
Exhibit of pathfinder trust department accounting system. 53p.+forms.
First edition, 1926.

1933

DODGE, Chester Joseph.
Estate administration and accounting; 2d ed. 450p.
First edition, 1932.

PROBATE ACCOUNTING, 1933 (continued)

GRANGE, William James, STAUB, Walter Adolph, and BLACKFORD, Eugene G.
Wills, executors, and trustees. 844p.

PUBLIC ACCOUNTANTS

1921

RUSSMAN, Albin.
The organization and accounts of a public accountant's office. (In Kester, Roy Bernard. Accounting theory and practice. v.3, p.423–464)

PUBLIC UTILITIES

1923

INTERNATIONAL TEXTBOOK COMPANY, Scranton.
Public-utility accounting practices. 85p.

1924

INTERNATIONAL TEXTBOOK COMPANY, Scranton.
Public-utility accounting principles. 107p.

1925

HAMMOND, W. M.
Accounting methods and procedure for electric, gas, and water utilities. 412p.

INTERNATIONAL TEXTBOOK COMPANY, Scranton.
Public utility accounting. Various pagings.

1926

BAILEY, Warren G., and KNOWLES, Daniel Emerson.
Accounting procedures for public utilities. 471p.

1933

WISCONSIN. PUBLIC SERVICE COMMISSION.
Depreciation; a review of legal and accounting problems. 196p.

1934

GRAHAM, Willard J.
Public utility valuation. 95p

RADIO DEALERS

1931

HADLEY, Charles R., company, Los Angeles.
Hadley's pathfinder accounting system for radio dealers. 63p.+forms.

RAILROADS

1903

KIRKMAN, Marshall Monroe.
Surplus material and track accounts. 67p.
Latest edition, 1904.

—Track accounts and returns. 39p.

1904

KIRKMAN, Marshall Monroe.
Surplus material and track accounts. 67p.
First edition, 1903.

RAILROADS (continued)

1906

KIRKMAN, Marshall Monroe.
Collection of revenue and other fiscal affairs. 470p.
Latest edition, 1907.

—General accounts and cash. 395p.
Latest edition, 1907.

—Passenger train traffic and accounts. 616p.
Latest edition, 1907.

—Safeguarding railway expenditures. 551p.
Latest edition, 1907.

1907

KIRKMAN, Marshall Monroe.
Collection of revenue and other fiscal affairs. 470p.
First edition, 1906.

—General accounts and cash. 395p.
First edition, 1906.

—Passenger train traffic and accounts. 616p.
First edition, 1906.

—Safeguarding railway expenditures. 551p.
First edition, 1906.

1908

PRICE, WATERHOUSE & co., New York.
Treatment of maintenance and depreciation accounts in the new classification of accounts prescribed for railroads by the Interstate commerce commission. 27p.

1911

COUNTY, Albert John.
Railway accounts and statistics. 67p.

1913

EATON, James Shirley.
Handbook of railroad expenses. 559p.

MOXEY, Edward Preston, GREELEY, Harold Dudley, JEFFERSON, Howard McNayr, and GRUNDMAN, Otto A.
Railroad accounting. (In their Practical accounting methods. p.243-330)

TATLOW, Herbert Johnson.
Institute of railway accounting: text-book of inter-line freight accounts. 86p.

1915

HOOPER, William Everett.
Railroad accounting. 461p

INTERNATIONAL TEXTBOOK COMPANY, Scranton.
Railroad agency accounting. Various pagings.

1917

SIKES, Clarence Steven.
Railway accounting. 2v.
v.1, 140p. v.2, 202p.
Latest edition, 1920.

1918

ADAMS, Henry Carter.
American railway accounting. 465p.

1920

SIKES, Clarence Steven.
Railway accounting. 2v.
v.1, 140p., 1920. v.2, 202p., 1921.
First edition, 1917.

RAILROADS (continued)

1924

GORDON, William Duncan, and LOCKWOOD, Jeremiah.
Railroads. (In their Modern accounting systems. p.329–390)
Latest edition, 1933.

INTERNATIONAL TEXTBOOK COMPANY, Scranton.
Station agents' accounting for freight and passenger business. Various pagings.

WERMUTH, Charles E.
Railroad accounts and statistics. 349p.

1925

WHITE, Joseph Lowell.
Analysis of railroad operations. 381p.

1929

LASALLE EXTENSION UNIVERSITY, Chicago.
Railway accounting. 33 pamphlets, c1929–31.
These pamphlets total 1052 pages.

1933

GORDON, William Duncan, and LOCKWOOD, Jeremiah.
Railroads. (In their Modern accounting systems; 2d ed. p.341–404)
First edition, 1924.

RANCHES

1921

COLLINS, Clem Wetzell.
Ranch cost accounting. (In Kester, Roy Bernard. Accounting theory and practice. v.3, p.226–274)

1930

WOODBRIDGE, Frederick Wells.
A system of accounting procedure for livestock ranches. 193p.

REAL ESTATE

1910

SWEETLAND, Charles Augustus.
Real estate accounting. (In his Insurance and real estate accounts. pt.2, p.1–46)

1917

MUCKLOW, Walter.
Real estate accounts. 357p.
Latest edition, 1924.

1924

HADLEY, Charles R., company, Los Angeles.
Pathfinder accounting manual for realtors and subdividers. 20p.+forms.

MUCKLOW, Walter.
Real estate accounts. 357p.
First edition, 1917.

RETAIL STORES

1910

SWEETLAND, Charles Augustus.
Department store accounts. 187p.
Latest edition, 1913.

RETAIL STORES (continued)

1913

MOXEY, Edward Preston, GREELEY, Harold Dudley, JEFFERSON, Howard McNayr, and GRUNDMAN, Otto A.
[Department store accounting] (In their Practical accounting methods. p.164–201)

NEWELL, George Griffiths.
"Department store auditing." 103p.

SWEETLAND, Charles Augustus.
Department store accounts. 187p.
First edition, 1910.

1914

JACKSON, Harry Albert.
Better store system and department accounting. 74p.

1917

HERZ, Eugene.
Controlling profits; simplified efficiency methods in store record keeping. 103p.

1920

CARTHAGE, Philip I.
Retail organization and accounting control. 349p.
Latest edition, 1924.

1921

BACAS, Paul E.
Principles of department store accounting. (In Kester, Roy Bernard. Accounting theory and practice. v.3, p.396–422)

MINSTER, Leopold.
Retail profits, turnover, and net worth. 48p.

1922

BOSTON. CHAMBER OF COMMERCE. Retail trade board.
Retail inventory shortages and remedies. 48p.

CHAMBER OF COMMERCE OF THE UNITED STATES OF AMERICA. Dept. of manufacture.
Perpetual inventory or stores control. 30p.
Latest edition, 1929.

NATIONAL RETAIL DRY GOODS ASSOCIATION. Controllers' congress.
A standard method of accounting for retail stores. 2v.
v.1, 52p. v.2, 22 charts (part fold.)

1923

HADLEY, Charles R., company, Los Angeles.
Exhibit and book of instructions of Hadley's pathfinder bookkeeping system, double entry; for wholesale and retail merchandising establishments. 36p.+forms.
Latest edition, 1930.

1924

ALTMAN, George T.
Cash records. 117p.

—Recording sales transactions. 92p.

CARTHAGE, Philip I.
Retail organization and accounting control. 349p.
First edition, 1920.

GORDON, William Duncan, and LOCKWOOD, Jeremiah.
Department store accounting. (In their Modern accounting systems. p.245–286)
Latest edition, 1933.

1925

COMSTOCK, Lynn M.
Modern retail methods, records, and accounting. 522p.

RETAIL STORES, 1925 (continued)

HODGE, Albert Claire.
Retail accounting and control. 545p.

LAZARUS, Arthur.
Stock control in department stores. 77p.

McNAIR, Malcolm Perrine.
The retail method of inventory. 143p.

THOMPSON, William Rodney, BENTON, A. C., HAIMAN, J. H., and SCHREFFLER, Robert Bruce.
Accounting for retail and department stores. 158p.

1928

NATIONAL RETAIL DRY GOODS ASSOCIATION. Controllers' congress.
Expense manual. 232p.

1929

CHAMBER OF COMMERCE OF THE UNITED STATES OF AMERICA. Dept. of manufacture.
Perpetual inventory or stores control. 26p.
First edition, 1922.

CONNER, A. H., and GORDON, Robert W.
Merchandise control. 42p.

SCHREFFLER, Robert Bruce.
The retail inventory. 40p.

1930

HADLEY, Charles R., company, Los Angeles.
Exhibit and book of instructions of Hadley's pathfinder bookkeeping system, double entry; for wholesale and retail merchandising establishments. 36p.+forms.
First edition, 1923.

1931

EGGLESTON, De Witt Carl.
Department store accounting. 422p.

1932

LIEBERMAN, Bernard.
Accounting system for retail stores. 26p.

1933

GORDON, William Duncan, and LOCKWOOD, Jeremiah.
Department store accounting. (In their Modern accounting systems; 2d ed. p.247–293)
First edition, 1924.

1934

ATKINSON, Sterling Krick.
A model cost control plan for delivery organizations of department stores doing an annual business of from two to ten million dollars. 124p.

LYANS, Cecil Kenyon, and BRISCO, Norris Arthur.
Retail accounting. 590p.

METROPOLITAN LIFE INSURANCE COMPANY, New York. Policyholders service bureau.
Inventory control methods. 30p.

RUBBER GOODS

1926

RUBBER MANUFACTURERS ASSOCIATION, INC.
Manual of accounts and budgetary control for the rubber industry. 257p.

SAWMILLS

1923

MAHONY, J.
A practical accounting system for the sawmill operator. 63p.

SCHOOLS, PUBLIC

1914

HUTCHINSON, J. Howard.
School costs and school accounting. 152p.

1924

FOWLKES, John Guy.
A handbook of financial accounting for schools. 56p.

1927

ENGELHARDT, Fred, and VON BORGERSRODE, Fred.
Accounting procedure for school systems. 130p.

—and ENGELHARDT, Nickolaus Louis.
Complete accounting system for public schools. 234p.

1930

KEMMERER, Walter William.
School accounting by machine methods. 179p.

FOWLKES, John Guy.
Principles and practices of financial accounting for schools. 238p.

SHEET METAL WORK

1914

METAL WORKER, PLUMBER AND STEAM FITTER.
Estimating, cost keeping, and profit making in the plumbing, heating, and sheet metal trades. 380p.

1923

BARUCH, Alfred.
Standard costs for sheet metal workers. 298p.

SHOES

1914

SMALL, Frederic Lincoln.
Treatise on comprehensive accounting methods; adapted to shoe manufacturing and other industries. 227p.

1924

COBB, Howard P.
Shoe factory accounting and cost keeping. 392p.

1928

BOLAND, Chester R.
Shoe industry accounting. 204p.

SILK

1912

DAY, Clarence Munro.
Silk mill costs. 70p.

SOCIETIES, ASSOCIATIONS, ETC.

1918

KRACH, Edward Tingey, compiler.
Standardized accounting system for country clubs. 32p.

SOCIETIES, ASSOCIATIONS, ETC. (continued)

1922

PIPER, Clarence Brett.
Manual explaining the use of an accounting system; designed for chapters of college fraternities. 159 l.+forms.

1925

HADLEY, Charles R., company, Los Angeles.
Exhibit and book of instructions; Hadley's pathfinder bookkeeping system for hotels [applicable also to hospitals and clubs] 82p.+forms.
Latest edition, 1928.

1926

CHAMBER OF COMMERCE OF THE UNITED STATES OF AMERICA. Organization service.
Financial control and accounting for a chamber of commerce. 65p.

1928

HADLEY, Charles R., company, Los Angeles.
Exhibit and book of instructions; Hadley's pathfinder bookkeeping system for hotels [applicable also to hospitals and clubs] 82p.+forms.
First edition, 1925.

1929

PHENEY, Edward Thomas.
College fraternity finances. 67p.

STOCK BROKERAGE

1916

TODMAN, Frederick Simson.
Brokerage accounts. 338p.
Latest edition, 1921.

1921

TODMAN, Frederick Simson.
Wall street accounting. 352p.
First edition, 1916.

1923

TODMAN, Frederick Simson.
The work of the cashier's cage. 77p.

1924

GORDON, William Duncan, and LOCKWOOD, Jeremiah.
Stock brokerage. (In their Modern accounting systems. p.193–244)
Latest edition, 1933.

HALSEY, STUART & co., INC., New York.
Investment bond accounting. 40p.
Latest edition, 1926.

1925

INTERNATIONAL TEXTBOOK COMPANY, Scranton.
Theory of accounts; operating on the New York stock exchange and stock brokerage accounting methods. Various pagings.

1926

HALSEY, STUART & co., INC., New York.
Investment bond accounting. 40p.
First edition, 1924.

1929

HERRICK, Anson.
An outline of brokerage accounting. 94p.

STOCK BROKERAGE (continued)

1930

EGGLESTON, De Witt Carl.
Wall street procedure; with special reference to brokers' accounts. 301p.

THORNTON, Frank Weldon.
Stock brokerage and investment house accounting; with notes on auditing procedure. 188p.

1933

GORDON, William Duncan, and LOCKWOOD, Jeremiah.
Stock brokerage. (In their Modern accounting systems; 2d ed. p.185-246)
First edition, 1924.

SUGAR

1922

WERMUTH, Charles E.
Classification of accounts for sugar estates. 30p.

TANNERIES

1913

STEWART, Ethelbert.
Tannery production costs and methods of accounting. 39p.

TELEPHONE COMPANIES

1908

MAYER, Clarence.
Telephone construction methods and cost. 281p.

1909

Tutt, R. G.
Telephone accounting. 27p.

TEXTILES

1916

Dale, Samuel Sherman.
Cost finding for textile mills; cotton, woolen, worsted, hosiery, underwear. 32p.

1922

Szepesi, Eugene.
Cost control and accounting for textile mills. 441p.

UNIVERSITIES AND COLLEGES

1910

Carnegie foundation for the advancement of teaching.
Standard forms for financial reports of colleges, universities, and technical schools. 37p.
Latest edition, 1921.

1921

Carnegie foundation for the advancement of teaching.
Standard forms for financial reports of colleges, universities, and technical schools. 37p.
First edition, 1910.

1922

Arnett, Trevor.
College and university finance. 212p.

UNIVERSITIES AND COLLEGES (continued)

1926

WASHBURN, Earle Leroy.
Accounting for universities. 126p.

1930

MOREY, Lloyd.
University and college accounting. 323p.

NATIONAL COMMITTEE ON STANDARD REPORTS FOR INSTITUTIONS OF HIGHER EDUCATION.
Bulletins. 8 nos.
For information concerning these publications issued between 1930 and 1934, see part I, 1930.

1933

AZIERE, Charles.
Accounting for Catholic institutions of higher education. 29p.

WATER WORKS

1916

WOLFF, Mark.
Interpretation of water-works accounts. 28p.

WOODWORKING

1915

TIMKEN, Frank Herrmann.
Accounting in the furniture and woodworking industries. 118p.

WOOLENS AND WORSTEDS

1918

DALE, Samuel Sherman.
Cost finding in woolen and worsted mills. 49p.

1923

SZEPESI INDUSTRIAL ORGANIZATION, Boston.
Cost and production standards ; worsted men's wear.
Portfolio of forms and charts, unpaged.

Part Two

CLASS 5a

Works dealing chiefly or wholly with general principles and procedure of auditing

1903

BEACH, Elmer Henry, and THORNE, William Winter.
The science and practice of auditing. 76p.

1905

MOULL, John.
Auditing for accountant students. 71p.
Latest edition, 1918.

RENN, George Benton.
Practical auditing. 32p.
Latest edition, 1909.

SOULÉ, George.
Soulé's manual of auditing; 6th ed. 24p.
First edition, 1892, 28 pages.

1908

DAY, Clarence Munro.
[Auditing] (In his Accounting practice. p.3–86)
Latest edition, 1924.

1909

COOLEY, Morgan L.
American audit record. 72p.

RENN, George Benton.
Practical auditing. 130p.
First edition, 1905.

1910

CHASE, William Arthur, and others.
Auditing and cost accounting. 517p.

COLE, William Morse.
Accounting and auditing. 479p.
Latest edition, 1921.

1912

MONTGOMERY, Robert Hiester.
Auditing theory and practice. 673p.
Latest edition, 1934.

SPEAR, Raymond Herbert.
Scientific auditing. 63p.

1913

HERTZ, Joseph Emmett.
Secrets of accounting. 37p.

1914

RACINE, Samuel Frederick.
Guide to the study of auditing. 63p.
Latest edition, 1916.

1916

RACINE, Samuel Frederick.
Guide to the study of auditing; 2d ed. 74p.
First edition, 1914.

WILDMAN, John Raymond.
Principles of auditing. 196p.
Latest edition, 1923.

1917

BENINGTON, Harold.
The detection of frauds. 30p.
Latest edition, 1921.

1917 (continued)

U. S. FEDERAL RESERVE BOARD.
Uniform accounting. 25p.
Reprinted in 1918 under title: "Approved methods for the preparation of balance sheet statements."
Latest edition, 1929.

1918

CASTENHOLZ, William Burtis.
Auditing procedure. 342p.
Latest edition, 1932.

MOULL, John.
Auditing for accountant students. 140p.
First edition, 1905.

REYNOLDS, Ward Burham, and THORNTON, Frank Weldon.
Duties of the junior accountant. 102p.
Latest edition, 1929.
See also 1933, Cipriani, Alfred B.

1919

BASSET, William Rupert.
How to audit. 112p.

1920

SHERWOOD, John F.
Public accounting and auditing. 2v.
v.1, 258p., 1920. v.2, 262p., 1921.
Latest edition, 1922.

1921

BELL, William Hansell.
Accountants' reports. 247p.
Latest edition, 1934.

BENINGTON, Harold.
The detection of frauds. 32p.
First edition, 1917.

COLE, William Morse.
Bookkeeping, accounting, auditing. 479p.
First edition, 1910.

SAXTON, Lynn Mateer.
Auditing. 88p.

TONER, James B.
Auditing. 45p.

1922

INTERNATIONAL TEXTBOOK COMPANY, Scranton.
Audit procedure and reports. 131p.

RICHARDSON, Franklin Whittemore.
The check list method of auditing & bookkeeping. 64p.
Latest edition, 1927.

ROBERT MORRIS ASSOCIATES.
The financial audit as viewed by bankers; statement analysis; suggested methods for a credit index. 56p.

SHERWOOD, John F.
Public accounting and auditing; 3d ed. 2v.
v.1, 264p. v.2, 266p.
First edition, 1920.

1923

ELLMORE, D. Carroll.
Audit program and specimen audit. 72p.

JACKSON, Jacob Hugh.
Audit working papers. 202p.

PALMER, Leslie E., and BELL, William Hansell.
Accountants' working papers. 194p.
Latest edition, 1929.

WILDMAN, John Raymond.
Principles of auditing. 196p.
First edition, 1916.

1924

BELL, William Hansell, and POWELSON, John Abrum.
Auditing, by William H. Bell [with] cases and questions, by John A. Powelson. 518p.
Latest edition, 1930.

DAY, Clarence Munro.
[Auditing] (In his Accounting practice. p.3–86)
First edition, 1908.

HILSEE, Donald Ashcraft.
Auditing; making an audit. 53p.
Latest edition, 1930.

KEISTER, David Armel.
Keister's corporation accounting and auditing; 17th ed. 569p.
First edition, 1894.

KILDUFF, Frederic W.
Auditing and accounting handbook. 813p.

KOHLER, Eric Louis, and PETTENGILL, Paul W.
Principles of auditing. 235p.
Latest edition, 1932.

KONOPAK, Lothar Theodore.
The auditor's working guide. 86p.

1925

BENNETT, George Edward.
Auditing. 377p.

INTERNATIONAL TEXTBOOK COMPANY, Scranton.
Auditing; auditing procedure [etc.] Various pagings.

1926

DAVIES, Ernest Coulter.
Auditing. 385p. (Complete accounting course; ed. by David Himmelblau, v.4)
(See part I, 1924, Himmelblau David, for the "Complete accounting course")

EGGLESTON, De Witt Carl.
Auditing procedure. 528p.

INTERNATIONAL TEXTBOOK COMPANY, Scranton.
Auditing practices. 191p.

RACINE, Samuel Frederick.
Junior auditing. 236p.

1927

HIMMELBLAU, David.
Auditors' certificates. 153p.

RICHARDSON, Franklin Whittemore.
The check list method of auditing & bookkeeping. 100p.
First edition, 1922.

VOKE, Albert F., and CUTRIGHT, Harold Glenn.
Auditing case—Ansted jewelry company. 29p.

1928

HIMMELBLAU, David.
Advanced auditing; financial investigation. 337p. (Complete accounting course, v.6)
(See part I, 1924, Himmelblau David, for the "Complete accounting course")

1929

EGGLESTON, De Witt Carl.
Auditors' reports and working papers. 305p.

JACKSON, Jacob Hugh.
Auditing problems. 534p.

MONTGOMERY, Robert Hiester, and GRAHAM, Willard J.
Auditing. 229p.

1929 (continued)

PALMER, Leslie E., and BELL, William Hansell.
Accountants' working papers. 313p.
First edition, 1923.

REYNOLDS, Ward Burham, and THORNTON, Frank Weldon.
Duties of the junior accountant. 107p.
First edition, 1918.

U. S. FEDERAL RESERVE BOARD.
Verification of financial statements (rev.) 26p.
First edition, 1917.

1930

BELL, William Hansell, and POWELSON, John Abrum.
Auditing, by William H. Bell [with] cases and questions, by John A. Powelson. 518p.
First edition, 1924.

BENNETT, George Edward.
Fraud; its control through accounts. 135p.

HANSON, Arthur Warren, and COFFMAN, Paul Brown.
Problems in auditing. 754p.

HILSEE, Donald Ashcraft.
Auditing; making an audit. 55p.
First edition, 1924.

MILLER, FRANKLIN & company, New York.
How to audit. 233p.

SHERWOOD, John F., and HORNBERGER, Donald Jay.
Fundamentals of auditing. 341p.
Latest edition, 1933.

1932

CASTENHOLZ, William Burtis.
Auditing procedure. 430p.
First edition, 1918.

GRAHAME, J. W. F., and MYERS, Preston E.
"Unaform" accounting schedules. 82p.

KOHLER, Eric Louis, and PETTENGILL, Paul W.
Principles of auditing; 3d ed. 298p.
First edition, 1924.

THORNTON, Frank Weldon.
Duties of the senior accountant. 91p.

1933

CIPRIANI, Alfred B.
Duties of the junior accountant. 170p.
Based to some extent on an earlier work under the same title by W. B. Reynolds and F. W. Thornton, first published in 1918.

HOGAN, Thomas J., and FINNEN, Malachi A.
Outline of audit procedure. 142p.

MCGINLEY, Lee.
Public accounting procedure. 169p.

SHERWOOD, John F., and HORNBERGER, Donald Jay.
Fundamentals of auditing; 2d ed. 363p.
First edition, 1930.

SMITH, Charles Aubrey.
Internal audit control. 205p.

THORNTON, Frank Weldon.
Financial examinations. 282p.

1934

BELL, William Hansell.
Accountants' reports; 3d rev. ed. 397p.
First edition, 1921.

MONTGOMERY, Robert Hiester.
Auditing theory and practice; 5th ed. 772p.
First edition, 1912.

Part Two

CLASS 5b

Treatises on auditing applicable to the following businesses and professions:

Banks
Electric railways
Government auditing (National, state, and municipal)
Insurance
Railroads
Stock brokerage

BANKS

1927

Millet, John I.
Bank audits and examinations. 490p.

ELECTRIC RAILWAYS

1908

Forse, William Harry.
Electric railway auditing and accounting. 157p.

GOVERNMENT AUDITING (NATIONAL, STATE, AND MUNICIPAL)

1933

Lafferty, William A.
The auditing of municipal accounts in New York state. 83p.

1934

MOORE, Franklin Frazee, and GILL, John Goodner, editors.
Municipal accounting and auditing. 321p.

NATIONAL COMMITTEE ON MUNICIPAL ACCOUNTING, Chicago.
Tentative outline of a suggested method of procedure for a detailed municipal audit. 26p.

INSURANCE

1910

WOLFE, Samuel Herbert.
The examination of insurance companies. 248p.

RAILROADS

1912

DAVENPORT, Reginald Arthur.
The railroad traveling auditor's work and methods, theory and practice. 66p.

STOCK BROKERAGE

1930

THORNTON, Frank Weldon.
Stock brokerage and investment house accounting; with notes on auditing procedure. 188p.

Part Two

CLASS 6

C. P. A. examination questions and answers

1902

TIPSON, Frederick Samson.
The theory of accounts. 134p.
Latest edition, 1922.

1904

BROAKER, Frank.
The technique of accountics; lessons 1–20. 262p.

TIPSON, Frederick Samson.
Auditing. 129p.

1907

ILLINOIS. UNIVERSITY.
Questions set at the examinations of candidates for the certificate of certified public accountant in Illinois, 1903–07. 65p.
Latest edition, 1920.

RAHILL, John Joseph.
Corporation accounting and corporation law . . . [with] an appendix on the California examinations for C. P. A. certificates; with a full set of questions and answers by Alfred G. Platt. 452p.
First edition, 1899.

1908

PENNSYLVANIA. STATE BOARD OF EXAMINERS OF PUBLIC ACCOUNTANTS.
Examination questions set at each examination from November, 1899, to November, 1907, inclusive. 158p.

1909

GREENDLINGER, Leo.
Accountancy problems; with solutions. 2v.
v.1, 323p., 1909. v.2, 445p., 1911.
Latest edition, 1911.

PENNSYLVANIA. STATE BOARD OF EXAMINERS OF PUBLIC ACCOUNTANTS.
Examination questions set at each examination from November, 1908, to November, 1909, inclusive. 50p.

1911

CHASE, William Arthur.
C.P.A. examinations and how to pass them. 89p.
Latest edition, 1915.

GREENDLINGER, Leo.
Accountancy problems; with solutions. 2v.
v.1, 393p., 1911. v.2, 459p., 1913.
First edition, 1909.

1913

BENNETT, Robert Joseph.
Pennsylvania C. P. A. examinations for 1912; with answers and solutions. 72p.

1914

BENNETT, Robert Joseph, and MORTON, Frederick W.
C. P. A. questions and answers. 310p.

BENTLEY, Harry Clark, compiler.
C. P. A. auditing questions to January 1, 1914. 247p.

1915

BROAKER, Frank.
The American accountants' manual; volume 1. 210p.
First edition, 1897.

1915 (continued)

BROAKER, Frank.
Post graduate expert accountancy course [with] C. P. A. exams. 2v.
v.1, 25p. v.2, 30p.

CHASE, William Arthur.
C. P. A. examinations and how to pass them. 93p.
First edition, 1911.

MICHIGAN. STATE BOARD OF ACCOUNTANCY.
Michigan C. P. A. manual, 1915. 183p.
Latest edition, 1920.

THE RONALD PRESS COMPANY, New York.
1914 C. P. A. problems and solutions. 2v.
v.1, 346p. v.2, 375p.

—C. P. A. problems with solutions, 1915. 2v.
v.1, 351p., 1915. v.2, 361p., 1916.

1916

COX, Henry Clay, compiler.
Classified C. P. A. problems and solutions, 1915. 414p.

TANNER, John B.
C. P. A. examinations and how to prepare for them. 70p.

1918

CASTENHOLZ, William Burtis, and MOREY, Lloyd.
C. P. A. problems and solutions; selected problems from American institute and state C. P. A. examinations. 457p.
Latest edition, 1932.

WISCONSIN. STATE BOARD OF ACCOUNTANCY.
Governmental accounting questions and answers; 1914, 1915, 1916, 1917, 1918. 50p.
Latest edition, 1922.

1920

ILLINOIS. UNIVERSITY.
Questions set at the examinations of candidates for the certificate of certified public accountant in Illinois, 1903–1918. 247p.
First edition, 1907.

MICHIGAN. STATE BOARD OF ACCOUNTANCY.
Michigan C. P. A. manual, 1920. 260p.
First edition, 1915.

1921

AMERICAN INSTITUTE OF ACCOUNTANTS. Board of examiners.
Examination questions prepared by the Board of examiners of the American institute of accountants for the examinations conducted from June, 1917, to May, 1921, inclusive. 204p.
Latest edition, 1928.

BLOCK, Milton D.
C. P. A. examinations and how to prepare for them. 76p.
Latest edition, 1922.

NEWLOVE, George Hillis.
C. P. A. accounting; theory, questions, and problems. 3v.
v.1, 367p., 1921. v.2, 331p., 1921. v.3, 333p., 1922.
Latest edition, 1930.

—and PRATT, Lester Amos.
Industrial accounting; with C. P. A. questions and problems. 266p

1922

BLOCK, Milton D.
C. P. A. examinations and how to prepare for them. 76p.
First edition, 1921.

TIPSON, Frederick Samson.
The theory of accounts. 271p.
First edition, 1902.

WISCONSIN. STATE BOARD OF ACCOUNTANCY.
Governmental accounting questions and answers; 1914, 1915, 1916, 1917, 1918, 1919, 1920, 1921. 87p.
First edition, 1918.

1927

BENTLEY, Harry Clark.
Massachusetts certified public accountant examination questions; with answers. 826p.

COLLINS, Clem Wetzell, and others.
C. P. A. review. 490p.
"C. P. A. review answers" was published in 1928. 955p.

1928

AMERICAN INSTITUTE OF ACCOUNTANTS. Board of examiners.
Examination questions prepared by the Board of examiners of the American institute of accountants for the examinations conducted from June, 1917, to November, 1927, inclusive. 555p.
First edition, 1921.
See 1932, American institute of accountants, for examinations conducted from May, 1927, to November, 1931.

1930

NEWLOVE, George Hillis.
C. P. A. accounting; theory, auditing, and problems; 3d ed. rev. and enl. 2d printing. 4v.
v.1, 698p. v.2, 279p. v.3, 616p. v.4, 278p.
First edition, 1921.

TAYLOR, Jacob Bacchus, and MILLER, Hermann Clinton.
C. P. A. problems and questions in theory and auditing. 603p.
"Solutions to C. P. A. problems" by Taylor and Miller was published in 1931. 486p.

WINTER, Sidney Graham.
C. P. A. review; questions and problems in auditing and in accounting theory and practice. 556p
"C. P. A. review; answers to questions and solutions to problems" by Winter was published in 1930. 763p.

1931

INTERNATIONAL TEXTBOOK COMPANY, Scranton.
C. P. A. questions and coaching. 187p.

1932

AMERICAN INSTITUTE OF ACCOUNTANTS. Board of examiners.
Examination questions prepared by the Board of examiners of the American institute of accountants for the examinations conducted from May, 1927, to November, 1931, inclusive. 281p.
See 1921, American institute of accountants, for examination questions prepared from June, 1917, to November, 1927.

CASTENHOLZ, William Burtis, and MOREY, Lloyd.
C. P. A. problems and solutions; selected problems from American institute and state C. P. A. examinations. 457p.
First edition, 1918.

DICKERSON, William E., and JONES, J. Weldon.
Ohio C. P. A. problems: an analytical study of and solution to the problems given by the Ohio state board of accountancy, 1928–1931. 252p.
1932 supplement and 1933 supplement published in 1933 and 1934.

FINNEY, Harry Anson, BAUMANN, Harry Paul, and GORDON, Spencer.
Unofficial answers to the examination questions of the American institute of accountants, May, 1927, to November, 1931. 423p.

SHERWOOD, John F.
C. P. A. problems. 108p.

1933

MYER, Joseph Charles.
New York C. P. A. theory questions with answers. 512p.

1934

SEIDMAN, Henry L.
New York C. P. A. problems and solutions, 1924–1933. 2v.
v.1, 296p. v.2, 341p.

Part Two

CLASS 7

Encyclopedias, handbooks, etc.

1901

BEACH, Elmer Henry, and THORNE, William Winter, compilers.
The American business and accounting encyclopaedia. 1090p.
Latest edition, 1908.

1908

BEACH, Elmer Henry, and THORNE, William Winter, compilers.
The American business and accounting encyclopaedia. 6v.
First edition, 1901.

SPEAR, Raymond Herbert, editor.
The Commercial world encyclopedia of accounting. 2v.
Latest edition, 1911.

1910

AMERICAN SCHOOL OF CORRESPONDENCE, Chicago.
Cyclopedia of commerce, accountancy, business administration. 10v.
Vol.2 and v.4–10 contain accounting material.
Latest edition, 1920.

INTERNATIONAL TEXTBOOK COMPANY, Scranton.
The bookkeeper's handbook. 302p.
Latest edition, 1920.

1911

SPEAR, Raymond Herbert, editor.
The Commercial world encyclopedia of accounting. 2v.
First edition, 1908.

1920

AMERICAN SCHOOL OF CORRESPONDENCE, Chicago.
Accountancy and business management. 7v.
Vol.2 and v.4 based on v.4 and v.6 published in 1910.
First edition, 1910.

INTERNATIONAL TEXTBOOK COMPANY, Scranton.
The bookkeeper's handbook; 2d ed. 302p.
First edition, 1910.

1922

BIENVENU, Emile.
Accounting and business dictionary. 314p.

KOEHLER, Theodore, and KOEHLER, Theodora.
The accounting quiz-answerer. 12v.

1923

SALIERS, Earl Adolphus, editor.
Accountants' handbook. 1675p.
For second edition, see 1932, Paton, William Andrew.

1924

KILDUFF, Frederic W.
Auditing and accounting handbook. 813p.

1925

JONES, Edwin E., and others.
American business accounting. 3v.

1927

CROW, William Henry.
Corporation treasurer's and controller's guide. 1657p.

1931

AMERICAN INSTITUTE OF ACCOUNTANTS. Special committee on terminology.
Accounting terminology. 126p.

1932

PATON, William Andrew, editor.
Accountants' handbook; 2d ed. 1873p.
For first edition, see 1923, Saliers, Earl Adolphus.
For latest edition of Paton's Accountants' handbook, see 1934, Paton, William Andrew.

1934

ALFORD, Leon Pratt, editor.
Cost and production handbook. 1544p.

PATON, William Andrew, editor.
Accountants' handbook; 2d ed., rev. printing. 1742p.
For first printing of Paton's Accountants' handbook; 2d ed., see 1932, Paton, William Andrew

SUPPLEMENT: UNIFORM SYSTEMS

SUPPLEMENT: UNIFORM SYSTEMS

INTRODUCTION

ONE of the outstanding developments in accounting since the beginning of the 20th century is the increasing interest in uniform accounting systems and methods. Trade associations and other voluntary groups as well as federal and state government bureaus have sponsored uniform cost-finding methods and uniform systems of accounts for the benefit of the various businesses or professions which they serve. Coincident with the growth of uniform accounting practice among associated industries has been the development of uniformity in accounting procedure for public utilities under the jurisdiction of federal and state government regulatory bodies.

Several treatises and surveys on accounting activities of trade associations and works dealing with the social and economic significance of public utility regulation have been written in recent years, but nothing approximating a comprehensive classification of what has been accomplished in uniform accounting practice and procedure has ever been published. That there is need for such information will be acknowledged by those who are interested in this phase of accounting activity. In an attempt to meet this need the compilers of this bibliography present in the form of a supplement two classified lists which are designated as follows:

LIST 1 Alphabetical list of the businesses and professions for which uniform accounting systems, or some phase of uniformity in accounting practice and procedure, have been sponsored, with the names of the sponsors listed alphabetically under each heading.

LIST 2 Alphabetical list of the public utility industries for which uniform systems or uniform classifications of accounts have been prescribed, with the names of the federal or state government regulatory bodies listed alphabetically under each heading.

The following sources of information, in addition to correspondence with trade associations, private industrial organizations, and state utility commissions, have aided in the compilation of this Supplement:

LIBRARIES

American institute of accountants.

Chamber of commerce of the United States of America. Dept. of manufacture.

Columbia university. School of business.

Ford, Bacon & Davis, inc., Engineers, New York.

Harvard university. Graduate school of business administration.

National association of cost accountants.

Price, Waterhouse & co., New York.

U. S. Bureau of railway economics.

U. S. Library of Congress.

REFERENCE SOURCES

Brundage, Henry M.
The why, who and when of the National classification of accounts for gas and electric utilities: an address delivered before the Accounting section of the Wisconsin utilities association, Eau Claire, Wisconsin on Thursday, June 19, 1930. [N. Y. American gas association, 1930]

Saliers, Earl Adolphus.
Accountants' handbook. N. Y. Ronald, 1923.

U. S. Dept. of agriculture.
Index to Farmers' bulletins, nos. 1–1000. Wash. Govt. print. off. 1920.

—Index to Farmers' bulletins, nos. 1001–1500. Wash. Govt. print. off. 1929.

—List of publications of the U. S. department of agriculture from January, 1901, to December, 1925, inclusive. Wash. Govt. print. off. 1927.

U. S. Library of Congress. Division of documents.
Monthly check-list of state publications. 1910–1934. Wash. Govt. print. off. 1910–1934.

U. S. Office of experiment stations.
Experiment station record. 1889–1934. Wash. Govt. print. off. 1890–1934.

U. S. Superintendent of documents.
Catalogue of the public documents of Congress and of all departments of the government of the United States for the period March 4, 1893, to June 30, 1931. Wash. Govt. print. off. 1896–1934. 20v.

—Monthly catalogue United States public documents. 1895–1934. Wash. Govt. print. off. 1895–1934.

LIST 1

Alphabetical list of the businesses and professions for which uniform accounting systems, or some phase of uniformity in accounting practice and procedure, have been sponsored, with the names of the sponsors listed alphabetically under each heading.

INTRODUCTION

THERE are two types of organizations which have sponsored uniform accounting practice and procedure for the use of various lines of business: (1) private organizations, such as trade associations, professional and industrial organizations, accounting firms, etc., and (2) federal and state government bureaus.

The works sponsored by the *private organizations* have little general reference value. Until recently the publications were of a confidential nature and their distribution was restricted to associated members. Though recent publications have been available for sale to the public, their chief use has been within the association. The majority of systems are either out of print or not available to the public. In general, however, works published since 1930 may be obtained by writing to the sponsoring organizations.

This list is merely suggestive of the lines of business and the associations which have been interested in uniform accounting activities. Under each business is listed whenever known the latest name of the sponsoring organization, with the former name or names noted in parentheses. The titles of the works published are not recorded because they would add no reference value. The date of the first and latest publication, however, is recorded whenever known because it is of some interest to know approximately the period during which the association was engaged in some form of uniform accounting activity. Since this record is in most cases based upon the publications examined, it does not necessarily indicate the period during which systems may have been attempted but never published. Moreover, it is impossible to present a complete and accurate record of what has been done, since the extent to which the uniform systems were adopted and used by members cannot be determined.

Development of uniform accounting methods has received impetus under the National Industrial Recovery Act, the precise result of which cannot be ascertained at the present time. Where possible, each "code authority" which has proposed a uniform system of accounts for its industry is listed separately regardless of whether the system is sponsored by a trade association already listed or is an entirely new organization formed under the N. R. A.

The second type of organization included in List 1 is the *federal or state government bureau.* Such federal departments as the Department of Agriculture and the Bureau of Mines have prepared uniform systems of accounting for the industries which they serve. State government agencies, such as agricultural extension divisions and bureaus of business research connected with state universities, have also sponsored uniform accounting procedure for the benefit of private industry. These government agencies are included with the private sponsoring associations in order that both types of organization which have promoted uniform accounting systems for specific lines of business may be listed together. The bulletin number and date of publication are given. Federal documents may be secured from the Superintendent of Documents, Washington, D. C., and state documents, from the various issuing state government agencies, if they are in print. They are indexed in the various government document catalogs.

The two types of organizations which have sponsored uniform accounting systems have published other works closely related to accounting which are excluded from this Supplement. Though books on such subjects as cost studies, cost reports, and business statistics compiled for specific lines of business are of material assistance in establishing uniform accounting practice and procedure, they are omitted because they are not essentially "works on accounting." The same type of business and financial data that is omitted from the main bibliography is omitted from this Supplement. Reports recommending uniform accounting systems which were not adopted are excluded as well as articles appearing in periodicals outlining uniform accounting procedure.

Cost systems and accounting manuals prepared by individual businesses and government departments for their own use only, and accounting systems offered for sale by companies selling bookkeeping machines and other mechanical devices are omitted.

List 1

(The *see* and *see also* references in the Subject Index at the back of the book should be used to direct the reader to works on related or subordinate subjects in this list)

ADVERTISING AGENCIES

American association of advertising agencies.

AGRICULTURAL MACHINERY AND EQUIPMENT

Farm equipment institute (formerly National association of farm equipment manufacturers which superseded the National implement and vehicle association) 1916.

National federation of implement dealers associations.

AGRICULTURE

U. S. Dept. of agriculture. Agricultural economics bureau. Farmers' bulletin no.511, 1912; 1923. Farmers' bulletin no.572, 1914; 1928.

U. S. Dept. of agriculture. Farm management and farm economics office. Farmers' bulletin no.782, 1917; 1921.

U. S. Dept. of agriculture. Office of cooperative extension work. The federal act of 1914, providing for "cooperative agricultural extension work," obligates cooperation between the state agricultural colleges and the federal government for the benefit of farmers and householders. Many state extension offices connected with state colleges and universities have sponsored accounting systems for farmers and householders which have been usually no more than simple account books and instructions to aid in keeping records. The publications of the state extension offices and the experiment stations have been indexed in the Monthly check-list of state publications and also in the Agricultural index since 1916. References are also to be found in the Experiment station record. The publications may be secured from the various issuing agencies.

AGRICULTURE (continued)

U. S. Dept. of agriculture. Office of experiment stations.
The Hatch act provided for the promotion of scientific investigation and experiment in agricultural science through agricultural experiment stations many of which have published simple systems of accounting for farmers.
The publications of the state extension offices and the experiment stations have been indexed in the Monthly check-list of state publications and also in the Agricultural index since 1916. References are also to be found in the Experiment station record. The publications may be secured from the various issuing agencies.

AIR TRANSPORTATION

Aeronautical chamber of commerce of America, inc. 1931.

U. S. Post office dept. Air mail service. 1929 (System approved 1930)

ALCOHOL

Hardwood distillation industry. Code authority. 1934.

Industrial alcohol institute, inc. 1928.

ARCHITECTS

American institute of architects. (System in preparation)

AUTOMOBILES
(DEALER SYSTEMS)

Chrysler corporation, Detroit. 1925.

Dodge brothers, inc., Detroit. 1923. 1926.

Ernst & Ernst, certified public accountants, Cleveland. 1922. 1924 (Ford dealer system)

Franklin automobile company, Syracuse, N. Y. 1928.

General motors management service (formerly Motor accounting company, a subsidiary of General motors corporation, Detroit) 1923. 1930.

McCurdy, Frank B., co., Houston, Tex. 1923 (Ford accounting system)

Motor world wholesale, New York (formerly Motor world publishing company) 1918. 1925.

Nash motors company, Kenosha, Wis. 1928.

National automobile dealers association. 1927. 1928.

AUTOMOTIVE REPLACEMENT PARTS

National standard parts association. 1926.

AWNINGS AND TENTS

National tent and awning manufacturers association, inc. 1924.

BAKERIES

American association of the baking industry. 1922(?)

American bakers association (formerly National association of master bakers) 1917.

Associated bakers of America. 1932.

Biscuit and cracker manufacturers association. 1921(?)

BANKS

U. S. Federal reserve board. Circular 7, 1914.

BARRELS

Associated cooperage industries of America. 1918.

BATTERIES

Electric storage battery company, Philadelphia. (Dealer system)

National battery manufacturers association, inc. 1930.

National battery manufacturers association. Code authority. 1934.

BELTING

American leather belting association. 1932.

Leather belting exchange. 1916.

BOOKBINDING

Employing bookbinders of America. 1923. 1928.

BOOKSELLING

National association of book publishers. 1926. 1932.

BOTTLING

American bottlers of carbonated beverages. 1929.

BOXES

National association of corrugated and fibre box manufacturers.

National association of wooden box manufacturers. 1917.

Wirebound box manufacturers association. 1918. 1926.

BREWERIES

Goettsche, H. C., & co., certified public accountants, Chicago. 1933. 1934.

United States brewers association. 1934.

BRICKS

American face brick association. 1916. 1922.

Brick manufacturers association (formerly Common brick manufacturers association) 1923.

National paving brick manufacturers association. 1921.

BRUSHES

American brush manufacturers association.

BUILDING AND LOAN ASSOCIATIONS

American savings, building and loan institute. 1931. 1932.

Ohio. State university. College of commerce and business administration. Bureau of business research. 1928.

CANNING AND PRESERVING

California sardine processing industry. Code authority. 1934.

National canners association. 1917. 1927.

National pickle packers association.

CANVAS GOODS

Retail canvas goods industry. Code authority. 1934.

CAR WHEELS

Association of manufacturers of chilled car wheels. 1920.

CARPETS, RUGS, ETC.

Institute of carpet manufacturers of America, inc. 1935.

CARRIAGES AND WAGONS

Baby vehicle manufacturers association (formerly Go-cart association)

Carriage builders national association of the United States of America. 1914.

CARS

Railway car manufacturers association. 1918. 1923.

CASKETS

Casket manufacturers association of America.

CEMENT

Cement industry. Code authority. 1934.

Portland cement association (formerly Association of Portland cement manufacturers) 1917. 1927.

CHARITABLE AND PENAL INSTITUTIONS

Bureau of municipal research, New York. 1917.

Illinois. Board of public charities. 1902.

Illinois. Dept. of public welfare. 1911. 1918.

Illinois. General assembly. Efficiency and economy committee. 1914.

Mississippi. State accounting dept. 1924.

New Jersey. Dept. of institutions and agencies.

New York (State) Comptroller's office. 1919 (System for institutional farms)

Patterson, Teele and Dennis, accountants and auditors, New York.
System for the use of charitable institutions receiving money from the city of New York.
System for the use of Catholic charitable institutions in New York.

Washington (State) Division of municipal corporations (formerly Bureau of inspection and supervision of public offices) 1920.

CHEESE

Wisconsin. Dept. of agriculture. Bulletin, v.1, no.8, 1920.

Wisconsin. University. College of agriculture. Agricultural extension service. Circular no.233, 1929.

CLAY

Clay products association.
Structural clay products industry. Code authority.
Tentative system proposed but not accepted to date.

CLOTHING

Clothing design company, inc. 1932.

Coat and suit industry. Code authority.
Uniform accounting methods promoted under the code.

International association of garment manufacturers.
System still in use, 1933.

National cloak, suit and skirt manufacturers association. 1912.

COAL TRADE

Coal merchants association, Chicago. 1920.

National retail coal merchants association. 1922.

Philadelphia retail coal conference. 1929.

Shepard and Hutchison's uniform cost sheet for coal yards in Chicago. 1916.

U. S. Fuel administration. 1917.

Washington (State) University. Bulletin, General ser. no.138, 1920.

CODE AUTHORITY OFFICES

Retail solid fuel industry. Code authority. 1934.
Accounting system prepared by Counselor & Buchanan, certified public accountants, for the code authority office and the divisional code authorities for the Retail solid fuel industry, applicable to other code authority offices.

COFFEE

Associated coffee industries of America. National coffee code authority. 1934.

National coffee roasters association. 1927(?)

CONFECTIONERY

Midland club, Sioux Falls, S. D. 1919.

National confectioners association of the United States. 1916. 1929.

CONSTRUCTION

Associated general contractors of America. 1927.
Standard accounting methods promoted under the code for general contractors.

Concrete masonry industry. Code authority.
Tentative system proposed but not accepted to date.

Contractors association of Northern California. 1924.

CONTAINERS

Cigar container industry. Code authority. 1934.

Glass container association of America. 1926.

Tin can club. 1924.

COOPERATIVE STORES AND SOCIETIES

Co-operative league of the United States of America (formerly Co-operative league of America) 1918. 1920.

U. S. Dept. of agriculture. Office of markets and rural organization. Bulletin no.381, 1916.

COTTON GINS

U. S. Dept. of agriculture. Bureau of markets and crop estimates. Bulletin no.985, 1921.

COTTON MILLS

Cotton-textile institute, inc. 1928. 1933.
Uniform cost accounting activities promoted under the code.

National association of cotton manufacturers. 1922.

National association of finishers of cotton fabrics. 1917. 1919.

CREAMERIES

Iowa. State college of agriculture and mechanic arts. Agricultural experiment station. Circular no.68, 1921.

U. S. Dept. of agriculture. Office of markets and rural organization. Bulletin no.559, 1917.

U. S. Dept. of agriculture. Bureau of markets. Bulletin no.865, 1920.

Wisconsin. Dept. of markets. Bulletin, v.2, no.13, 1921.

CURTAINS, DRAPERIES, ETC.

Ready-made furniture slip covers manufacturing industry. Code authority.
Uniform cost formula approved under the code.

Novelty curtain, draperies, bedspreads, and novelty pillow industry. Code authority. 1934.

DENTAL EQUIPMENT AND SUPPLIES

American dental trade association. 1931.

DRUGS

American drug manufacturers association (formerly National association of manufacturers of medicinal products) 1927.

American pharmaceutical manufacturers association (formerly American association of pharmaceutical chemists) 1920. 1923.

Federal wholesale druggists association.

National wholesale druggists association. 1919.

DRY GOODS

Butler brothers, Chicago. (System for retailers)

DRY GOODS (continued)

National retail dry goods association. Controllers' congress. 1922. 1931.

Retail research association. 1927.

Wholesale dry goods institute. (In print, 1934)

DYEING AND CLEANING

American dyes institute. 1920.

National association of dyers and cleaners of the United States and Canada. 1925. 1934.

ELECTRIC CONSTRUCTION

Association of electragists, International (formerly National association of electrical contractors and dealers) 1917. 1925.

Keller-Pike company, Philadelphia.

ELECTRIC EQUIPMENT AND SUPPLIES

Artistic lighting equipment association. 1928(?)

Delco-light co., Dayton, Ohio. 1919 (Dealer system)

National council of lighting fixture manufacturers.

National electrical manufacturers association. 1917. 1931.
The electrical manufacturing industry under the code has set up as a standard the methods of accounting prepared by the National electrical manufacturers association.

National electrical wholesalers association (formerly Electrical supply jobbers association) 1918. 1922.

ELECTRIC LIGHT AND POWER COMPANIES

Edison electric institute (formerly National electric light association) 1908 (Uniform classification of expense accounts) 1910 (Complete classification) 1914 (Standard classification of accounts) 1932 (Public utility salvage accounting)

The present "Uniform classification of accounts for electrical utilities" recommended for adoption by the National association of railway (later railroad) and utilities commissioners was formulated with the cooperation of the N.E.L.A. and was officially approved by the N.E.L.A. in 1923.
(See List 2, Electric light and power companies)

General electric company, Schenectady, N. Y.

Illinois gas association in joint convention with Illinois electric railways association and Illinois state electric association.

ELECTRIC RAILWAYS

American transit association (organized in 1882 as the American street railway association the name of which was changed to American street and interurban railway association and in 1910 to American electric railway association) 1904. 1907.
The 1914 classification of accounts prescribed by the I.C.C. was adopted as a standard by the Association.
The Committee on standard classification of accounts cooperates with the Interstate commerce commission in rendering interpretations and decisions on the I.C.C. classification of accounts for electric railways.
(See List 2, Electric railways)

EMERY WHEELS

Grinding wheel manufacturers association of the United States and Canada. 1918.

ENGINEERS

American engineering council.

FAIRS

International association of fairs and expositions. 1927.

FERTILIZERS

National fertilizer association. 1916. 1927.

National fertilizer association. Fertilizer recovery committee. 1934.

FINANCE COMPANIES

American association of personal finance companies (formerly American association of small loan brokers; American industrial lenders) 1931.

National association of finance companies.

FIRE APPARATUS

Fire extinguishing appliance manufacturing industry. Code authority. 1934.

Motor fire apparatus manufacturing industry. Code authority. 1934.

FISHING TACKLE

Fishing tackle industry. Code committee. 1934.

FLAVORING EXTRACTS

Flavoring extract manufacturers association of the United States. 1918.

FLOOD CONTROL

Ohio. Miami conservancy district. Technical reports, pt.9, 1922.

FLOUR MILLS

Millers national federation. 1926. 1929.

U. S. Food administration. Milling division. 1917.

FORGING

American drop forging institute. 1919. 1924.

Drop forging industry. Code authority. 1934.

FOUNDRIES

American foundrymen's association. 1919. 1928.

Gray iron institute. 1930.

Ingot brass and bronze industry. Code authority.
Tentative system proposed but not accepted to date.

Malleable founders society (an organization of malleable iron founders for the conduct of matters within the scope of the N.R.A.) 1934.

Malleable iron research institute (formerly American malleable castings association) 1917. 1927.

National association of brass manufacturers. 1917(?)

National founders association. 1917.

Southern metal trades association. 1923(?)

Steel founders society of America. 1902. 1930.

FOUNDRY SUPPLIES

Foundry supply manufacturers association. 1917.

FRUIT

California fruit growers exchange.

Dried fruit association of California. 1931.

U. S. Dept. of agriculture. Office of markets and rural organization. Bulletin no.225, 1915.

U. S. Dept. of agriculture. Bureau of markets. Bulletin no.590, 1918.

U. S. Dept. of agriculture. Bureau of markets and crop estimates. Bulletin no.1006, 1921.

FUNERAL DIRECTORS

National funeral directors association of the United States and Canada. 1925.

National selected morticians.

FUR

American fox institute. 1932.

FURNITURE

Central bureau of dining table manufacturers.

Metal bed and spring bed institute. 1924.

National association of chair manufacturers. 1916. 1917(?)

National association of furniture manufacturers. 1924. 1931.

National association of piano bench and stool manufacturers. 1917.

National association of steel furniture manufacturers. 1918.

National association of table manufacturers. 1923(?)

National association of upholstered furniture manufacturers.

National bureau of metal and spring bed manufacturers. 1911.

Ohio. State university. College of commerce and journalism. Bureau of business research. Monograph no.2, 1926.

GARAGES AND SERVICE STATIONS

Motor world wholesale, New York (formerly Motor world publishing company) 1918. 1925.

GAS COMPANIES

American gas association (formed in 1918 by the union of the American gas institute and the National commercial gas association) 1914. 1919.
The present "Uniform classification of accounts for gas utilities" recommended for adoption by the National association of railway (later railroad) and utilities commissioners was formulated with the cooperation of the American gas association and was officially approved by the American gas association in 1923.
(See List 2, Gas companies)

Illinois gas association in joint convention with Illinois electric railways association and Illinois state electric association.

GAS EQUIPMENT AND SUPPLIES

Gas appliance institute. Code authority.
Uniform system approved under the code.

GLASS AND GLASSWARE

American association of flint and lime glass manufacturers, inc.

Glass container association of America (formerly National bottle manufacturers association) 1926.

Illuminating glassware guild.

Mirror manufacturers association. 1920.

National glass distributors association, eastern division (formerly Eastern association of glass distributors) 1919.

GLOVES AND MITTENS

National glove and mitten manufacturers association. 1925.

GOVERNMENT ACCOUNTING (NATIONAL, STATE, AND MUNICIPAL)

Bureau of municipal research, New York. 1910. 1920.

California. State dept. of finance. Division of budgets and accounts. 1930. 1932.

Cincinnati bureau of governmental research. 1928. 1930.
Report no.11, 1928, prepared by Searle, Oakey and Miller, certified public accountants.

Colorado taxpayers protective league. 1916.

Committee on uniform street and sanitation records, Chicago. 1931. 1933.

Illinois municipal league, Urbana, Ill. Bulletin no.21, 1927.

Montana. State examiner. 1917.

Municipal finance officers' association, Chicago. 1933.

National association of state auditors, comptrollers, and treasurers. 1926.

GOVERNMENT ACCOUNTING (continued)

National committee on municipal accounting, Chicago. Bulletin no.1, 1934. Bulletin no.2, 1934.

National economy league. Massachusetts state branch, inc., Boston. 1933.

Nebraska. Auditor of public accounts. 1924.

New Jersey. Commissioner of municipal accounts. 1923. 1927.

New York (State) Comptroller's office. 1913. 1928.

New York state conference of mayors and other municipal officials, Albany. 1933.

Oregon. Secretary of state. 1930.

Portland, Or. Dept. of public works. Bureau of standards. 1928.

Public administration service, Chicago. 1933.

U. S. Bureau of the census. 1904. 1906.

U. S. Federal civil works administration. 1934.

U. S. Federal emergency administration of public works. 1934.

Washington (State) Division of municipal corporations (formerly Bureau of inspection and supervision of public offices) 1920. 1921. 1928.

GRAIN ELEVATORS

U. S. Dept. of agriculture. Office of markets and rural organization. Bulletin no.236, 1915. Bulletin no.362, 1916. Markets document 2, 1916.

U. S. Dept. of agriculture. Bureau of markets. Bulletin no.811, 1919.

GROCERIES

Harvard university. Bureau of business research. Bulletin no.3, retail grocers, 1916; 1922. Bulletin no.8, wholesale grocers, 1916. (Cost studies and statistics omitted)

National retail grocers association.

National wholesale grocers association (in cooperation with Harvard university. Bureau of business research) 1916.

New York wholesale grocers association. 1923.

U. S. Federal trade commission. 1916. 1920.

GUNITE CONTRACTORS

Cement gun contractors association.

HARDWARE

Advertising federation of America (formerly Associated advertising clubs of the world) 1917 (Retail dealer system)

Harvard university. Bureau of business research.
Bulletin no.11, hardware retailers, 1918.
(Cost studies and statistics omitted)

Iron plumbing specialty manufacturers association. 1930.

National association of kitchen equipment manufacturers.

National retail hardware association. 1919(?)

HEATING AND VENTILATING EQUIPMENT

American oil burner association. 1927.

National association of manufacturers of heating and cooking appliances (formerly National association of stove manufacturers) 1917. Also, "Standard accounting practice" still in print, 1933.

National warm air heating and air conditioning association (formerly National warm air heating and ventilating association) 1921. 1931.

HIGHWAYS

American road builders association. 1932.

Associated Pennsylvania constructors. 1926.

U. S. Dept. of agriculture. Bulletin no.660, 1918.

HOSIERY AND UNDERWEAR

Hosiery code authority. 1934.

National association of hosiery and underwear manufacturers. 1922(?) 1933.

HOSPITALS

American hospital association. 1921. 1926.

Cleveland hospital council. 1932 (Modified system based on that of the American hospital association)

Duke endowment. Hospital section, Charlotte, N. C. 1929.

Hospital Saturday and Sunday association of St. Louis. 1908.

New York (City) Bellevue and allied hospitals. 1915.

Pennsylvania. Dept. of public welfare. Bulletin no.2, 1922.

United hospital fund of New York. New York conference on hospital accounting (formerly Hospital Saturday and Sunday association) 1933.

HOTELS

Hotel association of New York City. 1926. 1933 (Uniform system . . . as prescribed by the American hotel association of the United States and Canada and the Hotel association of New York City)

United hotels company of America. 1926.

HOUSING PROJECTS

New York (State) Dept. of public works. Division of architecture. Board of housing. 1929.

ICE

National association of ice industries (in 1919 the Natural ice association of America united with the National association of ice industries) 1913. 1919.

ICE CREAM

International association of ice cream manufacturers (formerly the National association of ice cream manufacturers) 1925. 1926.

INSURANCE

U. S. Dept. of agriculture. Office of farm management. Bulletin no.840, 1920.

JEWELRY AND SILVERWARE

Advertising federation of America (formerly Associated advertising clubs of the world) 1916 (Retail dealer system)

American national retail jewelers association. 1920.

Ingersoll, Robt. H. & bro. 1913. 1918 (Retail dealer system)

New England manufacturing jewelers and silversmiths association. 1921. 1932.

Silverware manufacturing industry. Code authority. 1934.

Sterling silversmiths guild of America (formerly Sterling silverware manufacturers association) 1919.

KNIT GOODS

Associated knit underwear manufacturers of America. 1917. 1924.

Knit goods manufacturers of America. 1917. 1925.

National knitted outerwear association. 1924.

LACE

American lace manufacturers association. Code authority. 1934.

LAUNDRIES

Laundryowners national association of the United States and Canada. 1920. 1931.

LAUNDRY MACHINES

American washing machine manufacturers association. 1922.

Washing and ironing machine manufacturers industry committee. 1934.

LEATHER GOODS

Luggage and fancy leather goods industry. Code authority. 1933.

LIVE STOCK

Iowa. State college of agriculture and mechanic arts. Agricultural experiment station. Bulletin no.209, 1922.

Missouri. University. College of agriculture. Agricultural extension service. Circular 161, 1925.

Texas. University. Bureau of business research. Research monograph no.5, 1930.

U. S. Dept. of agriculture. Office of markets and rural organization. Bulletin no.403, 1916.

U. S. Dept. of agriculture. Agricultural economics bureau. Bulletin no.1150, 1923.

Wisconsin. Dept. of agriculture. Bulletin, v.1, no.4, 1920.

LOGGING

News print service bureau. 1922.

LUMBER

California white and sugar pine manufacturers association.

Millwork cost bureau. 1916. 1917.

National retail lumber dealers association. 1924.

National veneer and panel manufacturers association (with Plywood manufacturers association cooperating) 1922.

North Carolina pine association. 1917.

Northeastern retail lumbermen's association.

Retail lumber and building material code authority. 1934.

Shaw, A. W., company, Chicago. Bureau of business standards. 1920(?)

U. S. Dept. of agriculture. Office of markets and rural organization. Markets document 2, 1916.

West coast lumbermen's association. 1919.

MACARONI

National macaroni manufacturers association. 1930.
(In 1923 a system was published under the supervision of the National macaroni manufacturers association by National cereal products laboratories)

MACHINERY AND MACHINE TOOLS

American boiler manufacturers association. 1920.
Now use the system of the Machinery builders society.

American gear manufacturers association. 1920.

Conveyor machinery manufacturers association. 1916.

Electric overhead crane institute. 1928(?)

Gear manufacturing industry. Code authority. 1934.

Hydraulic society. 1919.
Now use the system of the Machinery builders society.

Machinery builders society. 1922. 1933.

National machine tool builders association. 1912. 1931.

Screw machine products institute (formerly Screw machine products association) 1924(?) 1929.

Stoker manufacturers association.

MEAT DEALERS

Northwestern university. School of commerce. Bureau of business research. 1923.

MEAT DEALERS (continued)

U. S. Dept. of agriculture. Bureau of agricultural economics. 1922. 1924.

MEAT PACKERS

Institute of American meat packers (formerly American meat packers association) 1920. 1929.

METAL WORK

National association of ornamental iron, bronze and wire manufacturers. 1930.

MILK

International association of milk dealers. 1923. 1931.

MILK SUBSTITUTES

American dry milk institute, inc. 1929.

MINING, COAL

Anthracite institute (formerly Anthracite operators' conference) 1919 (System prepared for the General policies committee of the Anthracite operators by R. H. Montgomery and R. V. Norris)

National coal association. 1919.

United mine workers of America. 1923.

MINING, METAL

Lake Superior iron ore association. 1920. 1923.

U. S. Bureau of mines. Technical paper 223, 1919. Technical paper 250, 1920. Bulletin 372, 1934.

MONUMENTS

Memorial craftsmen of America, inc.

MOTION PICTURES

Motion picture producers and distributors of America, inc.

MOTOR BUS TRANSPORTATION

American transit association (organized in 1882 as the American street railway association the name of which was changed to American street and interurban railway association and in 1910 to American electric railway association. American electric railway accountants association is an affiliated organization) 1925. 1926.
The two uniform classifications of accounts for bus companies promulgated by the A.E.R.A. were adopted by the National association of railway (later railroad) commissioners in 1926.
(See List 2, Motor transportation companies)

Main and company, certified public accountants, Pittsburgh. 1926.

Motor bus code authority. 1933.
Adopted the classification of accounts recommended by the members of the Accounting committee of the National association of motor bus operators representing independently owned bus operating companies.

MOTOR TRUCK TRANSPORTATION

Automobile journal publishing co., Pawtucket, R. I. 1919.

Commercial vehicle, New York. 1916.

Edison electric institute (formerly National electric light association) 1932.

Firestone ship-by-truck bureau. 1920.

Motor truck association of America. 1932.

New York (State) University. Bureau of business research and New York wholesale grocers association. 1924.

Purdue university. Engineering experiment station. Bulletin, v.7, no.1, 1923.

Truck owners conference, inc. 1920.

MUSIC TRADE

Music industries chamber of commerce. 1923.

NEWSPAPERS

United typothetae of America. 1924 (Adaptation of the system prepared for printers)

OIL

American petroleum institute. 1926. 1931.

National petroleum publishing company. 1924.

Pearce and Granata, certified public accountants, Chicago.

U. S. Bureau of mines. Bulletin 158, Petroleum technology 43, 1917.

OPTICAL EQUIPMENT AND SUPPLIES

American association of wholesale opticians. 1921.

Optical manufacturers association. 1918.

PAINTS AND VARNISHES

American paint and varnish manufacturers association (formed in 1926 by the merger of the Paint manufacturers association of the United States and the National varnish manufacturers association) 1917. 1924.

Paint industry recovery board. 1934.

PAPER

Abrasive paper and cloth manufacturers exchange.

American paper and pulp association.
The following affiliated organizations have published systems of accounting:
Bureau of envelope manufacturers of America.
Cost association of the paper industry. 1921. 1923.
Cover paper manufacturers association. 1918.
Glazed and fancy paper manufacturers. 1923.

Sulphite paper manufacturers association.
Tentative system proposed by the code authority but not accepted to date.
Writing paper manufacturers association. 1920(?)

Corrugated fibre company, Dayton, Ohio. 1916.

Label manufacturers national association (in cooperation with the Folding box manufacturers national association and National association of employing lithographers) 1919.

National association of loose leaf manufacturers. 1916.

National paper trade association of the United States. 1920.

News print service bureau. 1919. 1926.

Paper distributing trade code authority. 1934.

Paper stationery and tablet manufacturers association. 1934.

Rope paper sack manufacturers association. 1916.

Wrapping paper manufacturers association. 1916.

Writing tablet manufacturers association. 1918.

PAPER BOXES

National federation of paper box manufacturers association. 1917.

National paper box manufacturers association. 1922. 1933.

Paperboard industries association (organized in 1925 to cover the former activities of the National container association, Box board association, and Folding box manufacturers national association) 1924. 1929.

PENCILS

Lead pencil institute, inc.

PERSONAL AND HOUSEHOLD ACCOUNTING

Many state documents on accounting for householders prepared and sponsored by state extension offices in cooperation with the U.S.

PERSONAL AND HOUSEHOLD ACCOUNTING (continued)

Department of agriculture are not listed because they are usually no more than simple account books and instructions to aid in keeping records. These publications are indexed in the Monthly checklist of state publications and may be secured from the various issuing agencies.

PHOTOGRAPHIC STUDIOS

Eastman kodak company, Rochester, N. Y.

PLUMBING AND HEATING

Heating and piping contractors national association (formerly National association of heating and piping contractors)

National association of master steam and hot water fitters.

Plumbing and drainage specialty manufacturers association (formerly Plumbing and heating industries bureau which was the National trade extension bureau of the plumbing and heating industries) 1920. 1928 (The standard accounting system created by the bureau is now being distributed by the National association of master plumbers of the United States, inc.)

Power piping society. 1921 (?)

POULTRY

U. S. Dept. of agriculture. Bureau of animal husbandry. Circular 176, 1911.

U. S. Dept. of agriculture. Animal industry bureau. Farmers' bulletin no.1427, 1924 (Revision of circular 176)

U. S. Dept. of agriculture. Office of cooperative extension work. See note under the above office (listed under Agriculture) for information which applies to poultry accounting.

U. S. Dept. of agriculture. Office of experiment stations. See note under the above office (listed under Agriculture) for information which applies to poultry accounting.

PRINTING

American photo-engravers association (formerly International association of manufacturing photo-engravers) 1916. 1933.

American printers cost commission. 1910. 1913 (Adopted by the United typothetae of America in 1911)

Ben Franklin clubs of America. 1908.

Cost division of the color printing and lithographing industries. 1919. 1925.
(In 1920 the cost accounting activities of the National association of employing lithographers were consolidated with those of the Label manufacturers national association and the Folding box manufacturers, the activities of which have since operated under the name of Cost division of the color printing and lithographing industries)

Engraved stationery manufacturers association. 1921.

Engravographia. 1922.

International association of electrotypers of America.

National lithographic printing code authority. 1934.

Periodical publishers institute. Business publishers division.
Uniform system prepared under the code for graphic arts industries.

Printers board of trade of Philadelphia. 1909.

United typothetae of America. 1918. 1933.

United typothetae of America. National code authority of the commercial relief printing industry. 1934.

PRINTING INK

National association of printing ink makers. 1934.
Printing ink cost bureau. 1925. 1927(?)

PUBLISHING

Associated business papers, inc. 1932.

Book manufacturing industry. National code authority. 1934.

RADIO BROADCASTING STATIONS

National association of broadcasters, inc. 1929. 1932.

RADIO MANUFACTURE

Radio manufacturers association.
Uses system of the National electrical manufacturers association, listed under Electric equipment and supplies.

RAILROADS

Railway accounting officers association (formerly Association of American railway accounting officers)
From its organization in 1888 to the present time this association has been consistently "the clearing house of railway accounting ideas and experiences."
(See List 2, Railroads)

REAL ESTATE

Building managers association of Chicago. 1921. 1922.

National association of building owners and managers. 1922. 1925.

National association of real estate boards. 1931.

REFRACTORIES

American refractories institute (formerly Refractories manufacturers association) 1925.

REFRIGERATORS AND REFRIGERATING MACHINERY

Kelvinator sales corporation, Detroit. (Dealer system)

National refrigerator manufacturers association. 1931.

Refrigerating machinery association.

RESTAURANTS

National restaurant association. 1930.

ROOFING

Prepared roofing association.

RUBBER GOODS

Rubber manufacturers association, inc. (formerly Rubber association of America, inc.) 1920. 1933.

Rubber wire group (formerly association) 1918.

SAFES AND VAULTS

National association of safe and vault manufacturers. 1919.

SAND AND GRAVEL

Illinois concrete aggregate association. 1922.

National sand and gravel association (formerly National association of sand and gravel producers) 1930. 1933.

SAWMILLS

Hardwood manufacturers institute, inc. 1925.

SCHOOL SUPPLIES

National school supply association. 1921. 1925.

SCHOOLS, PUBLIC

Indiana. State board of accounts. 1924. 1931.

Iowa. Dept. of public instruction. Research bulletin no.15, 1934.

Iowa. University. Studies in education, v.3, no.1, First series no. 97, 1925.

SCHOOLS, PUBLIC (continued)

New York (State) University. 1916. 1934.

Ohio. Bureau of inspection and supervision of public offices. 1914.

Oklahoma. Dept. of education. Division of research and service. Bulletin no.135, 1933.

Pennsylvania. Dept. of public instruction. 1920.

Pittsburgh. Board of public education. 1913.

South Dakota. Dept. of public instruction. Committee on city school accounting. Bulletin no.5, 1931.

U. S. Bureau of the census. 1911.

Washington (State) Division of municipal corporations (formerly Bureau of inspection and supervision of public offices) 1915. 1920.

Wisconsin. University. Bureau of educational research. Bulletin no.4, 1924.

SEED TRADE

American seed trade association. 1925.

SHEET METAL WORK

Metalware institute, inc. 1928. 1930.

National association of sheet metal contractors of the United States. 1930.

National association of sheet and tin plate manufacturers. 1927.

Pressed metal institute (formerly association) 1917.
"A new one being prepared, 1931."

Sheet metalware association. 1919.

SHIPBUILDING

Atlantic coast shipbuilders association. 1919.

Shipbuilding and ship-repairing industry. Code authority.
Standard accounting methods promoted under the code.

SHOE REPAIRING

National leather and shoe finders association. 1917. 1933.

SHOES

Advertising federation of America (formerly Associated advertising clubs of the world) 1916 (Retail dealer system)

Harvard university. Bureau of business research. Bulletin no.2, shoe retailers, 1914; 1917. Bulletin no.6, shoe wholesalers, 1916. (Cost studies and statistics omitted)

National boot and shoe manufacturers association. 1919. 1924.

National shoe retailers association.

SILK

National federation of textiles, inc. (formerly Silk association of America, inc.) 1928. 1929.

Throwing industry code committee. 1934.

SLATE INDUSTRY

National slate association.

U. S. Bureau of mines. 1929.

SOCIAL AGENCIES

Wieboldt foundation, Chicago. 1924.

SOCIETIES, ASSOCIATIONS, ETC.

Chicago district golf association. 1918.

National federation of business and professional women's clubs, inc. 1930(?) 1933.

Treasurers society, Washington, D. C. 1926.

Young men's Christian association. 1919. 1928.

SPICE TRADE

American spice trade association.

STAMP AND DIE WORKS

International stamp manufacturers association. 1922.
(Various systems were prepared by Litle, Goodwin and company, financial and industrial accountants, Pittsburgh, and copyrighted by the International stamp manufacturers association)

STATIONERY TRADE

Bank and commercial stationery industry. 1934.

Engraved stationery manufacturers association. 1921.

National association of stationers and manufacturers of the U. S. A. 1915.

Paper stationery and tablet manufacturers association, inc. 1934.

STEEL BARRELS

Steel barrel manufacturers council (formerly Steel barrel manufacturers institute) 1920(?)

STEEL, STRUCTURAL

American institute of steel construction, inc. 1924.

Iron league of New York. 1924.

STONE INDUSTRIES

Greater New York cut stone contractors association. 1923.

Indiana cut stone club (in 1934 replaced by the Regional committee of the code authority for the limestone industry)

Limestone industry. Code authority. 1933.

National crushed stone association, inc. 1931.

National lime association (formerly National lime manufacturers association and Lime association) 1919.

STORE FIXTURES

National commercial fixture manufacturers association. 1922.

National retail dry goods association. Controllers' congress. Metropolitan controllers' association. 1931.

TAILORING

National association of merchant tailors of America. 1917.

TANNERIES

Tanners council of America. 1922 (Individual systems prepared for various divisions of the tanning industry)

TAXICAB COMPANIES

National association of taxicab owners. 1924.

TELEPHONE COMPANIES

American telephone and telegraph company. 1910. 1912 (effective January 1, 1913)

United States independent telephone association. 1926. 1929.

TERRA COTTA

National terra cotta society. 1917.

TEXTILES

National association of finishers of textile fabrics. 1934.

Textile bag manufacturers association. 1929.

Textile converters association. 1930.

THEATERS

Universal chain theatres corporation, New York. 1932.

TILES

Associated tile manufacturers, inc. 1919.

Structural clay tile association (formerly Hollow building tile association) 1925.

Tile contracting division of the construction industry. Code authority. 1934.

TIN PLATE

National association of sheet and tin plate manufacturers. 1927.

TIRES
(DEALER SYSTEMS)

Goodrich, B. F., company, Akron, Ohio.

Goodyear tire & rubber co., inc., Akron, Ohio.

United States rubber products, inc., Dayton, Ohio. 1932.

TUBES

Collapsible tube manufacturers institute (formerly National association of collapsible tube manufacturers) 1921.

WAREHOUSES

American warehousemen's association. 1918. 1921.

Association of refrigerated warehouses. 1921.

Merchandise warehousing trade. Code authority. 1934.

Michigan. State college of agriculture and applied science. Agricultural extension division. Bulletin no.106, 1930.

National furniture warehousemen's association. 1923(?)

National retail dry goods association. Controllers' congress. 1927.

U. S. Dept. of agriculture. Bulletin no.520, 1917.

Wisconsin. Dept. of markets. Bulletin, v.1, no.5, 1920. Bulletin, v.6, no.6, 1925.

WATER WORKS

American water works association. 1911 (Arranged by representatives of the United States bureau of the census, American water works association, New England water works association, American association of public accountants, Ohio bureau of uniform public accounting, and others)

WEBBING

Webbing manufacturers exchange. 1919.

WOODWORKING

Associated wooden ware manufacturers.

Hickory handle association. 1923.

National association of mopstick manufacturers. 1929(?)

National association of wood turners, inc. 1923.

WOOLENS AND WORSTEDS

Wool institute, inc. 1928.

LIST 2

Alphabetical list of the public utility industries for which uniform systems or uniform classifications of accounts have been prescribed, with the names of the federal or state government regulatory bodies listed alphabetically under each heading.

INTRODUCTION

THIS list consists of industries which are known as "public utilities" because their undertakings are characterized as having "public interest." They consist mainly of two types: the *common carriers,* such as electric and steam railways, express, sleeping car, telephone and telegraph, cable, pipe line, and automotive companies; and the *local utilities,* such as electric light and power companies, gas companies, and water works.

The purpose of this list is to record the progress of one important phase of public utility regulation, that of developing uniformity in accounting procedure for public utilities. Under each industry is listed alphabetically the names of the federal and state commissions which have prescribed uniform systems or uniform classifications of accounts for the public utilities under their jurisdiction. Since the recording of the titles would have no particular value for reference purposes, they are omitted. The date represents the year in which the classification of accounts prescribed became effective. Though this is a *20th century bibliography,* the federal and state commissions which prescribed classifications of accounts before 1901 are listed in order to have a complete record of what has been done and to give credit to the pioneers in this field.

Among the common carriers the steam railroads were the first to have their accounting practices regulated. The Massachusetts Board of Railway Commissioners received in 1876 the first grant of authority over railway accounts. The "uniform system" prescribed, however, was far from complete.

The 20th section of the Act to Regulate Commerce, enacted in 1887, authorized the Interstate Commerce Commission to prescribe for utilities under its jurisdiction "a uniform system of accounts and the manner in which such accounts shall be kept" and to require certain specific reports. The law, however, contained no provision for enforcement until 1906 when Congress made uniform accounts compulsory. In the meantime various state commissions prescribed their own "uniform classifications of accounts" for railroads and other common carriers under their jurisdiction, and these are listed where it is possible to determine what was prescribed independently by the various states. Publications, however, reprinting the "I.C.C. Classification" for use in various states are omitted because they are a duplication of reference material.

The jurisdiction of the Interstate Commerce Commission, formerly limited to the regulation of rail and joint rail and water carriers, was extended in 1906 to include express and sleeping car companies and pipe lines and, in 1910, to include telephone, telegraph, and cable companies. To avoid conflict of authority and duplication of effort many state commissions accepted the accounting rules of the Interstate Commerce Commission for the utilities engaged in both state and interstate commerce. These states and the states which have prescribed accounting regulations supplementing the "I.C.C. Classification" are not listed. States which have prescribed a different or modified classification of accounts for common carriers since the year in which the "I.C.C. Classification" was prescribed are listed.

The first state to prescribe a uniform classification of accounts for local utilities was Massachusetts which prescribed a system for gas companies in 1886 and one for electric companies in 1887. The uniform classifications of accounts for electric light and power companies and for gas companies prescribed by the Wisconsin and New York commissions in 1908 were, however, the beginning of the modern movement toward uniformity in accounting methods and procedure for local utilities regulated by state commissions. The separate efforts of the many states during the next decade resulting in many and varied interpretations of accounts tended to nullify the advantages of the uniform accounting practices prescribed by the separate states. To remedy this situation the utilities commissioners worked together for several years to bring about national uniformity in the classification of accounts for local utilities.

At the annual meeting of the National Association of Railway (later Railroad) and Utilities Commissioners held in November, 1920, uniform classifications of accounts for electric and gas utilities were recommended for adoption by the state commissions, and at the annual meeting in 1922 they were revised. The uniform classification of accounts for water utilities was recommended for adoption by state commissions at the annual meeting in 1921, and the uniform classification of accounts for bus companies, in 1926. In 1930 the association recommended for adoption a uniform classification of accounts for natural gas companies.

The National Association of Railroad and Utilities Commissioners is not a legislative body. It consists of the commissioners of all the states (except Delaware which has no commission) and the District of Columbia who hold annual meetings for the discussion of problems relating to public utility regulation in the various states. The classifications formulated in 1920 and revised in 1922 have served as a basis for other state classifications, for the Federal Power Commission's system of accounts, and for the accounting procedure of many operating companies located within states which have not adopted a uniform classification of accounts.

Each classification of accounts prescribed for a local utility under the jurisdiction of the state, together with its effective date and the effective date of each revision if any, is listed under the state. The "N.A.R.U.C. Classification," together with the date that it was put into effect, is listed under each state which adopted it. If a state is not listed under any local utility industry, it may be assumed that it prescribed neither its own classification of accounts nor the "N.A.R.U.C. Classification" for that industry.

Such works as orders, instructions, rules, regulations, interpretations, circulars, reports, and decisions issued from time to time to supplement the accounting systems are omitted from consideration in this list.

The publications of the federal commissions can be secured from the Superintendent of Documents, Washington, D. C., and those issued by the state commissions can be obtained, if they are in print, from the various state offices.

List 2

(The *see* and *see also* references in the Subject Index at the back of the book should be used to direct the reader to works on related and subordinate subjects in this list)

Date=Effective date.
N.A.R.U.C. classification=The classification recommended for adoption by the National association of railway (later railroad) and utilities commissioners.

ELECTRIC LIGHT AND POWER COMPANIES

Alabama. Public service commission.
N.A.R.U.C. classification adopted. 1924.

Arizona. Corporation commission.
Electric corporations. 1914.
N.A.R.U.C. classification adopted. 1926.

Arkansas. Corporation commission.
N.A.R.U.C. classification adopted. 1935.

California. Railroad commission.
Electric corporations. 1913.
Electrical corporations, class A (having annual operating revenues exceeding $250,000) 1923 (superseding the 1913 classification)
The 1923 classification was predicated upon and is substantially the same as the Federal power commission's uniform system of accounts. The California system has not been modified since 1923, except in one instance.
Electrical corporations, class B and class C. 1926.

Colorado. Public utilities commission.
Electric light and power utilities. 1916.
N.A.R.U.C. classification adopted. 1924.

Connecticut. Public utilities commission.
N.A.R.U.C. classification adopted. 1924.

District of Columbia. Public utilities commission.
Influenced by the accounting methods of the Interstate commerce commission and the Federal power commission under the jurisdiction of Congress.
N.A.R.U.C. classification adopted. 1930.

ELECTRIC LIGHT AND POWER COMPANIES (continued)

Georgia. Public service commission.
N.A.R.U.C. classification adopted. 1924.

Idaho. Public utilities commission.
Electric light and power companies. 1914.
N.A.R.U.C. classification adopted. 1923.

Illinois. Commerce commission (successor in 1921 to the Public utilities commission)
Electric utilities. 1919.
N.A.R.U.C. classification adopted (with minor modifications) 1923.

Indiana. Public service commission.
Electric utilities. 1913. 1920 (revised issue)
Electric utilities, class C, simplified method. 1924.
N.A.R.U.C. classification adopted (optional with utility) 1924.

Kansas. State corporation commission (successor in 1933 to the Public service commission which in 1925 superseded the Public utilities commission)
N.A.R.U.C. classification adopted. 1923.

Kentucky. Public service commission.
N.A.R.U.C. classification with modifications (being prepared for adoption, 1935)

Louisiana. Public service commission.
N.A.R.U.C. classification adopted. 1927.

Maine. Public utilities commission.
Electrical companies. 1915. 1917 (revised issue)
Electrical utilities. 1924.
N.A.R.U.C. classification not adopted but the classification prescribed in 1924 follows it closely, in some respects. Depreciation requirements differ.

Maryland. Public service commission.
Electrical corporations. 1911.
N.A.R.U.C. classification adopted. 1930.

Massachusetts. Board of gas and electric light commissioners (successor in 1887 to the Board of gas commissioners, established in 1885)
Electric companies. 1887.

Massachusetts. Dept. of public utilities (formed in 1919 by the consolidation of the Public service commission and the Board of gas and electric light commissioners)
Gas and electric companies. 1921. 1927 (revised issue) 1934 (revised issue)
N.A.R.U.C. classification followed closely but with modifications.
Municipal lighting plants. 1922. 1934 (revised issue)

Michigan. Public utilities commission (successor in 1919 to the Railroad commission)
Electric light and power utilities. 1915.
N.A.R.U.C. classification adopted. 1923.

Missouri. Public service commission.
Electrical corporations and municipalities. 1915. 1932 (1st revised issue)

Montana. Board of railroad commissioners (ex-officio Public service commission)
Electric utilities. 1913. 1919 (revised issue) 1922 (revised issue)

National association of railway (later railroad) and utilities commissioners.
Uniform system of accounts for electrical corporations, prepared by Committee on statistics and accounts of public utilities and recommended for adoption by state commissions at the annual meeting of the National association of railway and utilities commissioners in Washington, November 12, 1920.
Revised issue recommended for adoption at the annual meeting of the National association of railway and utilities commissioners held in Detroit, Mich., November, 1922. "Revision of 1922."
The "N.A.R.U.C. classification."

Nevada. Public service commission.
Electric utilities. 1911.
N.A.R.U.C. classification adopted. 1924.

New Hampshire. Public service commission.
Electric utilities. 1914. 1917 (revised issue) 1925 (revised issue)
Electric utilities (a new classification to be made effective, Jan. 1, 1935)

New Jersey. Board of public utility commissioners.
Electric light, heat, and power utilities. 1912. 1915 (revised issue)
N.A.R.U.C. classification adopted. 1925.

ELECTRIC LIGHT AND POWER COMPANIES (continued)

New York (State) Public service commission. 1st district.
Electrical corporations. 1909. 1919.

New York (State) Public service commission. 2d district.
Electrical corporations. 1909.
Electrical corporations, condensed scheme for corporations having gross operating revenues from electric operations amounting to less than $500,000 per annum. 1909.
Electrical corporations, second condensed scheme for corporations having gross operating revenues from electric operations amounting to less than $100,000 per annum. 1909.
Electrical corporations, third condensed scheme for corporations having gross operating revenues from electric operations amounting to less than $25,000 per annum. 1909.
The uniform systems of accounts prescribed by the Public service commission, 1st district, and the Public service commission, 2d district (listed above) superseded by the classification established by the Public service commission (listed below).

New York (State) Dept. of public service. Public service commission.
N.A.R.U.C. classification adopted (with minor modifications) 1924.
Electric corporations (all classes) 1934.
Tentative draft, 1933.
Superseded the N.A.R.U.C. classification.
Municipal electric utilities (tentative draft only, 1934)

North Carolina. Utilities commission (successor in 1934 to the Corporation commission which prescribed the system listed below)
N.A.R.U.C. classification adopted (with additional information required) 1931.

North Dakota. Board of railroad commissioners.
N.A.R.U.C. classification adopted. 1922.

Ohio. Public utilities commission.
Electric utilities. 1915.

Oklahoma. Corporation commission.
Public service companies. 1910.
Gas and electric utilities. 1922.
Electric and natural gas utilities. 1927.

Oregon. Public utilities commissioner (successor in 1931 to the Public service commission which in 1915 succeeded the Railroad commission)
Electric utilities. 1913.
Electric utilities, class D (abbreviated classification) 1915.
N.A.R.U.C. classification adopted (with minor modifications) 1925.

Pennsylvania. Public service commission.
Electric companies. 1919.
Tentative draft, 1917.

Rhode Island. Public utilities commission.
Prescribed a form for the annual reports of public utilities operating in the state. 1923.
(Does not have a "system")

South Carolina. Railroad commission. Electrical utilities division.
N.A.R.U.C. classification adopted.

Tennessee. Railroad and public utilities commission.
N.A.R.U.C. classification adopted. 1922.

U. S. Federal power commission.
System of accounts for licensees under the Federal water power act. 1922.
Tentative draft, 1921.

U. S. Interstate commerce commission.
Gas corporations and electric corporations in the District of Columbia. 1909.

Utah. Public utilities commission (successor to the Public service commission)
N.A.R.U.C. classification adopted. 1922.

Vermont. Public service commission.
N.A.R.U.C. classification adopted. 1929.
Adopted only for the use of companies having annual operating revenues in excess of $10,000 a year averaged over a period of five years.

Virginia. State corporation commission.
N.A.R.U.C. classification adopted. 1921.

Washington (State) Dept. of public works (successor to the Public service commission)
Electrical corporations, class C. 1922.
N.A.R.U.C. classification adopted. 1924.

ELECTRIC LIGHT AND POWER COMPANIES (continued)

Washington (State) Division of municipal corporations (successor in 1921 to the Bureau of inspection and supervision of public offices which prescribed the system listed below)
Municipal electric light and power utilities. 1916.

West Virginia. Public service commission.
N.A.R.U.C. classification adopted (with minor modifications) 1923.
Classification for income accounts revised, 1932.

Wisconsin. Public service commission (successor to the Railroad commission which prescribed the systems listed below)
Electric utilities, class A and class B. 1908. 1909 (revised issue, correcting ambiguities and defining terms more closely) 1912 (class C added)
N.A.R.U.C. classification adopted for class A and class B (with minor modifications) 1923.
Electric utilities, class A, partially revised (to account for Depreciation) 1932.
Electric utilities, class C. 1912.
Electric utilities, class C and class D. 1926.
New classification. For class C this supersedes the 1912 classification.

Wyoming. Public service commission.
N.A.R.U.C. classification adopted. 1923.

ELECTRIC RAILWAYS

New Jersey. Board of public utility commissioners.
Street or traction railway utilities. 1912. 1919 (revised issue to conform to the I.C.C. classification)

New York (State) Dept. of public service. Metropolitan division. Transit commission (successor in 1921 to the New York Public service commission, 1st district, which prescribed the 1909 classification listed below)
Street railway companies. 1909.

New York (State) Dept. of public service. Public service commission (successor in 1921 to the New York Public service commission, 2d district, which prescribed the classifications listed below)
Street railroad corporations. 1909.
Street railroad corporations, condensed scheme for corporations

having gross operating revenues from street railroad operations amounting to less than $500,000 per annum. 1909.

Street railroad corporations, second condensed scheme for corporations having gross operating revenues from street railroad operations amounting to less than $100,000 per annum. 1909.

Electric railroad corporations. 1919.

Follows closely the I.C.C. classification with modifications to comply with the New York statutes.

U. S. Interstate commerce commission.

The American transit association (formerly American electric railway association) cooperates with the I.C.C. in rendering interpretations and decisions on the I.C.C. classification of accounts.

Electric railways:

Expenditures for road and equipment. 1908.

Operating expenses. 1908.

Operating revenues. 1908.

Uniform system of accounts. 1914.

Orders, instructions, rules, regulations, interpretations, decisions, etc. issued from time to time to supplement the accounting classifications for electric railways are not listed. They are indexed in the Monthly catalogue of United States public documents and may be obtained from the Superintendent of documents, Washington, D. C.

Washington. Division of municipal corporations (successor in 1921 to the Bureau of inspection and supervision of public offices which prescribed the system listed below)

Municipal street railways. 1921.

Wisconsin. Public service commission (successor to the Railroad commission which prescribed the system listed below)

Electric railroads. 1909. 1912 (revised issue with no material changes)

EXPRESS COMPANIES

U. S. Interstate commerce commission.

Express companies:

Expenditures for real property and equipment. 1908.

Operating expenses. 1908.

Operating revenues. 1908.

Form of general balance sheet statement. 1911.

Uniform system of accounts. 1914.

Orders, instructions, rules, regulations, interpretations, decisions, etc. issued from time to time to supplement the accounting classifications for express companies are not listed. They are indexed in

EXPRESS COMPANIES (continued)

the Monthly catalogue of United States public documents and may be obtained from the Superintendent of documents, Washington, D.C.

GAS COMPANIES

Alabama. Public service commission.
N.A.R.U.C. classification adopted. 1924.

Arizona. Corporation commission.
Gas corporations. 1914.
N.A.R.U.C. classification adopted. 1926.

California. Railroad commission.
Gas corporations. 1913.
Gas corporations having annual operating revenues exceeding $250,000. 1924.
Gas corporations, class B and class C. 1926.

Colorado. Public utilities commission.
Gas utilities. 1916.

Connecticut. Public utilities commission.
N.A.R.U.C. classification adopted. 1924.

District of Columbia. Public utilities commission.
Influenced by the accounting methods of the Interstate commerce commission and the Federal power commission under the jurisdiction of Congress.
N.A.R.U.C. classification adopted. 1927.

Georgia. Public service commission.
N.A.R.U.C. classification adopted. 1924.

Idaho. Public utilities commission.
N.A.R.U.C. classification adopted. 1925.

Illinois. Commerce commission (successor in 1921 to the Public utilities commission)
Gas utilities. 1919.
N.A.R.U.C. classification adopted (with minor modifications) 1923.

Indiana. Public service commission.
Gas utilities. 1913. 1922 (revised issue)
N.A.R.U.C. classification adopted (optional with utility) 1924.

Kentucky. Public service commission.
N.A.R.U.C. classification with modifications (being prepared for adoption, 1935)

Louisiana. Public service commission.
N.A.R.U.C. classification adopted. 1927.

Maine. Public utilities commission.
Gas companies. 1915. 1917 (revised issue)
Gas utilities. 1924.
N.A.R.U.C. classification not adopted but the classification prescribed in 1924 follows it closely, in some respects. Depreciation requirements differ.

Maryland. Public service commission.
Gas corporations. 1911.
N.A.R.U.C. classification adopted. 1930.

Massachusetts. Board of gas and electric light commissioners (successor in 1887 to the Board of gas commissioners, established in 1885, which prescribed the system listed below)
Gas companies. 1886.

Massachusetts. Dept. of public utilities (formed in 1919 by the consolidation of the Public service commission and the Board of gas and electric light commissioners)
Gas and electric companies. 1921. 1927 (revised issue) 1934 (revised issue)
N.A.R.U.C. classification followed closely but with modifications.

Michigan. Public utilities commission (successor in 1919 to the Railroad commission)
Gas utilities. 1923. 1926 (revised issue)
This system is substantially the same as the N.A.R.U.C. classification.

Missouri. Public service commission.
Gas corporations and municipalities. 1915. 1932 (1st revised issue)

Montana. Board of railroad commissioners (ex-officio Public service commission)
Gas utilities. 1913.

GAS COMPANIES (continued)

National association of railway (later railroad) and utilities commissioners.

Uniform system of accounts for gas corporations, prepared by Committee on statistics and accounts of public utilities and recommended for adoption by state commissions at the annual meeting of the National association of railway and utilities commissioners, in Washington, November 12, 1920.

Revised issue recommended for adoption at the annual meeting of the National association of railway and utilities commissioners held in Detroit, Mich., November, 1922. "Revision of 1922."

The "N.A.R.U.C. classification."

Uniform classification of accounts for natural gas companies . . . recommended for adoption by state commissions by said National association . . . 1930.

Nevada. Public service commission.
Gas utilities. 1911.
N.A.R.U.C. classification adopted. 1924.

New Hampshire. Public service commission.
Gas utilities. 1915.

New Jersey. Board of public utility commissioners.
Gas utilities. 1912. 1915 (revised issue) 1925 (2d revised issue)

New York (State) Public service commission. 1st district.
Gas corporations. 1909. 1919.

New York (State) Public service commission. 2d district.
Gas corporations. 1909.

Gas corporations, condensed scheme for corporations having gross operating revenues from gas operations amounting to less than $500,000 per annum. 1909.

Gas corporations, second condensed scheme for corporations having gross operating revenues from gas operations amounting to less than $100,000 per annum. 1909.

Gas corporations, third condensed scheme for corporations having gross operating revenues from gas operations amounting to less than $25,000 per annum. 1909.

The uniform systems of accounts prescribed by the Public service commission, 1st district, and the Public service commission, 2d district (listed above) superseded by the classification established by the Public service commission (listed below).

New York (State) Dept. of public service. Public service commission.
N.A.R.U.C. classification adopted (with minor modifications) 1924.
Gas corporations (all classes, including natural gas) 1934.
Tentative draft, 1933.
Superseded the N.A.R.U.C. classification.

North Carolina. Utilities commission (successor in 1934 to the Corporation commission which prescribed the system listed below)
N.A.R.U.C. classification adopted (with additional information required) 1931.

North Dakota. Board of railroad commissioners.
N.A.R.U.C. classification adopted. 1922.

Ohio. Public utilities commission.
Natural gas utilities. 1921.

Oklahoma. Corporation commission.
Public service companies. 1910.
Gas and electric utilities. 1922.
Electric and natural gas utilities. 1927.

Oregon. Public utilities commissioner (successor in 1931 to the Public service commission which in 1915 succeeded the Railroad commission)
Gas companies. 1913.
N.A.R.U.C. classification adopted (with minor modifications) 1925.

Pennsylvania. Public service commission.
Natural gas companies. 1920.
Tentative draft, 1918.
Manufactured gas companies. 1924.
Tentative draft, 1923.

Rhode Island. Public utilities commission.
Prescribed a form for the annual reports of public utilities operating in the state. 1923.
(Does not have a "system")

Tennessee. Railroad and public utilities commission.
N.A.R.U.C. classification adopted. 1922.

U. S. Interstate commerce commission.
Gas corporations and electric corporations in the District of Columbia. 1909.

GAS COMPANIES (continued)

Utah. Public utilities commission (successor to the Public service commission)
N.A.R.U.C. classification adopted. 1922.

Vermont. Public service commission.
N.A.R.U.C. classification adopted. 1929.
Adopted only for the use of companies having annual operating revenues in excess of $10,000 a year averaged over a period of five years.

Virginia. State corporation commission.
N.A.R.U.C. classification adopted. 1921.

Washington (State) Dept. of public works (successor to the Public service commission)
Gas companies. 1913.
N.A.R.U.C. classification adopted (optional with utility) 1929.

West Virginia. Public service commission.
Natural gas companies. 1923. 1931.

Wisconsin. Public service commission (successor to the Railroad commission which prescribed the systems listed below)
Gas utilities, class A and class B. 1908.
N.A.R.U.C. classification adopted for class A and class B (with minor modifications) 1923.

HEATING COMPANIES

Illinois. Commerce commission (successor in 1921 to the Public utilities commission)
Heating utilities. 1919.
Heating utilities. 1923 (revision of 1919 classification to conform to structure and rules of electric and gas classifications)

Indiana. Public service commission.
Heating utilities. 1913. 1920 (revised issue)

Missouri. Public service commission.
Heating companies and municipalities. 1915.

New Jersey. Board of public utility commissioners.
Electric light, heat, and power utilities. 1912. 1915 (revised issue)
N.A.R.U.C. classification for electric utilities adopted. 1925.

New York (State) Dept. of public service. Public service commission.
Steam corporations. 1935.
Follows general principles established in the system for electric and gas corporations.

Pennsylvania. Public service commission.
Steam heating companies. 1926.

MOTOR TRANSPORTATION COMPANIES

Alabama. Public service commission.
Motor carriers. 1927.

California. Railroad commission.
Automotive transportation companies, class A. 1922.

Connecticut. Public utilities commission.
Motor bus operations. 1926.
Taxicab operations. 1932.

District of Columbia. Public utilities commission.
N.A.R.U.C. classification adopted. 1926.

Florida. Railroad commission.
Auto transportation companies. 1930.

Georgia. Public service commission.
N.A.R.U.C. classification adopted. 1929.

Idaho. Public utilities commission.
Auto transportation companies. 1930.

Kansas. State corporation commission (successor in 1933 to the Public service commission which prescribed the system listed below)
Motor carriers. 1926.

MOTOR TRANSPORTATION COMPANIES (continued)

Maine. Public utilities commission.
Motor vehicle operations (buses) 1926.
Common and contract carriers (trucks) 1933.

Maryland. Public service commission.
N.A.R.U.C. classification adopted (with minor modifications) 1930.

Massachusetts. Dept. of public utilities.
Motor vehicles. 1926.

Minnesota. Railroad & warehouse commission.
Auto transportation companies. 1927.
Also accepts reports filed on basis of the N.A.R.U.C. classification.

Missouri. Public service commission.
Motor bus carriers. 1929. 1933 (1st revised issue)

National association of railway (later railroad) and utilities commissioners.
Uniform classification of accounts for bus companies (with operating revenues of $100,000 or more) and for bus companies (with operating revenues of less than $100,000)—both systems prepared by a committee of and adopted by the American electric railway association, approved and submitted by the Committee on statistics and accounts of public utility companies of the National association of railroad and utilities commissioners, and recommended for adoption by state commissions by said National association at its annual convention held in Asheville, North Carolina, November, 1926.
The "N.A.R.U.C. classification."

New Jersey. Board of public utility commissioners.
Bus utilities. 1930.

New York (State) Dept. of public service. Public service commission.
Omnibus corporations, classes A, B, and C (annual operating revenues in excess of $25,000) 1934.
Tentative draft prepared, 1933.

New York (State) Dept. of public service. Metropolitan division. Transit commission.
Bus corporations. 1932.

North Carolina. Utilities commission (successor in 1934 to the Corporation commission which prescribed the system listed below)
N.A.R.U.C. classification adopted (with additional information required) 1931.

North Dakota. Board of railroad commissioners.
Auto transportation companies. 1923. 1928 (superseding the 1923 classification) 1932 (superseding the 1928 classification)

Oklahoma. Corporation commission.
Motor bus and truck companies. 1929.

Oregon. Public utilities commissioner (successor in 1931 to the Public service commission which prescribed the system listed below)
Automotive transportation companies, class A and class C. 1923.

Pennsylvania. Public service commission.
Passenger motor vehicles, class A and class B. 1928.
Tentative classification, class A, 1924.
Passenger motor vehicles, class C, optional. 1928.

Tennessee. Railroad and public utilities commission.
N.A.R.U.C. classification adopted. 1930.

Utah. Public utilities commission (successor to the Public service commission)
Automotive transportation companies. 1922.

Vermont. Public service commission.
N.A.R.U.C. classification adopted. 1929.
Adopted only for the use of companies having annual operating revenues in excess of $10,000 a year averaged over a period of five years.

Washington (State) Dept. of public works (successor to the Public service commission)
Unincorporated auto transportation companies, class B. 1922.
Incorporated auto transportation companies. 1922.
Auto transportation companies. 1926 (supersedes and cancels the 1922 classifications)

Wisconsin. Public service commission (successor to the Railroad commission which prescribed the system listed below)
N.A.R.U.C. classification adopted for class A and class B. 1928.

PIPE LINE COMPANIES, GAS

Oklahoma. Corporation commission.
Gas pipe lines. 1914.

PIPE LINE COMPANIES, OIL

U. S. Interstate commerce commission.
Pipe line companies (oil):
Operating revenues and expenses. 1911.
Investment in pipe lines, pipe line operating revenues, and pipe line operating expenses of carriers by pipe lines (in part, a revision of the 1911 classifications) 1915.
Uniform system of accounts. 1935 (1st revised issue)
Orders, instructions, rules, regulations, interpretations, decisions, etc. issued from time to time to supplement the accounting classifications for pipe line companies are not listed. They are indexed in the Monthly catalogue of United States public documents and may be obtained from the Superintendent of documents, Washington, D.C.

RAILROADS

Massachusetts. Dept. of public utilities.
(In 1869 the Railroad commission was established, this being the first regulatory body in the United States. In 1885 the Board of gas commissioners was established and its name was changed to the Board of gas and electric light commissioners in 1887. In 1913 the Railroad commission became the Public service commission, and in 1919 the Public service commission and the Board of gas and electric light commissioners were consolidated into the Department of public utilities.)
Railroads:
General instructions in regard to the keeping of railroad accounts. 1876.

Michigan. Public utilities commission (successor in 1919 to the Railroad commission)
Railroads. 1882 (handbook)
"Conforms to classification of accounts adopted at the Second national convention of Railroad commissioners at Saratoga Springs, N. Y., June 10, 1879, and also the system adopted by the Railroad commissioner of Michigan as provided by the law of 1881."

New York (State) Board of railroad commissioners (superseded in 1907 by the Public service commissions, 1st and 2d districts)
Railroads:
Explanations for the guidance of railroad companies in making reports. 1884. 1889 (revised issue)

New York (State) Public service commission. 2d district.
Railroads:
Expenditures for road and equipment, operating revenues, operating expenses, locomotive miles, car miles, train miles. 1908.

Oregon. Public utilities commissioner (successor in 1931 to the Public service commission which in 1915 succeeded the Railroad commission)
Railroads:
Rules governing the accounting for railroad lines within Oregon. 1910.
Rules governing accounting and apportionment of operating revenues and expenses and accounts of movement of traffic within Oregon. 1912.

U. S. Interstate commerce commission.
The Railway accounting officers' association (formerly Association of American railway accounting officers organized in 1888) has assisted and cooperated with the commission in regulating and systematizing the accounting affairs of the carriers. Its work and authority has so grown that it now prescribes mandatory rules covering many phases of railway accounting work.
"Railway accounting procedure," the principal publication of the Association, contains all the mandatory rules and a synopsis of its recommendations since 1888.
Railroads:
Operating expenses. 1888. 1894 (1st revised issue) 1901 (2d revised issue)
The 1888 classification is "substantially a reissue of the Classification as adopted by the Convention of State railroad commissioners held at Saratoga in June, 1879."
Construction expenses. 1901.
Construction and equipment expenditures. 1905.
Expenditures for road and equipment. 1907. 1908 (supplement to the 1st issue)
Locomotive-miles, car-miles, and train-miles. 1907.
Operating expenses. 1907 (3d revised issue) 1908 (3d revised issue, condensed)
Operating revenues. 1907. 1908 (supplement to the 1st issue)

RAILROADS (continued)

U. S. Interstate commerce commission (continued)
Revenues and expenses for outside operations. 1908.
Expenditures for additions and betterments. 1909. 1910 (1st revised issue)
Form of general balance sheet statement. 1909. 1910 (1st revised issue)
Form of income and profit and loss statement. 1912.
Income, profit and loss, and general balance sheet accounts. 1914.
Investments in road and equipment. 1914.
Operating revenues and expenses. 1914 (revised issue)
Also condensed classification for operating expenses, 1914.
Train-miles, locomotive-miles, and car-miles. 1914 (revised issue)
Orders, instructions, rules, regulations, interpretations, decisions, etc., issued from time to time to supplement the accounting classifications for railroads are not listed. They are indexed in the Monthly catalogue of United States public documents and may be obtained from the Superintendent of documents, Washington, D.C.

Washington (State) Dept. of public works (successor to the Public service commission which was, in turn, the successor to the Railroad commission which prescribed the system listed below)
Railroads:
Forms "A" and "B" (classification of units involved in construction, and additions and betterments) 1910.

SHIPPING (CARRIERS BY WATER)

California. Railroad commission.
Carriers by water, class B. 1923.

Maine. Public utilities commission.
Vessels. 1916.

U. S. Interstate commerce commission.
Water lines:
Operating revenues and operating expenses (tentative classification) 1908.
Carriers by water:
Operating expenses. 1911.
Operating revenues. 1911.
Expenditures for real property and equipment. 1913.
Form of general balance sheet statement. 1913.
Income and profit and loss accounts. 1913.

Alphabetical list of representative items chargeable to operating expenses. 1917. 1930.
Orders, instructions, rules, regulations, interpretations, decisions, etc. issued from time to time to supplement the accounting classifications for carriers by water are not listed. They are indexed in the Monthly catalogue of United States public documents and may be obtained from the Superintendent of documents, Washington, D.C.

United States shipping board emergency fleet corporation. Division of operations.
Vessel owners. 1918.

Washington (State) Dept. of public works (successor to the Public service commission)
Passenger, freight, and ferry service. 1928.

SLEEPING CAR COMPANIES

U. S. Interstate commerce commission.
Sleeping car companies:
Operating revenues and operating expenses. 1910.
Revenues and expenses of sleeping car operations, of auxiliary operations, and of other properties for sleeping car companies. 1912 (1st revised issue)
Orders, instructions, rules, regulations, interpretations, decisions, etc. issued from time to time to supplement the accounting classifications for sleeping car companies are not listed. They are indexed in the Monthly catalogue of United States public documents and may be obtained from the Superintendent of documents, Washington, D.C.

TELEGRAPH AND CABLE COMPANIES

Maryland. Public service commission.
Telephone and telegraph companies. 1911.

U. S. Interstate commerce commission.
Telegraph and cable companies:
Uniform system of accounts for telegraph and cable companies (exclusive of wireless telegraph companies) 1914.
Orders, instructions, rules, regulations, interpretations, decisions, etc. issued from time to time to supplement the accounting classifications are not listed. They are indexed in the Monthly catalogue of United States public documents and may be obtained from the Superintendent of documents, Washington, D.C.

TELEPHONE COMPANIES

California. Railroad commission.
Telephone companies. 1914.
I.C.C. classification adopted 1922 (setting aside the 1914 classification)
The I.C.C. "first revised issue" has not been adopted.

Georgia. Public service commission (successor to the Railroad commission which prescribed the system listed below)
Telephone companies. 1920.

Indiana. Public service commission.
Telephone companies, classes C and D simplified. 1924.

Kansas. State corporation commission (successor to the Public service commission which in 1925 superseded the Public utilities commission. The Court of industrial relations, created in 1920 and abolished in 1925, prescribed the 1920 classification listed below)
Telephone companies. 1913.
Telephone companies, class D. 1920.

Maine. Public utilities commission.
Telephone companies, class D. 1915. 1917 (revised issue)

Maryland. Public service commission.
Telephone and telegraph companies. 1911.

Minnesota. Railroad & warehouse commission.
Telephone companies, classes C and D. 1918. 1919 (reissue) 1921 (reissue)
Telephone companies, classes C, D, and E (supplement to the above) 1927.

Missouri. Public service commission.
Telephone corporations, class D. 1918.

Montana. Board of railroad commissioners (ex-officio Public service commission)
Telephone utilities. 1913.

Nebraska. State railway commission.
Telephone companies. 1909.
Telephone companies, classes C, D and E. 1919.
Based on the I.C.C. classification but in modified form.

New York (State) Dept. of public service. Public service commission.

Telephone corporations, classes A and B. 1935.

This entirely new system of accounts supersedes the I.C.C. system, effective 1913, which in turn superseded the system, effective 1912, prescribed by the New York Public service commission, 2d district.

Telephone corporations, other than classes A and B. 1912.

System of accounts for telephone companies, with annual operating revenues below $50,000 and with physical property devoted to the public service in excess of $10,000, which became effective January 1, 1912, still in effect.

North Dakota. Board of railroad commissioners.

Telephone companies, class D. 1916. 1926.

South Dakota. Board of railroad commissioners.

Telephone companies operating within the state of South Dakota. 1916.

U. S. Interstate commerce commission.

Telephone companies:

Uniform system of accounts (tentative) 1911.

Uniform system of accounts, class A and class B. 1913.

1915 (supplement)

Uniform system of accounts, class C. 1915.

Uniform system of accounts for telephone companies (tentative draft) 1930.

Uniform system of accounts, class A. 1933.

Uniform system of accounts, class B. 1934.

Orders, instructions, rules, regulations, interpretations, decisions, etc. issued from time to time to supplement the accounting classifications for telephone companies are not listed. They are indexed in the Monthly catalogue of United States public documents and may be obtained from the Superintendent of documents, Washington, D.C.

Utah. Public utilities commission.

Telephone utilities (small) 1928.

Based to a certain extent on the I.C.C. classification.

Wisconsin. Public service commission (successor to the Railroad commission which prescribed the systems listed below)

Telephone utilities. 1909.

Telephone utilities, class C. 1911.

WAREHOUSES

California. Railroad commission.
  Warehousemen operating in cities having a population of 25,000 or more. 1929.
  Cold storage warehousemen. 1933.

Maine. Public utilities commission.
  Warehousemen. 1916.

Washington (State) Dept. of public works (successor to the Public service commission)
  Incorporated public warehouse companies. 1923.
    Jurisdiction abolished in 1929.
  Storage warehouses. 1933 (new law)

WATER WORKS

Alabama. Public service commission.
  N.A.R.U.C. classification adopted. 1924.

Arizona. Corporation commission.
  Water corporations. 1914.
  N.A.R.U.C. classification adopted. 1929.

California. Railroad commission.
  Water corporations. 1913. 1920 (revised issue)

Colorado. Public utilities commission.
  Water utilities. 1916. 1920 (revised issue)

Connecticut. Public utilities commission.
  Water works. 1922.

Idaho. Public utilities commission.
  Water corporations. 1914.

Illinois. Commerce commission (successor in 1921 to the Public utilities commission)
  Water utilities. 1919.
  N.A.R.U.C. classification adopted (with minor modifications) 1923.

Indiana. Public service commission.
  Water utilities. 1913. 1920 (revised issue) 1926 (revised issue)
  Water utilities, class C, simplified method. 1924.

Kentucky. Public service commission.
N.A.R.U.C. classification with modifications (being prepared for adoption, 1935)

Maine. Public utilities commission.
Water companies. 1915. 1918 (revised issue)

Maryland. Public service commission.
Water companies. 1911. 1922 (reissue)

Massachusetts. Dept. of public utilities (formed in 1919 by the consolidation of the Public service commission and the Board of gas and electric light commissioners)
Water companies. 1923.
N.A.R.U.C. classification followed closely but with modifications.

Missouri. Public service commission.
Water corporations and municipalities. 1915. 1932 (1st revised issue)

Montana. Board of railroad commissioners (ex-officio Public service commission)
Water utilities. 1913. 1919 (revised issue) 1922 (revised issue)

National association of railway (later railroad) and utilities commissioners.
Uniform classification of accounts for water utilities, prepared by Committee on statistics and accounts of public utilities and recommended for adoption by state commissions at the annual meeting of the National association of railway and utilities commissioners in Atlanta, October, 1921.
The "N.A.R.U.C. classification."

Nevada. Public service commission.
Water utilities. 1911.
N.A.R.U.C. classification adopted. 1924.

New Hampshire. Public service commission.
Water utilities. 1915.

New Jersey. Board of public utility commissioners.
Water utilities. 1912. 1925 (revised issue)

New York (State) Dept. of public service. Public service commission.
Water-works corporations, classes A and B (annual operating revenues in excess of $50,000) 1934.

WATER WORKS (continued)

North Carolina. Utilities commission (successor in 1934 to the Corporation commission which prescribed the system listed below)
N.A.R.U.C. classification adopted (with additional information required) 1931.

North Dakota. Board of railroad commissioners.
N.A.R.U.C. classification adopted. 1922.

Oregon. Public utilities commissioner (successor in 1931 to the Public service commission which in 1915 succeeded the Railroad commission)
Water utilities. 1913.
N.A.R.U.C. classification adopted (with minor modifications) 1925.

Pennsylvania. Public service commission.
Water companies. 1918.

Rhode Island. Public utilities commission.
Prescribed a form for the annual reports of public utilities operating in the state. 1923.
(Does not have a "system")

Tennessee. Railroad and public utilities commission.
N.A.R.U.C. classification adopted. 1922.

Utah. Public utilities commission (successor to the Public service commission)
N.A.R.U.C. classification adopted. 1925.

Washington (State) Dept. of public works (successor to the Public service commission)
N.A.R.U.C. classification adopted. 1929.
Class D companies may keep only such accounts as are necessary to compile a simplified form of annual report.

Washington (State) Division of municipal corporations (successor in 1921 to the Bureau of inspection and supervision of public offices which prescribed the system listed below)
Municipal water utilities. 1916.

West Virginia. Public service commission.
N.A.R.U.C. classification adopted (with minor modifications) 1924.
Classification of income accounts revised, 1932.

Wisconsin. Public service commission (successor to the Railroad commission which prescribed the systems listed below)
Water utilities, class A and class B. 1908.
N.A.R.U.C. classification adopted for class A and class B (with minor modifications) 1925.
Water utilities, class C. 1911.
Water utilities, class C and class D. 1926.
New classification. For class C, this supersedes the 1911 classification.

WHARVES

Maine. Public utilities commission.
Wharfinger. 1916.

APPENDIX

This Appendix provides miscellaneous sources of reference for the accountant. It contains bibliographies and histories of accounting, miscellaneous works about accounting and accountants' services, financial and business management handbooks and dictionaries, published indexes which include references to accounting and related subjects, national associations of accountants, office managers, comptrollers, etc., with the names of the periodicals which they sponsor, and a selected list of publishers of works on accounting during the last decade.

BIBLIOGRAPHIES OF ACCOUNTING

The following are the only bibliographies published since the beginning of the 20th century in book or pamphlet form which include works on accounting by American authors. Various check-lists which have appeared in periodicals are omitted. Bibliographies of accounting for specific subjects, such as railroad accounting and municipal accounting, are omitted.

BENTLEY, Harry Clark, 1877– , and LEONARD, Ruth Shaw, 1906–
Bibliography of works on accounting by American authors . . . Bost. H. C. Bentley, 1934–35. 2v. 23½cm.
v.1, 1796–1900; v.2, 1901–1934.

COLUMBIA UNIVERSITY. Library. Montgomery library of accountancy.
A check list of books, printed before 1850, in the Montgomery library of accountancy at Columbia university . . . N. Y. Columbia univ. press, 1927. 46p. 24cm.

—A second check list of books, printed before 1850, in the Montgomery library of accountancy at Columbia university . . . N. Y. Columbia univ. press, 1930. 32p. 24cm.

MYER, Joseph Charles, 1893–1934, and HERWOOD, Herman.
The third American check-list of early bookkeeping texts. [N. Y. Herskowitz & Herskowitz, 1933] [8]p. 24cm.
Reprinted from the Certified public accountant, Apr. 1933.
The second author's name was formerly Hermann Herskowitz.

HISTORIES OF ACCOUNTING

The following are the only books which treat of the history of accounting in this country. Histories of business education and articles in periodicals are omitted.

ANYON, James T., 1851–
Recollections of the early days of American accountancy, 1883–1893. [N. Y.] Priv. print. 1925. 68p. 22cm.

GREEN, Wilmer L.
History and survey of accountancy. Brooklyn, Standard text press, 1930. 288p. 23½cm.

LITTLETON, Ananias Charles, 1886–
Accounting evolution to 1900. N. Y. Amer. institute pub. co. [c1933] 368p. 24½cm

MISCELLANEOUS WORKS ABOUT ACCOUNTING AND ACCOUNTANTS' SERVICES

Selected List

AMERICAN INSTITUTE OF ACCOUNTANTS.
Certified public accountant laws of the United States. N.Y. Century [1930] 247p. 24½cm.
Prefatory note signed: A. P. Richardson, editor.

THE ETHICAL PROBLEMS OF MODERN ACCOUNTANCY: lectures delivered in 1932 on the William A. Vawter foundation on business ethics, Northwestern university, School of commerce. N.Y. Ronald [c1933] 152p. 22cm.
Contents.—Accountancy as a profession, by Vanderveer Custis. —The accountant and the investor, by G. O. May.—The accountant and the stock exchange, by J. M. B. Hoxsey.—The accountant and his clientele, by Arthur Andersen.—The accountant and the investment banker, by E. M. Stevens.—The accountant and his profession, by J. H. Jackson.

RICHARDSON, Alphyon Perry, 1875–
The ethics of a profession. N.Y. Century [c1931] 159p. 17½cm.

SCOTT, D R, 1887–
The cultural significance of accounts. N.Y. Holt [c1931] 316p. 22½cm.

YOAKUM, Clarence Stone, 1879–
Business and the young accountant; vocational experiences of the college graduate. Ann Arbor, Mich. Univ. of Mich. School of business administration, Bur. of business research, 1929. 42p. 23cm. (Michigan. University. School of business administration. Bureau of business research. Michigan business studies, v.2, no.3)

FINANCIAL AND BUSINESS MANAGEMENT HANDBOOKS AND DICTIONARIES OF AID TO THE ACCOUNTANT

Selected List

(See also Part Two, Class 7, pages 288–290)

ALFORD, Leon Pratt, 1877– , editor.
Management's handbook. N. Y. Ronald [c1924] 1607p. 18cm.
"Devoted to classified knowledge and practice of management in manufacturing industries . . . practical working information for the use of executives."

ALSAGER, Christen Martin, 1871–
Dictionary of business terms; containing definitions of terms, phrases and abbreviations relating to accounting, banking, bonds, brokerage, business law, business organization, corporations, domestic and foreign exchange, economics, insurance, investments, money, mortgages, real estate, speculations, stock exchange operations, stocks, trusts, and other branches of business. Chic. Callaghan, 1932. 429p. 18cm.
"While the book is primarily intended for the use of students in schools of commerce and business administration of collegiate grade, it has, nevertheless, been written with the idea that it would be equally useful to law students, engineering students, business men, professional men, and the public in general."

CROWELL, Thomas Y., company, publishers.
Crowell's dictionary of business and finance; rev. ed. N. Y. Crowell [c1930] 601p. 23cm.
"This book is intended as a compendium in one handy volume of all important terms used in business and finance generally."

DONALD, William John Alexander, 1890– , and others, editors.
Handbook of business administration. N. Y. Pub. for the American management association by McGraw-Hill, 1931. 1753p. 18cm.
"Provides in a form convenient for study the fundamentals and the procedures of managerial policy and technique which may be put to use by business executives as problems arise and as the business process changes."

Montgomery, Robert Hiester, 1872– , editor.
Financial handbook; 2d ed. . . second printing. N. Y. Ronald, 1933. 1628p. 19cm.
"This hand book is intended for constant reference by all who have in any way to do with the finances of business. Its particular purpose is to provide readily and in sufficient detail serviceable information on all questions which are likely to arise in the financial management of business organizations whether large or small."

Munn, Glenn Gaywaine.
Encyclopedia of banking and finance; a reference manual comprising over 3,275 terms relating to money; credit; banking practice, history, law, accounting and organization; trusts, finance; foreign exchange; investments; securities; speculation; business organization; insurance; commodities; markets; brokerage. N. Y. Bankers pub. co. 1931. 765p. 27cm.
"First edition, published, 1924 . . . Third edition, revised, 1931."
Contains bibliographies.
"The essential function of this volume is to serve the banking, financial, and allied vocations by explanations of somewhat greater length than has heretofore been attempted—of the subjects that are comprehended within the limits of this department of economic life."

Parker, John Scott, 1873– , and Smith, Jay Braisted Roe, 1869– , editors.
The corporation manual; statutory provisions relating to the organization, regulation and taxation of domestic business corporations, and to the admission, regulation and taxation of foreign business corporations, in the several states, territories and districts of the United States, arranged under a uniform classification; the uniform stock transfer act; federal and state laws regulating the sale of corporate stocks and securities; with forms and precedents; ed. by John S. Parker and J. B. R. Smith, assisted by a board of associated editors in the several states; 36th ed. N. Y. U. S. corp. co. 1935. 2695p. 28cm.
"The only book which gives a complete compilation of the business corporation statutes of all the states and territorial possessions—all arranged according to a uniform classification which enables investigators readily to compare the statutes upon any particular subject in any state with legislation upon the same subject in all other states."

SALIERS, Earl Adolphus, 1884–   , editor.
The handbook of corporate management and procedure. N. Y. McGraw-Hill, 1929. 1237p. 21½cm.
"The purpose of this book is to provide ready reference to such facts as are needed in handling the everyday problems that confront all who are concerned in corporate affairs."

SMITH, Howard Irving.
Smith's financial dictionary; 2d ed. N. Y. Moody's magazine, 1908. 543p. 24cm.
First edition, 1903.
"Compiled for the purpose of assembling and interpreting the terms employed in financial and allied commercial affairs." One of the first works of its kind and it is still useful.

PUBLISHED INDEXES WHICH INCLUDE REFERENCES TO ACCOUNTING AND RELATED SUBJECTS

Selected List

ACCOUNTANTS' INDEX: a bibliography of accounting literature to December, 1920. N. Y. Amer. institute of accountants [c1921] 1578p. 23½cm.

—Supplement: a bibliography of accounting literature, January, 1921 —June, 1923. [N. Y.] Amer. institute of accountants, 1923. 599p. 23½cm.

—Second supplement: a bibliography of accounting literature, July, 1923—December, 1927 (inclusive) [N. Y.] Amer. institute of accountants [c1928] 789p. 23½cm.

—Third supplement: a bibliography of accounting literature, January, 1928—December, 1931 (inclusive) N. Y. Pub. for the Amer. institute of accountants by the Amer. institute pub. co. [c1932] 635p. 23½cm.

The Accountants' index with its three supplements is a comprehensive key to the literature on accounting and its related subjects. References include books, pamphlets, and periodical articles. For references to accounting literature since 1931, see the list, "Current literature compiled in the library of the American institute of accountants," appearing monthly in the Journal of accountancy.

INDUSTRIAL ARTS INDEX. N. Y. Wilson, 1913–

A subject index to a selected list of engineering, trade, and business periodicals, books, and pamphlets, with a list of important technical societies.

"Monthly index, cumulating throughout the year, with the December number forming an annual cumulation."

NATIONAL ASSOCIATION OF COST ACCOUNTANTS.

Complete topical index. N. Y. National assn. of cost accountants, 1930. (N.A.C.A. bulletin, v.12, no.3)

—Complete topical index, N.A.C.A. publications, April, 1920, to September, 1932. N. Y. National assn. of cost accountants, 1932. (N.A.C.A. bulletin, v.14, no.4)

—Topical index supplement, N.A.C.A. publications, October, 1932, to October, 1934; with corrections to the Complete topical index. N. Y. National assn. of cost accountants, 1934. (N.A.C.A. bulletin, v.16, no.4)

These indexes include references to all the material issued by the National association of cost accountants. Most of the mate-

National association of cost accountants (continued)
rial indexed will be found in the semi-monthly bulletins and the year books issued as part of the association's service to members. With some exceptions additional copies of the bulletins and year books are available for sale to non-members.

Newark, N. J. Free public library. Business branch.
Business books: 1920–1926; an analytical catalog of 2600 titles . . . comp. by Linda H. Morley and Adelaide C. Kight under the direction of John Cotton Dana. N. Y. Wilson, 1927. 592p. 26½cm.
Supplement to "2400 business books and guide to business literature," published in 1921. The first edition entitled "1600 business books" was published in 1916. These works index the important material in the field of business prior to 1927.

Public affairs information service.
Public affairs information bulletin. N. Y. Public aff. inform. serv. 1915–
"A combination of a subject index to the current literature in its field—books, documents, pamphlets, articles in periodicals, multigraphed material, etc.—and a digest of recent events and developments in the fields of sociology, political science and economics, particularly the practical sides of these subjects."
"Issued in three forms: (1) weekly bulletins (2) bi-monthly cumulations, cumulating throughout the year, the last issue, October, indexing the material of the twelve months and forming (3) the permanent annual volume."

The Publishers' trade list annual. N. Y. Publishers' weekly, 1873–
"A collection of publishers' catalogs, arranged alphabetically by publisher's name, and bound up in one large volume. Lists only books in print and so is primarily useful for finding quickly the price of a book and whether or not it is in print."

The publishers' weekly; the American book trade journal. N. Y. Publishers' weekly, 1872–
"The standard American book trade journal; containing lists of new publications of the week, lists of books announced for publication, news notes, editorials and articles, advertisements of books wanted, etc. The principal bibliographical list is the weekly list of new publications, which is an author list with full titles, imprint, collation, and descriptive notes."

U. S. Library of Congress. Division of documents.
Monthly check-list of state publications. Wash. Govt. print. off. 1910–

"A current bibliography, arranged alphabetically by the names of states, of the publications of the states, territories and insular possessions of the United States . . ." There is a full annual index.

U. S. SUPERINTENDENT OF DOCUMENTS.
Catalogue of the public documents of Congress and of all departments of the government of the United States for the period March 4, 1893, to June 30, 1931. Wash. Govt. print. off. 1896–1934. 20v.
"This index which is generally referred to by its binder's title as the Document catalogue forms the permanent and complete catalog of all government publications both congressional and departmental for the period covered." It is a dictionary catalog. As far as issued it supersedes the Monthly catalogue (see below).

—Monthly catalogue United States public documents. Wash. Govt. print. off. 1895–
"A current bibliography of all publications issued by all branches of the government, including both the congressional and the department and bureau publications. . . . There is a detailed author and subject index for each volume . . . Only the volumes since the latest Document catalogue are needed for constant use as the earlier volumes are superseded for most purposes by the Document catalogue."

UNITED STATES CATALOG; books in print January 1, 1928; ed. by Mary Burnham; 4th ed. N. Y. Wilson, 1928. 3164p. 36cm.
"1st ed. 1900; 2d ed. 1903; supplement to 2d ed. covering 1902–05, 1906; 3d ed. 1912; supplement, 1912–17, to the 3d ed. 1918, all ed. by Marion E. Potter; supplements to 3d ed. 1917–21, 1921–24, ed. by E. E. Hawkins, 1921, 1924. 2v."
"Forms an approximately complete record of books published in the United States which were in print January 1, 1928 . . ." An author, subject, and title list.

—Cumulative book index: a world list of books in the English language, 1928–1932, supplementing the United States catalog; 4th ed. N. Y. Wilson, 1933. 2298p. 36cm.
The scope of the Cumulative book index, beginning in 1930, was enlarged to include in its listing books published in Great Britain, Australia, Canada, South Africa, and the British dominions and colonies generally.
For works published since 1932, see the Cumulative book index issued monthly except August and cumulating throughout the year. The last number of each volume covers all the publications of the year and forms an annual supplement to the United States catalog.
An author, subject, and title list on the same plan as the United States catalog.

NATIONAL ASSOCIATIONS OF ACCOUNTANTS, OFFICE MANAGERS, COMPTROLLERS, ETC., WITH THE NAMES OF THE PERIODICALS WHICH THEY SPONSOR

American association of university instructors in accounting. *The Accounting review.* 214 Commerce building, University of Illinois, Urbana, Ill.

American institute of accountants. *The Journal of accountancy.* 135 Cedar street, New York.

American management association. *The Management review.* 20 Vesey street, New York.

American society of certified public accountants. *The Certified public accountant.* National press building, Washington, D. C.

Controllers institute of America. *The Controller.* 1 East 42 street, New York.

National association of cost accountants. *N.A.C.A. bulletin.* 385 Madison avenue, New York.

National association of state auditors, comptrollers and treasurers. Office of secretary, Union trust building, Baltimore. *Report of the annual convention.*

National office management association. Office of secretary, Wharton school of finance and commerce. University of Pennsylvania, Philadelphia. *Quarterly bulletin.* Indianapolis.

DIRECTORY OF PUBLISHERS

Selected list of the publishing houses which have published works on accounting in the last ten years and which are now located at the following addresses:

American book company, 88 Lexington avenue, New York.
American institute publishing co., inc., 135 Cedar street, New York. Publishers for the American institute of accountants whose publications were formerly distributed by the Century company.
American technical society, Drexel avenue & 58 street, Chicago.
Appleton, D.—Century company, inc., 35 West 32 street, New York.

Bankers publishing company, 465 Main street, Cambridge, Mass.
Brookings institution, 722 Jackson place, Washington, D.C.
Bruce publishing company, 524 North Milwaukee street, Milwaukee.
Business publications company, 400 West Madison street, Chicago.

Callaghan and company, 401 East Ohio street, Chicago.
Century company, *see* Appleton, D.—Century company, inc.
Chamber of commerce of the United States of America, 1615 H street, N. W., Washington, D.C.
Crowell, Thomas Y., company, 393 Fourth avenue, New York.

Dry goods economist, 239 West 39 street, New York.

Edwards bros., inc., 310 South State street, Ann Arbor, Mich.
Ellis publishing company, Battle Creek, Mich.

Financial publishing company, 9 Newbury street, Boston.

Ginn and company, 15 Ashburton place, Boston.
Globe book company, inc., 175 Fifth avenue, New York.
Government printing office, Washington, D.C.
Greenberg, publisher, inc., 449 Fourth avenue, New York.
Gregg publishing company, 270 Madison avenue, New York.

Hadley, Charles R., company, Los Angeles.
Hale, E. M., and company, 3100 West Cherry street, Milwaukee.
Harper & brothers, 49 East 33 street, New York.
Harvard university press, Randall hall, Cambridge, Mass.
Heath, D. C. and company, 285 Columbus avenue, Boston.
Holt, Henry, and company, inc., 1 Park avenue, New York.
Houghton Mifflin company, 2 Park street, Boston.

International textbook company, 1001 Wyoming avenue, Scranton.

Johns Hopkins press, Homewood, Baltimore.

LaSalle extension university press, 401 South Michigan avenue, Chicago.
Longmans, Green and co., 114 Fifth avenue, New York.
Lyons & Carnahan, 2500 Prairie avenue, Chicago.

McGraw-Hill book company, inc., 330 West 42 street, New York.
Macmillan company, 60 Fifth avenue, New York.
Merrill, Charles E., co., 381 Fourth avenue, New York.
Metropolitan life insurance company, Policyholders service bureau, 1 Madison avenue, New York.
Municipal finance officers' association of the United States and Canada, 850 East 58 street, Chicago.

National association of cost accountants, 385 Madison avenue, New York.
National committee on municipal accounting, 850 East 58 street, Chicago.

Ohio state university press, Columbus, Ohio.
Oxford book company, incorporated, 381 Fourth avenue, New York.

Pergande publishing co., 3331 North Bartlett avenue, Milwaukee.
Prentice-Hall, inc., 70 Fifth avenue, New York.
Princeton university press, Princeton, N. J.

Rand McNally & company, 111 Eighth avenue, New York.
Ronald press company, 15 East 26 street, New York.
Rowe, H. M., company, incorporated, 624 North Gilmor street, Baltimore.

Shaw, A. W., company, *see* McGraw-Hill book company, inc.
Simmons-Boardman publishing co., 30 Church street, New York.
South-western publishing co., incorporated, 201–203 West Fourth street, Cincinnati.
Spectator, 56 & Chestnut streets, Philadelphia.
Standard text press, 186 Joralemon street, Brooklyn.

United States corporation company, 150 Broadway, New York.
University of Chicago press, 5750 Ellis avenue, Chicago.
University of Michigan press, Ann Arbor, Mich.
University publishing co., 1126 Q street, Lincoln, Neb.

Wahr, George, 103–105 North Main street, Ann Arbor, Mich.
Walker, Frank R., company, 536 Lake Shore drive, Chicago.
White press company, Departmental bank building, Washington, D.C.
Wiley, John & sons, inc., 440 Fourth avenue, New York.
Winston, John C., co., 1006 Arch street, Philadelphia.

AUTHOR INDEX

AUTHOR INDEX

THIS alphabetical author index directs the reader to each author included in Part One, the chronological list, Part Two, the classified list, and the reference sources in the Appendix. Each number is the page reference to the author's work.

A joint author or one who has a subordinate relation to the work is indexed by means of a *see* or *see also* reference. For example, a work by Rittenhouse and Clapp is indexed under Rittenhouse, thus:

Rittenhouse, Charles Forest, 59

and under Clapp, thus:

Clapp, Philip Francis, *see* Rittenhouse, C. F., 59

A *see also* reference is used when an author is a main author or is a sole author but is also a joint author or subordinate author, thus:

Allen, Leslie Herbert, 44
See also Block, M. D., 97

SUBJECT INDEX

SUBJECT INDEX

THIS is an alphabetical list of the businesses and professions for which cost accounting systems and constructive accounting have been prepared and which are listed in Part Two and in the Supplement. Each number is the page reference.

See references are provided in this list for the purpose of directing the reader from his choice of subject to the compilers' choice of subject where the page references are given.

See also references are provided in this list for the purpose of directing the reader to related or subordinate subjects where page references are given.